T0316487

Non-Performance and Remedies under International Contract Law Principles and Indian Contract Law

Internationalrechtliche Studien

Beiträge zum Internationalen Privatrecht, zum Einheitsrecht und zur Rechtsvergleichung

Herausgegeben von Ulrich Magnus und Peter Mankowski

Band 60

PETER LANG
Frankfurt am Main · Berlin · Bern · Bruxelles · New York · Oxford · Wien

Lars Meyer

Non-Performance and Remedies under International Contract Law Principles and Indian Contract Law

A comparative survey of the UNIDROIT Principles of International Commercial Contracts, the Principles of European Contract Law, and Indian statutory contract law

PETER LANG
Internationaler Verlag der Wissenschaften

Bibliographic Information published by the Deutsche Nationalbibliothek
The Deutsche Nationalbibliothek lists this publication in the Deutsche Nationalbibliografie; detailed bibliographic data is available in the internet at http://dnb.d-nb.de.

Zugl.: Hamburg, Univ., Diss., 2010

D 18
ISSN 0947-0395
ISBN 978-3-631-60993-4

www.peterlang.de

Table of Contents

Acknowledgements

I would like to thank Professor Ulrich Magnus (University of Hamburg) for entrusting me with the idea of this survey and supportively supervising its preparation. Moreover, I would like to thank Professor Alejandro M. Garro (Columbia Law School in New York City) as well as Professor Ved P. Nanda (Ved Nanda Center of International Legal Studies at the University of Denver) for their valuable comments and trusting support. Professor Peter Mankowski (University of Hamburg) kindly prepared the second opinion required for the acceptance of this survey as a doctoral thesis by the Faculty of Law of the University of Hamburg.

Most of the research for this book was conducted at the Max Planck Institute for Comparative and International Private Law in Hamburg and during a visiting research fellowship at Columbia Law School in New York City. I would like to express my gratitude to the faculty, staff and sponsors of these two institutions and also to the faculty and staff of the Sturm College of Law at the University of Denver and the Institute of Advanced Legal Studies in London for their hospitality and courtesy.

Finally, I would like to sincerely thank my parents for their encouragement and generous support throughout my legal education.

Introduction

I. Generally

India's emergence as a major economy and promising trading partner especially of the Member States of the European Union (EU), the United States and its Asian neighbours has significantly accelerated the subcontinent's integration into the world economy. Following its recent conclusion of a free-trade agreement with the ten countries of the Association of South-East Asian Nations (ASEAN), the subcontinent's negotiations of a similar trade deal with the EU[1] therefore mark another significant step in perpetuating its position as a rising economic power that some expect to generate the fastest-growing gross domestic product (GDP) among large countries over the next 20 to 25 years and an estimated annual growth of as much as 10 per cent.[2]

Trade between India and the EU as a trade bloc has been growing constantly since India took up a reform process involving regulatory liberalization and a gradual decrease of restrictions on foreign investment in 1991.[3] Today, the EU is India's largest trading partner and biggest source of foreign direct investment, with India in turn being one of Europe's top ten trading partners.[4] Given the two regions' continuous efforts to further increase bilateral trade and economic cooperation between India and both the EU and the individual Member States, there is a vast array of issues calling for an examination of whether India's legal and regulatory environment is sufficiently calibrated to accommodating fast-growing trading activity between the two regions and the increasing inflow of European foreign direct investment into the subcontinent.

Simultaneously, businesses of all sizes are more and more often confronted with the question of whether and to what extent India's laws and judicial system provide reliable and predictable rules as well as effective protection for foreign

---

1 See *cf.* the European Commission's overview of the European Union's bilateral trade relations with India at http://ec.europa.eu/trade/issues/bilateral/countries/india/index_en.htm.

2 See, *e.g.*, *A bumpier but freer road*, The Economist (not attributed), 2 October 2010 at 67.

3 Following a drastic rise in foreign debt and inflation, India in 1991 instituted a new industrial policy aimed primarily at attracting foreign investment. This measure marked the beginning of a series of reforms aimed at opening up its previously restrictive policy on trade, industry and foreign investment.

4 See *cf.* European Commission, *supra* note 1.

investors and trading partners. While this general question obviously involves specific topics such as intellectual property protection or India's peculiar employment laws, it also appears useful to examine how similar or how different the general legal frameworks in India and the EU actually are. One such general area of law is that of contractual non-performance (or breach of contract) and remedies, which may well be regarded as the core part of any contract law regime[5] and is of particular interest to businesses and individuals involved in international transactions.[6] By comparing the UNIDROIT Principles of International Commercial Contracts[7] and the Principles of European Contract Law[8] with Indian statutory contract law – which is primarily embodied in the Indian Contract Act, 1872 and the Specific Relief Act, 1963[9] – this survey seeks to identify where and to what extent the "common core" of Europe's major contract law systems and Indian law provide identical, similar or diverging rules on non-performance and remedies.

At the same time, a comparative analysis of European contract law principles especially with the Indian Contract Act may be valuable for a few additional reasons. First, this survey might serve as a contribution to the discussion and evaluation of the actual dogmatic compatibility of the civil-law and common-law traditions in the area of contractual non-performance and remedies, which is especially interesting with a view on the process of international contract law harmonisation. Given that the Indian Contract Act was enacted under the British Empire's colonial rule and most of its provisions were therefore derived from English common law, it may be regarded as a source of "codified English common law" on contracts. In other words, given that existing English statutes such as the Sale of Goods Act, 1979 merely cover specific areas of contract law, the Indian Contract Act might provide a useful indication of how English contract law could actually be codified or transposed into more general statutory legislation. In fact, recent judgments containing references to the UNIDROIT Principles and the UN Convention on Contracts for the International Sale of Goods (CISG) can be perceived as demonstrating an "increasing openness of English courts towards

5 See, *e.g.*, Ulrich Magnus, *Das Recht der vertraglichen Leistungsstörungen und der Common Frame of Reference*, Zeitschrift für Europäisches Privatrecht 2007 at 260.

6 One observer has described the UNIDROIT Principles' provisions on non-performance as, "[i]n practical terms, (…) the substantive heart of the whole Principles. It is where the Principles' solutions to a large proportion of real world disputes in commercial transactions are to be found." See Arthur Rosett, *UNIDROIT Principles and Harmonisation of International Commercial Law: Focus on Chapter Seven*, Uniform Law Review 1997 at 441. Accordingly, the articles contained in Chapter 7 of the UPICC are among those cited most by arbitral award making reference to this instrument. See Michael Joachim Bonell, *The UNIDROIT Principles in Practice* (2002) at XIII.

7 Hereafter also referred to as "UNIDROIT Principles" or "UPICC."

8 Hereafter also referred to as "European Principles" or "PECL."

9 Hereafter also referred to as "Indian Contract Act" and "Specific Relief Act", respectively.

foreign and international sources of inspiration",[10] and perhaps even as signifying a growing relevance especially of the UPICC to English contract law.

Moreover, as the European Commission has called for a critical review of its so-called "sector-specific approach" in relation to EU legislation and is even contemplating the option of adopting a uniform (optional) instrument on contract law,[11] the question of whether English common law and the contract law statutes of the continental Member States could be integrated into a set of uniform rules has also attracted a high level of political interest throughout Europe.

From an Indian legal perspective, a comparison of Indian statutory contract law with the two sets of Principles might indicate whether the rules and concepts found in these two non-legislative instruments could actually serve as a source of reference or inspiration for courts and arbitral tribunals in India when deciding disputes pertaining to international contracts. This could be particularly interesting in light of the fact that India's new arbitration law[12] in principle permits the application of non-legislative "soft law" like the UNIDROIT Principles as a source of supplementary rules to fill gaps in Indian law, and possibly even to govern international disputes. This survey might therefore help answer the question of where and how the rules set forth in the UPICC actually differ from those found in Indian statutory contract law, and where they might provide a valuable alternative. (In fact, it is apparently a political intention to encourage Indian and foreign parties to make increasing use of arbitration as a means of resolving international commercial disputes[13] might further magnify the relevance of this particular issue.)

This survey thus compares European and international contract law principles with the Indian statutory laws on contractual non-performance, or breach of contract, and remedies. As the UPICC and the PECL are probably the most complete and elaborate collections of common rules and concepts found especially among the national laws EU Member States, the survey is concerned with those two instruments rather than any national systems. In fact, as the European Principles practically form the basis of the EU-endorsed Common Frame of Reference (CFR),[14] "the core of the non-performance concept in the [CFR] consists of the development of the ideas used in the PECL";[15] the latter will therefore play a

10 See Michael Joachim Bonell, *The UNIDROIT Principles and CISG – Sources of Inspiration for English Courts?*, Uniform Law Review 2006 at 305.

11 See generally *infra* Ch. I(I)(B)(1).

12 See *infra* Ch. II(I)(B).

13 See, *e.g.*, *Bhardwaj says prospects are bright for making India an arbitration hub*, IndLaw.com (not attributed), 20 October 2007, available at http://www.indlaw.com.

14 See *infra* Ch. I(I)(B)(1).

15 See Fryderyk Zoll, *The Remedies for Non-Performance in the System of the Acquis Group*, in Rainer Schulze (ed.), *Common Frame of Reference and Existing EC Contract Law* (2008) at 190.

pivotal role in the drafting of new EU legislation, new national laws, and possibly even a (optional) uniform European code on contracts.

The general finding of this survey is that the UNIDROIT and European Principles and Indian statutory contract law not only share a notable structural proximity in that their black letter rules are often accompanied by Explanations and Illustrations; the three regimes' rules on non-performance and remedies in many respects either appear to be derived from the same legal concepts or (are likely to) provide for quite similar outcomes.

II. Structure and methodology

The first Chapter of this survey gives a general overview of the UNIDROIT and European Principles and sets out the state of affairs in the ongoing process of harmonising (and possibly unifying) international and particularly European contract laws. It closes with an examination of the value of the Principles' approach to the process of legal harmonisation, *i.e.*, to developing uniform rules based on common concepts found in different contract law systems. Chapter II provides an introduction to the Indian Contract and Specific Relief Acts and their historic backgrounds, and Chapters III to VIII present a detailed comparison of the three regimes' rules on non-performance and remedies. Finally, a Conclusion recites the major findings of this survey.

Due to the substantive and structural parallels between the Principles and the relevant Indian statutes, the comparison is structured as a rule-by-rule presentation of their substantive rules, followed in each case by a "comparative analysis" of their major differences and similarities. While the Principles' provisions on a particular issue are generally presented and discussed in a single section, any substantive divergences between these two instruments are identified in the context where they appear. Given that, from a geographical perspective, the UNIDROIT Principles are intended to be applied universally and that their drafters drew from the most extensive pool of legal systems, the survey's mode of presentation roughly follows the structure of the UPICC by comparing each provision in their Chapter 7 with its counterparts in the European Principles and in Indian statutory contract law. Areas of focus include the particular concepts of non-

---

See also Ole Lando, *The Structure and Legal Values of the Common Frame of Reference (CFR)*, European Review of Contract Law 2007 at 246, according to whom "for the time being most of the rules [of the CFR] prepared are those of the PECL," and Ulrich Magnus (*supra* note 5 at 279), who has observed that the (preliminary) rules of the so-called *Acquis Principles*, too, largely correspond to the Principles' provisions on non-performance and remedies. See generally *infra* Ch. I(I)(B)(1).

performance and breach of contract underlying each regime, as well as their rules on specific performance and the (other) remedies available for non-performance.

Finally, as this survey is concerned with Indian *statutory* contract law as opposed the entire body of Indian law on contracts, references to any relevant Indian or English case law are being kept to a minimum and included only where they are essential for the understanding of the workings and implications of a particular statutory rule, or where their inclusion facilitates the comparison of a provision with the Principles.[16] The comparative analysis will focus less on evaluating the quality of each regime's provisions and rules but rather on identifying their similarities and divergences and assessing whether any of them might emanate from a superior idea or concept.

16 It should also be noted that especially court decisions and arbitral awards that may be relevant to this survey but were published after January 2009 are not reflected in this survey.

Chapter I: Overview of the UNIDROIT and European Principles

I. Generally

Today, it is commonly understood that globalization – being a phenomenon which brings about the emergence of integrated markets stretching across national borders and, as a result, an internationalization of economic activity – requires a more globalized regulatory framework. The main argument in this regard is that multiple and often diverging national legal systems create an unnecessarily high level of legal uncertainty among the parties in relation to the different national and international laws governing their transnational commercial interactions.[17] On a contractual level, such legal uncertainty leads to a higher level of transaction risk and, ultimately, higher transaction costs, and is therefore regarded as a "non-tariff trade barrier". Moreover, the persistence of diverging national laws often puts consumers and smaller businesses at a disadvantage when dealing with multinational corporations, which have better resources to assess the positions and peculiarities of different national laws and employ them for their benefit. Against this background, it has been widely acknowledged that more coherent laws that are equally accessible and comprehensible for actors across the world or at least throughout a particular trading bloc would help to reduce legal uncertainty as to the substance as well as the judicial application of the rules governing cross-border transactions.

If a benchmark for effective legislation on contracts is "to provide a means by which contracting parties may quickly and fairly arrive at a contractual agreement under rules and terms which are understood by and acceptable to all and which render predictable and enforceable outcomes",[18] it is evident that contract law is perceived to be one of the general areas of law that urgently ought to be further "internationalized" in response to the globalization of economic interaction. Consequentially, commentators and institutions all over the world argue in favour of continuous harmonisation or even a unification of international contract laws by way of both legislative and non-legislative instruments. On the one hand, this

17 The term "international contract" can be defined most practicably as any contractual relationship involving parties from more than one country or being otherwise connected to more than one country.

18 See Gregory G. Letterman, *UNIDROIT's Rules in Practice: Standard International Contracts and Applicable Rules* (2001) at 3.

approach involves the adoption of uniform laws by supranational regional bodies (such as the European Union) which directly penetrate into or even supersede the legal systems of the relevant member states. On the other hand, uniform international rules are established by way of international conventions and so-called "soft law", *i.e.*, through instruments gaining legal force only upon adoption or transposition into national laws or by being selected to directly govern particular contracts.

The term "soft law" is used to describe a variety of forms of non-legislative measures such as model laws (which countries are free to adopt to whatever extent and in whatever form suits them), restatements such as those presented by the American Law Institute, trade terms such as the Incoterms prepared by the International Chamber of Commerce, and, as in the case of the Principles, collections of common rules and best solutions stemming from a variety of national and international legal systems. Soft law is not passed or implemented by any lawmaking bodies, and the influence of any such instrument is therefore entirely dependent on its substantive quality and the institutions sponsoring it.

Various actors have taken on the task of pursuing further coherence among international contract laws.[19] This pool comprises official institutions and multinational organizations as well as institutes, professional networks and private working groups, or individuals. Trade organizations also play a part in the process, *e.g.*, through the elaboration of model contract terms.[20]

The enactment of international treaties has certainly been the most authoritative means of contract law harmonisation. In this regard, especially the United Nations Convention on Contracts for the International Sale of Goods (CISG)[21] has had significant success in synchronizing the signatories' rules on sale of goods contracts. On a more regional level, the European Union is continuously shaping the legal environment of its Internal Market,[22] and the mainly francophone West African members of the Organisation pour l'Harmonisation du Droit des Affaires en Afrique (Organization for the Harmonisation of Business Law in Af-

---

19 For a general overview of the process and methods of international contract law harmonisation, the institutions involved and the most important instruments brought forward by these institutions, see, *e.g.*, Roy Goode/Herbert Kronke/Ewan McKendrick, *Transnational Commercial Law – Text, Cases, and Materials* (2007) at 191 *et seq.* and 215 *et seq.*, and Michael Joachim Bonell, *An International Restatement of Contract Law* (2005) at 1 to 7.

20 See, *e.g.*, the "Incoterms" ("International Commercial Terms") provided by the *International Chamber of Commerce*.

21 As the first major multi-party treaty on contract law, CISG has been extraordinarily successful: various provisions have been transformed into national laws, and it serves as a standard instrument regulating for international sales transactions and, as a consequence, has been a guiding source also for the UPICC and PECL. Presented in 1980, the CISG has to this point been ratified by 71countries.

22 See *infra* B(1).

rica (OHADA))[23] have also enacted various uniform instruments regulating commercial, corporate and judicial matters.[24] The OHADA countries are, *inter alia*, considering the adoption of a uniform contract law[25], the first draft of which is strongly influenced by the CISG and the UNIDROIT Principles.[26]

Nonetheless, at least from a global perspective it appears that these various initiatives have not (yet) progressed the level of actual legislative harmonisation in relation to international contract law very far. Ole Lando, the leading force and chairman of the commission that drafted the PECL, even observed that, "in spite of these efforts, the harmonisation and unification of the various forms of contract law of the world have not yet progressed very far. There are still substantial differences not only between the Common Law of the English-speaking world and the Civil Law, which has its roots on the European Continent, but also between the contract laws of the countries belonging to this Civil Law Group. In fact, the contract laws of the world lag sadly behind the ongoing rapid growth of world trade and communication."[27]

The following sections therefore examine the particular value and relevance of the Principles to the pursuit of international contract law harmonisation.

II. History

A. UNIDROIT Principles

Based in Rome, the UNIDROIT Institute is an independent, intergovernmental organization preparing drafts for conventions, model laws and principles based

---

23 Created in 1993; currently 16 member states. See http://www.ohada.org.

24 Other regional trade blocs and multinational organizations such as *NAFTA*, *Mercosur* and *ASEAN* are mainly pursuing harmonisation of the commercial laws of their member countries. For a general overview, see Loukas A. Mistelis, *Regulatory Aspects: Globalization, Harmonisation, Legal Transplants, and Law Reform – Some Fundamental Observations*, 34 Int'l Lawyer (2000) at 1055, 1061.

25 See *cf.* Marcel Fontaine, *Le projet d'Acte uniforme OHADA sur les contrats et les Principes d'UNIDROIT relatifs aux contrats du commerce international*, Uniform Law Review 2004 at 253.

26 For a general overview of the arguments brought forth in favour and against international contract law harmonisation, see, *e.g.*, Sandeep Gopalan, *The Creation of International Commercial Law: Sovereignty Felled?*, 5 San Diego International Law Journal (2004) at 267; Sandeep Gopalan, *Transnational Commercial Law: The Way Forward*, 18 American University International Law Review (2003) at 803; and Michael Joachim Bonell, *supra* note 19 at 1 *et seq.*

27 See Ole Lando, *CISG and Its Followers: A Proposal to Adopt Some International Principles of Contract Law*, 53 American Journal of Comparative Law (2005) at 379, 383 *et seq.*

on comparative legal analysis. Prior to drafting the UPICC, it contributed substantially to, *inter alia*, the UN Convention on Contracts for the International Sale of Goods (CISG).[28] The self-proclaimed role of the institute is to study needs and methods for modernizing, harmonising and coordinating private law, and to promote the adoption of uniform rules of private law by single states or groups of states. It currently accounts for more than 60 member states from all continents, including all major industrialized nations and all Member States of the European Union.

In 1971, the UNIDROIT Governing Council started considering participation in the process of multilateral contract law harmonisation, which had been pursued by a growing number of socialist and capitalist countries alike, for instance in the form of the 1964 Hague Convention on the International Sale of Goods. As a first step, a committee was installed to assess the feasibility of a project like the UPICC; nine years later, a specific Working Group took up the drafting process. The Group consisted of contract law and international trade law experts from all continents, each one representing his/her respective socialist or market-economy, or civil-law or common-law, system. The members were not delegated from their countries of origin but participated in their private capacity.

The drafting process involved so-called *rapporteurs* conducting research on a certain area or issue of contract law and formulating a first version of the black letter rules and comments to be proposed for inclusion in the final set of principles. These drafts were then circulated and discussed within the Working Group as well as external experts, and eventually agreed upon and edited by the members of the Working Group. The drafters drew inspiration from the world's major contract law systems, focusing particularly on recently revised laws – *e.g.*, domestic codes like the United States Uniform Commercial Code (UCC) or statutes of a number of civil-law jurisdictions – on treaties such as the CISG, and even on existing non-legislative international trade rules.[29] Much like a restatement of contract law, the UPICC mostly contain the rules found in a majority of the systems examined. Yet, some provisions are based on innovative concepts that the Working Group autonomously considered to be best-suited to the specifics of international trade. (Unlike the Notes to the PECL, however, the UPICC do not provide any express references to the legal systems that influenced each provision.)

---

28 The UNIDROIT Institute and the UN are collaborating on the basis of a cooperation agreement.

29 See *cf.* Michael Joachim Bonell, *The UNIDROIT Principles of International Commercial Contracts and the Principles of European Contract Law: Similar Rules for the Same Purposes?*, Uniform Law Review 1996 at 229, 231. Ideas and experiences were also transferred from the UNIDROIT Institute to the Commission on European Contract Law and *vice versa*, and some participants were members of both institutions.

The UPICC were first presented in 1994,[30] and a revised and extended version was published in 2004.[31] This current edition is composed of ten chapters that include 185 articles dealing with the most relevant questions of international commercial contracts and obligations. According to the UNIDROIT Institute, they are intended to provide "a balanced set of rules designed for use throughout the world irrespective of the legal traditions and the economic and political conditions of the countries."[32]

Due to their non-legislative and hence non-binding nature, the UPICC, like the PECL, only bear persuasive authority, but their approach has received a considerable amount of international attention.[33] Consequently, the institute is working on a revised and extended edition that will comprise issues related to the unwinding of failed contracts, illegality, plurality of obligors and obligees, conditions, and termination of long-term contracts for cause.[34]

B. Principles of European Contract Law

The European Union (EU) has been enacting Directives and Regulations with effect on issues of contract law for more than two decades, thereby actively creating a system of EU contract law while at the same time shaping the domestic laws of its Member States in pursuit of facilitating the functioning of the Internal Market.[35]

---

30 International Institute for the Unification of Private Law (UNIDROIT), *UNIDROIT Principles of International Commercial Contracts* (1994).

31 International Institute for the Unification of Private Law (UNIDROIT), *UNIDROIT Principles of International Commercial Contracts 2004* (2004).

32 *Id.* at XV.

33 For a detailed account of the history of the UNIDROIT Principles and an assessment of their practical relevance, see *cf.* Bonell, *supra* note 19 at 27 *et seq.* and 362 *et seq.*, and *The UNIDROIT Principles and Transnational Law*, Uniform Law Review 2000 at 199. See also *infra* III(F).

34 See, *e.g.*, UNIDROIT International Institute for the Unification of Private Law, *Implementation of Work Programme 2006-2008 – UNIDROIT Principles of International Commercial Contracts* (not attributed), Uniform Law Review 2007 at 800; Reinhard Zimmermann, *The UNIDROIT Principles of International Commercial Contracts 2004 in Comparative Perspective*, 21 Tul. Eur. & Civ. L.F. (2006) at 1, 28 *et seq.* (2006); and Herbert Kronke, *A Bridge out of the Fortress: UNIDROIT's Work on Global Modernisation of Commercial Law and its Relevance for Europe*, Zeitschrift für Europäisches Privatrecht 2008 at 1.

35 Directive 85/374/EEC of 25 July 1985 on the approximation of the laws, regulations and administrative provisions of the Member States concerning liability for defective products was probably the first legislative act by the European legislator with direct effect on the Member States' contract laws.

In parallel to the enactment of uniform legislation by the European Commission, the Parliament and the Council of the European Union, various scholarly initiatives have also been discussing the question of whether and how, in the course of further political integration, European contract laws should be harmonised or perhaps even unified. One of the first groups examining this issue was the Commission on European Contract Law, which eventually presented the Principles of European Contract Law. In light of these parallel efforts, it appears appropriate to give an overview of the development of the PECL in the historical context of "contract law harmonisation" in the EU.

1. Harmonisation of contract laws in the European Union

The establishment and furtherance of a single Internal Market among its Member States constitutes a primary objective of lawmaking in the EU, and the existence of different national legal systems in the Member States is regarded as a barrier to the free flow of goods, services, people, and capital across the continent. *A fortiori*, the EU legislator aims to gradually establish a pan-European legal infrastructure in relation to any sectors that are relevant to cross-border transactions, while at the same time ensuring a high level of consumer protection. Self-evidently, many of the Directives and Regulations enacted for these two main purposes directly penetrate into or indirectly shape the substance of the Member States' laws on contracts.[36]

For the time being, however – and especially after the Union grew from 15 to 27 Member States in 2004 and 2007, respectively –, significant substantive differences among national contract law systems persist, with inconsistencies appearing even within the consistently growing *acquis communautaire*.[37] Such incoherence is magnified by the fact that each Member States individually implements each Directive and may derogate from many of the minimum standards imposed therein in favour of stricter rules. Moreover, despite the wide range of already harmonised sectors, European legislation remains sector-specific[38] and all fundamental issues of contract law and commercial law, such as formation of

36 See, *e.g.*, Reiner Schulze, *Common Frame of Reference and Existing EC Contract Law* (2008), and Bettina Heiderhoff, *Gemeinschaftsprivatrecht* (2007), for overviews of European legislation on contract law in general and on issues of non-performance and remedies in particular.

37 The term "*acquis communautaire*" refers to the entirety of existing EU legislation and the decisions of the European Court of Justice.

38 Current EU legislation is generally described as being "sector-specific", meaning that its Regulations, Directives and Recommendations each address only particular areas or issues of contract law (*e.g.*, e-commerce, travel contracts, consumer credits or employment) that are considered to require pan-European minimum standards in order to secure the functioning and further integration of the Internal Market.

contracts, performance or agency, are still regulated by the national laws of the Member States. After all, this is one reason why calls for further harmonisation and more coherence among European and domestic legislation on contracts as a means of facilitating inter-European trade are becoming more and more insistent.

In response, the European Commission – *i.e.*, the EU's executive body – has acknowledged the need for a more cohesive approach and taken the initiative to explore various options and alternatives on how to achieve it.[39] One of the options contemplated by the Commission is to abandon its current sector-specific approach to consumer and contract law harmonisation in favour of a more integrated, so-called "horizontal", approach to European contract law. For this purpose, it is even considering "full harmonisation" by way of adopting an optional horizontal instrument, or "28th contract law system", applicable to cross-border transactions throughout the Internal Market.[40]

While the vivid discussion of these options among EU officials, politicians, scholars and legal professionals is likely to continue for some time, a network of academics identified and supported by the Commission and also endorsed by the European Parliament and the Council[41] has already prepared a "Draft Common Frame of Reference" (DCFR), an outline edition of which was published in 2009.[42] In 2010, the Commission appointed a group of experts to support the

39 See generally European Commission, *Green Paper on the Review of the Consumer* Acquis, COM(2006) 744 final (8 February 2007); *Communication from the Commission to the European Parliament and the Council: European Contract Law and the revision of the* acquis*: the way forward*, COM(2004) 651 final (11 November 2004); *Communication from the Commission to the European Parliament and the Council: A more coherent European Contract Law – An Action Plan*, COM(2003) 68 final (12 February 2003); and *Communication from the Commission to the Council and the European Parliament on European contract law*, COM(2001) 398 final (11 July 2001). For an overview of the sequence of communications issued by the European Commission on the subject of European contract law, see, *e.g.*, Reinhard Zimmermann, *European Contract Law: General Report*, Europäische Zeitschrift für Wirtschaftsrecht 2007 at 459 *et seq*.

40 See, *e.g.*, European Commission, *Green Paper on the Review of the Consumer Acquis*, *id.* at Question A2, 14. See also European Commission, *Green Paper from the Commission on policy options for progress towards a European Contract Law for consumers and businesses*, COM(2010) 348 final (1 July 2010).

41 See, *e.g.*, European Parliament, *Resolution of 12 December 2007 on European Contract Law* (ref. no. P6_TA-Prov(2007)0615), and Council of the European Union, *(Draft) Report to the Council on the setting up of a Common Frame of Reference for European contract law* (as endorsed by the Council of the European Union as a Council position on 18 April 2008 (doc. no. 886/08)).

42 See Study Group on a European Civil Code/Research Group on EC Private Law (Acquis Group), *Principles, Definitions and Model Rules of European Private Law – Draft Common Frame of Reference (DCFR) – Outline Edition* (2009). See also Reiner Schulze, *Common Frame of Reference and Existing EC Contract Law* (2008); Hugh Beale, *The Future of the Common Frame of Reference*, European Review of Contract Law 2007 at 257; and Zimmermann, *supra* note 39 at 460 *et seq.*, for a discussion of the relation between the CFR and existing EU legislation.

Commission in preparing a proposal for a final Common Frame of Reference (CFR) by selecting, reviewing and amending certain parts of the DCFR.[43] The DCFR and CFR aim to provide common fundamental principles, definitions of key concepts and model rules found in EU legislation, the national contract laws of the Member States, and international treaties like the CISG. The intention is that both the DCFR and the CFR will initially serve, *inter alia*, as publicly accessible "tool boxes" of model rules and definitions for legislation on a European and a national level, *viz.* as a set of guidelines for the revision of existing laws and the drafting of new (and hence more coherent) legislation on contracts, and as a source of reference for the European Court of Justice in interpreting rules of, or based on, EU legislation on contracts. What is more, the CFR may well be a precursor to a possible optional horizontal instrument of European contract law.

Given that the PECL have served as the primary basis of the DCFR,[44] the structure of the two instruments is very similar. Looking ahead, this also means that the European Principles are also likely to form the foundation of the possible optional instrument of European contract law or even of a European contract code. Both of these roles clearly demonstrate their significance as a contribution to the process of contract law harmonisation in the EU.[45]

2. History of the European Principles

The First Commission on European Contract Law, consisting of legal scholars from every Member State of the European Communities at the time,[46] took up its work in 1982 following two years of preparations. The leading force and chairman of the Commission was Professor Ole Lando from Copenhagen, a long-time advocate of a uniform European contract law instrument. Co-funded by the European Commission, this so-called "Lando Commission" held frequent meetings in which members presented comparative examinations of different fields of contract law in the Member States. These comparative analyses were eventually transposed into black letter rules.

43 See European Commission, *Commission Decision 2010/233/EU of 26 April 2010 setting up the Expert Group on a Common Frame of Reference in the area of European contract law*, O.J. 2010, L-105 (26 April 2010). For a summary of the background, drafting process and prospects of the CFR, see, *e.g.*, Beale, *id.* at 257.

44 See, *e.g.*, Ole Lando, *supra* note 15 at 246, and *supra* note 27 at 382.

45 See, *e.g.*, European Commission, *Communication from the Commission to the Council and the European Parliament on European Contract Law*, *supra* note 39 at § 53; Zimmermann, *supra* note 34 at 31; and Lando, *supra* note 27 at 382.

46 Members of the EC (now the European Union) at the time were Belgium, Denmark, France, Germany, Greece, Ireland, Italy, Luxemburg, the Netherlands, and the United Kingdom.

The working procedures of the Lando Commission closely resembled those of the UNIDROIT Working Group, and inspiration, too, was drawn not only from the domestic laws and statutes of the existing Member States, but also from external sources like the CISG, the Uniform Commercial Code (UCC), or the American Restatements of the Law of Contracts.[47]

A Second Commission on European Contract Law took over in 1992 and published Part I of the PECL, dealing with performance, non-performance and remedies, in 1994. A revised edition of Part I and a second part (on the rules of formation of contracts, authority of agents, validity of contracts, and interpretation) were released in a single volume in 1999, followed by a third part dealing with plurality of parties, set-off, illegality, conditions, and capitalization of interest among other subjects, in 2003. Though, at least currently, the Commission on European Contract Law itself does not hold any further meetings, much of the substance of the PECL has been incorporated in various more recent instruments (including the Draft Common Frame of Reference[48]) and is therefore, at least indirectly, subject to continuing development.

According to their drafters, the PECL are intended to provide uniform principles with a uniform terminology, cutting across the legal systems and socio-economic conditions in the countries that were members of the European Union at the time when the rules were drafted.[49] Hence intended to embody the "common core" of contract law in Europe,[50] the European Principles aim to facilitate cross-border trade within the EU and strengthen the Internal Market, primarily by providing an alternative to national legislation as well as a source of reference on European contract law for legislators, practitioners and researchers.[51]

III. Methodology, authority, substance and applicability

The two sets of Principles share far-reaching similarities in relation to both substance as well as each instrument's drafting process, structure and scope of application. This section therefore provides an introduction to the substance and characteristics of both instruments, sets out their most significant divergences, and finally examines their slightly varying practical relevance.

47 See Ole Lando/Hugh Beale (eds.), *Principles of European Contract Law, Parts I and II, Prepared by the Commission on European Contract Law, Combined and Revised Edition* (2000) at Introd. XX.

48 See, *e.g.*, Ole Lando, *supra* note 15 at 246, and *supra* note 27 at 382.

49 See Lando/Beale, *supra* note 47 at Introd. XXV *et seq.*

50 See *id.* at Introd. XXIV.

51 See *id.*

A. Methodology of the Working Groups

The methodology underlying the Principles has been described as "functional legal comparison" as a somewhat elevated form of comparative analysis of different legal systems regarding certain features of contract law.[52] It is comparable to the method used in the elaboration of the American Restatements of the Law of Contracts[53] in that both produce a collection of black letter rules supplemented by explanatory "Comments" (and, as in the PECL, comparative "Notes") to each rule, stressing differences and similarities among the major contract law systems.[54] As opposed to the rather descriptive nature of the Restatements, however, the Principles are intended to present best solutions, *i.e.,* the most practicable rules found on each issue in the legal systems considered, thus transcending and at the same time amplifying these sources of inspiration.[55] What is more, where considered appropriate by the drafters, they offer entirely innovative solutions that were unknown to any of the sources.

Otherwise containing only little criticism or indications of certain preferences regarding the regimes examined, both sets of Principles focus exclusively on the presentation of the most practicable and most representative rules found in or inspired by a pool of different legal systems. The working groups' independence from political interests (the "representatives" of the different legal systems were not delegated by their countries but chosen by the working groups) have allowed for them to be broader and less compromising than most supranational legislation and treaties.[56] This approach has also resulted in an extraordinarily "autonomous", or "neutral", character, which is responsible for much of the Principles' persuasive value, and it renders their rules considerably more flexible to being expanded or revised in response to new developments than domestic laws and international treaties (any changes to which need to be ratified by all signatory states).

Both the UPICC and the PECL are formulated in a way that is intended to allow for their further development, future additions, and the inclusion of experi-

52 See *cf.* Klaus-Peter Berger, *The lex mercatoria Doctrine and the UNIDROIT Principles of International Commercial Contracts*, Law & Policy in International Business 1997 at 943, 950.

53 The Restatements are published by the *American Law Institute* (see http://www.ali.org); the current "Restatement (Second) of the Law of Contracts" was released in 1981.

54 See Lando/Beale, *supra* note 47 at Introd. XXVI.

55 See *id.* at Introd. XXV *et seq.*

56 For instance, the CISG only covers sales law, and EU legislation also follows a so-called "sector-specific" approach.

ences gained from their use in practice.[57] At the same time, the extensive time-frame[58] of and the amount of comparative substance considered in the respective drafting processes have led to fairly broad recognition of this methodological approach, particularly in relation to the Principles' value as model laws for lawmakers[59] and as resources the supplementation and interpretation of national laws and international treaties on contractual issues.[60]

B. Structure and language

Each provision of the European Principles comprises three levels: first, the black letter rule; second, Comments explaining the rule's purpose and systematic context and giving brief Illustrations; and finally, Notes referring to the source(s) that inspired the rule and simultaneously comparing it to the concepts found among other major legal systems. The UPICC are presented in the same structure except that their drafters have not provided any comparative notes.

The general language and simplistic terminology of each instrument's black letter rules marks one of the two instruments' main appeals. In conjunction with the concise structure and good translatability of their provisions, this virtue allows for the Principles to be adopted *verbatim* as contractual provisions even by parties that are not familiar with drafting contracts. A second notable asset is the Principles' availability in almost all major languages of the world.[61] Even most consumers and small or mid-size businesses can find the provisions translated into at least one language that is convenient to them, and corporations doing business in multiple countries can adopt them as identical contract terms in multiple languages.

---

57 See Lando/Beale, *supra* note 51 at Introd. XXVII. In this context, PECL Art. 1:106(1) states that the "Principles should be interpreted and *developed* in accordance with their purposes" (emphasis added).

58 While the UPICC were published after 15 years of work, and another 10 years passed before a revised edition was published, the complete version of the PECL is the product of frequent meetings over more than 20 years.

59 See *cf. infra* F.

60 See also *infra* D and F.

61 The black letter rules of the 2004 version of the UPICC are available in the UNIDROIT Institute's official languages, *i.e.*, English and French, as well as 13 other languages (available at http://www.unidroit.org/english/principles/contracts/main.htm). The European Principles, which were originally drafted in English as well, have so far been translated into Bulgarian, Dutch, French, German, Italian, and Spanish (available at http://frontpage. cbs.dk/ law/commission_on_european_contract_law/).

C. Legal character and authority

Evidently, neither the UNIDROIT Institute nor the Commission on European Contract Law bear any legislative authority. As a result, the Principles are merely "soft law"[62] representing a consensus between different national and international contract laws, and their authority remains purely persuasive, as their application is entirely optional.[63] Nevertheless, both instruments have gained certain "legal relevance" by being used as sources of inspiration in the drafting, revision and interpretation of contract laws by domestic legislators and courts as well as – especially in the case of the European Principles – by the European Commission and the European Court of Justice.[64]

Yet, their non-legislative origin is also the source of some of the main reservations toward the Principles. Some observers have criticized that this approach illegitimately "privatized" or at least decentralized lawmaking as the drafting process underlying the Principles neither builds upon any legislative authority nor involves any official ratification.[65] In light of this observation, some warn that the Principles might be employed as a means to bypass (elected) legislators by applying such non-legislative rules to international transactions.[66] In fact, it has even been argued that the use of soft law to supplement or interpret contract laws was entirely incompatible with the normative primacy of national legislation.[67]

In all, these concerns appear excessively cautious. First, the Principles are not intended to *replace* any mandatory forum, and, second, the reliance of parties, courts or arbitral tribunals on any rules of soft law is possible only within the boundaries of the applicable conflict of law rules and therefore ultimately at the competent legislatures' discretion.

Regarding the methodology underlying the principles, some observers have criticized their somewhat scholarly nature and far-reaching scope of applicability by arguing that attempting to harmonise international law by way of comparing and blending such a large variety of legal systems could never lead to sufficiently practical provisions.[68] Whether such criticism is still valid or will prevail is

---

62 See, *e.g.*, Ulrich Drobning, *The UNIDROIT Principles in the Conflict of Laws*, Uniform Law Review 1998 at 385.

63 See *cf.* Friedrich Blase, *Die Grundregeln des Europäischen Vertragsrechts als Recht grenzüberschreitender Verträge* (2001) at 16, and Katharina Boele-Woelki, *Principles and Private International Law*, Uniform Law Review 1996 at 652, 657 *et seq.*

64 See generally *infra* F.

65 See, *e.g.*, Berger, *supra* note 52 at 950 and 953.

66 See *id.* at 953.

67 See, *e.g.*, Bettina Heiderhoff, Grundstrukturen des nationalen und eurpäischen Verbrauchervertragsrechts (2004) at 214.

68 See *id.* at 212.

strongly dependent on the Principles' appreciation and application in practice. In any case, though, their multi-national, flexible and neutral approach corresponds with the ways in which convergence and harmonisation develop in other areas affected by the globalization of business: competing national or regional economic, cultural and policy standards are compared and a broadly acceptable international standard evolves on the basis of their "common core" or a compromise.

What makes the Principles stand out especially in comparison to other instruments aimed at harmonising international contract laws is their dual value: on the one hand, having been developed unhampered by singular economic interests or political bargaining, they have been accepted as a concise model or source of inspiration for new legislation. On the other hand, while the harmonisation process is continuing and more and more contract legislation draws from the concepts presented by the Principles, their provisions can already be applied and "field-tested", thereby gradually creating awareness and familiarity among practitioners.

A valuable rudimentary consequence of the Principles' non-binding character is that, ultimately, their influence depends on their quality. In other words, the better their substance serves their purposes, the more they will be actually relied upon.

D. Applicability and substantive scope

Each set of Principles offers a list of – partly overlapping – general purposes.[69] According to their Preamble, the UPICC are intended to (1) serve as general rules for international commercial contracts; (2) identify "general principles of law" or "the *lex mercatoria*" where selected in contracts; (3) fill gaps in the relevant domestic law; (4) interpret or supplement existing international uniform law instruments such as the CISG; and (4) serve as a model for legislation by national and international legislators. Quite similarly, the five purposes stated in Article 1:101 of the European Principles are to (1) to facilitate cross-border transactions within Europe; (2) strengthen the single European market; (3) create an infrastructure for Community laws governing contracts; (4) provide guidelines for national courts and legislatures and fill gaps in national laws; (5) construct a linkage between the civil law and common law; and (6) provide a modern formulation of "general principles of law" or "*lex mercatoria*" relating to contracts.

69 See *cf.* Comment 8 to UPICC Preamble (the Comments to the UPICC have been published in International Institute for the Unification of Private Law (UNIDROIT), *supra* note 31) and Lando/Beale, *supra* note 47 at Introd. XXIII *et seq.*

Evidently, the two instruments' primary area of application is their choice as the *lex contractus*, *viz.* as rules governing a particular contract or a dispute arising from an international transaction, or as a source of reference for courts and arbitral bodies in interpreting national laws or conventions such as the CISG.[70] The subsection that follows examines the extent to which conflict of law rules permit the application of the Principles to such international[71] contracts.

1. Applicability of the Principles to international contracts

a. Parties' express choice of the Principles as lex contractus

Due to their non-legislative, or non-binding, character, a genuine choice of the Principles (as well as other soft law) as the *lex contractus* is considered impermissible under the conflict of law rules applicable in most countries. As a result, the incorporation of the Principles' black letter rules into contracts or their application to contracts cannot supersede any mandatory or non-discretionary, rules of the governing law.[72]

In the Member States of the European Union except Denmark, any contractual choice of law is now subject to the "Rome I Regulation",[73] which was adopted in 2008 to succeed the so-called Rome Convention on the law applicable to contractual obligations. Rome I determines the *lex contractus* applicable to contracts entered into by two or more parties located in different Member States. Art. 3(1) of the Regulation establishes that "[a] contract shall be governed by the *law* chosen by the parties" (emphasis added). Despite earlier moves to extend this choice, *inter alia*, to the UPICC and PECL, Art. 3 – similar to the Rome Convention – is clearly intended to allow only the choice of national laws or international treaties such as CISG, and not any soft law.[74] Choosing the Princi-

70 In a footnote to the UPICC Preamble and in Comment C to PECL Art. 1:101 (the Comments and Notes to the PECL have been published in Lando/Beale, *supra* note 47), respectively, both sets of Principles even provide proposals for the wording of a choice of law clause subjecting the contract to their Provisions.

71 In fact, PECL Art. 1:101(1) implies that the PECL are even intended to be applied to purely domestic contracts.

72 See also UPICC Art. 1.4; PECL Art. 1:103. For a general overview of the different views and arguments regarding the choice of the Principles as the lex contractus, see, *e.g.*, Drobnig, *supra* note 62 at 387 *et seq.*

73 Regulation (EC) No 593/2008 of the European Parliament and of the Council of 17 June 2008 on the law applicable to contractual obligations (Rome I).

74 See generally Stefan Leible/Matthias Lehmann, *Die Rom I-Verordnung*, Recht der Internationalen Wirtschaft 2008 at 528, 533. This also means that, fort the time being, Art. 3(1) of the Rome I Regulation does not encompass the choice of the Common Frame of Reference (CFR)

ples to apply *instead* of any domestic regime is therefore not permitted;[75] within these bounds, however, the parties may certainly adopt or refer to the Principles' provisions if and to the extent that the laws of the governing *lex contractus* are non-mandatory and allow for deviation as a matter of party autonomy or contractual freedom.

National or international conflict of law rules applicable in most other countries and regions impose similar limitations regarding the choice of soft law as the governing law.[76]

b. Applicability in absence of express choice by the parties

In the absence of any express (or valid) contractual choice of law clause, domestic courts may – if and to the extent that this is permitted by the applicable choice of law regime, autonomously decide that the contract shall be governed (entirely or in part) by the Principles.[77] The same applies if the contract provides or implies that disputes arising from it shall be governed by "general rules of (international) law", "the *lex mercatoria*", or "principles of international law".[78] While the Rome I Regulation rules out the application of the Principles in such instances, too,[79] observers have argued that the courts are allowed to rely on the Principles as

---

as the "law" governing a particular contract. See *cf.* Dieter Martiny, *Europäisches Vertragsrecht in Erwartung der Rom-I-Verordnung*, Zeitschrift für Europäisches Privatrecht 2008 at 79, 88.

75 This view has been expressly confirmed, *inter alia*, by the *Tribunale of Padova* (Italy), which declared a choice of the Principles as the lex contractus invalid and consequently considered their rules as merely bearing the authority of contractual provisions (see Tribunale di Padova, n. 40287 del 2001 (2005)).

76 In contrast to the Rome I Regulation, other conflict of law rules are conceived as being more liberal, most notably the 1994 Inter-American Convention on the Law Applicable to Contracts, ratified to this point by five members of the Organization of American States (OAS), namely Bolivia, Brazil, Mexico, Uruguay and Venezuela. This treaty is generally interpreted as allowing for an express choice of the UNIDROIT Principles as the *lex contractus* by the parties. Moreover, Comment 2 to § 1-302 of the United States Uniform Commercial Code (UCC) makes express reference to the possibility of agreeing upon the applicability of the UPICC. See generally Michael Joachim Bonell, *Towards a Legislative Codification of the UNIDROIT Principles?*, Uniform Law Review 2007 at 233, and *supra* note 19 at 180 *et seq.*

77 UPICC Preamble; PECL Art. 1:101(3)(b). See *cf.* Bonell, *supra* note 19 at 202; Drobnig, *supra* note 62 at 392 *et seq.*; and Ana M. López Rodriguez, *Lex Mercatoria and Harmonisation of Contract Law in the EU* (2003) at 343.

78 UPICC Preamble; PECL Art. 1:101(3)(a).

79 Art. 4(1) of the Rome I Regulation expressly states that the absence of a contractual choice of law by the parties leads to the application of a particular national law. This rules out the application of the Principles or other soft law as the governing law.

sources of reference for interpreting domestic laws[80] or international treaties such as the CISG.[81]

c. *Incorporation as contract terms and applicability under the lex contractus*

Most jurisdictions allow for the parties to derogate extensively from the rules of the applicable domestic law as a matter of party autonomy. Hence, subject to any non-derogable laws, the parties may incorporate soft law such as the Principles' black letter rules or the Incoterms provided by the International Chamber of Commerce while subjecting the contract to a domestic *lex contractus*.[82] In such cases, the Principles' provisions are binding to the extent that they are not contradictory to the relevant regime's mandatory rules.

---

80 For a discussion of the Principles' applicability to supplement or interpret purely domestic law, see *cf.* Boele-Woelki, *supra* note 63 at 670 *et seq.* In a notable *obiter dictum* (which stands in contradiction to the general attitude of English courts), an English judge has suggested to apply the UPICC or the CISG in interpreting English law in a purely domestic dispute. This opinion has prompted Michael Joachim Bonell (*supra* note 12 at 317) to observe an "increasing openness of English courts towards foreign and international source of inspiration".

81 UPICC Preamble; PECL Art. 1:101(4); CISG Art. 7(2). CISG Art. 7 provides the following rules:
"(1) In the interpretation of this Convention, regard is to be had to its international character and to the need to promote uniformity in its application and the observance of good faith in international trade.
(2) Questions concerning matters governed by this Convention which are not expressly settled in it are to be settled in conformity with the general principles on which it is based or, in the absence of such principles, in conformity with the law applicable by virtue of the rules of private international law."
For instance, CISG Art. 78 on interest, which does not contain any rules on when interest starts to accrue or on the method to determine the interest rate and the currency in which it is to be calculated, could be supplemented by the Principles' provisions (UPICC Art. 7.4.9 and PECL Art. 4:507). See generally Bonell, *supra* note 19 at 228 *et seq.*, and López Rodriguez, *supra* note 77 at 344. (See also Robert Koch, *Whether the UNIDROIT Principles of International Commercial Contracts may be used to interpret or supplement Article 25 CISG*, Internationales Handelsrecht 2005 at 65, arguing in favour of the supplementation of CISG Art. 25 by the UPICC.) However, see Rolf Herber, *„Lex mercatoria" und „Principles" – gefährliche Irrlichter im internationalen Kaufrecht*, Internationales Handelsrecht 2003 at 1, for a number of arguments invoked against the supplementation of CISG by the Principles.

82 See *cf.* Bonell, supra note 19 at 248, and Herbert Kronke, *UNIDROIT Principles: New Developments and Applications*, International Court of Arbitration Bulletin 2005, Special Supplement at 58. For a list of model clauses for international commercial contracts making reference to or being based on the UNIDROIT Principles, see Letterman, *supra* note 18.

d. Applicability in arbitral proceedings

In arbitral proceedings, the grounds for applying the Principles are somewhat broader than in disputes before courts of law, because arbitration statutes – particularly those based on the 1985 UNCITRAL Model Law on International Commercial Arbitration[83] – often allow for selection of soft law even as the exclusively applicable regime.[84] Against this background, it is widely recognized that an arbitration and choice of law clause according to which the Principles shall govern the contract in its entirety is binding upon the respective arbitral tribunal.[85]

In the absence of an express choice of the regime applicable in arbitral proceedings, the question of whether the arbitral body may autonomously apply the Principles as governing "law" is again dependent on the applicable national or international arbitration laws.[86]

2. Substantive scope

The Principles are intended for application to all types of contractual relationships, including contracts involving third parties[87] and contracts of indefinite validity.[88] Strictly speaking, parts of the Principles are not limited to contracts as they provide rules pertaining to obligations in general, *e.g.,* on set-off (UPICC Chapter 8; PECL Chapter 13) or assignment of rights (UPICC Chapter 9; PECL Chapter 11).

Geographically, the PECL are intended to apply if at least one of the parties is based in the European Union.[89] Within the borders of the EU, they may be applied to both cross-border and domestic contracts, and irrespective of whether the contract relates to a commercial or to a non-commercial transaction.[90] In this

83 See Art. 28(1) of the UNCITRAL Model Law on International Commercial Arbitration (amended version, 2006), according to which the arbitral tribunal is to decide the arbitral dispute in question "in accordance with such rules of law as are chosen by the parties as applicable to the substance of the dispute."

84 See generally Bonell, *supra* note 19 at 192 *et seq.*, and Drobnig, *supra* note 62 at 390, for further references. Art. 17 of the ICC Rules of Arbitration expressly permits the application of Principles in ICC arbitration as well. See also Comment 4 to UPICC Preamble.

85 For further references, see *cf.* Boele-Woelki, *supra* note 63 at 672 *et seq.*; Hein Kötz/Axel Flessner, *European Contract Law* (vol. I, 1997) at 19 *et seq.*; and Drobnig, *id.* at 389.

86 See *cf.* Drobnig, *id.* at 394, for further references.

87 See, *e.g.*, UPICC Art. 5.2.1; PECL Art. 10:101 *et seq.*

88 See, *e.g.*, UPICC Art. 5.1.8; PECL Art. 6:109 and 9:302.

89 PECL Art. 1:101(1).

90 See Lando/Beale, *supra* note 47 at Introd. XXV. Though the PECL are also intended for application to consumer transactions, some of the provisions aimed to ensure consumer protection appear not to provide for an appropriate level of consumer protection, and to contravene relevant

context, it has been emphasized that the PECL "will assist both the organs of the [European] Community in drafting measures and the courts, arbitrators and legal advisers in applying Community measures."[91] The UPICC are only concerned with *international commercial* transactions, but they are wider in the sense that their proposed scope of applicability is universal and not limited to the EU.[92]

If they are chosen to apply to a particular contract, both sets of Principles are intended to be of autonomous character like any domestic contract law system; hence, they comprise a number of mandatory provisions[93] and principles[94] from which the parties may not derogate. Similarly, the Principles are to be interpreted on the basis of and according to the general ideas and purposes embodied in their own provisions as well as the basic concepts underlying them.[95] However, neither the UPICC nor the PECL can at this stage be treated as being all-embracing or entirely self-contained contract law regimes.[96]

3. Further scope of applicability

Apart from the aforementioned proposed purposes, the Principles are intended to provide a source of reference for lawmakers, researchers and academics,[97] and they are supposed to contribute to the ongoing process of formulating a modern *lex mercatoria*.[98]

EU legislation. For instance, as opposed to most EC Directives, the PECL do not require consumer contracts to be in written form (PECL Art. 2:101(2)). Ole Lando has acknowledged this concern in relation to the PECL's possible lack of "social justice" due to their being too liberal (*supra* note 15 at 251). See also Dieter Medicus, *Voraussetzungen einer Haftung für Vertragsverletzung*, in Jürgen Basedow (ed.), *Europäische Vertragsrechtsvereinheitlichung und deutsches Recht* (2000) at 191 *et seq.*, and Zimmermann, *supra* note 34 at 30 *et seq.*

91 See Lando/Beale, *supra* note 47 at XXIII.

92 Being deliberately left undefined, the terms "international" and "commercial" shall be construed extensively (Comment 1 to UPICC Preamble), *i.e.*, they do not necessarily require the involvement of a merchant with all attributes required by most commercial codes.

93 UPICC Art. 1.5; PECL Art. 1:102(2).

94 For instance, the principle of good faith and fair dealing or the duty to cooperate.

95 UPICC Art. 1.6.2; PECL Art. 1.106(2). For a detailed overview of the basic ideas underlying the UPICC (and, equally, the PECL) – *viz.* freedom of contract; openness to usages; preservation of contracts; good faith and fair dealing; and policing against unfairness –, see Bonell, *supra* note 19 at 87 *et seq.*

96 See, *e.g.*, Bonell, *supra* note 19 at XIV.

97 See generally *id.* at 243 *et seq.*

98 See *cf.* Lando/Beale, *supra* note 47 at Introd. XVIII. In this context, see also the various databases collecting rules of international law, *e.g.*, http://www.lexmercatoria.org, http://www.transnational-law.de, or http://www.cisg.law.pace.edu, which also include the UNIDROIT Principles and European Principles.

On a critical note, it appears worth noting that neither Principles' own provisions and explanatory Comments provide any normative references or explanations whatsoever regarding their applicability. As a consequence, their actual sphere of applicability can be identified only with reference to the applicable domestic laws or treaties themselves or to secondary sources. In fact, more than anything else, the UPICC's Preamble and PECL Art. 1:101 come across more like appeals to contracting parties, legislators or arbitral judges to make us of the two instruments. For the purpose of minimizing uncertainty and increasing the Principles' practicability, future editions should provide a more precise determination of their sphere of applicability, *viz.* by including the positions of the major conflict of law regimes and arbitration rules on the question of whether the Principles may be chosen or applied as the *lex contractus*.

E. Differences in substance

Primarily due to their different regional and substantive scopes of applicability, the UPICC and the PECL account for a number of mostly slight divergences in substance. In most cases, however, their provisions closely correspond (in some parts even literally), and the expanded 2004 edition[99] of the UPICC now covers most of the issues addressed by the PECL.[100] What is more, any remaining substantial differences are almost entirely due to the differences in the two instruments' dogmatic backgrounds and proposed spheres of applicability.

The first group of divergences is due to their slightly different geographical scopes: whereas the UPICC's scope is universal and their rules are therefore designed to cover cross-border transactions all over the world, the PECL relate to (transnational and domestic) contracts that bear a connection to the European Union.[101] As a consequence, the PECL's general provision on good faith and fair dealing states that the meaning and implications of these terms should be determined according to European standards; conversely the UPICC expressly refer to "good faith and fair dealing in international trade".[102] This difference in perspective reappears in the two instruments' provisions on the relevance of usages: whereas the PECL establish that "[t]he parties are bound by a usage (…) considered generally

99 Provisions on authority of agents (Chapter 2 Sec. 2); third party rights (Chapter 5 Sec. 2); set-off (Chapter 8); assignment of rights; transfer of obligations and assignment of contracts (Chapter 9); and limitation periods (Chapter 10) were first included in the 2004 edition of the UPICC.

100 Issues of plurality of parties, illegality, conditions and interest are covered by the PECL but are not (yet) addressed by the UPICC.

101 UPICC Preamble; Comment A to PECL Art. 1:101(1).

102 PECL Art. 1:201(1); UPICC Art. 1.7(1).

applicable by persons in the same situation" and thereby refer to usages within the EU, the UPICC permit only the consideration of any "usage that is widely known to and regularly observed in international trade".[103] Furthermore, the European Principles need not take into account currencies that are not freely convertible[104] or countries without an average banking short rate or statutory rate of interest.[105] Finally, only the UNIDROIT Principles deal with permission requirements in relation to the performance of a contract[106] or with the determination of the relevant time zone.[107]

A second category of divergences arises from the aspect that, whereas the UPICC are strictly limited to commercial contracts,[108] the PECL are intended to provide rules for both commercial and non-commercial transactions.[109] As a result, the UPICC can afford to take a more liberal stance toward the validity of subsequently inserted deviant terms in confirmation letters,[110] or toward the validity of merger clauses.[111]

This difference regarding in their substantive scope of applicability is also responsible for the two instruments' diverging provisions on the incorporation of standard terms. The UPICC's general rules on formation of contracts apply also to the incorporation of standard terms; the PECL (also in line with the EU legislator's emphasis on consumer protection) are comparably more protective of consumers by stipulating that terms that are not negotiated individually are valid only if they were explicitly brought to the other party's attention.[112] By the same token, the UPICC provide that unfair contract terms are invalid only if (1) they are substantially unfair and (2) one party has taken advantage of an imbalance between its own position and the other party's position. Under the PECL, a significant imbalance alone entitles the inferior part avoid an unfair term.[113] Finally,

103 PECL Art. 1:105(2); UPICC Art. 1.9(2).

104 UPICC Art. 6.9.1(1)(a); PECL Art. 7:108.

105 PECL Art. 9:508(1); UPICC Art. 7.4.9(2).

106 UPICC Art. 6.1.14 *et seq.*

107 UPICC Art. 1.12(3).

108 UPICC Preamble. However, the Illustrations to various provisions of the UNIDROIT Principles indicate that this term is to be construed extensively, and it has even been observed that "[s]o wide-ranging are the illustrations that there is little room for international non-commercial contracts." See Joseph M. Perillo, *Force Majeure and Hardship under the UNIDROIT Principles of International Commercial Contracts*, Tulane J. of Int'l and Comp. L. (1997) at 5, 7.

109 PECL Art. 1:101(1).

110 UPICC Art. 2.1.12; PECL Art. 2:210 (which validate such terms only in relation to contracts between professionals).

111 UPICC Art. 2.1.17; PECL Art. 2:105(1) (which require a merger clause to be individually negotiated if it is to exclude the validity of any additional agreements).

112 UPICC Art. 2.1.19; PECL Art. 2:104.

113 UPICC Art. 3.10; PECL Art. 4:110(1).

UPICC Art. 6.1.7(1) (on payment) would appear to be appropriate in consumer transactions because it determines that the relevant currency shall be the currency used at the place of payment, which is usually the *seller's* place of business. By contrast, the PECL allow debtors to make payment "in any form used in the ordinary form of business".[114]

Other significant differences, such as the two sets of Principles' divergent rules on restitution,[115] are apparently due to no particular policy reason and thus of purely "technical" nature.[116]

F. Practical relevance

The extent to which both sets of Principles have been welcomed and are actually being applied in practice has prompted their drafters as well as external observers to express both satisfaction and confidence in their growing relevance.[117] In accordance with the purposes already proposed in each instrument, the Principles have been employed in a number of ways.[118] First, they have come to be frequently applied and referred to by arbitral bodies as the rules governing contractual dis-

114 PECL Art. 7:107(1).

115 UPICC Art. 9.3.6; PECL Art. 7.3.6 to 7.3.9.

116 For extensive rule-by-rule comparisons between the UPICC and the PECL, see Bonell, *supra* note 19 at 235 *et seq.*, and Bonell/Roberta Peleggi, *UNIDROIT Principles of International Commercial Contracts and Principles of European Contract Law: a Synoptical Table*, Uniform Law Review 2004 at 315; both articles characterize the differences between the two instruments as being either of merely "technical nature" or due to "policy" reasons. For a more general comparison, see also Arthur S. Hartkamp, *The UNIDROIT Principles for International Commercial Contracts and the Principles of European Contract Law*, European Review of Private Law 1994 at 341.

117 For the UPICC, see, *e.g.*, Michael Joachim Bonell, *UNIDROIT Principles 2004 – The New Edition of the Priniciples of International Commercial Contracts Adopted by the International Institute for the Unification of Private Law*, Uniform Law Review 2004 at 5, 7; Bonell, *supra* note 76 at 234; and Roy Goode, *International Restatements of Contract Law and English Contract Law*, Uniform Law Review 1997 at 232, according to whom the "response [to the UPICC] has been overwhelmingly favourable". For the PECL, see, *e.g.*, Lando/Beale, *supra* note 47 at XII *et seq.*, and Reinhard Zimmermann, *Die UNIDROIT-Grundregeln der internationalen Handelsverträge 2004 in vergleichender Perspektive*, Zeitschrift für Europäisches Vertragsrecht 2005 at 264.

118 See also a world-wide survey conducted by the *Center for Transnational Law (CENTRAL)* at the University of Münster/Germany on the use of transnational law in international contract practice and arbitration (Klaus Peter Berger/Holger Dubberstein/Sascha Lehmann/Viktoria Petzold, *The CENTRAL Study on the Use of Transnational Law in International Contract Law and Arbitration: Background, Procedure and Selected Results*, International Arbitration Law Journal 2000 at 145).

putes, and by national courts to supplement national or foreign contract laws or the CISG.[119] Second, especially the UPICC have on numerous occasions served as a model or source of reference in drafting or revising national contract laws.[120] Finally, both instruments are referred to in model contracts provided by international trade organizations.[121]

An online database, UNILEX,[122] gives an idea of how well especially the UNIDROIT Principles have been received by arbitral bodies in many parts of the world. The database currently carries a selection of well over 200 cases in which arbitrators or even courts of law[123] have applied or made reference to this instrument in decisions regarding contractual disputes. Other surveys and commentaries have also confirmed this wide-ranging recognition of the UPICC in each of the fields of application envisaged by their drafters.[124]

As for the European Principles, even affirming observers have stated that they have not gained similar practical relevance.[125] This might be due to their more narrow geographical focus on contracts with a connection to the European Union, where shared legal traditions and EU legislation already account for a fairly high level of harmonisation and where there is thus less need

---

119 See generally the database on the CISG maintained at *Pace University* (available at http://www.cisg.law.pace.edu), which frequently makes reference to the UPICC and PECL as supplementary sources to the CISG, and the summaries of major decisions or awards combining references to the UPICC provided by Bonell, *supra* note 19 at 262 *et seq.* and *supra* note 33.

120 Particularly the UPICC's rules and underlying research material have served as model laws and drafting guidelines for a number of reforms and new legislation such as the civil and contract codes of Argentina, China, Estonia, Germany, Israel, Lithuania, Mexico, the Netherlands, New Zealand, the Russian Federation, Vietnam, and the Canadian province of Quebec. See, *e.g.*, Ole Lando, *Salient Features of the Principles of European Contract Law*, 13 Pace Int'l L. Rev. (2001) at 339, 341; Reinhard Zimmermann, *Die „Principles of European Contract Law", Teil III*, Zeitschrift für Europäisches Privatrecht 1995 at 707, 712 *et seq.*; and Herbert Kronke, *supra* note 82 at 7. Moreover, the UPICC have formed the basis of a uniform contract law statute for the member states of the *Organisation pour l'harmonisation en Afrique du droit des affaires (OHADA)*, an organization of mostly francophone African countries (see Fontaine, *supra* note 25).

121 The Principles are now habitually referred to in the model contracts of both the *International Chamber of Commerce (ICC)* and the WTO/UNCTAD-related *International Trade Center (ITC)* as sources of rules that are eligible to be chosen to govern a particular contract. See *cf.* Kronke, *id.* at 58 and 61.

122 Maintained by the UNIDROIT Institute and available at http://www.unilex.info.

123 See especially Bonell, *supra* note 12, for a discussion of an *obiter dictum* in a decision of the English Court of Appeal (*ProForce Recruit Ltd. v. The Rugby Group Ltd.*, EWCA Civ. 69 (2006)) making reference to the UPICC.

124 See, *e.g.*, the survey carried out by the *Center for Transnational Law (CENTRAL)* at the University of Münster/Germany (*supra* note 118).

125 See, *e.g.*, Lando/Beale, *supra* note 47 at XII *et seq.*; Bonell, *supra* note 117 at 36; and Goode, *supra* note 117 at 232.

for parties or arbitral bodies to rely on uniform rules of soft law. Similarly, the PECL's more narrow geographical focus and their self-proclaimed footing on the "economic and social conditions prevailing in the Member States"[126] may also have had a limiting effect on their popularity among non-European stakeholders. Finally, the PECL's intended applicability to both commercial and non-commercial transactions – which made it necessary to include certain rules aimed at ensuring a minimum level of consumer protection – certainly reduces their value in disputes or questions regarding purely commercial contracts. Ultimately, the bundle of the aforementioned factors may simply render the PECL somewhat less practicable to arbitrators than the purely commercially oriented UPICC.

Nonetheless, the general appreciation of the PECL among observers and the fact that their substance has – albeit only occasionally – been considered even by courts outside Europe,[127] suggests that their substance is held in high esteem even where they "compete" with the UPICC. What is more, the PECL's ultimate "breakthrough" may be yet to come as they practically form the basis of the Common Frame of Reference (CFR) and thus perhaps even of an (optional) uniform instrument on European contract law.[128] By contrast, the conversion of the UPICC into a binding instrument appears to be highly unlikely.[129]

As for their proposed use as comparative sources of reference and their express adoption into international contracts, it is obviously difficult to assess the true extent to which the Principles have been employed for these purposes. Nonetheless, it appears fair to conclude that especially the UPICC have succeeded in all of their intended fields of application.

In any case, it is worth citing one commentator's straightforward verdict regarding the Principles' value and relevance to the process of international contract law harmonisation: "[a]s the market changes from the gathering of merchants in a limited geographical spot to a global interchange of communications, the myriad local laws of the marketplace are no longer adequate to assure the commercial community that even-handed rules will govern their transactions. Principles [are] one step toward such assurance."[130]

---

126 See, *cf.*, Lando/Beale, *supra* note 47 at XX.

127 See, *e.g.*, *GEC Marconi Sys. Pty Ltd. v. BHP Info. Tech Pty Ltd.*, Fed. Ct. Austl. (2003), available at http://www.unilex.info.

128 See, *e.g.*, Zimmermann, *supra* note 34 at 31, and *supra* II(B)(1).

129 See, *cf.*, Bonell, *supra* note 76 at 244.

130 See Joseph M. Perillo, *UNIDROIT Principles of International Commercial Contracts: The Black Letter Text and a Review*, Fordham Law Review 1994 at 281, 316.

IV. Alternatives worth coexisting, or competing variations of similar content?

The preceding comparison of the Principles' most significant divergences[131] shows that, particularly after the completion of the 2004 version of the UPICC, the two instruments are indeed very similar and the great majority of substantive differences are not due to the two drafting groups' dogmatic preferences but rather to their different scopes of application. This observation certainly raises the question of whether there is a need to retain and keep developing both instruments.

The historical explanation for why two such similar projects were carried out in parallel has been recited in numerous articles and treatises: whereas the UNIDROIT Institute had considered taking up work on the UPICC since the early 1970s, many observers were sceptical toward the feasibility and the chances of success, mainly because previous comparable efforts had received only little appreciation. At the same time, however, harmonisation of contract law in the European Union was already gaining momentum, and the pursuit of harmonising contract laws in this region seemed both more promising and more feasible. Eventually, the UNIDROIT Working Group and the Lando Commission took up work simultaneously and were even interconnected as a result of the dual membership of some of their respective members. When it emerged later that both instruments would be very similar in structure, contents and purposes, both were apparently already too far advanced to justify the abandonment of either one of them.[132]

Some observers have expressed a concern that the existence of two similar but yet not entirely identical sets of rules that may in many respects be applied alternatively might increase the very legal uncertainty and confusion they are intended to reduce.[133] The most frequent response to this concern has been that the two instruments' different regional and substantive scopes provide sufficient space for a non-competing coexistence; while most of the arbitral awards referring to the UPICC do not make mention of the PECL,[134] the PECL play an important role in the EU's harmonisation efforts.

Hence, it appears as though the UPICC and PECL never really competed for exclusiveness, for instance by seeking to provide rivalling ideas or striving to be

---

131 See *supra* III(E).

132 See *cf.* Bonell, *supra* note 29 at 241 *et seq.*

133 See *cf.* Letterman, *supra* note 18 at 268, and Kessedijan, *Un exercise de rénovation des sources du droit des contrats du commerce international: Les Principes proposés par l'Unidroit*, Revue critique de droit international 1995 at 641, 669.

134 See *cf.* Michael Joachim Bonell, *The UNIDROIT Principles in Practice: The Experience of the First Two Years*, Uniform Law Review 1997 at 34, 35.

the better of two equivalent alternatives.[135] Rather, it is fair to say that, due to their different fields of use and the passing of more than 15 years of "peaceful" coexistence in spite of their close resemblance, each set of Principles has gained its own share of recognition and practical significance.

135 See, *e.g.*, Bonell, *supra* note 19 at XII.

Chapter II: Overview of Indian statutory contract law

I. Indian Contract Act, 1872

A. History

A blend of Hindu[136] and English law, the Indian Contract Act was enacted in the course of a move toward codification of Indian law in 1872.[137] It came into force on 1 September of that year.

Indian law in general has emerged in conjunction with the evolution of a culture that is now well over 3,000 years old. In the centuries following the medieval period of Indian history, Hindu laws were continuously recorded and collected in a body of literature named *Dharmashastras*, a part of which, the *Vyavaharmayukha*, also contained rules on contracts. The only secular collection of rules on politics and government, the *Arthshastra of Kautilya*, which was written around 300 B.C., provides another source of principles of Hindu contract law, for instance in relation to contractual relationships in villages.[138]

English law was introduced to India in the 18th Century, when the British Crown established so-called *Mayor's Courts* in Calcutta (now Kolkata), Madras (Chennai), and Bombay (Mumbai).[139] Where appropriate, these tribunals were to apply, where appropriate, British statutory law being in effect since before or in 1726.[140] This creeping introduction of English common law[141] as the "primary"

136 For a cursory overview of Hindu law, see, *e.g.*, Konrad Zweigert/Hein Kötz, *Introduction to Comparative Law*, (3rd ed., 1998) at 306 *et seq.*

137 For a concise overview of the history of Indian contract law, see *cf.* Nilima Bhadbhade (ed.), *Mulla Indian Contract and Specific Relief Acts*, vol. I (12th ed., 2001) at 1 *et seq.*

138 For a discussion of Hindu contract law, see, *e.g.*, P.V. Kane, *History of Dharmashastras*, vol. III (1946) at 411 *et seq.* Conversely to Hindu law, Islamic (or Mahomedan) law in India contained detailed rules on contracts, which included general principles of contract law and rules applicable only to certain types of contracts like commercial contracts (see *cf.* Tahir Mahmood, *The Muslim Law of India* (3rd ed., 2002).

139 In the 18th and 19th centuries, these three *Mayor's Courts* in the three cities were replaced by today's High Courts.

140 In some matters, including contracts, the traditional laws and usages of Hindus or Mahommedans were to be applied when both parties involved in a dispute were Hindus or Mahommedans, respectively.

141 The term "common law" may be defined as "[t]he body of law derived from judicial decisions, rather than from statutes or constitutions" or as "[t]he body of law based on the English legal

Indian law continued until the mid-1800s, when the Indian Law Commission, which was first established in 1834, took up the task of codifying the law in certain areas (that were designated by what is known as the Charter of 1865).

Codification had become necessary because after 1726, competing legislative bodies had independently enacted various different and in some parts contradicting laws that were in turn applied individually by the chief courts and the tribunals instated by the Crown.[142] As a result, Indian law today is a system of codified law with a common-law tradition.

As part of the codification effort, the Law Commissions was also mandated to prepare a statute on contractual relationships. The final draft of the Contract Act drew from suggestions by the Third Indian Law Commission as well as various codes of other countries, including Field's Civil Code for New York. Nevertheless, it closely corresponded to English common law. Prior legislation relating to particular types of contracts[143] was partly repealed by the Indian Contract Act and partly remained in force. The Act generally superseded Hindu and Mahomedan law as it applied to all persons irrespective of their religion or heritage. However, some traditional Hindu and Mahomedan laws, especially the respective personal laws, remained in effect.[144] On the basis of the principles of "justice, equity and good conscience", courts were to apply English law in cases where the Contract Act did not offer a solution that was to be considered as being satisfactory with a view on Indian customs.

Since its enactment in 1872, the Indian Contract Act has been amended various times. The most substantial change was the transfer of its provisions on sale of goods and on partnerships into the Sale of Goods Act, 1930, and the Partnership Act, 1932 respectively.[145] After India's independence from Britain in 1947, the Contract Act practically remained in force in both India and Pakistan, and it became subject to the concurrent authority of the federal and state legislatures in India under the Constitution of 1950.[146] Since then, the trend toward enacting rules on general issues of contract law in the Contract Act and supplementing it

system, as distinct from a civil-law system." See Bryan A. Garner (ed. in chief), *Black's Law Dictionary* (2nd ed., 2001) at 114.

142 Based on the combination of its common-law tradition and codification, Indian private law today is a system of codified law derived from common-law tradition.

143 *E.g.*, the Interest Act, 1839; the Indian Bills of Lading Act, 1856; the Carriers Act, 1865; and the Workman's Breach of Contract Act, 1859.

144 For instance, the "*damdupat* rule", which holds that interest may not exceed the principal, is still valid in the state of Maharashtra, and in the Presidency Town of Calcutta.

145 In addition, several specific statutes including the Negotiable Instruments Act, 1881, the Transfer of Property Act, 1882, and the Specific Relief Act, 1877 were enacted after the Contract Act.

146 The Indian Constitution subjects the areas of civil law and procedural law to the concurrent authority of the *Lok Sabha* and the state parliaments.

with more specific statutes on particular types of contract has been upheld. Most notably, the remedy of specific performance is regulated by the Specific Relief Act, 1963.[147] Similarly, special courts dealing with specific matters have been established.[148]

Recurring calls a uniform contract code that would incorporate the various specific acts have so far not generated any tangible action.[149] However, observers have questioned especially the Contract Act's capacity to adequately deal with more recent contractual issues of growing significance. For instance, while other countries have enacted special laws regulating franchising contracts – a contract type that is particularly relevant with regard to information technology services and the subcontinent's growing retail sector –, India still lacks a specific regulatory framework on the subject.

B. Scope and structure

The Indian Contract Act applies to all Indians, regardless of their religion, in all states and provinces except the State of Jammu and Kashmir (Indian Contract Act Sec. 1). As India has not ratified the CISG, domestic statutes are the only source of rules applicable to contractual relationships.

Supplemented by the Specific Relief Act, 1963, which regulates the remedy of specific performance, and other specific statutes,[150] the Contract Act provides rules on all general matters of contract law including specific types of contracts, and on its own interpretation and applicability. Yet, the Act is not intended to exhaustively regulate every issue related to contract law; rather, as stated in its Preamble, it is intended to "define and amend certain parts of the law relating to contracts".[151] Though being the primary source of law, the statute thus permits the courts to adhere to Indian case law and consider persuasive external sources. In interpreting the Contract Act, reliance upon principles of English law is generally

147 See also *infra* II and Ch. V. Other specific acts passed after 1950 include the Forward Contracts (Regulation) Act, 1952; the Multimodal Transportation of Goods Act, 1993; the Securities Contracts (Regulation) Act, 1956; and the Consumer Protection Act, 1986.

148 *E.g.*, the *Railways Claims Tribunal.*

149 In fact, ongoing discussion about a uniform instrument for India almost exclusively relate to a unification of Indian personal and family laws. See *cf.* The Times of India (not attributed), *Nobody can direct House on uniform civil code: SC*, The Times of India, 18 October 2008 at 15.

150 See *supra* notes 147 and 145. Particularly the sale of goods and the law of partnerships are regulated by specific statutes, namely the Sale of Goods Act, 1930 and the Partnership Act, 1932.

151 Contracts under the Indian Contract Act are agreements that are "enforceable by law" (Sec. 2(h)); agreements are "every promise and every set of promises, forming the consideration of each other" (Sec. 2(e)).

not permitted unless the statute cannot be understood without an examination of English common law as its doctrinal foundation.[152] What is more, when deciding disputes that are clearly addressed by the Contract Act, Indian courts are not required to refer to previous judicial decisions. On the other hand, Indian courts frequently make reference to English law where the issue in question is not covered by any statutory provision, and it is acknowledged that relevant decisions of other Commonwealth courts or courts in the United States of America may also bear persuasive value in a particular case.[153]

As the Indian Contract Act does not contain any choice of law provision, the corresponding rule of English common law is generally applied. In this context, the Indian Supreme Court has held that an express or implied *bona fide* and legal choice by the parties that does not oppose public policy shall be the primary indicator for the applicable law. Other indicators such as the type of transaction or its closest connection are to be considered only to supplement such an express choice, or if neither the parties' choice nor their intentions can be determined.[154]

In 1996, India enacted a new arbitration law, which is based on the UNCITRAL Model Law on International Commercial Arbitration (1985).[155] Apart from setting the stage for arbitration as an efficient alternative in a jurisdiction where trials in courts usually last a decade and the courts are overwhelmed by a high volume of litigation, the enactment of the Indian Arbitration and Conciliation Act as well as India's accession to the New York Convention on Recognition of Foreign Arbitral Awards are exemplary of India's continuing efforts to reform its judicial and administrative environment with a view on its integration into global markets.

The Arbitration and Conciliation Act does not expressly prohibit the application of the UNIDROIT Principles or Principles of European Contract Law: in international (commercial) disputes, arbitrators are to make a decision that is in conformity with the rules of law designated in the contract.[156] In absence of such an express choice by the parties, arbitral tribunals are supposed to apply the rules of law that they consider appropriate in the circumstances.[157]

---

152 See generally Bhadbhade, *supra* note 137 at 15 *et seq.*, for further references.

153 See Manmohan Lal Sarin, *Contract Unconscionability in India*, 14 Loyola Los Angeles International & Comparative Law Journal (1992) at 569, 570.

154 For the scope of the choice of law by the parties and references to English and Indian case law, see *cf.* Bhadbhade, *supra* note 137 at 16 to 27.

155 For the background and an overview of Indian arbitration law, see, *e.g.*, Tracy S. Work, *India Satisfies Its Jones for Arbitration: New Arbitration Law in India*, 10 Transnational Law (1997) at 217.

156 Indian Arbitration and Conciliation Act Part I Ch. VI Sec. 28(1)(b)(i) to (ii).

157 Indian Arbitration and Conciliation Act Part I Ch. VI Sec. 28(1)(b)(iii).

The Indian Contract Act provides comments, explanations and illustrations to certain sections, often integrating case law into the provisions. Explanations and comments are intended to concretize or supplement the respective section, while illustrations represent general common-law rules to be considered in construing the rule. This format closely resembles that of the Principles, where each provision is accompanied by explanatory comments and, as in the European Principles, by comparative notes referring to the legal systems examined, and it constitutes a rare body of law blending statutory rules and codified (English) common law.

II. Specific Relief Act, 1963

Under common-law tradition, specific relief with regard to obligations other than those to pay money is treated as a form of judicial redress. As a consequence, the decision of whether a contract should be enforced is left entirely to the courts' discretion, specific performance being ordered only where awarding monetary compensation appears inadequate.[158] Even though specific relief is thus practically a matter of civil procedure, the Indian legislature enacted a separate code for this remedy in as early as 1877, at a time when English courts had just started to recognize that contracts should be specifically enforced in certain instances.[159] The Specific Relief Act, 1877 was replaced by a revised statute in 1963. The most significant difference between the Act of 1877 and the Specific Relief Act, 1963 is that the illustrations included in the first Act were not adopted into its successor.

The Indian Supreme Court has held that the Specific Relief Act, 1963 – just as the Indian Contract Act – is neither complete nor exhaustive; it is thus open to judicial interpretation and allows for the courts' decisions to be guided by English law as well as persuasive case law from other Commonwealth jurisdictions or from the United States of America.[160]

---

158 See generally infra Ch. V(B)(1).

159 See *cf.* Bhadbhade, *supra* note 137 at 2366, for further references. For an overview of the development and the substance of the law of specific relief in England, see, *e.g.*, Guenter H. Treitel, *The law of contract* (5th ed., 1979) at 752 *et seq.*

160 See Bhadbhade, *id.* at 2370, for references to decisions of the Indian Supreme Court, and *supra* I(B).

Chapter III: Non-performance in general

I. Generally

A. Principles

1. Unitary concept of non-performance

The Principles' notion of "non-performance" is based on a unitary concept: any failure to perform or any non-conforming performance of a contractual obligation, irrespective of its cause or consequences, constitutes non-performance.[161] The particular cause (*e.g.*, delay, defectiveness or impossibility) and the substantiality of the failure are relevant only to the determination of which and to what extent remedies are available to the aggrieved party, or whether the particular non-performance merely constitutes a "remedy-less" failure. While the term non-performance thus serves as a general designation for what is described as "breach of contract", "default" etc. in other contract law systems,[162] each remedy[163] has particular requirements and it is only in this context that a distinction between excused or unexcused or fundamental or non-fundamental non-performance is of relevance.[164]

The Principles' rules on non-performance and its remedies gravitate around the objectives of preserving the contract (*favor contractus*) and encouraging

161 See UPICC Art. 7.1.1; PECL Art. 8:101(1). This unitary concept, which is also found in other international instruments such as the CISG (*e.g.*, Art. 45 and 61) as well as in the American Uniform Commercial Code (UCC) and in EC legislation (*e.g.*, Directive 99/44/EC on certain aspects of the sale of consumer goods and associated guarantees), differentiates between different types of non-performances only with regard to the remedies available for the default ("remedy approach"). See generally Perillo, *supra* note 130 at 302; Reinhard Zimmermann, *Konturen eines europäischen Vertragsrechts*, Juristenzeitung 1995 at 477, 481; and Constantin Düchs, *Die Behandlung von Leistungsstörungen im Europäischen Vertragsrecht* (2006) at 51 *et seq.*

162 The rather neutral term "non-performance" was apparently chosen because – unlike the common-law term "breach of contract" – it also comprises excused failures to perform, *e.g.* those due to *force majeure* (UPICC Art. 7.1.7; PECL Art. 8:108). See also *infra* B.

163 The four general remedies provided in UPICC Chapter 7 and PECL Chapter 9 are: right to withhold performance; recovery of money due or specific performance; termination of the contract; and damages. Unlike the UPICC, the PECL also expressly provide a remedy of reduction of price (PECL Art. 9:401).

164 See generally *infra* Ch. IV(I).

completion of performance (*pacta sunt servanda*) by any means.[165] For instance, it is provided that the contract remains valid in any case of non-performance, including initial impossibility (UPICC Art. 3.3; PECL Art. 4:102). As a result, each party is strictly liable to perform its contractual obligations ("no-fault liability"[166]) or pay damages unless the failure to perform is excused.[167] On another note, the promisor's general right to cure before the promise is entitled to terminate the contract (UPICC Art. 7.1.4; PECL Art. 8:104) illustrates the fundamental status of the principle of *favor contractus* within the Principles' rules on non-performance.

2. *What constitutes non-performance*

The Principles' general conceptions and terminology of non-performance closely resemble each other and may well be considered as being identical with respect to their substantive cornerstones.

Art. 7.1.1 of the UNIDROIT Principles defines non-performance as a "failure by a party to perform any of its obligations under the contract, including defective performance or late performance". Non-performance is thus constituted by any type of default regarding a party's contractual or statutory obligations, including complete failure to perform, fully or partially non-conforming performance, or violation of a secondary obligation.[168] Similarly, the term does not distinguish between excused and non-excused, or fundamental and non-fundamental non-performance; these qualifications are relevant only with regard to the consequences of the particular failure to perform.[169] However, if the failure is caused by the promisee or by an event for which the oblige bears the risk, it does not constitute non-performance in the sense of Art. 7.1.1.[170]

The European Principles provide a definition of non-performance in Art. 1:301(4): "'non-performance' denotes any failure to perform an obligation under

165 See *cf.* Arthur Rosett, *supra* note 6 at 447 *et seq.* See generally Bonell, *supra* note 19 at 87 *et seq.*

166 Being found also in the CISG and a number of recently revised domestic legal systems, the concept of no-fault liability appears to steadily replace civil-law systems' traditional conception of requiring fault or responsibility for liability for performance. See *cf.* Zimmermann, *supra* note 161 at 481.

167 UPICC Art. 7.4.1; PECL Art. 8:101(1) and 8:108(1). The most significant causes of excused non-performance are interference or withholding of performance by the other party (UPICC Art. 7.1.2-3); PECL Art. 8:108(3)) and *force majeure* (UPICC Art. 7.1.7; PECL Art. 8:108). See *infra* III and VII.

168 See Comment to UPICC Art. 7.1.1.

169 See UPICC Art. 7.1.2, 7.1.3, 7.1.7, 7.3.1 and 7.4.1.

170 Though this result does not emanate directly from the black letter rule of UPICC Art. 7.1.2, it is clearly contemplated by Comment 1, according to which "the relevant conduct does not become excused non-performance but loses the quality of non-performance altogether." See generally *infra* II(A).

the contract, whether excused or not excused, and includes delayed performance, defective performance and failure to co-operate in order to give full effect to the contract." Just as under the UPICC, the cause of the non-performance is irrelevant with regard to the terminology, and the qualification of a failure to perform in accordance with the contract as non-performance is neither dependent on its being excused or unexcused nor does it presuppose a minimum degree of gravity.[171]

However, despite the fact that the wording of UPICC Art. 7.1.1 ("failure to perform *any* of its obligations under the contract" (emphasis added)) and PECL Art. 8:101(1) ("does not perform *an* obligation under the contract" (emphasis added)) appear to imply that the term non-performance does not necessarily require a remedy to be attributed to the particular non-compliance with the contract, Ole Lando among others has stated that non-performance under the Principles – similar to breach of contract under the CISG and common-law tradition – in fact does presuppose the availability of at least one remedy.[172]

The Principles also state that violation of an *accessory obligation* such as the duty not to disclose the other party's trade secrets, the duty of good faith and fair dealing,[173] or, on the promisee's part, the duty to receive or accept a valid tender of performance,[174] or violation of the duty to act in good faith and maintain fair dealing (UPICC Art. 1.7; PECL Art. 1:201),[175] may also constitute non-performance. The same applies if the oblige terminates the contract and subsequently abandons its performance without actually being entitled to do so.[176]

As a basis of their provisions on non-performance, both sets of Principles set out detailed rules on performance (UPICC Chapter 6; PECL Chapter 7), *e.g.*, on the time or quality and quantity of performance. These rules are applicable to the extent that they have not been altered or excluded by the parties.[177] If a party

171 See, *e.g.*, award of *Centro de Arbitraje de México* of 30 November 2006, available at http://www.unilex.info: "[I]ndeed, as stated in Article 7.1.1 of the UNIDROIT Principles, any failure by a party to perform any of its obligations under the contract is a non-performance" (emphasis added).

172 See, *e.g.*, Ole Lando, *Non-Performance (Breach) of Contracts*, in Arthur S. Hartkamp *et al.* (eds.), *Towards a European Civil Code* (3rd ed., 2004) at 509; Lando, *supra* note 120 at 359; and Lando, *The European Principles in an Integrated World*, European Review of Contract Law 2005 at 3, 12.

173 See, *e.g.*, Comment 2 to UPICC Art. 7.3.2.

174 See Comment 1 to UPICC Art. 7.3.4 and Comment A to PECL Art. 8:105.

175 See, *e.g.*, Comment 2 to UPICC Art. 7.3.2.

176 See Comment A to Art. 8:101.

177 Unlike the PECL, the UPICC draw a general distinction between two kinds of contractual obligations, namely "duties to achieve a specific result" (UPICC Art. 5.1.4(1)), which are violated if the obligor fails to achieve the promised result, and "duties of best efforts" (Art. 5.1.4(2)), which are violated if the obligor has failed to apply the agreed level of care or skill. Nonetheless, Ole

entrusts performance of a particular obligation to a third party, the other party nevertheless retains its claim against the actual promisor.[178]

B. Indian statutory law

As opposed to the Principles, the Indian Contract Act does not provide an express definition of what this statute describes as "non-performance"[179] or "breach of contract".[180] Its Chapter IV (Sec. 37-67; "Of the Performance of Contracts") only sets out a collection of rules on performance of and failure to perform contractual obligations. These provisions hence establish the requirements of conforming performance as well as the consequences of a breach of contract.

As a basic rule, parties to a contract must perform, or offer to perform, their respective promises unless performance is dispensed with or excused under the Contract Act or any other statute such as the Indian Sale of Goods Act, 1930 (Indian Contract Act Sec. 37).[181] This absolute duty to perform is violated by any (total or partial and actual or anticipatory) failure or refusal to perform a contractual obligation. Any action by which a party disables itself or prevents the other party from performing a contractual obligation also constitutes a breach of contract.[182] Unless the non-performance is excused, a party is strictly liable for any such failure to perform its obligations, and the other party is discharged from its own obligation and may invoke the remedies provided by the Indian Contract Act as well as the Specific Relief Act.

Lando (*supra* note 172 at 509) has made the same distinction in relation to the European Principles.

178 UPICC Art. 9.2.6(2); PECL Art. 8:107.

179 In common-law jurisdictions, the term "non-performance" or "nonperformance" generally denotes any "[f]ailure to discharge an obligation (esp. a contractual one)." See Garner, *supra* note 141 at 480.

180 The term "breach of contract" may be generally defined as "[v]iolation of a contractual obligation, either by failing to perform one's own promise or by interfering with another party's performance." See *id.* at 77.

181 The sections following Sec. 37 provide rules on the following subjects: death of the promisor (Indian Contract Act Sec. 37(2)); requirements for the tender to perform (Sec. 38); which person must perform (Sec. 40-45); the time and place for performance (Sec. 46-50); performance under contracts in which time is essential (Sec. 55); impossible acts (Sec. 56); performance under contracts containing illegal terms (Sec. 57-58); monetary obligations (Sec. 59-61); and contracts which need not be performed (Sec. 62-67), including the effect of the promisee's failure to provide facilities necessary for the performance (Sec. 67).

182 See generally R. K. Bangia, *Indian Contract Act* (11th ed., 2004) at 242, and Bhadbhade, *supra* note 137 at 993. See also *infra* II(B).

While the term "non-performance" itself is used only sporadically,[183] "breach of contract", in accordance with English common law, requires a failure to perform *and* a cause of action for the promisee to claim damages.[184] This conception implies that breach of contract – just as under English common law[185] – is to be asserted only if the non-performance is unexcused.[186] The question of *discharge*, or termination, of the contract, on the other hand, is independent from the question of whether a breach of contract has occurred. For instance, frustration may entail discharge of the contract, but the respective failure to perform does not necessarily constitute a breach.

If the contract is substituted, rescinded[187] or altered, or to the extent that the promisee makes use of its right to dispense with or remit performance in part or in full, breach or non-performance of the respective obligations cannot be argued (Sec. 62 *et seq.*).

The doctrines of *impossibility* and *frustration* inherit a somewhat specific status within the Indian Contract Act. If performance is (or subsequently becomes) physically impossible, impossible because of frustration, or unlawful, the contract is inevitably considered as being void (Sec. 56(1) and (2)) and performance is therefore excused from the time of occurrence of impossibility or unlawfulness. Hence, unless the contract involves *alternative* promises and performance of at least one of these promises would not be unlawful (Sec. 58), frustration and impossibility do not constitute breach but automatically terminate the contract.[188]

While the remedies available for a party's failure to perform a contractual obligation are generally laid out in Chapter VI of the Indian Contract Act (Sec. 73 to 75 ("Of the Consequences of Breach of Contract")), provisions on the consequences of a breach of contract in specific situations, *e.g.*, where the promisor knew of an impediment that led to impossibility of performance (Sec. 56(3)), are also disseminated throughout Chapter IV.

183 See, *e.g.*, Indian Contract Act Sec. 56(3).

184 See the Comment to Indian Contract Act Sec. 73: "Breach of contract naturally entails payment of compensation by the defaulting party for any loss or damages occasioned by the breach." See also Bangia, *supra* note 182 at 242, and Bhadbhade, *supra* note 137 at 994.

185 See, *e.g.*, Treitel, *supra* note 159 at 772.

186 See, *e.g.*, Indian Contract Act Sec. 67.

187 The term "rescission" may generally be defined as "[a] party's unilateral unmaking of a contract for legally sufficient reason, such as the other party's material breach." See Garner, *supra* note 141 at 606.

188 See generally *infra* VII(B).

C. Comparative analysis

The Indian Contract Act's concept of breach of contract principally corresponds with the unitary notion of non-performance found in the Principles: both terms presuppose a total or partial failure to fulfil a contractual obligation in the manner agreed upon or required by the respective instrument, irrespective of the cause and type of this failure. The actual cause of the non-performance[189] and the question of whether it is unexcused or fundamental are relevant only with regard to the remedies available as a consequence of the particular situation.[190]

With regard to the terminologies used in the three instruments, there is in fact only one slight divergence: The Indian Contract Act, in accordance with common-law tradition, qualifies failure or defective performance as breach of contract if a remedy for damages is attributed to the situation, *i.e.*, there is no breach if the aggrieved party is not entitled to damages. The Principles' drafters refrained from using the term "breach of contract"; yet, it is not entirely clear whether non-performance necessarily presupposes a remedy.[191] However, as UPICC Art. 7.1.7(1) and PECL Art. 8:101(1) state that both excused and unexcused failure to perform or defective performance may constitute non-performance, it appears as though the term does not presuppose a right to damages.

At the same time, all three instruments' notions of non-performance or breach of contract and the respective systems of remedies are based on the common-law doctrine of no-fault liability, according to which each party is strictly liable to perform its contractual obligations unless performance is *excused*. The only notable exception to this congruence is that whereas under the Principles impossibility of performance has no impact on the validity of the contract but may only excuse non-performance and entitle the promisee to terminate,[192] Indian law generally pronounces the contract automatically void in cases of both initial or subsequent impossibility, including frustration.[193]

---

189 As the structure of this survey is based on that of the UNIDROIT Principles, their terminology – where differing from the terms found in the PECL and in Indian statutory contract law – will be used in the comparative sections as general designations to include the corresponding terms found in the other two instruments (*e.g.*, "non-performance" for "breach of contract").

190 See *infra* Ch. V to VII.

191 In fact, it has been argued that the concept of non-performance under the Principles also requires a remedy to be attributed to the failure to perform. See, *e.g.*, Lando, *supra* note 172 at 509.

192 UPICC Art. 3.3 and 7.1.7(1); PECL Art. 4:102 and 8:108(1). For the only exception in cases where a total and permanent impediment prevents performance, see PECL Art. 9:303(4). See generally *infra* VII(A).

193 Indian Contract Act Sec. 56(1) and (2). See generally *infra* VII(B).

Generally, however, it can be summarized that – as a natural consequence of the impact of English law on both the Principles and Indian statutory contract law – the three instruments' basic conceptions of non-performance and breach of contract are consistent to a large extent.

II. Other party being responsible for the non-performance

A. Principles

1. Prevention of performance by the promisee

According to the UPICC, "[a] party may not rely on the non-performance of the other party to the extent that such non-performance was caused by the first party's act or omission" (Art. 7.1.2(1)). The PECL provide a similar rule by stating that the remedies available to a party are limited to the extent that its own act[194] caused the other party's non-performance (Art. 8:101(3)). As illustrated in the Comments to UPICC Art. 7.1.2, these provisions address two types of situations: actual prevention of performance by the promisee and mere failure to accept performance.

First, performance can become fully or partially impossible due to a preventive act committed by the promisee, *e.g.*, if it locks the gate to the land on which the promisor is to perform construction work. The PECL address this case as well, and Comment B(iii) to Art. 8:101 makes express reference to the civil law doctrine of *mora creditoris*.[195] The Comments also state that Art. 8:101(3) covers both direct (and intentional) prevention of the performance by the promisee as well as any other conduct impacting the other party's performance, *e.g.*, the promisee's failure to provide information that is necessary for the promisee's ability to perform.

In many cases, such conduct violates the promisee's duties of good faith and to cooperate, thus constituting a violation of contractual obligations or even non-performance[196] on its own part (UPICC Art. 1.7; PECL Art. 1:201 and 1:202).[197] But even if the promisee's preventive act does not amount to a violation of a con-

---

194 According to PECL Art. 1:301(1), the term "act" as used in the PECL includes omissions.

195 See also *infra* 2.

196 As Comment B to PECL Art. 1:202 states that a "failure to cooperate is a breach of contractual duty," a promisee's failure to cooperate may be treated as a non-performance (and may thus even entitle the promisor to invoke remedies) at least under the PECL. See generally Antoni Vaquer, *Tender of Performance, Mora Creditoris and the (Common?) Principles of European Contract Law*, 17 Tul. Eur. & Civ. L.F. (2002) at 83, 88.

197 See, *e.g.*, Comment D to PECL Art. 9:301.

tractual duty, or if its behaviour is excused, it has the effect that the other party's failure to perform is not to be considered as a non-performance.[198]

The second group of cases addressed by UPICC Art. 7.1.2 (and also by Art. 7.4.7) are those where the promisee is responsible for the promisor's non-performance because it is caused by an event for which, according to the contract, the former bears the risk.[199] While the PECL do not provide any express provision dealing with this situation, a similar rule can be derived from Illustration 4 to their Art. 8:101.

While Comment 1 to UPICC Art. 7.1.2 clearly states that the promisor's failure to perform "loses the quality of non-performance altogether" if it is caused by the promisee's conduct or by an event for which the latter bears the risk, Ill. 3 to Art. 8:101(3) PECL appears to imply that the promisor's failure is technically still to be considered a non-performance.[200] In any case, as the consequences attributed to this case by both sets of Principles are similar, the difference may well be regarded as being of merely technical nature.

2. Creditor's failure to accept tender of performance

Perhaps the practically most relevant case in which a promisor's failure to perform is a result of the promisee's conduct is where the latter rejects a valid tender of performance.

Similar to French and English law,[201] the UPICC do not provide an express rule on this issue. Rather, since the rejection of a valid tender constitutes a conduct by the promisee that causes the promisor's failure to perform, this case is governed by Art. 7.1.2.[202] As a basis for determining whether there has been a failure to accept a tender, Art. 6.1.1 *et seq.* provide requirements for a valid tender of performance and determine the grounds on which the same may be refused.

The PECL, in Comment B(iii) to Art. 8:101, make express reference to the civil law doctrine of *mora creditoris*, which circumscribes the specific case where a party omits the other party's performance by preventing the same or by failing to supply necessary cooperation. The Comment's reference to the doctrine em-

198 See Comment 1 to UPICC Art. 7.1.2.

199 For instance, the promisee is responsible for the non-performance if its house in which the promisor is to perform renovation work collapses.

200 As the phrasing of the third section of Comment B(iii) to Art. 8:101(3) ("in the case where there is also a non-performance of the debtor" (emphasis added)) appears to contradict the last sentence of Ill. 3 to this article, it is unclear in this respect whether the PECL qualify the promisor's failure to perform only as excused non-performance or whether it shall lose the quality of non-performance altogether.

201 See *cf.* Zimmermann, *supra* note 161 at 489, and Vaquer, *supra* note 196 at 85.

202 See *supra* 1.

phasizes that PECL Art. 8:101(3) is intended to include cases where the promisee rejects a tender of performance or refuses to cooperate.

PECL Art. 7:110 and 7:111 provide the debtor with a detailed catalogue of "self-help" rights and establish additional duties for the case that the creditor fails to accept a tender or to fulfil its own part necessary to enable performance. Most importantly, the promisor has to be ready and willing to perform, and it needs to express this status by way of a tender that complies with the contract (PECL Art. 8:104) or the requirements set out in Art. 6:108, 7:103 and 8:104 as well as the general provisions on performance in Chapter 6.[203]

3. *Consequences*

a. *Prevention of performance by promisee*

The rule under both sets of Principles is that a promisee's prevention of or interference with the other party's performance or the occurrence of an event for which it bears the risk, deprive the promisee of its remedies for that non-performance.[204]

If the promisee is only partly responsible for the non-performance, remedies are only available to it to a limited extent and the promisor still owes performance of the remaining part of the obligation (UPICC Art. 7.4.7).[205] What is more, the promisee may not terminate the contract even if it is only partly responsible for the non-performance (Comment 1 to UPICC Art. 7.1.2) unless the promisor's own contribution to its default still amounts to fundamental non-performance.[206]

As for the PECL, their Chapter 9 contains various provisions that are consistent with the rules and principles set forth by the UNIDROIT Principles, particularly those with respect to the limitation of the promisee's right to terminate the contract if it is partly responsible for the non-performance (Comment D to Art. 9:301) and those establishing limitations of its right to damages (*e.g.*, Comment B(iii) to PECL Art. 8:101; Art. 9:504(1) and Art 9:505(1)). If the promisee's contribution is to be qualified as non-performance on its own part, *e.g.*, because it violates a contractual obligation to provide cooperation, the promisee may claim

203 See generally Vaquer, *supra* note 196 at 88 *et seq.*

204 Comment 1 to UPICC Art. 7.1.2 even states that in the case of complete prevention of the performance by the promisee, the failure loses the quality of non-performance altogether. On the other hand, PECL Art. 7:110 and 7:111 indicate that under the European Principles, a refusal of a valid tender of performance excuses non-performance but does not discharge the obligation of the promisor as the latter still has to deposit the object in order to free itself of the obligation. See *cf.* Christoph Coen, *Vertragsscheitern und Rückabwicklung* (2003) at 259 *et seq.*

205 Guidelines for the apportionment of the contribution of each party to the non-performance are provided by the Comments and Illustrations to Art. 7.4.7. See *infra* Ch. VII(V)(A).

206 See UPICC Art. 7.3.1(1).

remedies as well (Comment B(iii) to PECL Art. 8:101). In this context, Comment D to Art. 1:301 contains a general assumption that the refusal to accept a tender constitutes a non-performance on the promisee's part.

While neither set of Principles makes a statement as to whether the party whose performance is prevented must remain willing and able to perform if it is not entitled to terminate the contract (*i.e.*, if the promisee's contribution to the promisee's failure to perform does not constitute a fundamental non-performance), a look at other provisions indicates that it is indeed obliged to do so: both the PECL and the UPICC convey great importance to the subsistence and performance of the contract (*pacta sunt servanda* and *favor contractus*)[207] and contain only few provisions allowing the contract to be terminated or the parties' obligations to be discharged before it has been performed. Hence, as there is no express provision (or mention in the Comments) on the fate of the duty to perform if performance has been (in part) prevented by an act or omission of the promisee, it has to be asserted that, if performance remains possible, the debtor shall not be automatically discharged from its own obligations.

In fact, this presumption is consistent with the Principles' common rule that performance is only temporarily excused if it is prevented by a temporary impediment.[208]

b. Promisee's rejection of a tender

As for the rejection of a valid tender or unreasonable refusal of a non-conforming tender[209] by the promisee, the European Principles provide rules not found in the UPICC: PECL Art. 7:110 (for non-monetary obligations) and 7:111 (for monetary obligations) contain certain duties of care of the debtor for the case that it retains possession of the money or goods due to a refusal or failure of the promisee to accept the former's tender.

The stipulation of these duties implies that the debtor shall not (yet) be discharged from the respective obligation but shall rather remain willing and able to perform.[210] Nonetheless, it may deposit the money or resell or deposit the goods

207 See, *e.g.*, UPICC Art. 1.3, 6.2.1 and 7.1.7(1); PECL Art. 6:111 and 8:108(1). See also Rosett, *supra* note 6 at 448.

208 UPICC Art. 7.1.7(1); PECL Art. 8:108(1).

209 The principle that even a non-conforming tender, *e.g.*, early performance, may only be refused reasonable grounds is perpetuated in PECL Art. 7:103(1) and also emanates from Art. 1:201. In fact, this principle also constitutes the major difference between the treatment of a mere tender and that of performance itself: while a performance which, however slightly, diverges from the contractual requirements is considered non-performance and therefore directly gives rise to remedies, a non-conforming tender may only be rejected on reasonable grounds.

210 See, *e.g.*, Comments E and F to PECL Art. 7:110. See also Vaquer, *supra* note 196 at 102.

in order to free itself from the obligation, and it may claim reimbursement for any reasonable expenses. (Unfortunately, though, the PECL fail to provide a rule on the essential question of how the risk for accidental destruction or damage of the goods after a refusal of a tender is to be allocated.[211])

Even though the UPICC do not provide any express rules on this issue, the same rights and duties of the promisee ought to be comprised by its general duties to cooperate (UPICC Art. 5.1.3) and to act in good faith and fair dealings (UPICC Art. 1.7 and 5.1.2).

Hence, while the European Principles provide a much more concise catalogue of rules for the case that the creditor fails to accept a tender or provide necessary cooperation, the UPICC and the PECL are to be considered generally congruent with regard to the full array of cases where the promisee is fully or partly responsible for the promisee's failure to perform.

B. Indian statutory law

1. Prevention of performance by the creditor

Sec. 53 of the Indian Contract Act addresses those cases where, under a contract involving reciprocal promises,[212] one party prevents the other party that is ready and willing to perform from doing so.[213]

The promisee's preventive conduct may take various forms, *e.g.*, withdrawal of prerequisites for the other party's performance or prevention of the occurrence of a condition precedent to which the contract was subjected.[214] Violation of a contractual "duty to cooperate" to the extent that the contract cannot be fulfilled also constitutes a preventive act or omission.[215]

According to the common-law rule established by English courts, the act must be *wrongful* in order to give rise to the consequences set forth in Sec. 53;[216] none-

---

211 See also *id.* at 110.

212 According to Sec. 2(f) of the Indian Contract Act, "reciprocal promises" are promises which form the consideration or part of the consideration for each other. See also *infra* III(B).

213 The official heading of Indian Contract Act Sec. 53, "Liability of party preventing event of which contract is to take effect", does not constitute a sufficient summary because it circumscribes only one of the situations that are covered by this provision.

214 See Bhadbhade, *supra* note 137 at 1073.

215 See *id.* at 1074.

216 The term "wrongful" in this context relates to a breach of the promisee's contractual duties, *e.g.*, the duty to cooperate, as well as to any preventive act outside the sphere of the contract. See *Mona Oil Equipment & Supply Co. Ltd. v. Rhodesia Rlys. Ltd.*, 2 All ER (All England Reporter) (1949) at 1014, 1016.

theless, "the rule extends to default or neglect in doing or providing anything which a party ought under the contract to do or provide, and without which the other party cannot perform its part."[217] For instance, courts have assumed wrongful prevention of performance where necessary machinery or materials to be supplied by the promisee were inadequate.[218]

Any such act or omission preventing a party from performing exempts this party from liability and entitles it to terminate the contract and claim compensation for any loss incurred as a result of its inability to perform, including any expenses and losses of profit it might have incurred (Indian Contract Act Sec. 53). Alternatively, the promisee may keep the contract alive and request further performance of the promisee's obligations as well as damages.[219]

2. Promisee's failure to provide necessary facilities for performance

Sec. 67 of the Indian Contract Act deals with a special case among those addressed by Sec. 53, namely the refusal or neglect of the promisee to "provide reasonable facilities" required for the promisor's performance. The Illustration to Sec. 67 of the Act demarcates the scope of this provision by referring to failure of the promisee to inform the promisor about aspects that are within its exclusive knowledge.

If performance cannot be tendered without certain information to which the promisor has access only through the promisee, the latter has to provide this knowledge even if there is no express contractual obligation to this extent.[220] Similarly, a buyer's failure to obtain import licenses, which makes it impossible for the seller to ship the goods, is also subject to Sec. 67.

If the promisee negligently fails or refuses to provide the required facilities, any non-performance caused by such negligence or refusal is excused[221] with the effect that the promisee does not commit a breach of contract and is exempt from liability.

3. Promisee's refusal to accept tender of performance

Finally, Sec. 38 of the Indian Contract Act addresses cases where the promisee refuses to accept a tender of performance. A valid tender generally requires that the promisor makes an unconditional offer at the proper time and place and gives

217 See generally Bhadbhade, *supra* note 137 at 1072.

218 See, *e.g.*, Avtar Singh, *Law of Contract and Specific Relief* (9th ed., 2005 (2006 reprint)) at 321.

219 See also *infra* Ch. VI(I)(B)(3)(b) and Ch. VII(I)(B)(1).

220 See Bhadbhade, *supra* note 137 at 1334.

221 See *cf.* Bangia, *supra* note 182 at 217 ("excused"), and Bhadbhade, *id.* at 1333 ("absolved").

the promisee reasonable opportunity to perform its own obligations; furthermore, the promisee needs to be able to make sure that it is actually being offered performance in accordance with the contract (Sec. 38(2)). It is sufficient if the offer is made to one of several joint promisees (Sec. 38(3)).[222]

If the promisee refuses to accept such a tender, "the promisor is not responsible for non-performance" and retains its "rights under the contract" (Sec. 38(1)). The rejection thus excludes a breach of contract on the promisor's part and the latter therefore generally exempt from liability and from having to perform the respective obligation, which in turn means that the promisee is deprived of its remedies for non-performance.[223] However, commentators have stated that the promisee's refusal of a tender of money – as opposed to goods or services – does not discharge the debtor from its obligation to pay.[224]

The wording of Sec. 38(1) also implies that the contract itself shall remain valid with the effect that the promisor may still demand performance from the promisee. However, it may also choose to terminate the contract and claim damages for breach of contract.[225]

C. Comparative analysis

With regard to *prevention* of performance by the promisee, the scope of the Indian Contract Act corresponds to that of the Principles.[226] All three instruments refer to an intentional and direct act of prevention as well as to any indirect conduct by the promisee that causes a failure of the other party to perform.[227] However, Indian (and English) courts require any such conduct to be *wrongful*. This requirement differs from the Principles, under which, if the promisee bears the *risk* for the occurrence of the particular event preventing the performance (*e.g.*, the collapse of its house in which the promisor was to render construction services), the provisions on interference with or prevention of performance are applicable and it is deprived of its remedies even if its conduct is excused.

Under Indian law, a party's wrongful preventive conduct by the creditor always constitutes a breach of contract that renders it liable to pay damages. This is

222 For a concise overview of the requirements for a valid tender, see *cf.* Bhadbhade, *id.* at 987 to 991.

223 See *cf.* Bhadbhade, *id.* at 975, and Bangia, *supra* note 182 at 217.

224 See Bhadbhade, *id.*

225 See *id.*

226 The only slight difference among the three instruments is the more limited scope of application of Sec. 53 of the Indian Contract Act, which is applicable only to reciprocal promises.

227 UPICC Art. 7.1.2(1); PECL Art. 8:101(3); Indian Contract Act Sec. 53.

a significant difference to the Principles, which provide that the preventive conduct is to be treated as a non-performance only if it actually amounts to a failure to perform a contractual obligation on promisee's part. Under the Principles, the question of whether the promisor may invoke any remedies for the preventive conduct hence depends on the circumstances of the particular situation.

As a consequence of any preventive conduct in the aforementioned sense, the Indian Contract Act also allows the promisor to avoid the contract (which is the first of two remedies awarded by Sec. 53) and thereby entitles it to decide for itself whether its obligation shall be discharged as a result of a wrongful act of prevention. By contrast, neither set of Principles expressly regulates the question of whether the obligation shall be discharged; however, their structure implies that the promisor must remain ready and willing to perform, and it may therefore be asserted that under the Principles, the promisor is only exempt from its obligation to perform if the promisee's conduct amounts to a fundamental non-performance on its own part and entitles the former to terminate the contract.

Finally, all three instruments grant the promisor a right to compensation for expenses and any losses sustained as a result of the preventive act, and they contain very similar rules in relation to cases where both parties are in part responsible for the non-performance.

As for the promisee's rejection of a valid tender of performance, all three instruments set forth requirements for a valid tender and agree that the promisee may not claim any remedies in this case. However, the Principles provide that the rejection of a valid tender – just like a prevention of performance – does not discharge the promisor from its obligation. This means that it has to remain ready and willing to perform (for a reasonable time) if the nature of the obligation permits it to do so.[228] By contrast, the consequence of the rule provided by Sec. 38 of the Indian Contract Act is that the obligation in question is discharged unless it is for payment of money. In turn, all three instruments entitle the promisor to still claim performance from the promisee.

Though neither the UPICC nor the Indian Contract Act address the issues of whether the promisor may deposit the goods or money in order to free itself from the obligation – which is expressly permitted by PECL Art. 7:110(2) – it can be asserted that this option is in fact available under all three instruments.[229]

---

228 In turn, it is evident that if the refusal of a valid tender constitutes fundamental non-performance on the promisee's part, the promisor may terminate the contract and thereby free itself of the respective obligation.

229 The permissibility of depositing the goods or money under the UPICC and the Indian Contract Act can be derived from the fact that both instruments generally recognize the applicability of (international) trade usages to contracts governed by these two instruments. See UPICC Art. 1.8 and, for the Indian Contract Act, Bhadbhade, *supra* note 137 at 36. For the permissibility

In all, particularly the fact that the UPICC and PECL do not discharge the promisor from its obligation if it rejects a valid tender or is otherwise responsible for its failure to perform, constitutes a practically very relevant difference between the Principles and Indian statutory contract law. In fact, the relevance of this difference is magnified by the fact that the rejection of a tender of performance is responsible for a large number of trade disputes and therefore frequently subject to litigation.

III. Right to withhold performance

A. Principles

Both two sets of Principles, in almost identical black letter rules, arrange for multiple grounds on which a party is entitled to withhold performance of its own obligations. UPICC Art. 7.1.3 and PECL Art. 9:201 are both based on the civil-law doctrine of *exceptio non adimpleti contractus*, the purpose of which is to protect the promisor from the risk of performing (*e.g.*, advancing money) without knowing whether the other party will do so as well.[230]

Accordingly, both sets of Principles entitle the parties to withhold performance in three general situations:[231] first, if the parties are to perform *simultaneously*, each of them may withhold performance until the other tenders performance or actually performs (UPICC Art. 7.1.3(1); PECL Art. 9:201(1)). Second, if the parties are to perform *consecutively*, the promisor may withhold performance until the party that is to perform first has performed its obligations (UPICC Art. 7.1.3(2); PECL Art. 9:201(1)). Finally, the promisor may, to a reasonable[232] extent, partially withhold its performance if the promisee that is to perform first fails to perform fully.[233]

---

of a deposit or "payment of money due in court" under English common law, see also Vaquer, *supra* note 196 at 107.

230 See Comment A to PECL Art. 9:201.

231 With a view on two more specific situations, performance may also be withheld (1) if and for as long as the promisor fails to provide adequate assurance of performance if such assurance was requested by the promisee in reaction to its reasonable belief that there will be fundamental non-performance on the promisor's part (UPICC Art. 7.3.4; PECL Art. 8:105(1); see *cf. infra* Ch. VI(I)(A)(2)(d)) and under the UPICC, (2) if and for as long as the promisor invokes its right to cure (UPICC Art. 7.1.4(4); see *infra* IV(A)).

232 According to PECL Art. 1:302, "[u]nder these Principles reasonableness is to be judged by what persons acting in good faith and in the same situation as the parties would consider to be reasonable. In particular, in assessing what is reasonable the nature and purpose of the contract, the circumstances of the case, and the usages and practices of the trades or professions involved should be taken into account."

233 See Comment to UPICC Art. 7.1.3 and PECL Art. 9:201(1).

1. Requirements for withholding performance

The test for the right to withhold performance in these three instances is practically identical under UPICC Art. 7.1.3 and PECL Art. 9:201(1):[234]

(1) The promise of which performance is to be withheld and the promise that the other party (completely or partly) fails to perform must arise from a single, synallagmatic contract.[235]
(2) It is irrelevant whether the parties are to perform simultaneously or consecutively. Nevertheless, the Principles' rules on order of performance (UPICC Art. 6.1.4 and PECL Art. 7:104) state that, generally and unless otherwise agreed, the parties are to perform simultaneously.
(3) The party that is to perform first entirely or partially *fails* to perform (UPICC Art. 7.1.3(2); PECL Art. 9:201(1))[236], or the parties are to perform simultaneously, one of them is *not able or willing* to do so (UPICC Art. 7.1.3(1); PECL Art. 9:201(1)). In principle, the promisor's failure, inability or unwillingness to perform need not amount to fundamental non-performance in either of these cases.[237]
(4) The promisor's failure to perform or make a valid tender of performance must not be caused by the withholding party's own conduct. This requirement stems from the Principles' rules on interference by the other party (UPICC Art. 7.1.2; PECL Art. 8:101(3)).[238]
(5) Withholding performance must be reasonable[239] (PECL Art. 9:201(1)) or done in good faith[240], respectively. The Comments to both sets of Principles indicate that if a party *entirely* fails to perform the respective obligation, it is reasonable for the other party to withhold the whole of its own performance

234 See also Düchs, *supra* note 161 at 214.
235 See Comment A to PECL Art. 9:201.
236 See also *id.*
237 See Comment B to PECL Art. 9:201. For the UPICC (which do not contain any express stipulation in this regard), this assumption stems from the fact that where fundamental non-performance is required, the respective provisions explicitly state so (*e.g.*, UPICC Art. 7.3.1(1)). Accordingly, the right to withhold performance in the specific circumstances addressed by UPICC Art. 7.3.4 – *viz.* where the promisee reasonably believes that the promisor will fail to perform – does indeed require the prospective non-performance to be fundamental.
238 See *supra* II(A).
239 According to PECL Art. 1:302, "[u]nder these Principles reasonableness is to be judged by what persons acting in good faith and in the same situation as the parties would consider to be reasonable. In particular, in assessing what is reasonable the nature and purpose of the contract, the circumstances of the case, and the usages and practices of the trades or professions involved should be taken into account."
240 See Comment to UPICC Art. 7.1.4.

in return. However, the Principles differ with regard to the case where only *a part* of an obligation remains unperformed: according to the European Principles' reasonability test, the other party may withhold only *an appropriate portion* of its own performance.[241] The Comment to UPICC Art. 7.1.4, on the other hand, permits withholding of the *entire* performance even in response to a mere partial failure to perform by the other party so long as this conduct does not pose a violation of the withholding party's duty of good faith (UPICC Art. 1.7).[242] Nevertheless, both notions will often lead to similar results. For instance, if a party withholds the entire payment only because the other party has failed to deliver a last missing part of a house it was to construct, this reaction is both unreasonable and contrary to good faith. In any case, both instruments certainly allow for a modification of these rules by way of contractual stipulations.

With regard to cases where the party that is to perform first seeks to withhold performance because it is *already clear* that the other will fail to perform its part, the UPICC and PECL account for a notable difference: whereas PECL Art. 9:201(2) grants a right to withhold performance (and, for that matter, a choice between keeping the contract alive or terminating it for anticipatory non-performance under Art. 9:304 if the prospective non-performance would be fundamental) if and for as long as it is *clear*[243] that there will be non-performance on the other end, the UPICC do not address this case. Yet, there are some good arguments in favour of extending the scope of this article beyond the express wording of its black letter rule. This is primarily because it appears as somewhat contrary to the UNIDROIT Principles' gravitation around the principles of good faith and fair dealing (Art. 1.7)[244] and *favor contractus*[245] to conclude that they are intended to permit termination even before performance is due (UPICC Art. 7.3.3) but not the less "rupturing" measure of withholding performance. If it is clear at one point before performance is due that the other party will fail to perform or if it refuses to do so (which usually also means that adequate assurance of due performance – a fruitless request of which is the only way of obtaining a right to withhold performance

241 See Comment B to PECL Art. 9:201.

242 See *cf.* Lando, *supra* note 172 at 13.

243 Unfortunately, PECL Art. 9:201(2) lacks a definition of the term "clear". (In fact, it is a general shortcoming of both sets of Principles that they lack definitions of a number of key abstract terms that are used in their provisions on non-performance.

244 As a fundamental concept, the principle of good faith and fair dealing recurs as a guiding principle throughout the UNIDROIT Principles. See, *e.g.*, Goode, *supra* note 117 at 238 *et seq.*, and Zimmermann, *supra* note 161 at 491.

245 See, *e.g.*, Bonell, *supra* note 19 at 117.

under the UPICC[246] – can or will not be provided), it is hard to see why the promisee should not be allowed to withhold performance and wait to see if there may eventually be performance without first having to demand assurance of performance. Hence, any other interpretation of UPICC Art. 7.1.3 would unnecessarily narrow the aggrieved party's choices and prompt it to terminate the contract.

There are also compelling arguments supporting a more narrow interpretation of Art. 7.1.3(2): first, the unambiguous express phrasing of the black letter rule does not leave much doubt about the drafters' intention to grant a general right to withhold performance only to the "party that is to perform *later*" (emphasis added). What is more, Art. 7.3.4 confers a right to withhold performance to the party that is to perform *first* only if additional requirements are met[247] and hence also indicates that the UPICC's drafters did indeed contemplate that there are situations where it may be equitable to allow this party to withhold performance but decided not to adopt a rule as general as that of PECL Art. 9:201(2).[248] Finally, the fact that the concept of withholding performance as devised by Art. 7.1.3, 7.3.3 and 7.3.4 was not changed in the revised version of the UPICC may also be perceived as an indicator of the drafters' intention not to grant a right to withhold performance if it is clear that the party that is to perform first will fail to do so.

2. *Consequences*

If either of the tests discussed above are met and the aggrieved party is thus entitled to withhold performance, its own non-performance is *excused* until the other party actually performs or tenders performance, depending on the order of performance. On this note, the *ICC International Court of Arbitration*, in an arbitral award making reference to UPICC Art. 7.1.3, has ruled that the buyer may withhold payment of the price if the seller delivers non-conforming goods.[249] In another award, the same tribunal has held that UPICC Art. 7.1.3 entitles the seller to withhold delivery of the goods if the buyer fails to pay the price.[250] Moreover, the UPICC expressly state that a party is entitled to withhold performance if and for as long as the other party invokes its right to cure its non-performance.[251]

---

246 UPICC Art. 7.3.4.

247 *I.e.*, under the condition that the promisee has demanded adequate assurance of due performance; see infra Ch. VI(I)(A)(2)(d).

248 See also Düchs, *supra* note 161 at 215.

249 ICC Int'l Court of Arbitration, arbitral award no. 8547 (1999), available at http://www.unilex.info.

250 ICC Int'l Court of Arbitration, arbitral award no. 7110 (1998), available at http://www.unilex.info.

251 UPICC Art. 7.1.4(4). See generally *infra* IV(A).

In addition to withholding performance, the promisee may certainly rely on all other remedies that it is entitled to as a result of the promisor's non-performance, *i.e.*, to terminate the contract, claim damages or ask for assurance of performance, if the respective requirements are met.[252]

B. Indian statutory law

The Indian Contract Act expressly entitles the parties to withhold performance in cases where the promisor (1) fails to perform a reciprocal promise that is to be performed simultaneously with the promisee's promise (Indian Contract Act Sec. 51), or (2) fails to perform a reciprocal promise that is to be performed first (Sec. 54).

The order of performance of reciprocal promises is determined by Sec. 52 of the Contract Act, according to which, unless the contract expressly stipulates a certain order (*i.e.*, simultaneous or consecutive performance), the order of performance depends on what "the nature of the transaction requires" or what was intended by the parties.

Both Sec. 51 and 54 of the Contract Act require reciprocal promises. This term is defined in Sec. 2(f) as "promises which form the consideration or part of the consideration for each other".[253] The types of promises covered by these sections must hence be dependent, or conditioned upon one another, *i.e.*, performance of one of them, necessarily or as per contractual provision depend on the (simultaneous or prior) performance of the reciprocal promise.[254]

Indian courts have held that unless the parties agree otherwise, giving possession of the goods and payment of the price are concurrent promises (Ill. (a) to Sec. 51),[255] and the burden of proof for any agreement to the contrary lies with the plaintiff. If the price is to be paid in instalments, the delivery of the goods and

252 Some commentators have argued that the UPICC do not treat the right to withhold performance as a remedy. This view mainly draws from the structural aspect that Art. 7.1.3 is included in the UPICC's section on "Non-Performance in General" instead of the specific sections devoted to each of the other remedies. However, the identical conception of UPICC Art. 7.1.3 and PECL Art. 9:201 and the Comment to Art. 7.1.3 ("[t]he present article is concerned with remedies"), *inter alia*, imply that it is indeed intended to provide a remedy for non-performance.

253 The term "consideration" may generally be defined as "[s]omething of value (such as an act, a forbearance, or a return promise) received by a promisor form a promisee." See Garner, *supra* note 141 at 131.

254 Reciprocal promises under which the performance of one promise is conditioned upon the performance of the other are also referred to as "dependent promises" or "concurrent promises" as opposed to independent promises. See *cf.* Bhadbhade, *supra* note 137 at 136 and 1077 *et seq.*

255 See also Sale of Goods Act, 1930 Sec. 32.

the first instalment are reciprocal promises in the sense of Sec. 51 (Ill. (b) to Sec. 51). On the other hand, work and the respective compensation are generally not considered to be concurrent promises with the effect that work must be completed before payment may be claimed.[256]

The following two subsections set out and discuss the requirements for withholding performance in the two scenarios addressed by Sec. 51 and 54 of the Indian Contract Act.

1. Parties to perform simultaneously (Indian Contract Act Sec. 51)

Sec. 51 of the Contract Act establishes a right to withhold performance of a promise that is to be performed simultaneously with another reciprocal promise if and so long as the other party is not ready and willing to perform.

As stated above, these promises must be reciprocal, *i.e.*, conditioned upon one another. The term "willing" refers to the mental state of intending to do an act, whereas being "ready" to perform requires close proximity of such willingness and the actual performance of the respective act.[257] Readiness and willingness do not presuppose that the respective party is on point and at any time capable of performing, *e.g.*, that it is in constant possession of the purchase price. Rather, it is sufficient that the buyer has arranged for making payment, or that the seller can deliver the goods without undue delay.[258]

2. One promise to be performed first (Indian Contract Act Sec. 54)

Indian Contract Act Sec. 54 applies to cases where one party is to perform *first* and fails to do so. The provision establishes that ruling that this party may not claim performance of the reciprocal promise and is liable to compensate the promisee for losses that the latter sustains because of the non-performance.[259]

Sec. 54 relates to reciprocal, concurrent promises of which (1) one can only be performed after the other, or (2) one can only be claimed upon performance of the other.[260] Indian courts have held that, provided the obligations in question are concurrent reciprocal promises, the promise that is to be performed first need neither be of any particular significance as compared to other duties arising

256 *JG Hashman v. Lucknow Improvement Trust*, All India Reporter (AIR) 1927 Oudh 616 (1927).
257 For an overview of case law on these terms, see *cf.* Bhadbhade, *supra* note 137 at 1066 *et seq.*
258 *Nathulal v. Phoolchand*, AIR 1970 S.C. 546 (1970).
259 See also *infra* Ch. VII(B)(I).
260 The sequence in which reciprocal promises are to be performed (*e.g.*, that a permission shall be obtained prior to the agreed transfer of property) may also be stipulated in the contract. See *Bishambar Nath Agrawal v. Kishan Chand*, AIR 1998 All 195 (1998).

from the contract nor of the same quality as the other.[261] Practical examples of contracts covered by Sec. 54 are those where one party is to supply something, *e.g.*, the cargo that is to be transported, before the other can commence with its own performance, or where payment is to be made in advance or upon delivery of the goods.

Unlike the above-mentioned Sec. 51, Sec. 54 requires that the promise is fully performed at the time of performance before performance of the reciprocal promise can be claimed. A mere tender or an indication of readiness and willingness to perform do not suffice.

3. *Consequences*

If the party that is to perform first fails to do so at the time of performance, it may not claim performance of the reciprocal promise and must compensate the promisee for losses sustained by the failure. If, in addition, the parties have agreed upon a fixed time for performance, the promisee of the obligation that is to be performed first may avoid the contract or a part of it (Indian Contract Act Sec. 55). Similarly, if the failure amounts to a refusal to perform the contract in its entirety, the promisee may also be entitled to terminate the contract as per Sec. 39 of the Indian Contract Act.

Unlike Sec. 51, Sec. 54 does not explicitly confer a right to withhold performance to the promisee. However, case law[262] (including Ill. (c) and (d) to Sec. 54 ("need not be performed")) indicates that the promisee may withhold performance of its own reciprocal promise until the party that is to perform first has done so. However, there are exceptions to this interpretation: where a party that is entitled to repudiate[263] the contract for non-performance (*e.g.*, under Sec. 39) chooses to uphold it, it is, in turn, not discharged of its own performance but only entitled to damages. Accordingly, once it chooses not to terminate the contract, it may not withhold performance but must tender further performance.[264]

The Indian Contract Act does not expressly limit the degree to which performance may be withheld to any level of appropriateness or reasonableness. Moreover, case law applying Sec. 54 indicates that, as long as the promises are reciprocal, their quality and significance with regard to each other are irrelevant to

---

261 See, *e.g.*, Bhadbhade, *supra* note 137 at 1078.

262 See *id.* at 1080.

263 The term "repudiation" may be defined as "[a] contracting party's words or actions that indicate an intention not to perform the contract in the future; a threatened breach of contract." See Garner, *supra* note 141 at 604.

264 See *cf.* Bhadbhade, *supra* note 137 at 1006 *et seq.*

whether the aggrieved party may withhold performance of its promise.[265] These decisions lead to the conclusion that performance of the whole reciprocal promise may be withheld regardless of whether the other party fails to or is unready or unwilling to perform only a part of its own promise.

C. Comparative analysis

The Indian Contract Act as well as the Principles generally allow for withholding of performance if the other party fails or is not ready and willing to perform its own promise.[266]

If the promises are to be performed simultaneously, it is sufficient under all three instruments if the respective promisor does not tender performance (UPICC Art. 7.1.3(1); PECL Art. 9:201(1)) because is not ready and willing to do so (Indian Contract Act Sec. 51). In cases where one party is to perform first under to the contract or due to the nature of the transaction, the party that is to perform subsequently may withhold performance only if there is an actual failure to perform on the other's part (UPICC Art. 7.1.3(2); PECL Art. 9:201(1); Indian Contract Act Art. 54).

As for the situation where it is clear that there will be a non-performance by the other party, only the PECL allow the party that is to perform first to withhold performance of its own obligations (PECL Art. 9:201(2)).[267] The Indian Contract Act contains an explicit rule only for the case where the promisor refuses to perform (Sec. 39). In such cases, the promisee has the right to either terminate the contract or to uphold it and claim damages. If it opts for the latter, it is still obliged to tender performance of its own obligation.[268] Apart from this provision, there is no indication whatsoever that the Indian Contract Act is intended to allow the party that is to perform first to withhold performance, especially as Indian law, in the tradition of English common law, does not recognize a general duty of good faith:[269] in this

265 See, *e.g.*, *id.* at 1078.

266 The linguistic difference between the civil-law term "synallagmatic" (as also used by the Principles) and "reciprocal" (being the corresponding common-law concept adopted by the Indian Contract Act) is of purely technical nature; both terms circumscribe interdependent promises, that is, promises being conditioned upon one another (see also Comment B and Note 2(b) to PECL Art. 9:201). Moreover, see UPICC Art. 7.1.5(2) and PECL 8:106(2), both of which use the term "reciprocal" for what their black letter rules on the right to withhold performance refer to as "synallagmatic".

267 See *supra* A.

268 See Bhadbhade, *supra* note 137 at 1006 *et seq.*

269 As opposed to UPICC Art. 7.3.3, which grants the potentially aggrieved party a right to terminate the contract in all situations where it is "clear" that there will be a non-performance, Sec.

respect, Indian statutory contract law thus corresponds to the rule found in Art. 7.1.3 of the UNIDROIT Principles.

The *order of performance* principally depends on the parties' intentions, *i.e.*, on what is fixed in or implied by the contract or by the circumstances of the particular case (UPICC Art. 6.4.1; PECL Art. 7:104; Indian Contract Act Sec. 52).

If there has only been partial non-performance on the other side, PECL Art. 9:201 limits the extent to which performance may be withheld to a *reasonable* extent, *viz.* an extent corresponding to the promisor's partial default. As opposed to this concept, both the Comments to UPICC Art. 7.1.3 and case law pertaining to Sec. 54 of the Indian Contract Act indicate that performance may in principle be withheld in full for the time of non-performance and regardless of whether the promisor fails to perform its promise entirely or only in part; however, the UPICC still require the reaction to be in good faith.

On another note, neither set of Principles limits the right to withhold performance if the party intending to do so is also entitled (*e.g.*, under UPICC Art. 7.3.3 or PECL Art. 9:304) but chooses not to terminate the contract. Indian courts, on the other hand, have ruled that the promisee, if it has the right but decides not to terminate the contract, must perform and is hence entitled to withhold performance of its reciprocal promise but may only claim damages for the non-performance.[270]

Despite the few aforementioned – and certainly practically relevant – divergences, the analysis of the right to withhold performance hence shows again that there is a high degree of resemblance among the three instruments with regard to the fundamental concepts their drafters were seeking to incorporate: while, in accordance with the principle of *favor contractus*, all three aim to preserve the contract to the largest possible extent, they do not do so at the cost of the aggrieved party and therefore protect it from suffering a loss or damage by the other's failure or unwillingness to perform its obligations.

---

39 of the Indian Contract Act only refers to a promisor's actual refusal to perform. Therefore, and especially as the Contract Act's Sec. 51, 54 and 39 all contain a negative implication to the extent that the rights to terminate the contract or withhold performance are only available if there is an actual refusal or failure to perform by the other party (or, in other words, only if performance is already due), even a contextual interpretation of the the Contract Act is not as convincing as the aforementioned interpretation of the UPICC.

270 See Bhadbhade, *supra* note 137 at 1006 *et seq.*, for references to Indian case law.

IV. Right to cure

A. Principles

In accordance with their focus on encouraging performance and preserving the contract, both sets of Principles comprise a right to cure non-performance. However, the scope of their respective rules differs considerably.

Subject to a fourfold test and provided that the contract does not require timely performance,[271] UPICC Art. 7.1.4(1) provides a comparably far-reaching right to cure:

(1) Notice of cure (UPICC Art. 7.1.4(2)(a)): after learning of its non-performance, the promisor is required to give notice to the promisee without undue delay and indicate the proposed means and timing of the cure to the extent that appropriate information is available to it.[272]

(2) Cure appropriate in the circumstances (UPICC Art. 7.1.4(2)(b)): an additional attempt to perform must appear reasonable in the particular case. In this context, Art. 7.1.4(2) establishes that a right to cure may be available even if the promisee is entitled to terminate the contract, thereby implying that even fundamental non-performance does not necessarily render a possible cure unreasonable.[273] Two core factors relevant to determining whether cure is appropriate are whether the cure promises to successfully eliminate the impediment to proper performance and whether the period required to cure would be unreasonably long, and thereby perhaps even elevates the non-performance to the level of fundamental non-performance.[274]

(3) No legitimate interest in refusing cure (UPICC Art. 7.1.4(2)(c)): even though a right to cure is presumed if it is to be considered appropriate and if the promisor has given proper notice, the promisor may nevertheless be barred from being entitled to cure its non-performance if the aggrieved party can show that it has a legitimate interest in rejecting the cure.[275]

(4) Cure effected promptly after notice (UPICC Art. 7.1.4(2)(d)): while the cure must be effected promptly, *i.e.*, without any extensive waiting period, the UPICC even allow for multiple attempts if this appears reasonable in the

271 See Comment 1 to UPICC Art. 7.1.4.

272 See Comment 2 to UPICC Art. 7.1.4.

273 See Comment 3 to UPICC Art. 7.1.4 and the black letter rule of Art. 7.1.4(2), according to which a termination notice (and therefore also fundamental non-performance) does not exclude the right to cure.

274 See Comment 3 to UPICC Art. 7.1.4.

275 See *cf.* Comment 4 to UPICC Art. 7.1.4, which also clarifies that the promisee is required to show that it has a legitimate interest in refusing cure ("if the aggrieved party can demonstrate a legitimate interest").

particular case; however, mere verbal expression of the intention to cure does not suffice.[276]

Whereas the promisee retains the right to withhold its own performance until cure has been effected (UPICC Art. 7.1.4(4)), all other remedies – including termination – are suspended for the period within which the promisor may reasonably repair its non-performance, or until it is clear that the failure to perform will be permanent (Art. 7.1.4(2) and (3)). At the same time, the promisor remains liable to pay any damages caused by the initial non-performance and the delay as well as for any damages that may be caused by the cure itself (Art. 7.1.4(5)).

The promisee's duty to cooperate (UPICC Art. 5.1.3) compels it to permit and, if necessary, enable the promisor to cure.

Based on a somewhat narrower concept than the UNIDROIT Principles, Art. 8:104 of the PECL entitles the promisor to cure its non-performance only (1) if it has previously made a non-conforming tender that was rejected by the promisee[277] and (2) if "the time for performance has not yet arrived or the delay would not be such as to constitute a fundamental non-performance", *viz.* time is not of the essence of the contract.[278]

Whereas the latter restriction basically corresponds to a similar reasoning underlying UPICC Art. 7.1.4,[279] the European Principles' exclusion of the right to cure at any time after the time of performance has passed (and unless the promisee opts to grant the promisor an additional period for performance[280]) denotes a considerable divergence between the two sets of Principles and appears to be due mainly to the broader scope of the PECL, which are intended to cover commercial as well as consumer contracts.[281]

By the same token, the European Principles do not contain a rule corresponding to the one established by UPICC Art. 7.1.4(2). As a result, the relation between the promisor's right to cure and the aggrieved party's right to terminate the contract in the first category of cases addressed by Art. 8:104, *viz.* where the non-

276 See Comments 5 and 6 to UPICC Art. 7.1.4.

277 The phrasing of PECL Art. 8:104 ("A party whose tender of performance is not accepted") signifies that the promisor shall not be entitled to cure its non-performance where it had not tendered performance at all. Conversely, Comment 1 to UPICC Art. 7.1.4 – in stating that, "[i]n effect (...), the non-performing party is able to extend the time for performance for a brief period beyond that stipulated in the contract" – indicates that the right to cure does not presuppose a previous tender, so that delay may in principle be cured as well.

278 See PECL Art. 8:103 and *infra* Ch. VI(I)(A)(2)(a).

279 See Comment 3 to UPICC Art. 7.1.4, according to which the question of whether "the necessary or probable delay in effecting cure would be unreasonable or would itself constitute a fundamental non-performance" is a factor to be considered in determining the appropriateness of cure.

280 UPICC Art. 7.1.5; PECL Art. 8:106.

281 See, *e.g.*, Bonell/Peleggi, *supra* note 116 at 323 *et seq.*

performance is fundamental but the time for performance has not yet arrived, remains unclear: shall fundamentality or the issuance of a termination notice categorically exclude a right to cure? Or shall the right to cure in turn preclude the right to terminate the contract? With a view on the rule found in UPICC Art. 7.1.4(2) and in light of the Principles' general emphasis on the principle of *favor contractus*, it appears fair to assume that even if the non-performance is fundamental and the aggrieved party wishes to terminate the contract, the promisee is nevertheless entitled to cure until the date or time when performance is actually due. In accordance with this interpretation, the aggrieved party would be entitled to terminate the contract only if the promisor has not cured its fundamental non-performance by the time when performance is due or if the delay caused by the cure would itself constitute fundamental non-performance.[282]

B. Indian statutory law

While a general right to cure appears to be generally recognized by English law[283] and has also become statutory law in Sec. 2-508 of the American Uniform Commercial Code (UCC), the Indian Contract Act contains no express provision on the matter.

However, Sec. 55(2) of the Contract Act acknowledges that there are cases where the promisee must accept performance even if it is delayed. This provision states that if a party fails to perform at a time specified in the contract but time is not of the essence of the contract, the promisee is not automatically entitled to terminate the contract but may only claim damages or loss caused by the default.[284] Practically, this rule hence grants a right to cure that is to be effected within a reasonable time.[285]

If time is of the essence of the contract, the aggrieved party has the right to terminate the contract (Indian Contract Act Sec. 55(1)), or it may accept the delayed performance (Sec. 55(3)).

C. Comparative analysis

Sec. 55 of the Indian Contract Act thus essentially corresponds to UPICC Art. 7.1.4 in that, unless time is of the essence, performance may be rendered or non-

282 See also Coen, *supra* note 204 at 269 *et seq.*

283 See generally Roy Goode, *Commercial Law* (3rd ed., 2004) at 342 *et seq.*, and *supra* note 117 at 242.

284 The question of whether time is of the essence of the contract generally depends on the parties' intention. Absent any clear provision in the contract, Indian courts generally presume that time is of the essence in commercial contracts and not so in non-commercial matters and in contracts concerning the sale of immovable property. See *cf.* Singh, *supra* note 218 at 325 and 333.

285 See Bhadbhade, *supra* note 137 at 1100, and Bangia, *supra* note 182 at 234.

performance cured even after the time when performance was due.[286] As a consequence, both Indian law and the UPICC are plainly contrary to the strict rule set forth in PECL Art. 8:104.

V. Additional period for performance

A. Principles

As another implication of their emphasis on preserving the contract and encouraging performance, both sets of Principles present almost identical provisions in respect of the aggrieved party's right to grant its counterpart an additional period to tender or complete performance.[287]

Based on the assumption that, if there is a delay in performance, the promisee is generally still interested in the performance of the contract, it may, without losing any of its remedies, give the other party a second chance to perform (and thereby indicate its continuing interest in performance). For this purpose, both UPICC Art. 7.1.5(1) and PECL Art. 8:106(1) require that the promisee, upon

(1) a fundamental or non-fundamental non-performance[288] of a contractual obligation,[289]

---

286 Comment 1 to UPICC Art. 7.1.4.

287 According to Comment to UPICC Art. 7.1.5, this provision is inspired by the German concept of "*Nachfrist*".

288 Whereas the black letter rule of UPICC Art. 7.1.5(1) speaks of "non-performance," the respective Comments only address delay, *i.e.*, one particular type of non-performance. However, Ill. 2 to UPICC Art. 7.1.5 clearly indicates that incomplete non-performance also gives rise to the option of granting of an additional period for performance. In fact, as the Comment to UPICC Art. 7.1.1 expressly states that the term "non-performance" comprises all forms of defective performance, it is to be assumed that, just as under the PECL (which clearly state so also throughout the Comments to Art. 8:106), this option is available to the aggrieved party in all cases of non-performance. Still, though, this issue needs to be distinguished from the question of whether the aggrieved party may terminate the contract upon fruitless expiration of the additional period; according to Art. 7.1.5(3) and 7.3.1(3), a right to termination upon expiration of an extra period arises only if the non-performance was caused by *late* performance. See also Coen, *supra* note 204 at 238 *et seq.*

289 While this interpretation of UPICC Art. 7.1.5(1) and (2) is clearly purported by Comment 2 to UPICC Art. 7.1.5 ("The party who grants the extension of time cannot terminate (...) during the extension time."), the European Principles are more unclear – in fact, even contradictory – in this respect. Whereas on the one hand, Note 3 to PECL Art. 9:301 expressly states that "it should be noted that the Principles do not permit the non-performing party to be given extra time once the non-performance is fundamental," Comment C to PECL Art. 8:106 clearly indicates that this is indeed possible: "[E]ven where the delay or other non-performance is fundamental, and thus the aggrieved party has the right to terminate immediately, it may not wish to do so (...).

(2) gives notice[290] to the promisor
(3) allowing an additional period of time for performance.

During the extra period, the aggrieved party may withhold performance of its own reciprocal obligations and recover damages for any loss caused by the delay; however, it is barred from invoking any other remedies such as terminating the contract or claiming specific performance. Instead, it is only upon the expiration of the extension or once the promisor indicates by way of a notice that it will indeed remain unable or unwilling to perform that it may resort to any of the remedies available for non-performance, including termination of the contract by way of a notice of termination if the non-performance is fundamental (UPICC Art. 7.1.5(2); PECL Art. 8:106(2) and 9:301(2)).[291]

Apart from the possibility of keeping the contract alive and the prospect of perhaps still receiving performance in accordance with the contract, there is a second incentive for the aggrieved party to grant the promisor additional time for performance: in cases of *delay*[292] of performance,[293] the former may, upon

---

The procedure set out in Article 8:106 permits it to give the debtor a final chance to perform." Against this background, the most convincing interpretation of PECL Art. 8:106 appears to be that – just as under UPICC Art. 7.1.5 – the right to fix an additional period is also available where the non-performance is fundamental.

290 For the form of a notice, see UPICC Art. 1.10 and PECL Art. 1:303.

291 For a different – yet somewhat incomprehensible – interpretation of (the German translation of) PECL Art. 8:106(2), see Coen, *supra* note 204 at 276 to 277, who apparently misread the relevant passage ("If it receives notice from the other party that the latter will not perform within (the additional) period, or if upon expiry of that period due performance has not been made, the aggrieved party may resort to any of the remedies that may be available under chapter 9.") as implying that even where the non-performing party declares that it will not perform, the aggrieved party may terminate the contract only *after* the expiration of the additional period. An interpretation to this extent is unconvincing particularly because the differentiation between the two situations addressed by the aforementioned passage would not have been necessary if the aggrieved party were in any case obliged to wait and see whether the defaulting party indeed fails or refuses to perform by the end of the additional period.

292 Neither the black letter rules nor the Comments to UPICC Art. 7.1.5 and PECL Art. 8:105 provide a clear definition of "delay of performance" and therefore leave open especially the crucial question of whether the term is intended to comprise only lateness of the tender of performance or also lateness of completion of performance, *e.g.*, cases where performance was merely incomplete at the time when it was due. However, Ill. 3 to PECL Art. 8:104 and Ill. 3 to Art. 8:106 as well as Ill. 2 to UPICC Art. 7.1.5 indicate that late completion of performance also enables the promisee to grant an additional period (and to terminate the contract upon expiration of the respite). On the other hand, it is unclear whether this also applies to cases of lateness of a *conforming* performance, *e.g.*, where the performance, though it was tendered on time and accepted by the aggrieved party, had been (non-fundamentally) non-conforming and this non-conformity was not cured by the time when the performance was due. See also *infra* Ch. VI(I)(A)(2)(b).

293 Whereas Comment B to this provision expressly underscores that PECL Art. 8:106(3) shall apply even if the default is excused because it is due to a temporary impediment to performance

expiry of an additional (fixed)[294] reasonable period,[295] terminate the contract even if the delay was not to be considered a fundamental non-performance (UPICC Art. 7.1.5(3); PECL Art. 8:106(3)).[296] This additional right constitutes an exception to the general rule that termination presupposes *fundamental* non-performance, *i.e.,* that time is of the essence of the contract (UPICC Art. 7.3.1(1); PECL Art. 9:301(1)).[297] It is valuable especially where the promisee is unsure whether the initial delay already constitutes fundamental non-performance; upon elapse of the extension, it may terminate the contract without any risk.

According to UPICC Art. 7.1.5(3) and PECL Art. 8:106(3), termination in this respect is to be effected by way of an additional notice unless it was already announced in the notice by which the extra period was granted. If this period is unreasonably short, it is to be extended to a reasonable extent before the contract may be terminated.[298]

(Art. 8:108(2)), this is equally clear under the UNIDROIT Principles, Art. 7.1.7(4) of which states that "(n)othing in this article prevents a party from exercising a right to terminate the contract." See also Coen, *supra* note 204 at 243.

294 The PECL require the extra period to be fixed, *i.e.*, of definite length (*e.g.*, to request performance "within a week" or "by July 1" as opposed to "as soon as possible"). See *cf.* Comment D to PECL Art. 8:106. Both the black letter rule and the Comments of the UPICC remain silent in this regard.

295 As in the first case, the extension needs to be granted by way of a notice to the promisor. According to PECL Art. 1:302, "[u]nder these Principles reasonableness is to be judged by what persons acting in good faith and in the same situation as the parties would consider to be reasonable. In particular, in assessing what is reasonable the nature and purpose of the contract, the circumstances of the case, and the usages and practices of the trades or professions involved should be taken into account."

296 Because it is usually in the promisor's interest to allow an extension and thereby maintain a chance of eventually receiving proper performance, it may certainly do so even if the initial delay already constituted a fundamental non-performance. However, if it grants an additional period for performance, it is barred from terminating the contract during this period.

297 UPICC Art. 7.1.5(4) provides that Art. 7.1.5(3) does not apply where the non-performance concerns only a minor part of the respective obligation. As UPICC Art. 7.1.5 and PECL Art. 8:106 are almost verbatim, the absence of a corresponding paragraph in the PECL may also be perceived as indicating that they indeed do not impose any such limitation. Even so, however, it can safely be assumed that termination of the entire contract due to a trivial non-performance would normally be a violation of the duty of good faith and fair dealing (PECL Art. 1:201) and therefore equally impermissible under the PECL. See also Hartkamp, *supra* note 116 at 352.

298 The question of what period of time is to be considered "reasonable" can be determined best with reference (1) to Ill. 2 to UPICC Art. 7.1.5 (which implies that reasonableness depends on the time required by the promisor to make a conforming tender) and to (2) the factors set out in Comment E to PECL Art. 8:106, namely the period of time originally set for performance, the need of the aggrieved party to obtain performance quickly (provided that this is apparent to the other party), the nature of the goods, services or rights to be performed or conveyed (*i.e.*, the complexity of performance), and the event which caused the delay.

B. Indian statutory law

Sec. 63 of the Indian Contract Act permits the promisee to grant an extension of the time for performance. According to the Indian Supreme Court, the extension of time requires an *agreement* comprising mutual consent by the parties, which must be expressed orally, in writing or through their conduct.[299] The agreement may be arranged at or after the time of performance fixed by the contract has elapsed. What is more, it may be conditioned and there need not be any consideration for the granting of the additional period.[300] Yet, the mere fact that the non-performing does not sue the defaulting party or does not issue a formal termination notice do not suffice.[301] Instead, it is imperative that the agreement comprises a specified period or date after or on which performance shall be due; if the extension is unspecified, it is to be extended to a reasonable period.[302] The non-performing party may express its acceptance of the offer of an extension simply by performing or by making and effort to do so.

Once due date of performance has been effectively postponed by way of such an agreement, the promisee may withhold performance of its own reciprocal promise(s) subject to Sec. 51 and 54.[303] At the same time, it is bound by the extension and is therefore barred from claiming performance until the additional period has expired.

If time was originally of the essence of the contract,[304] Sec. 55(3) provides that if the promisee chooses not to terminate the contract but instead to accept performance at a later stage, it is barred from claiming damages for the delay as per Sec. 55(1) unless it had, at or before the time of actual acceptance, given notice to the promisor of its intention to actually claim compensation.[305] In turn, if the promisor fails to perform within the additional period, the new timeline replaces the period or date that were originally intended to be of the essence of the contract, and the promisee's rights remain unaffected.

---

299 See *cf.* Bhadbhade, *supra* note 137 at 1265, and Bangia, *supra* note 182 at 232 and 263, for further references.

300 The common-law term "consideration" may be defined as "[s]omething of value (such as an act, a forbearance, or a return promise) received by a promisor from a promise." See Garner, *supra* note 141 at 131. "Consideration, or a substitute such as promissory estoppel, is necessary for an agreement to be enforceable." See *id.*

301 See Bhadbhade, *supra* note 137 at 1098 and 1266.

302 See *id.* at 1098 for further references.

303 See *supra* IV(B).

304 See *supra* IV(B).

305 See *cf.* Bhadbhade, *supra* note 137 at 1101 *et seq.*, and *infra* Ch. VII(I)(B)(1). According to the Amendment to Indian Contract Act Sec. 55(3), this rule does not apply in the state of Uttar Pradesh.

If time was initially not agreed to be of the essence of the contract, the promisee may not terminate the contract. Yet, it is entitled to compensation for any losses incurred because of the delay (Indian Contract Act Sec. 55(2)). What is more, it may issue a notice to the promisor fixing a reasonable time for performance and announcing that the contract shall be terminated after the respective period or date has elapsed.[306]

In case time for performance has been extended, the amount of damages is to be calculated with reference to the end of the extension, *i.e.*, compensation cannot be claimed for losses incurred at a time between the original due date and the end of the extra period.[307]

C. Comparative analysis

While the Principles allow the promisee to unilaterally extend the time for performance by issuing a notice to the promisor, Indian law requires an agreement between the parties. However, as this agreement presupposes neither any consideration for the extension nor the express (written or verbal) consent of the promisor, the latter's mere move or effort to perform within the additional period would constitute its acceptance of the additional period and render the extension effective under all three instruments.

As for the effects of an extension, Indian law corresponds to the Principles: if the respective requirements are met, the promisee may withhold performance of its own reciprocal or synallagmatic promise(s),[308] but it may not terminate the contract (or claim specific performance of the contract or reduce the price for performance) until the additional period has expired.[309] However, Sec. 55(3) of the Indian Contract Act excludes the right to claim damages where, time being of the essence of the contract, the promisee accepts the late tender but did not notify the promisor of its intention to claim damages for losses sustained as a result of the delay.

Finally, in cases of late performance where time was not of the essence of the contract, all three instruments grant the promisee an option for the promisee to fix a specified and reasonable period for performance upon the expiry of which it may terminate the contract.[310]

---

306 See *cf.* Bhadbhade, *id.* at 1101, for further references. See also *infra* Ch. VI(I)(B)(3)(c).
307 See *cf.* Bangia, *supra* note 182 at 233, and Bhadbhade, *id.* at 1098 and 1267.
308 UPICC Art. 7.1.5(2); PECL Art. 8:106(2).
309 UPICC Art. 7.1.5(2); PECL Art. 8:106(2); Indian Contract Act Sec. 63 and 55.
310 UPICC Art. 7.1.5(3); PECL Art. 8:106(3); Indian Contract Act Sec. 63.

VI. Exemption clauses

A. Principles

Art. 7.1.6 of the UNIDROIT Principles, which is entitled "Exemption Clauses", addresses clauses that

(1) limit a party's liability for non-performance;
(2) exclude a party's liability for non-performance; or
(3) permit a party to render performance substantially different from what the other party reasonably expected.

According to the black letter rule of Art. 7.1.6, such clauses may not be invoked if they are "grossly unfair" in relation to the purpose of the contract, and the restrictions imposed by this provision may not be waived by the parties.[311] In principle, the PECL provide a similar rule: "clauses excluding or restricting remedies" for non-performance may not be invoked if this were contrary to good faith and fair dealing (PECL Art. 8:109).

With these express rules on exemption and limitation clauses, both instruments acknowledge the practical significance of this specific type of potentially unfair contract terms, for which neither Principles provide any other general rules.[312] Yet, the extraordinarily broad and abstract wording of UPICC Art. 7.1.6 and PECL Art. 8:109 has also been subject to some criticism. While acknowledging that it is impossible to specifically cover all the various types of exemption and limitation of liability clauses occurring in contract practice,[313] it has been argued that the Principles' rather vague terminology – which is intended to grant courts "broad discretionary power" and does not set forth a precise test for determining when a clause may not be invoked[314] – results in a high level of uncertainty in this crucial field of international transactions.[315] Such criticism has a point

311 See Bonell, *supra* note 19 at 94 *et seq.* and 159.

312 Apart from cases where unfair contract terms violate the general principle of good faith, the UPICC grant a right to avoid them only if they lead to "gross disparity" between the parties' gains from the contract (UPICC Art. 3.10). Similarly, the PECL allow avoidance in cases of "excessive benefits or unfair advantage" of one party (PECL Art. 4:109) and of "unfair terms not individually negotiated" (Art. 4:110).

313 See *cf.* Marcel Fontaine, *Les clauses exonératoires et les indemnités contractuelles dans les Principes d'UNIDROIT: Oberservations critiques*, Uniform Law Review 1998 at 405, 406. See also Comment 1 to UPICC Art. 7.1.6 and Comment A to PECL Art. 8:109.

314 Comment 1 to UPICC Art. 7.1.6.

315 See, *e.g.*, Ernst A. Kramer, Die *Gültigkeit der Verträge nach den UNIDROIT Principles of International Commercial Contracts*, Zeitschrift für Europäisches Privatrecht 1999 at 209, 214; and Fontaine, *supra* note 313 at 410.

particularly with view on the Principles' purpose of contributing solutions to the process of contract law harmonisation, as there are still considerable divergences in domestic rules on exemption clauses even between the EU Member States' systems.[316] Unfortunately, UPICC Art. 7.1.6 and PECL Art. 8:109, which fail to offer uniform specific criteria but require substantial interpretation themselves, neither offer a solution to diminishing these divergences nor appear eligible to serve as a source of rules which, if chosen to govern a contract, reduce the uncertainty caused by these very divergences.

1. Clauses covered

As for the types of clauses covered, UPICC Art. 7.1.6 refers to exemption and limitation clauses, *i.e.*, "terms which directly limit or exclude the non-performing party's liability in the event of non-performance" and clauses that "permit a party to render performance substantially different from what the other party reasonably expected."[317] The latter type is especially relevant to terms that allow one party to unilaterally re-determine the character of its performance. Penalty clauses stipulating a fixed payment for non-performance are also subject to the conditions set out in Art. 7.1.6 if, in effect, they limit the compensation owed to the aggrieved party.[318]

According to Comment 2 to UPICC Art. 7.1.6 exemption clauses are to be distinguished from (1) clauses which merely define or concretize a party's obligation (*e.g.*, clauses defining the scope of a hotelkeeper's responsibility for losses its guests suffer from theft), and from (2) forfeiture clauses, *viz.* "clauses which permit one party to withdraw from a contract on payment of an indemnity".[319]

Similar to the UPICC, Art. 8:109 of the European Principles refers to both exemption and limitation clauses, that is, "all clauses which in practice prevent the aggrieved party from obtaining the normal remedy".[320] The provision is not limited to (liquidated) damages but applies to all possible remedies. The PECL, too, stress the need to distinguish clauses that merely define a party's obligation from clauses intended to exclude or restrict liability for non-performance.[321] Pen-

316 Particularly Council Directive 93/13/EEC of 5 April 1993 on unfair terms in consumer contracts, which harmonised the EU Member States' domestic consumer protection regimes, did not entirely abolish the fundamental divergences with regard to commercial contracts. See generally Fontaine, *id.* at 409 *et seq.*

317 Comment 2 to UPICC Art. 7.1.6.

318 See *cf.* Comment 4 to UPICC Art. 7.1.6.

319 See *cf.* Comments 2 and 3 to UPICC Art. 7.1.6.

320 Comment B to PECL Art. 8:109.

321 See Comment A to PECL Art. 8:109.

alty clauses, which are expressly addressed by PECL Art. 9:508, must also meet the requirements set forth in PECL Art. 8:109.

2. Clauses which may not be invoked

Both sets of Principles start out from the general assumption that, as a matter of freedom of contract, exemption and limitation clauses are valid unless invoking them would be grossly unfair or contrary to good faith and fair dealing.

The UPICC merely provide that *grossly unfair* contract terms may not be invoked. These are clauses that are inherently unfair and would, if applied, lead to an evident imbalance between the performances of the parties, or clauses that are not manifestly unfair but entail unfair results in certain circumstances, *e.g.*, if the non-performance was caused by gross negligence of the promisor. Unfairness is to be determined by examining the purpose of the contract and the parties' expectations.[322]

Quite similarly, PECL Art. 8:109 asks "whether it would be *contrary to good faith and fair dealing* to invoke the clause" (emphasis added), *i.e.*, whether their invocation in the particular case would be inequitable under Art 1:201. In addition, the PECL, unlike the UPICC,[323] provide general rules on unfair contract terms that were not negotiated individually.[324]

In practice, the standard of "contrary to good faith and fair dealing" found in the PECL poses a higher bar for the validity of clauses than the UPICC's "gross unfairness". This divergence is also a consequence of the PECL's proposed applicability to non-commercial contracts and their consequential need to ascertain a higher level of protection of the weaker party.

An important clarification found in the Comments to PECL Art. 8:109 is that *intentional* non-performance, including non-performance caused by a reckless act as per Art. 1:301(c) generally bars the reliance of an exemption of limitation clause because this would be contrary to good faith and fair dealing.[325] The UPICC do not explicitly mention this case; however, as the employment of the clause

322 See Comment 5 to UPICC Art. 7.1.6.

323 This difference is a result of the different scopes of application of the two instruments: While the UPICC only apply to commercial contracts, the PECL also address consumer and all other contracts and therefore are intended to ensure a higher level of protection of the weaker party.

324 PECL Art. 8:109 needs to be distinguished from Art. 4:110. While the latter deals with unfair clauses that have not been individually negotiated, including clauses which restrict or exclude liability for non-performance, Art. 8:109 is applicable irrespective of whether or not the clause was negotiated individually. If both Art. 8:109 and Art. 4:110 are applicable to a particular clause, it must satisfy the requirements of both provisions. Terms restricting or limiting remedies for mistake and incorrect information are covered by Art. 4:118(2).

325 Comment C to PECL Art. 8:109.

in favour of a party that intentionally or recklessly rendered itself unable to perform would certainly be "grossly unfair", it is fair to assert that the UNIDROIT Principles, too, intend to prevent such a party from doing so.[326]

Finally, while only the PECL's drafters have explicitly stated that the parties may not exclude or derogate from PECL Art. 8:109,[327] it may be assumed that this rule applies equally to UPICC Art. 7.1.6.

3. Consequences

If doing so would be grossly unfair or against good faith and fair dealing, an exemption clause may not be invoked and the respective party remains fully liable for its non-performance. As they are per se *invalid*, such exemption or limitation clauses may – as opposed to unreasonable penalty clauses (UPICC Art. 7.4.13; PECL Art. 9:508) – not be modified by the court.

B. Indian statutory law

Unlike the Principles, Indian statutory contract law does not provide an express rule on the validity of exemption or limitation clauses.[328]

Instead, the only provisions specifically dealing with the validity of unfair contract terms are Sec. 16 and 19A of the Indian Contract Act,[329] which establish that contract clauses are void if they create unfair advantages because they are the result of a party's undue influence on the free will of the other party.[330] This rule is similar to the common-law principle of contractual unconscionability, which applies to clauses to which one party "consented" only because of the other party's unconscionable conduct, *i.e.*, the latter's exploitation of an imbalance in bargaining positions.[331]

---

326 See, *e.g.*, Kramer, *supra* note 315 at 214. See also Bonell, *supra* note 29 at 237, who classifies this difference as a mere technical divergence between the PECL and the UPICC, *i.e.*, as one of multiple "divergences not originating from any policy considerations."

327 Comment D to Art. PECL 8:109.

328 However, the Law Commission of India has published a detailed study in relation to the possible elaboration of an Indian legislative act on the subject. See, *e.g.*, Law Commission of India, *199th Report on Unfair (Procedural & Substantive) Terms in Contract* (2006), available at http://lawcommissionofindia.nic.in/ reports/rep199.pdf.

329 For an overview of the requirements of a valid construction of exemption clauses in standard term contracts and their inclusion in the contract, see *cf.* Bhadbhade, *supra* note 137 at 149 *et seq.*

330 See *cf.* Sarin, *supra* note 153 at 573.

331 *Syed Noor v. Qutbuddin*, AIR 1956 AP 114 (1956).

In this context, the Indian Supreme Court has held that courts may strike down an unfair or unreasonable clause in a contract between parties of unequal bargaining positions only if there has also been *undue influence* exercised by the stronger party.[332] The Law Commission of India has affirmed this view.[333]

In another decision, the Supreme Court has also ruled that "terms which are so unfair and unreasonable that they shock the conscience of the court" are to be regarded as being opposed to public policy and therefore void as per Sec. 23 of the Contract Act.[334] Hence, unless there has been any undue influence or unconscionable conduct, the question of whether exemption and limitation clauses may be invoked is left entirely to the discretion of the courts. As Indian law, in accordance with its common-law tradition, does not recognize a general duty of good faith, the English common-law principles of "justice, equity and good conscience" are to be considered as guidelines in determining whether a clause may be invoked.[335]

C. Comparative analysis

Unlike the Principles, the Indian Contract Act does not provide any general guidelines on which exemption or limitation clauses may or may not be invoked. It is therefore left to the courts' discretion to decide – with reference to the common-law principles of justice, equity and good conscience – whether such terms may be invoked. In principle, however, the broad discretion conferred to the courts in this gray area of Indian statutory law does not appear to be very different from the wide judicial prerogative granted by UPICC Art. 7.1.6 and PECL Art. 8:109.

---

332 See, *e.g.*, *Central Inland Water Transport Corp. Ltd. v. Brojo Nath Ganguly*, AIR 1986 SC 1571 (1986).

333 See Law Commission of India, *13th Report (Contract Act, 1872)* (1958) at para. 43.

334 *Central Inland Water Transport Corp. Ltd. v. Brojo Nath Ganguly*, *supra* note 332 at 1613.

335 See Sarin, *supra* note 153 at 580. The Specific Relief Act, 1963 gives the courts somewhat broader discretion over unfair terms if a plaintiff seeking specific relief would gain an unfair advantage if the defendant would be ordered to perform. According to Sec. 20(2) of the Act, "the Court may properly exercise discretion not to decree specific performance (...) where the terms of the contract or the conduct of the parties at the time of entering into the contract or the other circumstances under which the contract was entered into are such that the contract, though not voidable, gives the plaintiff an unfair advantage over the defendant."

VII. *Force majeure*

A. Principles

1. Generally

Situations referred to, *inter alia*, as *force majeure* or impossibility due to unforeseen supervening events in civil-law systems or as frustration under English common law[336] are addressed by UPICC Art. 7.1.7 ("Force majeure") and PECL Art. 8:108 ("Excuse Due to an Impediment"), respectively.[337] These situations need to be distinguished from those underlying "hardship" (UPICC Art. 6.2.1 to 6.2.3) or a "change of circumstances" (PECL Art. 6:111); whereas the category of hardship relates to cases where performance is still possible but has become more onerous or impracticable due to a supervening event that could not be foreseen at the time of conclusion of the contract, "*force majeure*" or "excuse due to an impediment" relate to situations where circumstances that are beyond the parties' control actually *prevent* performance.[338]

Under the PECL, *force majeure* and hardship are strictly exclusive and it is left to courts to decide whether performance has become impossible or only excessively onerous.[339] This is different under the UPICC, where a particular situation

336 See generally *infra* Ch. VI(I)(B)(2)(a).

337 As the two terms are practically merely two ways of describing the same concept, the term "*force majeure*", as used in the UNIDROIT Principles, is hereafter used as a unitary designation that also covers the term "excuse due to an impediment" used in PECL Art. 8:108.

338 Whereas their respective provisions on *force majeure* are included in the Principles' sections on non-performance, the rules on hardship are part of their respective sections on performance. Generally speaking, hardship in this sense requires that "performance of the contract becomes excessively onerous because of a change of circumnstances" (see PECL Art. 6:111(2)) or that "the occurrence of events fundamentally alters the equilibrium of the contract either because the cost of a party's performance has increased or because the value of the performance a party receives is diminished" (see Comment 1 to UPICC Art. 6.2.1). The reasoning behind this separation of the Principles' provisions on *force majeure* on the one hand and hardship on the other is that the effects of hardship, where performance is still possible but only more burdensome, are a question of performance, whereas force majeure renders performance impossible and thus constitutes a form of non-performance. Being based on the structure of the UNIDROIT Principles, this survey only examines the implications of *force majeure* as a type of non-performance. For a discussion of the Principles' provisions on hardship, see, *e.g.*, Denis Tallon, *Hardship*, in Hartkamp *et al.* (eds.), *supra* note 172 at 499 *et seq.* For a comparative discussion of hardship and *force majeure* under common law and the UPICC as well as of the corresponding concepts found in other regimes, see also Perillo, *supra* note 108 and Hannes Rösler, *Hardship in German Codified Private Law – In Comparative Perspective to English, French and International Contract Law*, European Review of Private Law 2007 at 483.

339 See Comment A to PECL Art. 6:111.

may fall under UPICC Art. 6.2.2 *et seq.* and Art. 7.1.7 at the same time.[340] Here, the disadvantages party is entitled to choose which defence it wants to invoke, *viz.* whether it wishes to renegotiate the contract (UPICC Art. 6.2.3(1)) or have its non-performance treated as excused due to *force majeure* (UPICC Art. 7.1.7(1)).[341] In any case, though, the two sets of Principles fully concur in that only *force majeure* operates as an excuse to performance.

2. *Requisites of force majeure*

Despite their use of different designations, the two sets of Principles' provisions on *force majeure* are very similar. According to UPICC Art. 7.1.7(1) and PECL Art. 8:108(1), non-performance of any contractual obligation[342] – including a total failure to perform or mere delay – is generally *excused* under the following conditions:

(1) the non-performance is due to a supervening impediment which is beyond the promisor's sphere of control,[343] and
(2) the promisor could not reasonably[344] have been expected to take the impediment into account at the time of conclusion of the contract or to avoid or overcome the impediment or its consequences.[345]

---

340 See Comment 6 to UPICC Art. 6.2.2.

341 See *id.* For a comparative analysis of the Principles' differences in this respect, see, *e.g.*, Rösler, *supra* note 338.

342 This includes monetary obligations. See UPICC Art. 7.1.7(4) and Comment B to PECL Art. 8:108.

343 Comment B to PECL Art. 8:108 underscores that the rules on force majeure are inapplicable to situations where the impediment already existed at the time of conclusion of the contract without the parties' knowledge. Instead, such cases are treated as matters of mistake as to facts or law with the effect that the contract may be avoidable subject to PECL Art. 4:103. The UPICC's position in this regard is unclear: Whereas Ill. 1 and 2 to Art. 7.1.7 indicate that this provision is also not intended to encompass cases of initial impossibility or unlawfulness, Comment 1 to Art. 3.3 (according to which "initial impossibility of performance is equated with impossibility occurring after the conclusion of the contract," and which stresses that "the fact that the promisor (or the promisee) already knew of the impossibility of performance at the time of contracting" is to be taken into account in determining the effects of impossibility) suggests the opposite. See also Coen, *supra* note 204 at 388 *et seq.*

344 According to PECL Art. 1:302, "[u]nder these Principles reasonableness is to be judged by what persons acting in good faith and in the same situation as the parties would consider to be reasonable. In particular, in assessing what is reasonable the nature and purpose of the contract, the circumstances of the case, and the usages and practices of the trades or professions involved should be taken into account."

345 UPICC Art. 7.1.7(1); PECL Art. 8:108(1).

The requisites for a *force majeure* defence are thus rather rigid. Anything short of an impediment that actually (temporarily or permanently) prevents performance[346] may not be invoked to excuse a non-performance. Below this threshold, the promisor may resort only to the Principles' rules on hardship or change of circumstances. Impediments which are eligible to excuse the failure if they could not have reasonably been foreseen or avoided may be due to subsequent changes in law that render performance *illegal* as well as to physical factors that render it *impossible*. For instance, *force majeure* is constituted by foreign exchange controls in cases where the contract requires payment in a currency that is later subjected to such controls;[347] (civil) wars;[348] embargoes;[349] unexpected strikes that are beyond the promisor's influence;[350] or natural disasters.[351] Certainly, neither the financial capacity to perform monetary obligations[352] nor any actions of people to whom the promisor has entrusted performance (*e.g.*, its employees or a subcontractor[353]) are generally considered to be beyond the promisor's sphere of control. Under the UPICC, impossibility of performance due to governmental or administrative refusal of a permission may also constitute *force majeure* if all other conditions are met.[354]

However, the non-performance is not excused if the impediment merely leads to a delay in performance.[355]

The *reasonableness* test pertaining to the question of whether the impediment could have been foreseen, avoided or overcome limits the precautions that the promisee must take to those being proportionate to the risk, and it requires the

346 See, *e.g.*, Ill. 1(1) and (3) to UPICC Art. 7.1.7.

347 See Ill. 1(2) to UPICC Art. 7.1.7 and Ill. 3 and Comment B to PECL Art. 8:108.

348 See Ill. 2 to UPICC Art. 7.1.7.

349 See Ole Lando, *supra* note 172 at 515.

350 See Ill. 1 to PECL Art. 8:108.

351 See Comments C(ii) and C(iii) to PECL Art. 8:108. However, it has been held with respect to UPICC Art. 7.1.7 that the destruction of crops due to rainstorms and flooding caused by recurring meteorological events like the phenomenon known as "El Niño" shall not be considered unforeseeable (and shall therefore not give rise to the *force majeure* defense) for a seller who "in the course of its long-standing activity in the agricultural sector had already several times experienced similar events". See an arbitral award of the *Centro de Arbitraje de México* of 30 November 2006, available at http://www.unilex.info.

352 See Comment B to PECL Art. 8:108. See Perillo, *supra* note 108 at 16 for a similar interpretation of UPICC Art. 7.1.7.

353 See Comment C(i) to PECL Art. 8:108 and PECL Art. 8:107. Despite the absence of any express reference to this notion in the UPICC, this rule may be derived from UPICC Art. 3.11(1) as well as from Comment 1 to this provision.

354 See UPICC Art. 6.1.17(2).

355 See Comment C(i) to PECL Art. 8:108. For the application of this rule to UPICC Art. 7.1.7, see Perillo, *supra* note 108 at 18 (with reference to United States case law).

promisee to contemplate only what could have been foreseen by a normal person placed in the same situation.[356]

The burden of proof for the requirements under UPICC Art. 7.1.7 and PECL Art. 8:108 lies with the promisor, and the terms of the contract may derogate from or vary the allocation of risk or the effects of *force majeure*.[357]

3. Consequences of *force majeure*

a. Specific performance and damages

In the absence of any contrary contractual stipulation, *force majeure* operates as an excuse to non-performance. As a result, the promisor is not liable to pay any damages, liquidated damages or penalties. Evidently, *force majeure* also constitutes a defence against a claim of specific performance.[358] This may be different under the UPICC if a particular situation constitutes both *force majeure* and hardship.[359] In such cases, the disadvantaged party is entitled to choose whether to invoke the *force majeure* defence (with the effect that its non-performance is excused) or hardship (with the effects set out in UPICC Art. 6.2.1 *et seq.*). If the disadvantaged party opts for the latter set of consequences, the promisee cannot terminate the contract but is compelled to enter into renegotiations of the contract (UPICC Art. 6.2.2) and remain ready to perform.[360]

Yet, if the promisor fails to give notice of the impeding event and of its inability to perform to the promisee within reasonable time after it knew or should have known of their occurrence, the latter may claim compensation for any losses incurred because of the former's failure to issue such a warning (UPICC Art. 7.1.7(3); PECL Art. 8:108(3)).

Both sets of Principles also entitle the promisee to withhold its own performance subject to UPICC Art. 7.1.3 and PECL Art. 9:201.[361] If the impediment only affects a part of the contract, the PECL also allow for a reduction of the price by the aggrieved party (PECL Art. 9:401).[362]

---

356 See Comments C(ii) and C(iii) to PECL Art. 8:108. For the application of this rule to UPICC Art. 7.1.7, see Perillo, *id.* at 17.

357 UPICC Art. 7.1.7(1) (and Comment 4 to Art. 7.1.7); PECL Art. 8:108(1) (and Comment A to Art. 8:108).

358 UPICC Art. 7.1.7(1); PECL Art. 8:108(1) and 8:101(2). See also Comment D to PECL Art. 8:108 and *infra* Ch. V(I)(A)(3)(a) and Ch. VII(I)(A)(5).

359 See *supra* 1.

360 See *cf.* Comment 6 to UPICC Art. 6.2.2.

361 UPICC Art. 7.1.7(4).

362 See Comment D to PECL Art. 8:108.

b. Termination of the contract

Provided the non-performance caused by the impediment is fundamental, the promisee may unilaterally terminate the contract (UPICC Art. 7.1.7(4) and 7.3.1; PECL Art. 8:108(2), 8:103 and 9:301(1) *et seq.*).[363] By contrast, hardship (UPICC Art. 6.2.3) or change of circumstances (PECL Art. 6:111) permit termination only as a result of a *mutual* decision by the parties, or by way of a court order.[364]

If performance is impeded only partly, both sets of Principles give the promisee a choice: it may either terminate the contract as a whole by issuing a notice of termination to the promisor, or it may uphold the contract to maintain a chance of receiving the remaining portion of the performance and meanwhile withhold its own performance or an appropriate portion of it (UPICC Art. 7.1.7(4); PECL Art. 8:101(2)).[365]

As for cases where performance is prevented altogether, the Principles provide slightly different rules: whereas PECL Art. 9:303(4) stipulates that the contract is terminated automatically at the time when the impediment occurs, the UNIDROIT Principles nevertheless require the promisee to formally terminate the contract by way of a termination notice to the promisor.[366]

If the impediment is only of *temporary* nature, non-performance is excused temporarily. While the wording of PECL Art. 8:108(2) could be conceived as stating that the non-performance shall only be excused for as long as the impediment persists, Comment E to this provision clarifies that the consequences of the event also need to be taken into account if they prevent performance beyond the time of cessation of the actual impediment. Likewise, UPICC Art. 7.1.7(2) states that "the excuse shall have effect for such period as is reasonable having regard to the effect of the impediment on the performance of the contract."[367]

363 See also *infra* Ch. VI(I)(A)(2)(a).

364 As stated above (*supra* a), there are a few cases under the UPICC where the aggrieved party may not be entitled to terminate the contract for *force majeure*, namely if the situation constitutes both *force majeure* and hardship. See generally Düchs, *supra* note 161 at 210 *et seq.*

365 See *supra* II(A) and IV(A). Under the European Principles, the promisee may also reduce the price to a proportionate extent in accordance with PECL Art. 9:401.

366 While Michael Joachim Bonell has qualified this divergence between the Principles as being of merely technical nature (*supra* note 19 at 346), other commentators have argued that PECL Art. 9:303(4) actually constituted a "non-convincing" exception to the general rules on force majeure shared by th two sets of Principles, namely because it unnecessarily deprived the promisee of the option to tender its own performance in cases where it might still have an interest in doing so. See, *e.g.*, Hartkamp, *supra* note 116 at 353 *et seq.*

367 Strictly construed, the European Principles in this respect do not require that the period during which non-performance may be excused beyond the time of cessation of the impediment must be of "reasonable" duration. Such an interpretation of PECL Art. 8:102(2) might lead to outcomes that are substantially different from those under UPICC Art. 7.1.7(2) in relation to the

However, if the delay caused by a temporary impediment constitutes fundamental non-performance, the promisee is entitled to terminate the contract subject to the conditions set out in UPICC Art. 7.1.7(4) and 7.3.1 as well as PECL Art. 8:108(2), 8:103 and 9:301(1), respectively.[368] Conversely, if the delay does not constitute fundamental non-performance, the aggrieved party may either render time of the essence of the contract by granting an additional period for performance or demand assurance of due performance, and subsequently terminate the contract upon expiry of the extension[369] or if the promisor fails to provide adequate assurance.[370]

B. Indian statutory law

1. Subsequent impossibility and frustration

In synchrony with its common-law tradition, Indian law subjects cases where performance of a valid contract subsequently becomes impossible due to a supervening event beyond the parties' control to the doctrine of *frustration.* Sec. 56(2) of the Indian Contract Act, which stipulates: "[a] contract to do an act which, after the contract is made, becomes impossible (…), becomes void when the act becomes impossible (…)."[371] The section thus marks an exception to the general common-law principle of no-fault liability, *i.e.,* absolute liability of the parties for their obligations under a contract.[372]

Sec. 56 of the Indian Contract Act should be examined in its historical context, *i.e.*, with a view on the rules under English common law. Initially, English law treated contractual obligations as absolute in the sense that subsequent events could not excuse the parties from having to perform their obligations under an existing and valid contract.[373] Yet in 1863 this so-called "doctrine of absolute liability" was substantially modified in *Taylor v. Caldwell*,[374] where Blackburn J

---

time from which damages are to be calculated. Indeed, Michael Joachim Bonell has also noted a "technical divergence" between these two provisions with respect to "the effects of a temporary impediment." See, *e.g.*, Bonell, *supra* note 19 at 346, and Bonell/Peleggi, *supra* note 15 at 320.

368 See also *infra* Chapter VI(I)(A)(2)(a).

369 See *supra* V(A).

370 UPICC Art. 7.3.4; PECL Art. 8:105. See also *infra* Ch. VI(I)(A)(1)(d).

371 For a discussion of "initial impossibility" and "unlawfulness" (Indian Contract Act Sec. 56(1)) as well as "subsequent unlawfulness" (Sec. 56(2)), see *infra* Ch. VI(I)(B)(2).

372 For a general overview of the common-law doctrine of frustration, see *infra* Ch. VI(I)(B)(2)(a).

373 See *Paladine v. Jane*, Aleyn 29 (1647).

374 *Taylor v. Caldwell*, 3 B. & S. 826 (1863). In this case, the defendants contracted to let the plaintiffs use their music hall on four days for the purpose of giving concerts. Before the first day, the

held that it was inapplicable to contracts that are contingent upon an express or implied condition, *e.g.*, the persistence of the subject matter of the contract.[375] On these grounds, it became a matter of common law that physical impossibility of performance renders a contract void. Accordingly, it was held a few years later in *Robinson v. Davison*[376] that an agreement becomes void in cases of death or incapacity of a person whose personal performance was required under it. Finally, in 1903, *Krell v. Henry*[377] curbed the principle of absolute contractual duties even further. Here it was held that an unforeseeable destruction of the commercial object, that is, the foundation of the contract (*e.g.*, uselessness of performance due to a supervening change of circumstances), should also discharge the parties from their obligations. *Taylor v. Caldwell* and *Krell v. Henry* hence constituted what is known under English common law as the "doctrine of frustration".

The Indian Supreme Court has held that Sec .56(2) of the Indian Contract Act transposes the English doctrine of frustration into a general rule of statutory law.[378] Consequently, "impossibility" in the sense of Sec. 56(2) is not confined to its literal meaning. Instead, it addresses what is known under English law as frustration either due to physical impossibility of performance or to mere destruction of the commercial object of the contract. Illustrations (d) and (e) to Sec. 56(2) reflect this broad range of applicability of this provision. Physical impossibility relates to situations where a supervening event subsequently prevents performance, for instance because of destruction of the subject matter of the contract as a result of the event.[379] Frustration of the object of the contract, on the other hand, is caused by a subsequent supervening event that – though not impeding performance itself – destroys the object or the foundation of the

---

music hall was accidentally destroyed by fire. The plaintiffs' action for damages was dismissed because it was held that the defendants were discharged from their obligations as a result of the destruction of the music hall.

375 See generally Treitel, *supra* note 159 at 649 *et seq.*

376 *Robinson v. Davison*, L.R. 6 Ex. 269 (1871).

377 *Krell v. Henry*, 2 K.B. 740 (1903). In Krell v. Henry, the defendant, for the purpose of watching the procession for the coronation of King Edward VII, had rented the plaintiff's flat – which was located along the projected path of the procession – for the days on which the event was to take place. When the coronation procession was cancelled due to illness of the King, the contract was held to be frustrated despite the fact that the defendant could still have used the flat and performance was therefore not physically impossible.

378 *Satyabrata Ghose v. Mugneeram Bangur & Co.*, AIR 1954 S.C. 44 (1954). The transposition of the doctrine of frustration into an exhaustive rule of statutory law also has the effect that the different legal theories underlying that doctrine are inapplicable in India. See generally Bhadbhade, *supra* note 137 at 1117 *et seq.*

379 *E.g.*, the destruction due to fire of a music hall that had been let for a series of concerts (see *Taylor v. Caldwell*, 3 B. & S. 826 (1863)). See also Singh, *supra* note 218 at 341, and Bhadbhade, *supra* note 137 at 1146, for further references.

contract.[380] Against this background, Indian courts have applied the doctrine of frustration to the following cases:

- destruction of subject-matter that was assumed by the parties to exist or continue to exist;
- non-existence of circumstances that were assumed as the foundation of the contract;
- occurrence of circumstances rendering performance impossible in the way in which it was contemplated and despite the fact that literal performance may still be possible (*e.g.*, intervention of war);
- subsequent changes in law or government intervention rendering the contract or its performance unlawful, including refusal of an official permission; and
- death or incapacity of a party whose personal performance was required by the contract.[381]

Mere commercial difficulty, *i.e.*, the fact that performance has only become unprofitable, more costly or otherwise more onerous, does not constitute frustration due to a change of circumstances.[382] Neither do a party's mere insolvency[383] or disappointed expectations.[384] Finally, if the intervention of the frustrating event was made possible only because of a delay in performance caused by the promisor, the principle of frustration is generally inapplicable.[385]

2. Consequences

Impossibility and frustration in the above sense lead to *automatic* termination of the contract from the time of the occurrence of the supervening event (Indian Contract Act Sec. 56(2)). As a result, the failure to perform is excused and the promisor is not liable to pay damages; in other words, the promisor does not com-

380 See *Satyabrata Ghose v. Mugneeram Bangur & Co.*, AIR 1954 S.C. 44 at 46 (1954):
"This much is clear that the word 'impossible' has not been used here in the sense of physical or literal impossibility. The performance of an act may not be literally impossible but it may be impracticable and useless from the point of view of the object and purpose which the parties had in view; and if an untoward event or change of circumstances totally upsets the very foundation upon which the parties rested their bargain, it can very well be said that the promisor found it impossible to do the act which he promised to do."

381 See Ill. (d) and (e) to Indian Contract Act Sec. 56 and Bhadbhade, *supra* note 137 at 1143.

382 See *cf.* Bangia, *supra* note 182 at 254, and Singh, *supra* note 218 at 339, for further references.

383 See *cf.* Bhadbhade, *supra* note 137 at 1136, for further references.

384 See *cf.* Singh, *supra* note 218 at 340 for further references to specific instances where Indian courts have refused to apply the doctrine of frustration and thus held that the contract was not to be considered as being automatically void.

385 See *cf.* Singh, *id.* 218 at 351, and Bangia, *supra* note 182 at 251, for further references.

mit a breach of contract. Consequently, the aggrieved party's obligations are also discharged.[386]

If the impossibility of performance are self-induced, *i.e.*, if one party caused the supervening event or carried the risk for its occurrence,[387] or if the event could have reasonably been foreseen by an average person,[388] the failure to perform is generally not excused. However, the parties may derogate from Sec. 56(2) and modify the allocation of the risk.[389] For instance, if the contract contains an absolute promise to perform, the promisor may not invoke the defence of frustration even if performance becomes impossible without its own fault.[390] Similarly, if the contract makes reference to particular grounds of frustration or indicates that the parties contemplated the particular situation, performance is not discharged unless the contract also contains a provision to this extent.[391]

If, prior to the occurrence of impossibility or a supervening event, parts of the contract had already been performed, frustration does not invalidate the transfers of performance that were already completed.[392] If only a divisible part of the contract is frustrated, the unaffected parts may remain valid and thus enforceable.[393]

Evidently, the automatic termination of the contract neither affects the validity of a clause stating that the doctrine of frustration shall not be applicable, nor does it invalidate an arbitration clause or any other clauses pertaining to the resolution of the dispute.[394]

C. Comparative analysis

Aside from the different theoretical foundations of the underlying concepts, the basic notion of what Indian law calls frustration or impossibility principally corresponds to the concepts of "*force majeure*" under the UNIDRIOIT Principles and "excuse due an impediment" under the PECL.

386 See generally *infra* Ch. VI(I)(B)(2)(b).

387 See *cf.* Singh, *supra* note 218 at 358, for references to Indian case law.

388 See *cf.* Bhadbhade, *supra* note 137 at 1174.

389 In this context, Sec. 56(2) also needs to be distinguished from Sec. 32 of the Indian Contract Act: whereas Sec. 56(2) applies to cases where a supervening event renders performance impossible or causes frustration of the purpose of the contract, Sec. 32 deals with the dissolution of contracts which impliedly or expressly stipulate that their enforcement depends on the absence or impossibility of a certain contingency. See *cf.* Bhadbhade, *id.* at 1143.

390 See *cf. id.* at 1178.

391 See generally *id.* at 1128 and 1135.

392 See *cf.* Bangia, *supra* note 182 at 252; Bhadbhade, *supra* note 137 at 1135, for further references.

393 See Specific Relief Act Sec. 12(4) and Expl. to Specific Relief Act Sec. 12 (see infra Ch. VI(I)(B)(2)(a)).

394 See *cf.* Singh, *supra* note 218 at 360, for references to Indian case law.

Yet, there is an obvious difference between UPICC Art. 7.1.7 and PECL Art. 8:108 on the one hand and Sec. 56(2) of the Indian Contract Act on the other with regard to the range of cases to which the consequences set out under these provisions are attributed. In determining whether an impediment to performance actually operates as an excuse to performance, the Principles strictly distinguish situations where performance is actually prevented by a supervening event (*force majeure* or excuse due to an impediment) from cases where, due to "hardship" or "change of circumstances", it has only become more onerous; whereas non-performance is actually excused in the former category of cases, mere hardship, however grave it may be, can only give rise to a right to renegotiation or judicial adjustment of the contract.[395]

Just as English law,[396] Indian law does not make this strict distinction. Hence, while many of the cases in which Indian courts have applied the doctrine of frustration resemble the examples provided by the Comments and Illustrations to the Principles' provisions on *force majeure*, the Indian Supreme Court has extended the scope of Sec. 56(2) of the Contract Act beyond the literal meaning of the term "impossibility" by also applying it to frustration due to a fundamental change of circumstances striking the object of the contract.[397] The Principles, on the other hand, generally treat a non-performance as being excused only if performance has become physically impossible.[398]

To the extent that their scope of applicability concurs, UPICC Art. 7.1.7, PECL Art. 8:109 and Sec. 56(2) of the Indian Contract Act provide quite similar requirements for non-performance to be excused due to subsequent supervening impossibility of performance. The supervening event must (1) have occurred after the formation of the contract, (2) not be caused by or part of the risk borne by one of the parties, and (3) not have been reasonably foreseeable by either party.[399] What is more, neither the Principles nor Indian law recognize mere financial incapacity or difficulty as an excuse to a failure to perform.

395 For a comparison of the Principles' concept of hardship (or change of circumstances) with English common law, see, *e.g.*, Joseph M. Perillo, *Hardship and its Impact on Contractual Obligations: A Comparative Analysis* (1996), and Rösler, *supra* note 338.

396 See, *e.g.*, Rösler, *id.* at 497, for further references.

397 *E.g.*, frustration of a contract for lease of an apartment for the purpose of viewing a coronation procession due to subsequent cancellation of the procession because of the King's illness (*Krell v. Henry*, 2 KB 740 (1903)). See also *supra* note 377.

398 See, *e.g.*, Comment A to PECL Art. 8:108 ("Article 8:108 has to apply only in cases where an impediment prevents performance." (emphasis added)). Under the UPICC, there may be cases constituting both *force majeure* and hardship at once (see Comment 6 to UPICC Art. 6.2.2 and *supra* A(1) and A(3)(a)).

399 UPICC Art. 7.1.7(1); PECL Art. 8:108(1), and Indian Contract Act Sec. 56(2) and relevant Indian case law (see *supra* B(2)).

As for the consequences of frustration and *force majeure* in cases where performance is physically impossible, there is correlation only insofar as non-performance is excused and the promisor therefore not liable to pay damages. However, there are substantial divergences as to the fate of the contract. Whereas Sec. 56(2) of the Indian Contract Act provides that the contract is *automatically* void without any further action required from the parties and regardless of their intentions,[400] the UNIDROIT Principles grant the aggrieved party a choice: it may terminate the contract by giving notice to the promisor if the failure constitutes a fundamental non-performance, or it may, where appropriate, keep the contract alive to maintain a chance of eventually receiving the outstanding portion of performance (UPICC Art. 7.1.7(1)). The PECL take yet another slightly different approach: if performance is prevented permanently and entirely, the contract terminates automatically (PECL Art. 9:303(4)) just as under Sec. 56(2) of the Indian Contract Act. However, if the impediment is not total and permanent, the European Principles reflect the UPICC's rule by leaving the decision over the fate of the contract with the aggrieved party (PECL Art. 8:108(1)).

Yet, despite this difference in policy, the practical outcome will often be identical under all three regimes. This is because unless the impediment affects only a minor part of the contract, impossibility normally constitutes fundamental non-performance, with the effect that termination of the contract – which occurs automatically under Indian law – will usually be the aggrieved party's only effective option under the Principles.

In contrast to UPICC Art. 7.1.7(2) and PECL Art. 8:108(2) – according to which performance is excused only temporarily if the impediment is not permanent –, Sec. 56(2) of the Indian Contract Act does not expressly address cases where performance is prevented only temporarily. However, the Indian Supreme Court has held that a temporary impediment leading to mere delay in performance does not frustrate the contract.[401] What is more, if the contract is divisible into performable portions and portions whose performance has become impossible, the former remain valid and thus enforceable unless the contract is to be considered as being frustrated in its entirety.[402]

Finally, unlike the Principles, Indian statutory contract law does not establish a general duty of the promisor to give notice to the promisor once it has or could reasonably have become aware of the impediment to performance.

---

400 In fact, the parties need not even be aware of the occurrence of the supervening event. See Bhadbhade, *supra* note 137 at 1185, for references to English case law.

401 See *Satyabrata Ghose v. Mugneeram Bangur & Co.*, AIR 1954 S.C. 44 (1954). See also Bangia, *supra* note 182 at 253.

402 See Specific Relief Act Sec. 12(4) and Expl. to Specific Relief Act Sec. 12. See generally *supra* Ch. VI(I)(B)(2)(a)).

Chapter IV: Overview of the systems of remedies

I. Principles

The UNIDROIT and European Principles present widely identical systems of remedies. Both instruments provide four remedies for non-performance: the right to withhold performance;[403] specific performance;[404] termination;[405] and damages.[406] Unlike the UPICC, the PECL arrange for a fifth remedy, namely the aggrieved party's right to reduce the price in exchange for accepting a non-conforming tender of performance.[407]

The aggrieved party has a general right to (specific) performance unless performance is impossible or unlawful and if none of the exceptions set out in the respective black letter rules apply. The question of whether the promisor has at all caused or is responsible for its non-performance is irrelevant as it is only excused if the failure is due to an event that is beyond its control.[408] In providing that specific performance is unavailable if the non-performance is excused, the Principles basically follow the common-law doctrine of "absolute contractual liability" in that they hold a party strictly liable to fulfil its obligations unless certain exceptional circumstances exculpate it from this liability.[409]

The remedy of damages also primarily requires that the promisor's failure to perform in accordance with the contract is not excused. However, in order for the aggrieved party to be entitled to damages – and thus to claim its reliance interest as opposed to mere performance of the contract[410] – it is also necessary that

403 UPICC Art. 7.1.3; PECL Art. 9:201. See *supra* Ch. III(III)(A). Some commentators have stressed that the UPICC do not qualify the right to withhold performance as a remedy. This assumption mainly draws from the positioning of Art. 7.1.3 within the UPICC's section on non-performance in general instead of within a separate section comparable to those devoted to the other remedies. Yet, especially the identical conception of UPICC Art. 7.1.3 and PECL Art. 9:201 (see *supra* Ch. III(III)), and the Comment to Art. 7.1.3 ("[t]he present article is concerned with remedies"), among others, imply that it was indeed designed as a regular remedy to non-performance.

404 UPICC Art. 7.2.1 to 7.2.3; PECL Art. 9:101 to 9:103. See *infra* Ch. V.

405 UPICC Art. 7.3.1 to 7.3.6; PECL Art. 9:301 to 9:309. See *infra* Ch. VI.

406 UPICC Art. 7.4.1 to 7.4.13; PECL Art. 9:501 to 9:510. See *infra* Ch. VII.

407 PECL Art. 9:401. See *infra* Ch. VIII(A).

408 UPICC Art. 7.1.7(1); PECL Art. 8:101 and 8:108. See also Magnus, *supra* note 39 at 264.

409 See, *e.g.*, Zimmermann, *supra* note 161 at 481. See also *infra* Ch. VII(I)(A)(5).

410 See *infra* Ch. VII(A)(I)(6).

the promisor bears a certain degree of responsibility for the non-performance, namely that it could reasonably have foreseen the harm caused by the default.

Conversely, termination of the contract is permitted even if the non-performance is excused but presupposes that the failure is of "fundamental" scale.

If the promisor can prove that its non-performance is excused and not fundamental, the promisee is only entitled to withhold performance of its own synallagmatic promises or, under the PECL, reduce the price payable in exchange for the former's performance. In certain cases, a non-performance may even be entirely "remedy-less", *e.g.*, if it consists of a party's mere failure to receive performance[411] or if it is so immaterial that the withholding of the synallagmatic promise would be contrary to good faith or unreasonable.[412]

The general structure underlying the Principles' system of remedies is yet another implication of the fundamental status both instruments confer to the concept of *pacta sunt servanda*.[413] A contract may be terminated only if non-performance reaches a level of fundamentality where it would not make any sense for the parties to keep it alive. Likewise, the configuration of specific performance as a fully-fledged remedy[414] supplemented by the notion of assurance for performance, the right to cure and the option to grant an additional period for performance invites the aggrieved party to opt for claiming performance as a coequal alternative to claiming damages or terminating the contract.

Still, though, the promisee is generally free to choose from and between the remedies available to it in the particular situation. Aside from being subject to the specific requirements of each remedy, this freedom of choice is limited only by the principle of good faith and fair dealing, which is embodied in terms like reasonableness[415] or fundamentality[416] and generally prescribed by the general provisions of UPICC Art. 1.7 and PECL Art. 1:201.[417] Moreover, the aggrieved party may freely cumulate any remedies that are logically compatible[418] or shift from one remedy to another.[419]

The Principles generally permit the parties to modify any of the remedies, *e.g.*, to agree that termination of the contract shall be allowed in any case of non-

411 See, *e.g.*, Lando, *supra* note 172 at 509.

412 See Comment to UPICC Art. 7.1.3 and Comment B to PECL Art. 9:201.

413 See *cf.* Rosett, *supra* note 6 at 448.

414 The conception of a right to specific performance as a primary remedy corresponds to most continental European civil-law systems and also the CISG. See generally *infra* Ch. V(I)(A)(1).

415 *E.g.*, UPICC Art. 7.1.3; PECL Art. 9:201.

416 *E.g.*, UPICC Art. 7.3.1; PECL Art. 9:301

417 See *cf.* Lando/Beale, *supra* note 47 at XXXIX.

418 UPICC Art. 7.3.5(2) and 7.4.1; PECL Art. 8:102.

419 UPICC Art. 7.2.5; Comment C to PECL Art. 8:102. See also *infra* Ch. V(II)(A).

performance or only in specific circumstances.[420] This right to derogate from the black letter rules is limited only by general principles such as good faith and fair dealing[421] and under a small number of specific provisions, for instance on grossly excessive penalties or unfair limitation clauses.[422]

II. Indian statutory law

Indian law distinguishes between damages as the presumptive remedy for breach of contract on the one hand and specific relief, preventive injunction[423] and termination[424] (which are available only in specific circumstances) on the other hand.[425]

In accordance with its common-law tradition, damages, *viz.* the recovery of losses or damages sustained as a result of a breach of contract, are the primary remedy under the Indian Contract Act.[426] In fact, the term "breach of contract" presupposes a cause of action for damages.[427] Alternatively, the aggrieved party

---

420 For instance, it has been confirmed that the right to terminate the contract may be replaced by an express provision compelling the parties to renegotiate the contract in certain events. See *Camera Arbitrale Nazionale ed Internazionale di Milano*, arbitral award no. A-1795/51 (1 December 1996), available at http://www.unilex.info.

421 See also Magnus, *supra* note 39 at 269.

422 See, *e.g.*, UPICC Art. 7.2.4 and 7.1.6; PECL Art. 9:509 and 8:109.

423 See generally Bhadbhade, *supra* note 137 at 2423.

424 The Indian Contract Act and Specific Relief Act as well as the standard commentaries on Indian contract law use a variety of terms to describe what the Principles unitarily refer to as termination of a contract for non-performance. For the sake of conformity and comparability, this survey consistently applies the term "termination" for what Indian statutory contract law also terms "putting an end to the contract" (*e.g.*, Indian Contract Act Sec. 39, 53), "rescission" of a voidable contract (*e.g.*, Specific Relief Act Sec. 27 *et seq.*) or "voidance" (*e.g.*, Indian Contract Act Sec. 53 and 55).

425 In common-law jurisdictions, the use of the term "remedy" appears to very even among commentators. According to Ole Lando (*supra* note 172 at 514.), "[i]n the *Common Law* some authors use the term remedy to describe the various types of relief which an aggrieved party can obtain in case of a breach of contract. Such relief may be the very performance he contracted for or something in substitution of the promised performance, *i.e.*, damages and restitution. Other authors use the term remedy for other rights of an aggrieved party as well, for instance the right of an aggrieved party to withhold performance and to terminate the contract." In India, the prevailing view appears to be that at least damages, specific relief and injunction to prevent a breach are considered as remedies for breach of contract. (See, *e.g.*, Bhadbhade, *supra* note 137 at 2421, and Singh, *supra* note 218 at 399.)

426 Indian Contract Act Sec. 73 to 75. See generally *infra* Ch. VII.

427 See, *e.g.*, Bhadbhade, *supra* note 137 at 994.

may also claim restitution of the value of what had been performed by the aggrieved party prior to the breach (claim of *quantum meruit*).[428]

Specific performance is an exceptional remedy that is – in accordance with common-law tradition[429] – left exclusively to the courts' discretion and awarded only where damages are deemed to provide inadequate relief to the aggrieved party.[430] The awarding of an injunction as a means of perpetually or temporarily preventing the other party from committing a breach is also left to the courts' discretion.[431]

Termination of the contract, on the other hand, may take effect by force of law, *i.e.*, automatically, or at the option of the aggrieved party. In adopting the doctrine of frustration, Indian statutory law is based on the assumption that not every breach of contract justifies discharging the parties' liabilities under it. Instead, automatic termination comes into question only in a limited number of instances, namely in cases of frustration due to a supervening event that was not contemplated by the parties at the time of conclusion of the contract, or where performance is or becomes impossible or unlawful, the contract is *automatically* void.[432] Alternatively, termination may take effect at the option of the aggrieved party in cases of (1) delay where timely performance was of the essence of the contract, (2) refusal or self-induced failure to perform ("repudiation"[433]), and (3) prevention of performance by the promisor's conduct.[434] In these cases, the aggrieved party is given a choice: first, it may keep the contract alive in order to see whether the party in default might eventually become willing or able to perform. (However, exercising this option also means that the latter may take advantage of any potential circumstances in which non-performance is excused, *e.g.*, frustration due to a supervening event.) Alternatively, the aggrieved party may choose to terminate the contract and immediately sue for damages.

As under the Principles, the aggrieved party's right to sue for damages is therefore independent from its possible right to terminate the contract. Similarly, a suit for specific performance does not bar a suit for damages in addition to or in the alternative to specific performance, and the courts may award damages in addition to specific performance if they consider the latter remedy to be "not sufficient

428 See generally *infra* Ch. VI(B)(2)(c).

429 The rules found in the Specific Relief Act generally correspond to but are perceived as simplifying the exceptions acknowledged by English courts. See *cf.* Bhadbhade, *supra* note 137 at 2420.

430 Specific Relief Act Sec. 20 and 10 *et seq.* See generally infra Ch. V.

431 Specific Relief Act Sec. 36 *et seq.* See generally Bhadbhade, *supra* note 137 at 2754 *et seq.*

432 Indian Contract Act Sec. 56(1) and (2). See generally *infra* Ch. VI(I)(B)(2).

433 The term "repudiation" may be defined as "[a] contracting party's words or actions that indicate an intention not to perform the contract in the future; a threatened breach of contract." See Garner, *supra* note 141 at 604.

434 Indian Contract Act Sec. 55(1), 39, and 53, respectively. See generally *infra* Ch. VI(I)(B)(3).

to satisfy the justice of the case".[435] Termination and specific performance, on the other hand, are alternative remedies and therefore incompatible.[436]

435 Specific Relief Act Sec. 21(1), (2) and (3). See generally *infra* Ch. V(I)(B)(3).

436 Specific Relief Act Sec. 29. However, a suit for termination in the alternative to specific performance, *i.e.*, for the case that the court decides that the contract should not be specifically enforced, is permitted.

Chapter V: Specific performance

I. Specific performance of monetary and non-monetary obligations

A. Principles

1. Generally

The Principles' provisions on "specific performance" mark a primary example of how the two instruments' Principles are intended to integrate different legal systems and strike a practicable balance especially between the civil-law and common-law traditions. In fact, UPICC Art. 7.2.2 *et seq.* and PECL Art. 9:102 *et seq.* are probably the Principles' single most innovative approach to tackling persisting discrepancies among the world's major contract law systems, and numerous commentators have stated that – though it remains to be seen to what extent courts in common-law jurisdictions will actually acknowledge the conception proposed by the Principles – they were indeed offering a practically-oriented, workable compromise between the civil and common-law traditions.[437]

As emphasized already by the headings to their respective sections on the subject of specific performance,[438] both sets of Principles grant the promisee a *right to performance* as a primary remedy where the non-performance is "unexcused".[439] This right is excluded only by an exhaustive set of exceptions (as set out in UPICC Art. 7.2.2 and PECL Art. 9:102(2) and (3)) in which, broadly speaking, enforcing performance of the obligation would appear unreasonable or contrary to good

437 See, *e.g.*, Arthur S. Hartkamp, *Principles of Contract Law*, in Hartkamp *et al.*, *supra* note 172 at 125, 136; Blase, *supra* note 63 at 86; and Rosett, *supra* note 6 at 448 *et seq.* From a common-law perspective, see Perillo, *supra* note 130 at 304, and Goode, *supra* note 117 at 241. See also Zimmermann, *supra* note 161 at 482, arguing that the proximity of the Principles' concept of specific performance to civil-law tradition actually corresponds to a general trend because a number of jurisdictions influenced by common-law tradition were shifting toward the continental European conceptualization of specific performance as a (non-discretionary) primary remedy.

438 UPICC Ch. 7 Sec. 2; PECL Ch. 9 Sec. 1 ("Right to Performance").

439 See, *e.g.*, Lando/Beale, *supra* note 47 at XXXIX, and Goode, *supra* note 117 at 241. See also PECL Art. 8:101(2).

faith.[440] The decision of whether or not to award specific relief is therefore not left to the discretion of the courts. Instead, provided none of the aforementioned exceptions applies, the promise is free to choose whether it wants to claim performance of the contract or damages. This conception is yet another an expression of how the Principles' provisions gravitate around the basic principle of *pacta sunt servanda* and aim to preserve the contract alive by encouraging performance as far as this appears reasonable.[441]

The structuring of specific performance as a non-discretionary, primary remedy corresponds to the rules found in most civil-law countries.[442] Common-law tradition, on the other hand, treats damages as the primary and universal remedy for breach of contract and leaves it to the courts to decide whether, in exceptional cases where damages are deemed to pose inadequate relief, specific performance should be awarded.[443]

Under CISG Art. 28,[444] on the other hand, the question of whether or not the awarding of specific performance shall be in the courts' discretion is deferred to the *lex fori* (*i.e.*, the laws of the jurisdiction of the competent court). Especially in comparison with CISG Art. 28, the Principles' provisions on specific performance certainly present a fairly more stringent approach to contract law harmonisation.[445] As a result – and because the enforcement of foreign judgments and arbitral awards ordering specific performance of a contract is guaranteed in most countries of the world – especially arbitrators may resort to UPICC Art. 7.2.1 *et seq.* and PECL Art. 9:101 *et seq.* as sources of practicable compromise when deciding international trade disputes that bear a connection to both civil-law and common-law jurisdictions.[446]

---

440 See UPICC Art. 7.2.2; PECL Art. 9:102(2) and (3).

441 See generally Lando, *supra* note 172 at 509; Rosett, *supra* note 6 at 447 *et seq.*; and Comment B to PECL Art. 9:102.

442 See, *e.g.*, Luisa Antoniolli/Anna Veneziano (eds.), *Principles of European Contract Law and Italian Law* (2005) at 400, and Zimmermann, *supra* note 161 at 482.

443 See also *supra* B.

444 CISG Art. 28 establishes the following rule:

> "If, in accordance with the provisions of this Convention, one party is entitled to require performance of any obligation by the other party, a court is not bound to enter a judgment for specific performance unless the court would do so under its own law in respect of similar contracts of sale not governed by this Convention."

445 See *cf.* Comment 2 to UPICC Art. 7.2.2 and Comment D to PECL Art. 9:102.

446 See *cf.* Perillo, *supra* note 130 at 305, and Goode, *supra* note 117 at 241.

2. *Right to performance of monetary obligations*

a. *Requisites of specific performance*

Art. 7.2.1 of the UNIDROIT Principles and Art. 9:101(1) of the European Principles establish the general rule that a creditor has a general right to demand payment of money owed to it is entitled to enforce this right by way of legal action in court. Monetary obligations covered by these two provisions include secondary debt such as interest or a fixed sum of damages.[447]

According to UPICC Art. 7.2.3, the right to payment of contractual debt also entitles the creditor to cure a non-conforming payment, *e.g.*, if a payment has been made in a different currency or to a different account than agreed.[448] The right to payment generally requires the payment to be due, but it is irrespective of the currency in which it is owed.[449]

b. *Exceptions*

The UNIDROIT Principles merely acknowledge that usages in the sense of UPICC Art. 1.9 may in some cases exclude the right to recover the price payable for certain goods or services.

By contrast, PECL Art. 9:101(2) expressly sets out two cases where a creditor may not enforce its contractual right to payment of money owed to it. First, even where the debtor refuses or is clearly unable to accept the creditor's performance, a claim for the price is barred if the creditor could have made a cover transaction that (1) would have been reasonable[450] and (2) could have been concluded without

---

447 See Comment to UPICC Art. 7.2.1 ("money which is due under a contractual obligation") and Comment A to PECL Art. 9:101 ("every obligation to pay money").

448 See also Comment 3 to UPICC Art. 7.2.3. Despite the absence of an explicit stipulation to this extent, it appears appropriate to interpret Art. 9:101 of the European Principles so as to also entitle the creditor to claim cure of a non-conforming payment. This is primarily because neither PECL Art. 8:104 (on the promisor's right to cure) nor the Comments to that provision contain any limitation to non-monetary obligations, and because Comment A to Art. 8:101 states that defective performance in the sense of Art. 8:101 may occur with regard to *any* obligation under the contract. See generally *supra* Ch. III(IV)(A).

449 See Comment to UPICC Art. 7.2.1 and Comment A to PECL Art. 9:101.

450 According to PECL Art. 1:302, "[u]nder these Principles reasonableness is to be judged by what persons acting in good faith and in the same situation as the parties would consider to be reasonable. In particular, in assessing what is reasonable the nature and purpose of the contract, the circumstances of the case, and the usages and practices of the trades or professions involved should be taken into account."

significant effort or expense (PECL Art. 9:101(2)(a)).[451] Second, money cannot be recovered if performance of the creditor's own obligation would be unreasonable in the particular circumstances (PECL Art. 9:101(2)(b)). The second exception is especially relevant where performance of the counter-performance for which the payment in question is owed would be unreasonably expensive or is of no further interest to the debtor.[452]

In spite of this remarkably structural divergence with respect to the exceptions imposed on the right to performance of monetary obligations, it is worth emphasizing that UPICC Art. 7.2.1 and PECL Art. 9:101 agree on the exemption that is most relevant from a commercial perspective: where the creditor can reasonably be expected to dispose of the goods by way of a cover transaction, it must do so if it wants to retain its own right to claim the price.[453]

c. Consequences

Provided that none of the above-mentioned exceptions applies, the creditor may claim payment and – instead or at the same time – invoke any other remedies except damages for the debtor's failure to pay. The creditor may, for instance, terminate the contract after making a cover transaction and recover the difference between the contract price and the cover price plus any further loss it may have incurred as a result of the debtor's failure or refusal to accept the creditor's performance.[454] If there is a current price for performance, the creditor may also simply opt to terminate the contract and claim the current price prevailing at the time of termination plus any additional loss it has incurred as a result of the debtor's refusal or failure to accept its performance.[455]

Where payment cannot be claimed due to one of the exceptions recognized under UPICC Art. 7.2.1 and PECL Art. 9:101(2), the creditor certainly retains a right to recover any damages caused by the non-payment.[456]

---

451 The PECL do not take a firm stance on the question of the fate of the contract in cases where the aggrieved party has actually concluded a cover transaction. Comment B to PECL Art. 9:103 merely suggests that the contract may be considered to be automatically terminated because as the debtor can no longer tender performance.

452 See Ill. 2 and Comment B(iii) to PECL Art. 9:101.

453 Under the UPICC, this rule stems from a relevant usage (see Comment to UPICC Art. 7.2.1); in the PECL, it is provided in Art. 9:101(2)(a).

454 UPICC Art. 7.4.5; PECL Art. 9:506. See *infra* Ch. VII(IV)(A)(1).

455 UPICC Art. 7.4.6; PECL Art. 9:507. See *infra* Ch. VII(IV)(A)(2).

456 UPICC Art. 7.4.1; PECL Art. 9:103.

Finally, any delay in the payment of a primary monetary obligation entitles the creditor to interest on the amount of the debt (UPICC Art. 7.4.9; PECL Art. 9:508).[457]

3. Right to performance of non-monetary obligations

The Principles also grant the promisee a right to claim and enforce performance of obligations other than those to pay money. Under UPICC Art. 7.2.2 and PECL Art. 9:102, the aggrieved party may demand performance unless one of the exceptions and limitations prescribed by these provisions applies. The right to performance includes the right to claim cure, *i.e.*, repair or replacement, of any defective or non-conforming performance that the promisor has delivered or the promisee has validly rejected (UPICC Art. 7.2.3; PECL Art. 9:102(1)).[458]

According to UPICC Art. 7.2.2 and PECL Art. 9:102(2), the right to specific performance of non-monetary obligations is excluded in the five situations described in the following sections.

a. Performance impossible or unlawful

Factual or legal impossibility excludes the right to specific performance indefinitely or, if performance is only temporarily impossible, for as long as the impediment persists (UPICC Art. 7.2.2(a); PECL Art. 9:102(2)(a) and Art. 8:108(2)).

As opposed to the Principles' respective provisions on *force majeure* (UPICC Art. 7.1.7; PECL Art. 8:108),[459] the impossibility defence against a claim of specific performance does not only relate to a subsequent impediment to performance, but also to initial impossibility. In both cases, impossibility generally does not affect the validity of the contract (UPICC Art. 3.3 and 7.1.7(4); PECL Art. 4:102 and 8:108);[460] hence, where the aggrieved party is not entitled to claim performance, other remedies may still be available.

---

457 See *infra* Ch. VII(VII)(A)(1).

458 See also Comment 3 to UPICC Art. 7.2.3 and Comment C to PECL Art. 9:102. Repair in this context includes, *inter alia*, cure of insufficient services, removal of third-party rights, and the provision of a necessary public permission. For the promisor's right to cure, see UPICC Art. 7.1.4 and PECL Art. 8:104 (*supra* Ch. IV(IV)(A).

459 See *supra* Ch. IV(VII)(A).

460 For the only exception to this rule under the PECL, see Art. 9:303(4), according to which the contract is automatically void in case of a total and permanent impediment occurring after its conclusion. Under the UPICC, on the other hand, the refusal of a mandatory public permission may invalidate the entire contract (UPICC Art. 6.1.17(1) and (2) and also Comment 3(a) to UPICC Art. 7.2.2). See also the Comments to UPICC Art. 3.3 and PECL Art. 4:102.

For impossibility to constitute a defence against a claim of specific performance, neither the UPICC nor the PECL distinguish between cases where the promisor is only personally incapable of performing and cases where performance is altogether impossible or prohibited by law.

b. Performance unreasonably burdensome or expensive

The second exception to the promisee's right to performance of non-monetary obligations relates to cases where, due to a grave change of circumstances after the conclusion of the contract, performance is still possible but onerous or expensive to an extent where claiming or enforcing it would be contrary to good faith and fair dealing (UPICC Art. 7.2.2(b); PECL Art. 9:102(2)(b)).[461]

The Principles refrain from providing clear-cut definitions of the terms "unreasonable" or "unreasonably burdensome or expensive".[462] While the PECL underscore that this gap is intentional as "[n]o precise rule can be stated on when the effort or expense is unreasonable",[463] a few indicators can be derived from the Comments and Illustrations to the two aforementioned provisions. For instance, if the expenses the promisor would incur if it indeed performed would vastly exceed the value that performance has for the promisee, the latter's right to performance of this obligation may be excluded in the particular circumstances.[464] According to Comment F accompanying PECL Art. 9:102, "considerations as to the reasonableness of the transaction or of the appropriateness of the counter-performance are irrelevant."

What is more, this second category of exceptions to the right to performance goes hand in hand with the Principles' rules on hardship (UPICC Art. 6.2.1 to 6.2.3; PECL Art. 6:111). If performance would be so onerous or impracticable that compelling the promisor to perform would constitute hardship, UPICC Art. 6.2.1 *et seq.* and PECL Art. 6:111 provide for renegotiation or judicial adaptation of the contract but do not permit the promisee to terminate the same.[465] Moreover,

461 See Comment 3(b) to UPICC Art. 7.2.2 and Comment F to PECL Art. 9:102.

462 PECL Art. 1:302 merely provides that "[u]nder these Principles reasonableness is to be judged by what persons acting in good faith and in the same situation as the parties would consider to be reasonable. In particular, in assessing what is reasonable the nature and purpose of the contract, the circumstances of the case, and the usages and practices of the trades or professions involved should be taken into account."

463 Comment F to PECL Art. 9:102.

464 See Comment 3(b) and Ill. 1 to UPICC Art. 7.2.2; and Comment F and Ill. 3 to PECL Art. 9:102.

465 See *supra* Ch. III(VII)(A). Generally speaking, hardship in this sense occurs when "performance of the contract becomes excessively onerous because of a change of circumstances" (see Comment A to PECL Art. 6:111), or where "the occurrence of events fundamentally alters the equilibrium of the contract either because the cost of a party's performance has increased or

hardship also bars a claim of specific performance under the present exception. For instance, if a ship which is to deliver the goods contracted for sinks to sea bottom and can only be retrieved at a cost that vastly exceeds the value of the goods, the parties are compelled to renegotiate the contract and specific performance cannot be claimed either because it would be unreasonable to compel the seller to perform.[466]

Yet, the scope of UPICC Art. 7.2.2(b) and PECL Art. 9:102(2)(b) also extends beyond the situations addressed by the two instruments' provisions on hardship. For instance, specific performance may also be barred if the supervision of the promisor's compliance with an award of performance (for which the courts are responsible in most common-law jurisdictions) would be exceptionally burdensome,[467] or if performance has become useless to the aggrieved party.[468] In such cases, the PECL expressly state that Art. 6:111 on hardship shall prevail over Art. 9:102(2)(b) if both rules are applicable.[469] This means that the promisor is bound to perform unless performance has become so onerous or expensive that renegotiation or judicial adjustment of the contract have become impossible or useless and the parties have subsequently failed to reach a mutual decision to nullify the contract. Conversely, the Comment to Art. 7.2.2(b) of the UNIDROIT Principles indicates that this provision stands on an equal footing with their articles on hardship (Art. 6.2.1 *et seq.*).[470] As a result, the promisee has a choice to either assume hardship and renegotiate the terms of the contract while still claiming performance, or to forgo its right to performance and claim damages instead. Considering that the UPICC are applicable only to commercial transactions, this ample conception seems appropriate in spite of the fact that a right to choose between these two essentially different remedies in favour of the promise necessarily increases uncertainty on the promisor's end. In turn, the PECL's categorical stipulation of a superior status of the right to performance may have been driven by the need to provide a set of clear-cut, definite rules to avoid any unnecessary uncertainty among consumers or among individual parties to work or service contracts.

because the value of the performance a party receives is diminished" (see Comment 1 to UPICC Art. 6.2.1).

466 See Ill. 1 to UPICC Art. 7.2.2 and Ill. 3 to PECL Art. 9:102.

467 See Comment 3(b) to UPICC Art. 7.2.2.

468 See Comment F and Ill. 4 to PECL Art. 9:102.

469 Comment F to PECL Art. 9:102. For a critical discussion of the primacy of PECL Art. 6:111 over Art. 9:102(2)(b), see Düchs, *supra* note 161 at 164 *et seq.*

470 See Comment 3(b) to UPICC Art. 7.2.2 ("As to other possible consequences arising from drastic changes of circumstances amounting to a case of hardship, see Arts. 6.2.1 *et seq.*").

c. Cover transaction

UPICC Art. 7.2.2(c) and PECL Art. 9:102(2)(d) provide in almost identical terms that specific performance may not be claimed where the aggrieved party may reasonably obtain performance from an alternative source.[471] The rule draws from the assumption that most of the goods and services contracted for in international (commercial) transactions are of standard type and quality and usually freely available on the market.[472] If a supplier fails to deliver such goods or services, the aggrieved party is often able and usually even prefers to abandon the contract and obtain them from another supplier. Where this poses a reasonable alternative or is in fact easier than obtaining performance from the promisor,[473] the promisee may not invoke its right to request performance, but instead has two options: it may either (1) terminate the contract, conclude a cover transaction and claim damages for the difference between the contract price and the price of the cover transaction or the current price,[474] or (2) choose not to procure the goods or services from an alternative source and simply claim damages for non-performance.

"Reasonableness" in this respect goes beyond the question of whether it is possible to obtain the respective goods or services from another supplier. It also requires that the promisor is actually able to resort to the alternative source at reasonable logistic and financial conditions, and it takes into account the question of whether the promisor will eventually be indeed able to compensate the former for a possibly higher cost of the cover transaction.[475]

d. Performance being of exclusively personal character

A claim of specific performance is also barred if the underlying obligation is for work or services that bear an exclusively personal character or based on a personal relationship between the parties (UPICC Art. 7.2.2(d); PECL Art. 9:102(2)(c)). This rule emanates from three considerations. First, it is aimed at protecting the personal liberty of the promisor. Second, it acknowledges that the quality of performance of an obligation of purely personal character will often be impaired if the promisor is reluctant but nevertheless ordered to perform. Finally, it takes

471 Neither set of Principles takes a defnite stance on what shall be the fate of the contract if the aggrieved party has actually concluded a cover transaction. Comment B to PECL Art. 9:103 merely suggests that the contract may be considered as being automatically terminated because the non-performing party can no longer tender performance,.

472 See Comment 3(c) to UPICC Art. 7.2.2.

473 See Comment H to PECL Art. 9:102.

474 UPICC Art. 7.4.5 and 7.4.6; PECL Art. 9:506 and 9:507. See *supra* Ch. VII(IV)(A).

475 See Comment 3(c) and Ill. 2 to UPICC Art. 7.2.2, and Comment H to PECL Art. 9:102.

into account that the enforcement of the performance of this type of obligations is practically difficult especially where the courts are to supervise the parties' compliance with an award of specific performance.[476]

Both sets of Principles require performance to be of an exclusively personal character. Hence, this term neither includes work or services that are to be delivered by a company or ordinary obligations that can also be performed by any other professional with similar qualifications, *e.g.*, another engineer, lawyer or surgeon. Rather, performance must require "individual skills of an artistic or scientific nature" or involve a "confidential and personal relationship". In other words, performance must be non-delegable.[477] The PECL add that requiring an individual to enter or continue a personal relationship, *e.g.*, a partnership based on or requiring a close personal relation between the parties, is also impermissible.[478]

In principle, UPICC Art. 7.2.2(d) and PECL Art. 9:102(2)(c) may not be invoked against the performance of negative obligations like those constituted by an exclusivity clause. Yet, if the enforcement of such an obligation in relation to services, work or a personal relationship would practically result in the indirect enforcement of a positive act to provide or maintain the same, the PECL prescribe that Art. 9:102(2)(c) shall apply.[479]

e. Performance not being requested within reasonable time

Finally, the aggrieved party loses the right to performance if it fails to claim specific performance within reasonable time after it got to know or ought to have known of the promisor's failure to perform (UPICC Art. 7.2.2(e); PECL Art. 9:102(3)). This limitation allows the non-performing party to assume after a certain period of time that the promisee will not seek specific performance and thus spares the former from having to remain ready to perform indefinitely. What is more, the rule is intended to disable the aggrieved party from speculating upon a favourable development of the market before taking a final decision on whether it opts for claiming performance or damages.[480]

What is a "reasonable" period in this context depends on the circumstances of each particular case.[481] In any case, however, it is to be assumed that, if the

---

476 See Comment 3(d) to UPICC Art. 7.2.2, and Comment G to PECL Art. 9:102.

477 See Comment 3(d) and Ill. 3 and 4 to UPICC Art. 7.2.2, and Comment G and Ill. 5 to PECL Art. 9:102.

478 See Comment G and Ill. 6 to PECL Art. 9:102.

479 See Comment 3(d) to UPICC Art. 7.2.2 and Comment G and Ill. 7 to PECL Art. 9:102.

480 See Comment 3(e) to UPICC Art. 7.2.2. UPICC Art. 7.2.2(a) and PECL Art. 9:102(3) correspond to UPICC Art. 7.3.2(2) and PECL Art. 9:303(2), which subject the aggrieved party's right to terminate the contract to a similar limitation. See *infra* Ch. VI(I)(A)(2)(f).

481 See Comment I to PECL Art. 9:102.

aggrieved party has set an additional period for performance as per UPICC Art. 7.1.5 and PECL Art. 8:106, the "reasonable" period of time under UPICC Art. 7.2.2(e) and PECL Art. 9:102(3) starts to run only after the expiration of the respite.[482]

f. Consequences

In principle, the exception to the parties' general right to performance do not affect the validity of the contract. Instead, the contract remains valid (though usually terminable) even if performance is impossible.[483] Yet, the aggrieved party is still entitled to withhold performance, terminate the contract if the non-performance is of fundamental scale, and claim damages if it is unexcused.

Where the right to performance is excluded because performance would be unreasonably onerous but the particular situation also constitutes hardship, the PECL – unlike the UNIDROIT Principles – compel the aggrieved party to request renegotiation and judicial adaptation or termination of the contract before being allowed to terminate it unilaterally and claim damages for non-performance.[484]

If the promisee has makes a cover transaction, it may, subject to UPICC Art. 7.4.5 and PECL Art. 9:506, respectively, recover the difference between the contract price and the price of the substitute transaction.[485]

4. Judicial penalty

Unlike the PECL, the UNIDROIT Principles allow the courts to order that the defaulting party shall pay a penalty on top of damages if it fails to comply with an award of specific performance (UPICC Art. 7.2.4).[486] This option is intended to complement the right to performance by providing "an effective means of ensuring compliance with (such) judgments".

482 See also Coen, *supra* note 204 at 241 and 273 *et seq.*

483 UPICC Art. 3.3 and 7.1.7(4); PECL Art. 4:102 and 8:108. For the only exception to this rule under the PECL, see Art. 9:303(4), according to which the contract is terminated automatically if a total and permanent impediment occurs after its conclusion. Under the UPICC, the refusal of a mandatory public permission may invalidate the entire contract (UPICC Art. 6.1.17(1) and (2); see also Comment 3(a) to UPICC Art. 7.2.2).

484 See also *supra* b.

485 See also *infra* Ch. VII(IV)(A).

486 However, this divergence between the two sets of Principles is classified as being of merely technical nature and due to no particular policy reason. See *cf.* Perillo, *supra* note 130 at 306; Bonell, *supra* note 29 at 238; and Bonell/Peleggi, *supra* note 116 at 320.

B. Indian statutory law

1. Generally

In India, the remedy of specific relief is regulated by the Specific Relief Act, 1963.[487] As opposed to the primary, or presumptive, remedy of damages for breach of contract, specific performance of obligations other than those to pay money is equitable *judicial* relief and thus a matter of discretion of the courts. As a consequence, it may be awarded only in exceptional cases where the plaintiff seeking specific relief shows that damages would provide inadequate relief.[488] The only exception to this rule occurs in relation to contracts for the sale or lease of immovable property; in this respect, the general presumption is that damages provide inadequate relief and the promise may choose between damages and a claim of performance of the contract as alternative remedies (Specific Relief Act Sec. 10)). Termination of the contract precludes a claim of specific performance.

The conception of specific relief as an exceptional remedy corresponds to English common-law tradition. The underlying consideration is that compensation[489] in money therefore usually provides adequate relief because there are usually alternative sources from which the aggrieved party can obtain the goods or services contracted for.

The Specific Relief Act applies to all enforceable contractual obligations other than those to pay money owed in exchange for the supply of goods or services,[490] including duties to abstain from doing a certain act.[491] The Act also recognizes that there may be instances where the promisor, in order to avoid being compelled to pay damages, has an interest in the court's ordering performance of the contract, *e.g.*, if it was initially unable but later becomes able to perform. In other words, a suit for specific performance may be brought by both the aggrieved party and the non-performing party (Specific Relief Act Sec. 15). The limitation period for such a suit is three years from the date when performance was due, or,

---

487 See *supra* Ch. II(II).

488 For an overview of the English law of specific relief, see, *e.g.*, Treitel, *supra* note 159 at 752 *et seq.*

489 In common-law jurisdictions, the term "compensation" may be defined as "[p]ayment of damages, or any other act that a court orders to be done by a person who has caused injury to another and must therefore make the other whole." See Garner, *supra* note 141 at 118.

490 See generally Bhadbhade, *supra* note 137 at 1634. See generally *infra* 4.

491 See Singh, *supra* note 218 at 730. In this regard, Sec. 11 of the Specific Relief Act provides that a trustee's obligation under a contract connected to the trust is specifically enforceable unless the trustee entered it "in excess of its powers or in breach of trust".

if there was no fixed date for performance, from the time when the promise knew that the promisor would refuse to perform.[492]

The Mumbai High Court has ruled that specific relief may also be awarded in arbitration proceedings.[493]

2. When specific relief may be awarded

a. Specifically enforceable contracts

Sec. 10 of the Specific Relief Act lists a number of exceptional instances where, subject to the other provisions of the Act, contracts are specifically enforceable. The courts may at their discretion order specific performance (1) if there is no standard for ascertaining the actual damage caused by the breach, or (2) where compensation in money would not provide adequate relief for the same (Specific Relief Act Sec. 10(a) and (b)).[494]

With regard to the second of the aforementioned categories of exceptions, the Explanation to Sec. 10(b) stresses two particular refutable presumptions, namely that (1) compensation in money is presumed to be inadequate relief for a breach of contract to transfer *immovable* property,[495] and that (2) failure to perform an obligation to transfer *movable* property can be remedied by compensation in money unless the property (a) is not an "ordinary article of commerce",[496] (b) consists of goods that are not easily accessible on the market,[497] or (c) is of special value or interest to the aggrieved party.[498] The

492 See Sec. 54 of the Schedule to the Limitation Act, 1963, which prescribes the following limitation period (and the relevant starting dates) in relation to a suit relating to specific performance of a contract:

"Three years. The date fixed for the performance of a contract, or, if no such date is fixed, when the plaintiff has noticed that performance is refused.

493 *Farohar & Co. v. Hemant Manohar Nabar*, AIR 1992 Bom 8 (1992). See also Bhadbhade, *supra* note 137 at 2426.

494 For exemplary case law pertaining to Specific Relief Act Sec. 10(a) and (b), see, *e.g.*, Bhadbhade, *id.* at 2446 *et seq.*

495 See Expl. (i) to Specific Relief Act Sec. 10(b).

496 Goods which were manufactured or produced solely at the request or specification of the purchaser do not necessariyl bear the degree of particularity required for "property [which] is not an ordinary article of commerce." See *Maheswari & Co. Pvt. Ltd. v. Corpn of Calcutta*, AIR 1975 Cal 165 (1975).

497 For instance, shares in a private company are not considered to be "easily obtainable in the market," and specific performance of a contract for the sale of such shares may therefore be awarded. The same applies to a contract for supply of a vessel, a plant and machinery, or commodities that are not readily available from another source. See generally Bhadbhade, *supra* note 137 at 2450 *et seq.*, and Singh, *supra* note 218 at 733 *et seq.*

498 See Expl. (ii)(a) to Specific Relief Act Sec. 10(b).

burden of proof for the inadequacy of damages lies with the plaintiff seeking specific relief.[499]

If the promisor can only perform a portion of its obligation or obligations, the courts shall generally not award specific performance of only a part of the contract (Specific Relief Act Sec. 12(1)).[500] "Inability to perform" a part of a contract in this sense may be due, *inter alia*, to insufficient quantity or minor quality of the subject matter of the contract, or to defect in title, impossibility or unlawfulness. Sec. 12 does not apply if the *promisee's* conduct has caused the promisor's inability to perform.[501]

However, there three exhaustive exceptions to the rule set forth in Sec. 12(1) of the Specific Relief Act, all of which are calibrated to the proportion of the performable part in relation to the portion which cannot be performed. In these instances, the court may exercise its discretion and award specific performance. First, where the value of the part that cannot be performed bears only a small proportion in relation to the entire obligation and can be adequately compensated in money, specific performance of the performable part may, at the suit of either party, be ordered together with compensation of the non-performable portion (Sec. 12(2)).[502]

If, by contrast, the portion that cannot be performed represents a *considerable part* of the whole obligation, the court is to examine first whether this portion can be compensated in money (Sec. 12(3)). Provided this is the case, specific performance of the remaining part may be ordered at the suit of the aggrieved party if it pays or has already paid the consideration owed for the portion of the contract that cannot be performed. If, on the other hand, the non-performable part cannot be compensated by way of damages (*e.g.*, where it is impossible to determine a fair and reasonable amount of compensation for the unperformed part), specific relief may only be awarded if the aggrieved party pays or has paid the consideration without any deduction. In either of the two aforementioned instances, the aggrieved party must also relinquish all claims for performance regarding the part for which monetary compensation is awarded, as well as any right to compensation for any additional losses that were caused by the promisor's failure to perform that part. As opposed to Sec. 12(2), the exceptions set out in Sec. 12(3) of

499 See Bhadbhade, *supra* note 137 at 2448 for further references.

500 According to the Explanation to Sec. 12 of the Specific Relief Act, "a party to a contract shall be deemed unable to perform (...) if a portion of its subject-matter existing at the date of [conclusion of] the contract has ceased to exist at the time of its performance."

501 See Bhadbhade, *supra* note 137 at 2458.

502 A frequently cited example where a combination of specific performance and compensation should be awarded as per Sec. 12(2) of the Specific Relief Act is a fictional case where it turns out that two out of 100 parcels of land sold under a contract cannot be transferred to the purchaser due to the seller's lack of title to the two parcels.

the Specific Relief Act operate only for the benefit of the promisee and may not be invoked by the non-performing party.

Finally, if a part of a single contract can be specifically performed and stands on a "separate and independent footing" from the remaining parts, the court may order specific performance of that divisible part only (Sec. 12(4)). As this subsection is considered to be merely an exception to the principal rule that specific performance of a part of a contract is undesirable, Indian courts have been very reluctant to apply it in spite of its quite straightforward phrasing.[503]

In principle, the test applicable to Sec. 12 of the Specific Relief Act is always "whether the [aggrieved party] gets substantially what he contracted to buy".[504] If the combination of specific performance and monetary compensation does not pass this threshold, the courts are to award only damages for breach of contract. In fact, an award for only damages also gives the promise the opportunity to terminate the contract and thereby avoid being bound to perform its own obligation (which it necessarily would be required to do under a judgment awarding specific performance and damages in accordance with Sec. 12(2) to (4) of the Specific Relief Act).[505]

Sec. 13 of the Specific Relief Acts prescribes that if a party contracts to sell or let immovable or movable property but lacks the title or the power to transfer the same, the promisee may nevertheless claim specific performance if the seller or lessor subsequently obtains the necessary authority, *e.g.*, by acquiring a title to the property, by obtaining a permission it was to furnish, or by producing a third person's consent to validate the title.[506]

b. Contracts which cannot be specifically enforced

Specific Performance being an exceptional remedy under Indian law, Sec. 14(1)(a) of the Specific Relief Act – similar to Sec. 10(b) – stipulates the general rule that "a contract for the non-performance of which compensation is an adequate relief" cannot be specifically enforced. For instance, compensation in money is the only remedy available for non-performance of a contract to lend money (with or without security).[507]

---

503 See Bhadbhade, *supra* note 137 at 2467 *et seq.*

504 See generally *id.* at 2458.

505 From the promisee's perspective, this option is especially valuable if the *promisor*, having initially been unable but now being able to perform at least a part of its obligations, sues for specific relief.

506 See *cf.* Singh, *supra* note 218 at 741.

507 See *cf.* Bhadbhade, *supra* note 137 at 2486.

On this basis, Sec. 14(1) rules out specific performance with a view on certain types of contracts. First, contracts involving a high level of detail or depending on the personal qualifications or volition of the parties are not specifically enforceable (Sec. 14(1)(b)). On the one hand, this category emanates from the principle that, as a matter of human dignity and personal liberty, no person should be compelled to provide work or maintain a personal relationship against his or her will. On the other hand, Sec. 14(1)(b) takes into account the practical difficulties that the courts would incur if they were to supervise specific performance of an obligation involving particular personal skill or a high level of detail. Subsection (1)(b) therefore comprises contracts for personal services, artistic contracts, agency contracts as well as construction contracts that require certain personal qualities or technical knowledge of the builder or engineer.[508]

Second, contracts which are "in their nature determinable", *i.e.*, revocable, cannot be specifically enforced (Specific Relief Act Sec. 14(1)(c)). If, for instance, a lease contract or an agreement on a certain business partnership contains a clause under which the defendant is entitled to revoke the contract at any time after its execution, an award ordering specific performance would practically be ineffective and is therefore excluded.

Finally, specific relief is barred where the contract involves a continuous obligation the performance of which the courts are practically incapable of supervising (Specific Relief Act Sec. 14(1)(d)). Courts in India and England have relied on the rule codified in this subsection where they refused to enforce agreements under which the defendant was to keep a building in repair or a railway company was to operate signals and provide engine power.[509]

An arbitration clause bars a suit for enforcement of the contract except if the Indian Arbitration and Conciliation Act, 1996 provides that it is specifically enforceable (Sec. 14(2)).

If the contract in questions falls under any of the aforementioned categories, it cannot be enforced and damages are the only available remedy unless specific performance may be granted under Sec. 14(3), which sets out five exceptional instances where specific performance is nevertheless presumed to provide more equitable relief than compensation in money.[510]

---

508 See also *id.* at 2490 *et seq.* for further examples derived from Indian case law.

509 See Singh, *supra* note 218 at 747 *et seq.* for references to Indian and English cases.

510 Notwithstanding the stipulations contained in Sec. 14(1)(a), (c) and (d) of the Specific Relief Act, Subsection 3 of Art. 14 prompts the courts to enforce the following types of contracts:
- Mortgage agreements, provided that the borrower refuses to execute the mortgage although the lender has already advanced the entire loan or, having furnished a part of it, is willing to advance the remaining amount (Sec. 14(3)(a)(i));
- Contracts to buy debentures of a company (Sec. 14(3)(a)(ii));
- Formal deeds of partnership (Sec. 14(3)(b)(i));

Sec. 17 of the Specific Relief Act ("Contract to sell or let property by one who has no title, not specifically enforceable") establishes that specific performance of a contract to sell or let immovable property shall not be awarded unless the vendor or lessor doubtlessly possesses a title to the property.

c. *Judicial discretion*

Specific performance being a discretionary remedy, the court is by no means compelled to enforce the contract (Specific Relief Act Sec. 20(1)), that is, even if the contract does not fall under any of the categories listed in Sec. 14(1) and (2) of the Act.

However, the court is bound to decide reasonably and based on sound judicial principles (Sec. 20(1)), and to consider the circumstances of the case as well as the conduct of the parties and their respective interests in relation to the contract.[511] Sec. 20(2) lists three illustrative situations where, provided an award of specific performance is not barred by Sec. 14, the court may choose to refrain from enforcing the contract. First, specific performance may be refused if the contract gives the party suing for specific performance an *unfair advantage* over the other (Sec. 20(2)(a)). Unfairness in this sense may result from the terms of the contract, the conduct of the parties or the circumstances prevailing at the time of conclusion of the contract. Indian courts have considered contract as being unfair particularly where one party aimed to delude the other or exploit its inferior bargaining position, distress, illiteracy or tension in order to obtain an unconscionable and oppressive bargain.[512]

Second, the courts may exercise their discretion not to order specific performance where performance, considering the circumstances present at the time of conclusion of the contract,[513] would cause unforeseeable hardship for the promisor while non-performance would in turn not constitute hardship for the promisee (Sec. 20(2)(b)). Being applicable even if there is no improper conduct at all on the promisee's end, this clause relates to instances where the contract is unconscionable as a result of circumstances that were neither caused nor foreseen by the promisor.[514] However, it has been held that neither a mere depreciation of the value of the sale price nor forfeiture of the purpose for which

- Contracts to purchase shares of a partner of a company (Sec. 14(3)(b)(ii));
- Subject to certain conditions enumerated in Sec. 14(3)(c)(i) to (iii), construction contracts.

511 See, *e.g.*, *Jehtalal Nanshah Modi v. Bachu*, AIR 1945 Bom. 481 (1945).

512 See, *e.g.*, Bhadbhade, *supra* note 137 at 2573 *et seq.*, for references to relevant case law.

513 See Expl. 2 to Specific Relief Act Sec. 20(2).

514 See Singh, *supra* note 218 at 764 *et seq.* Where hardship occurs only *after* the conclusion of the contract, Sec. 20(2)(c) may be applicable.

the defendant entered the contract may constitute hardship in this sense.[515] Similarly, inadequacy of the consideration or the fact that performance has simply become onerous to the promisor do not lead to hardship as under Sec. 20(2)(a) and (b) of the Act.[516]

Third, the courts may refuse to enforce a contract where certain circumstances, though not providing grounds for termination, would render specific performance *inequitable* (Sec. 20(2)(c)). In this context, a mere delay of performance does not suffice as a reason for the courts to refuse to award specific performance.[517]

If the party seeking specific relief has already completed "substantial acts" in reliance on the enforceability of the contract or incurred losses as a result of performing its own obligations under it, Sec. 20(3) expressly entitles the court to order specific performance.[518] Finally, the mere fact that the contract is not equally enforceable at the instance of both parties – that is, the absence of what is called mutuality of remedy – does not bar a court to award specific relief in either party's favour. In this respect, Sec. 20(4) of the Specific Relief Act, 1963 has replaced the (non-codified) principle of mutuality in India.

d. General requirements of and defences against claim of specific performance

The Specific Relief Act also stipulates certain requirements with respect to a person's eligibility to claim specific performance. Sec. 15 set out a non-exhaustive list of the individuals and legal entities that may sue for specific performance of a particular contract. In turn, Sec. 19 of the Act specifies the individuals and legal entities against whom and which a contract may be specifically enforced.

Sec. 16 lists a number of "personal bars" to the enforcement of the contract in favour of the promisee, thereby providing defences for the promisor against a suit for specific relief. As per this provision, specific performance may not be awarded if the aggrieved party

- would not be entitled to compensation for breach of contract under the Indian Contract Act, especially if it has itself committed a breach (Sec. 16(a));[519]

515 See *id.* for references to case law.

516 See Expl. 1 to Specific Relief Act Sec. 20(2).

517 See, *e.g.*, Bhadbhade, *supra* note 137 at 2583, for references to Indian case law.

518 See, *e.g.*, Ill. to Sec. 22(3) of the repealed Specific Relief Act, 1877: "A sells land to a railway company, who contract to execute certain works for his convenience. The company take the land and use it for their railway. Specific performance of the contract to execute the works should be decreed in favour of A."

519 See also *infra* Ch. VII(I)(B).

- is incapable of performing its own obligation under the contract, has itself acted fraudulently or unjustly, or has violated essential terms of the contract (Sec. 16(b));[520] or
- fails to aver and prove that it has at all times been unconditionally ready and willing to perform all of its own obligations under the contract (Sec. 16(c)).[521]

Sec. 9 of the Specific Relief Act further stresses that the promisor may counter a claim of specific performance with any defence available under the laws that are applicable to the contract, *e.g.*, incapacity, mistake, undue influence, fraud, misrepresentation or illegality. The most essential requirements derived from this section are that a contract that is to be specifically enforced must be valid and enforceable under the Indian Contract Act and that the respective obligation must be due.[522] On the other hand, any unreasonable delay on the aggrieved party's end in performing its own obligations bars it from claiming specific performance if time was of the essence of the contract.[523] If time is not of the essence of the contract, the aggrieved party is required to claim specific performance within reasonable time, *i.e.*, as soon as it knew or ought to have known of the circumstances entitling it to claim performance.[524]

Provided it was only intended to secure performance and not to entitle the non-performing party to pay a specified sum in lieu of performing its obligations, a liquidated damages clause does not categorically prevent the court from enforcing the contract even if the non-performing party is willing to pay the stipulated amount. Evidently, however, specific relief and payment of the fixed sum may not be awarded simultaneously (Specific Relief Act Sec. 23).[525]

---

520 In India, the term "violation of essential terms" is commonly construed as referring to a "violation which is absolutely vital to the bargain and which will absolutely alter the mutual relationship of the parties so that it will become inequitable to decree specific performance." See Bhadbhade, *supra* note 137 at 2519.

521 According to Expl. (i) to Sec. 16(c) of the Specific Relief Act, readiness and willingness to perform a *monetary obligation* do not require the plaintiff to actually tender payment or deposit the money except if a court has ordered it to do so. For case law on the Section, see, *e.g.*, Singh, *supra* note 218 at 752 *et seq.* With a view on Sec. 16(c), Indian courts have also held that the plaintiff must be ready and willing to perform (or in possession of the money) at all times from the date of conclusion of the contract to the date of the judgment ordering specific performance even if the non-performing party wrongfully repudiates the contract. See *cf.* Bhadbhade, *supra* note 137 at 2532, for references to case law.

522 See *cf.* Singh, *supra* note 218 at 730 *et seq.*

523 See, *e.g.*, Bhadbhade, *supra* note 137 at 2433, for references to Indian case law.

524 See *cf.* Singh, *supra* note 218 at 734 *et seq.*

525 See also *infra* Ch. VII(X)(B).

3. Consequences of a suit for specific relief

In a suit for specific performance, the promisee may alternatively sue for termination of the contract for the case that it cannot be specifically enforced, or that the court refuses to award specific relief (Specific Relief Act Sec. 29).

Furthermore, Sec. 21(1) of the Specific Relief Act gives the aggrieved party suing for specific relief a right to simultaneously claim damages either instead of or in addition to performance of the contract.[526] Subsections 2 and 3 of Sec. 21 underscore that the option of claiming damage in addition to specific relief is not intended to allow the plaintiff to claim the two remedies for breach of the same obligation; instead, Sec. 21(1) entitles it to sue for specific performance and at the same time recover any losses incurred in addition to the value of the non-performance, *e.g.*, losses caused by a delay in performance. Monetary compensation in substitution of specific relief, unlike damages for breach of contract, presupposes the persistence of a valid and enforceable contract.[527] If performance becomes impossible without the promisee's fault, the court may award damages in lieu of specific performance.[528]

Provided the plaintiff sues for damages in addition or in the alternative to specific relief, the court may at its discretion award damages instead of or in addition to performance of the contract if or to the extent that it opines that specific performance ought not be awarded (Sec. 21(2) and (5)).[529] For instance, in a suit for possession of a house where the agreed lease period is soon to expire, the court may thus award compensation instead of performance.[530]

If, on the other hand, the court decides that specific performance ought to be ordered but would not entirely "satisfy the justice of the case", it may award compensation in addition to specific relief (Sec. 21(3)), *e.g.*, damages for late performance. Accordingly, it has been held that where a buyer sues for performance of a contract for the sale of immovable property and the suit is decided one year after the property was to be transferred, the court may award damages for any loss it incurred by the buyer as a result of the delay.[531]

---

526 As opposed to Sec. 21, which allows for claiming and/or awarding damages in addition to or in substitution of performance of a contract that can be performed *in full*, Sec. 12 of the Specific Relief Act permits the courts to award damages in substitution of a *part* of the contract which cannot be performed. For an overview of Specific Relief Act Sec. 12, see *supra* 2(a).

527 See, *e.g.*, Bhadbhade, *supra* note 137 at 2599 and 2601.

528 See Explanation to Specific Relief Act Sec. 21.

529 According to Sec. 21(4), the amount of damages awarded in lieu of specific relief is to be determined with reference to the principles set out in Sec. 73 of the Indian Contract Act.

530 See, *e.g.*, Bhadbhade, *supra* note 137 at 2602, for references to Indian case law.

531 See, *e.g.*, Ill. to Sec. 19(3) of the repealed Specific Relief Act, 1877 and Singh, *supra* note 218 at 774.

To avoid multiple proceedings, Sec. 24 provides that the aggrieved party must sue for damages and specific performance simultaneously if it wants to retain the option to claim damages at a later stage. This is because if a suit for specific relief is dismissed and the plaintiff did not also claim damages in accordance with Sec. 21(1) and (5), it is barred from bringing a separate action for damages later but may only sue for termination of the contract or for any other remedies that may be available for the breach.[532] A plaintiff suing for specific performance and damages in the alternative to each other must elect between them before the end of the trial.[533]

4. Claim for agreed sum of money

Indian law (just as under English common law) allows for the specific enforcement of obligations to pay a fixed amount of money in exchange for the performance of a particular contractual duty or upon the occurrence of a certain event by way of an action for an agreed sum. The term "agreed sum" in this context comprises the price of goods, the repayment of a debt, or the remuneration owed to an employee.[534]

The promisee actually has a *right* to performance of such monetary obligations due to their being primary contractual duties. As a result and unlike generally, specific performance of these obligations is neither an exceptional remedy nor left to the courts' discretion. Rather, the courts are bound to order payment of the debt if the creditor proves that payment is due, *e.g.*, that it has actually performed its own obligation under the contract or that the relevant event has occurred.

C. Comparative analysis

1. Monetary obligations

The Principles' provisions on the creditor's right to the performance of monetary obligations widely correspond to the situation under Indian law. Under UPICC Art. 7.2.1 and PECL Art. 9:101(1), the creditor is entitled to claim payment of any monetary obligation once the same is due. While neither the Indian Contract Act nor the Specific Relief Act contain any statutory rule in this regard, Indian courts have recognized a similar rule that also corresponds to English common law: as opposed to non-monetary obligations, the creditor has a right to the performance

532 Specific Relief Act Sec. 24.

533 See, *e.g.*, Bhadbhade, *supra* note 137 at 2602, for further references.

534 See generally *id.* at 1634 *et seq.* and 2422.

of a contractual duty to pay an agreed sum of money.[535] The only difference between Indian law and the concept found in the Principles is that whereas UPICC Art. 7.2.1 and PECL Art. 9:101(1) relate to primary as well as secondary monetary obligations, the rule under Indian law is limited to contractually agreed, or primary, duties to pay money.[536]

Commentaries also indicate that Indian courts have at least not generally recognized any of the exceptions that the UPICC (*i.e.*, usages as per UPICC Art. 1.9, including usages requiring the creditor to resell goods that the debtor fails or refuses to pay for) and PECL (*viz.* reasonableness of a cover transaction and unreasonableness of performance of the creditor's obligation (Art. 9:101(2)) impose on to the creditor's right to payment.[537]

2. Non-monetary obligations

Unlike their rules on the performance of monetary obligations, the Principles' rules on specific performance of non-monetary obligations are structurally diametric to those under Indian law. Whereas the UPICC and PECL grant the promisee a non-discretionary right to performance under the sole condition that the contract is valid and has not been terminated, Indian law generally qualifies specific relief as an exceptional remedy awarded at the sole discretion of the courts and only where damages would provide inadequate relief or in lack of a standard for determining the exact amount of payable damages.[538] Consequently – and similar to English and Scottish law[539] but in contrast to the Principles[540] – neither the Specific Relief Act nor Indian case law provide any indication whatsoever as

535 Under English common law, too, an action for an agreed sum is regarded as a form of specific relief (as opposed to damages). See generally Treitel, *supra* note 159 at 745.

536 See Bhadbhade, *supra* note 137 at 1634 *et seq.* and 2422.

537 According to Note 3 to PECL Art. 9:101, courts in the European common-law jurisdictions have acknowledged that, in order to prevent impracticable or unjust outcomes, the right to performance of contracts other than for the sale of goods needs to be limited in certain instances. Hence, where a party had announced in advance that it was no longer interested in performance of a particular service, it has been ruled that the other party may complete performance nonetheless (and subsequently claim the price) only if it has a legitimate interest in doing so. Whereas PECL Art. 9:101(2)(b) expressly reflects the consideration underlying this rule of common law, the UPICC and Indian case law apparently do not generally ask whether the creditor's own performance and the debtor's acceptance of the same are reasonable in the particular circumstances.

538 Specific Relief Act Sec. 20 and 10. Indian courts, for that matter, also require the contract to be valid and enforceable, and that the obligation in question is due. (See *cf.* Singh, *supra* note 218 at 730 *et seq.*)

539 See, *e.g.*, Note 5 to PECL Art. 9:102.

540 UPICC Art. 7.2.3; PECL Art. 9:102(1).

to whether the promisee shall have a right to claim cure of defective performance of non-monetary obligations. [541]

However, in spite of their fundamentally different conceptions of this remedy, the Principles and the Indian Specific Relief Act share a number of very similar rules in relation to the instances in which the promisee's right to specific performance is excluded (Principles) or in which the courts shall not award specific relief (Indian law), respectively.

a. Performance impossible or unlawful

According to the Principles, the right to performance is excluded if performance initially is or subsequently becomes impossible or unlawful.[542] Nonetheless, the contract remains valid in either case.[543] Indian law, too, recognizes that impossibility and unlawfulness render the contract unenforceable. As opposed to the Principles' provisions, though, the Indian Contract Act provides that a contract is automatically void if performance is impossible[544] or the object contracted for unlawful,[545] *viz.* if performance would violate any statute or public policy.[546]

b. Performance unreasonably burdensome or expensive

If performance of the contract is indeed possible but has become onerous or expensive to the extent that to enforce it would be contrary to good faith and fair dealing, the right to performance is also excluded under the Principles.[547] Sec. 20(2)(a) to (c) of the Indian Specific Relief Act provide a similar rule: the courts may refuse to enforce a contract if performance of the obligation in question would constitute an unfair advantage to the promisee or hardship for on the promisor's end, or if they deem awarding specific relief otherwise inequitable.[548]

For instance, if the price for performance vastly exceeds[549] or is wholly out of proportion to[550] the value of performance for the promise, both sets of Principles

541 Specific Relief Act Sec. 12. For the question of whether Indian law confers a *right to cure* to the promisor, see *supra* Ch. III(IV)(B).

542 UPICC Art. 7.2.2(a); PECL Art. 9:102(2)(a).

543 UPICC Art. 3.1 and 7.1.7(4); PECL Art. 4:102 and 8:108.

544 Indian Contract Act Sec. 56. See generally *supra* Ch. III(VII)(B) and *infra* Ch. VI(I)(B)(2).

545 Indian Contract Act Sec. 23 and 24.

546 See Ill. (e) to (k) to Indian Contract Act Sec. 23. See also Bangia, *supra* note 182 at 165.

547 UPICC Art. 7.2.2(b); PECL Art. 9:102(2)(b).

548 See Bhadbade, *supra* note 137 at 2596.

549 SeeComment 3(b) and Ill. 1 to UPICC Art. 7.2.2, and Ill. 3 to PECL Art. 9:102.

550 See Singh, *supra* note 218 at 764, stating that Specific Relief Act Sec. 20(2)(b) applies to this case.

and Indian statutory law provide that specific performance should not be awarded. What is more, Indian law also recognizes the Principles' notion that a contract is unenforceable if supervising its performance would be practically impossible or unduly burdensome for the court.[551]

c. Performance readily available on the market or from an alternative source

The third scenario where the Principles do not grant the promisee a right to performance is where it may reasonably obtain performance from an alternative source by way of a cover transaction.[552] A similar though somewhat narrower rule can be derived from the Indian Specific Relief Act is similar: the (refutable) presumption that damages provide adequate relief for breach of a contract for the transfer of movable property does not apply where the goods are not readily available on the market or no ordinary articles of commerce.[553] In other words, specific relief is unavailable in a contract for the transfer of movable property if the property can be obtained from an alternative source. However, it should be noted that the courts are by no means bound to award specific performance if the goods are not readily available elsewhere. As the aforementioned refutable presumption does not generally apply to service contracts – a category which comprises most business process outsourcing (BPO) and research and development (R&D) assignments and is therefore relevant to a large portion of Indian international trade – this also means that service contracts are more likely to be enforced than sale of goods contracts.

d. Performance being of exclusively personal character

All three instruments also recognize that, as a matter of personal liberty of the promisee as well as in order to prevent the practical difficulties in supervising adherence to an order of performance, there are obligations where the exclusively personal character of performance renders specific enforcement of the contract inadequate.

Under the Principles, the promisor's right to performance of such obligations is excluded if performance is *non-delegable* because (1) it depends on individual artistic or scientific skill going beyond the ordinary expertise of individuals work-

551 See Comment 3(b) to UPICC Art. 7.2.2; Comment F to PECL Art. 9:102; and Specific Relief Act Sec. 14(1)(d). See also Bhadbhade, *supra* note 137 at 2447 *et seq.*, making reference to the general principle that, due to the practical impossibility of supervising an order of performance, Indian courts should not award specific relief in relation to work contracts.

552 UPICC Art. 7.2.2(c); PECL Art. 9:102(2)(d).

553 See Expl. (ii)(a) to Specific Relief Act Sec. 10(b).

ing in a particular field, or because (2) it is based on a confidential or personal relationship between the parties.[554] The Indian Specific Relief Act provides a similar principle. Any contract which is *dependent* on the personal qualifications or volition of the parties cannot be enforced.[555] In fact, consequences under this provision and the Principles diverge only with regard to partnership contracts. Whereas the Specific Relief Act expressly permits awarding of specific performance of a formal deed of partnership if the partners have already commenced business,[556] the PECL expressly rule out the enforcement of partnership contracts concluded by individuals and which are based on or require a close personal contact.[557]

It is therefore fair to conclude that under all three instruments, the question of specific enforceability of many of the types of service contracts that are relevant to international trade with India today – *e.g.*, BPO contracts, R&D contracts, or software engineering contracts – will generally depend on the level of sophistication of the assignment and the expertise required for the particular service.

e. Performance to be requested within reasonable time

Another restriction to the right to performance of the contract[558] under the Principles is derived from a common-law concept[559] and consequentially corresponds to an identical rule established by Indian courts:[560] the aggrieved party loses the right to claim specific performance if it fails to do so within a reasonable period of time.

f. Personal bars to specific relief

Specific Relief Act's list of "personal bars to (specific) relief" set out in Sec. 16 is not expressly reflected in the Principles; nevertheless, the UNIDROIT and European Principles' general emphasis on good faith and fair dealing as well as their provisions on the right to withhold performance[561] suggest that they take a similar

554 UPICC Art. 7.2.2(d); PECL Art. 9:102(2)(c). According to Note 3(d) to PECL Art. 9:102, this principle is also recognized in England, Ireland, Scotland and the United States.

555 Specific Relief Act Sec. 14(1)(b).

556 Specific Relief Act Sec. 14(3)(b)(i).

557 See Comment G and Ill. 6 to PECL Art. 9:102. The UPICC do not address partnership contracts in this context.

558 UPICC Art. 7.2.2(e); PECL Art. 9:102(3).

559 See *cf.* Note 4 to PECL Art. 9:102.

560 See, *e.g.*, Singh, *supra* note 218 at 734 *et seq.*

561 See, *e.g.*, *supra* Ch. III(III)(A).

position at least in relation to cases where the aggrieved party has itself failed to honour the contract.

g. Implications of a claim of or suit for specific performance

As a valid and enforceable contract is an indispensable requisite of specific enforcement of the contract under both the Principles and Indian law, it is self-evident that neither regime allows the aggrieved party to terminate the contract and claim specific performance at the same time.[562]

Under the Principles, damages and specific performance pertaining to the same obligation are also treated as strictly incompatible (albeit interchangeable) remedies.[563] Evidently, however, a claim of specific performance may be complemented by a claim for damages for any additional losses caused by a delay in performance or wasted expenditures made in contemplation of performance. Under the Indian Specific Relief Act, "the plaintiff may also claim compensation of [the] breach, either in addition to, or in substitution of, (…) performance" as well; this means that the aggrieved party may either (1) claim damages instead of performance, or (2) supplement its claim for specific performance with a possible claim for the recovery of any losses exceeding the plain value of the performance, *e.g.*, damages for late performance.[564]

Hence, all three instruments consider termination and damages (except compensation for the value of the performance itself) to be incompatible with a claim of specific performance.

Whereas the UPICC grant the courts the discretion to complement an award of specific performance with a judicial penalty to be paid by the non-performing party if the latter still fails or refuses to perform,[565] this measure is unknown to both the PECL and Indian law.

3. Evaluation

The comparison of the Principles and Indian statutory contract law regarding the area of specific performance highlights one of the most fundamental structural differences between the three instruments, namely the conception of specific performance as a primary remedy to which the aggrieved party has a right on the one hand, and as an exceptional, entirely discretionary remedy on the other.

562 UPICC Art. 7.3.5(1); Comment B to PECL Art. 8:102; Specific Relief Act Sec. 29.

563 See, *e.g.*, Comment 2 to UPICC Art. 7.4.1.

564 Specific Relief Act Sec. 21(1). See also *supra* B(3).

565 UPICC Art. 7.2.4.

However, the practical consequences under these conceptions, especially with regard to commercial transactions, are nonetheless very similar. First, the exceptions to the promisee's right to performance under the Principles essentially present a reverse image of the instances where Indian law allows for the awarding of specific relief, thereby largely balancing the three regimes' fundamentally different starting points. Second, parties to customary commercial sales or services transactions usually prefer damages for breach of contract – often preceded by a cover transaction – over specific performance, so that the latter remedy bears only limited practical significance.[566]

Still, though, the influence of both common and civil-law systems on the Principles[567] has accounted for some innovative, conciliate solutions to be found in these two instruments. For instance, this civil-law like provision of a *right* to performance also of non-monetary obligations (which may even be backed up by financial penalties)[568] can serve as an efficient means of discouraging so-called "profitable contract-breaking".[569] This concept has a point especially with a view on contracts for services where performance often depends on the specific skill and knowledge of the service provider and the promisor's interest usually goes beyond a purchaser's mere focus on immediate financial profit. On the other hand, the UPICC and PECL also acknowledge the somewhat more commercial and pragmatic approach of (English) common-law systems, which prescribe damages as the presumptive remedy unless compensation in money is inadequate to remedy the breach.

The amenities of the common-law approach are obvious: it is simpler and provides more stringent results as there are a number of instances where specific relief is inadequate, *e.g.*, where performance is impossible or useless, where it is difficult for the courts to supervise their award for performance, or where such an award restricts personal liberty. Nonetheless, even commentators from common-law jurisdictions have commended the Principles as presenting "a reasonable compromise between the common-law and the civil-law approaches to specific performance"[570] and embodying "true harmonisation made possible by simply placing less em-

566 See, *e.g.*, Note 2 to PECL Art. 9:102; Zimmermann, *supra* note 161 at 482; Rosett, *supra* note 6 at 448; and – from a common lawyer's perspective – Goode, *supra* note 117 at 241.

567 See, *cf.*, Lando, *supra* note 172 at 509.

568 See *supra* A(4).

569 The term "profitable contract-breaking" describes cases where the assignee, having completed part of the work, abandons the contract in order to take on a more lucrative assignment and at the same time retain the remuneration received in advance; under common-law tradition, the remuneration may be recovered only in case of total failure of consideration, and damages are available only if the assignee's default has actually caused additional costs, *e.g.*, for completion of the work by a another person. See *cf.* Goode, *supra* note 117 at 241.

570 See Perillo, *supra* note 130 at 304.

phasis on familiar historic doctrine and stressing the practical outcome of cases instead."[571] Evidently, however, the actual success of this approach will strongly depend on the extent to which it will be adopted by the courts in common-law jurisdictions where specific performance is devised as a discretionary remedy.

II. Change of remedy

A. Principles

What options are available to the aggrieved party if an obligation remains unperformed in spite of its having claimed or even successfully sued for performance of the contract?

Pursuant to Art. 7.2.5(1) of the UNIDROIT Principles, a party may abandon its claim for performance and instead invoke any other remedy subject to the following test:

(1) the non-performance in question concerns a non-monetary obligation;
(2) the aggrieved party has claimed (or already sued for) performance of the contract, but a judgment ordering the other party to perform has not yet been rendered;
(3) performance has not been received within an additional period for performance fixed by the aggrieved party[572] or otherwise within a reasonable period of time, *e.g.*, because the promisor becomes unable to perform only after the aggrieved party's claim or suit or because such inability becomes evident only at a later stage.[573]

If the aggrieved party has already obtained a judgment ordering performance of the contract, Art. 7.2.5(2) allows for an *immediate* shift to another remedy. This is because it is presumed that in this case the party in default has had enough time to assess its ability to perform and make arrangements for a possible change of remedy. The test under UPICC Art. 7.2.5(2) is as follows:

---

571 See Rosett, *supra* note 6 at 448 *et seq.*

572 UPICC Art. 7.1.5; PECL Art. 8:106. See *supra* Ch. III(V)(A).

573 These two conditions imposed by UPICC Art. 7.2.5(1) basically subject the right to shift from claiming specific performance to another remedy to the principle of good faith and fair dealing (UPICC Art. 1.7; PECL Art. 1:201), thereby seeking to protect the interests of a promisor acting in reliance on a claim of performance. Accordingly, the required duration of both the additional period fixed by the aggrieved party and the reasonable period of time otherwise required to expire before a change of remedy is to be determined in light of the particular case, and with reference especially to the difficulty involved in performance. See *cf.* Comment 2 to UPICC Art. 7.2.5.

(1) the non-performance in question concerns a non-monetary obligation;
(2) a court (or arbitral tribunal) has ordered the promisor to perform;
(3) the judgment or award ordering performance turns out to be unenforceable, *i.e.*, the aggrieved party has unsuccessfully attempted to enforce it.[574]

The black letter rules of the European Principles do not expressly address the option of shifting from specific performance to another remedy. However, Comment C to PECL Art. 8:102 contains statements that closely resemble the stipulations of UPICC Art. 7.2.5, and any substantive divergences between the two instruments have been characterized as emanating from "no particular 'policy' reason" and therefore being of merely "technical nature".[575]

As specific performance requires a valid and enforceable contract, and because a termination notice often leads the other party to act in reliance on the termination of the contract, Comment C to PECL Art. 8:102 also underscores that exercising the right to terminate the contract usually precludes a later change to claiming specific performance.

B. Indian statutory law

Absent any express rule to the contrary, Indian law generally allows for free shifting between different remedies until a court has passed a judgment ordering performance of the contract.

Provided that the plaintiff has sued for compensation in the alternative to specific performance or amended its plaint accordingly during the proceedings (Specific Relief Act Sec. 21(5)), the court may at its discretion award damages if it opines that specific relief should not be awarded but that there has indeed been a breach of contract for which the aggrieved party should be compensated (Specific Relief Act Sec. 21(2)).[576] Unlike a judgment ordering damages for breach of contract, an award of monetary compensation in lieu and substitution of specific

574 See Comment 3 to UPICC Art. 7.2.5.

575 See, *e.g.*, Bonell, *supra* note 29 at 238, and Bonell/Peleggi, *supra* note 116 at 320. Notwithstanding the accuracy of this characterization, it is worth noting that the PECL's drafters appear to have taken a more liberal position in relation to a change of remedy than the UNIDROIT Working Groups. According to Comment C to PECL Art. 8:102, the aggrieved party is already allowed to shift to damages if the promisor is "*not likely* to [perform] within a reasonable time" (emphasis added). By contrast, the wording of the second alternative of UPICC Art. 7.2.5(1) unequivocally requires that the aggrieved party *did not receive* performance within a reasonable period of time.

576 According to Sec. 21(4) of the Specific Relief Act, damages awarded in lieu and in substitution of specific relief are to be assessed with reference to the principles set out in Sec. 73 of the Indian Contract Act. See *infra* Ch. VII(I)(B)(6).

performance presupposes that the court could generally order performance of the contract but decides not to do so. Hence, there must be a valid contract and a refusal of the performance of the same defendant (Specific Relief Act Sec. 21(2)).

A deviation from English law,[577] the Explanation to Sec. 21 of the Specific Relief Act emphasizes that compensation may be awarded even if performance of the obligation has become impossible. As a consequence, the court may award compensation in lieu and in substitution of specific performance even in cases where performance becomes impossible without the plaintiff's fault, *e.g.*, due to the promisee's conduct.[578] For this purpose, the plaintiff needs to amend its plaint for specific relief by a claim of damages pursuant to Sec. 21(5); it need not abandon the former plaint and convert it into a suit for compensation for breach of contract (which would be subject to Sec. 73 of the Indian Contract Act).[579] For instance, if "(...) a purchaser sues (...) his vendor, for specific performance of a contract for the sale of a patent, and before the hearing of the suit the patent expires, the court may award compensation (...) for the non-performance of the contract, and may, if necessary, amend the plaint for this purpose."[580]

Similarly, where a property is attached and sold in a court auction during the pendency of a suit for specific relief, the plaintiff is entitled to claim damages and amend its plaint accordingly.[581]

A plaintiff claiming damages and specific relief in the alternative may elect between the two remedies at any time during the proceedings.[582] Once the suit for specific performance of the contract or part of it has been dismissed, Sec. 24 of the Specific Relief Act bars a subsequent suit for damages for breach of contract; however, any other remedies may still be invoked. On the other hand, once a judgment awarding specific relief has been passed and the plaintiff had not claimed damages in the alternative (or, as the case may be, amended its plaint accordingly), a subsequent claim of damages is barred as per Order II, Rule 2(3) of the Code of Civil Procedure, 1908.[583]

---

577 See Bhadbhade, *supra* note 137 at 2599.

578 See Singh, *supra* note 218 at 773, and Bhadbhade, *id.* at 2600 and 2602, for references to Indian case law.

579 See, *e.g.*, Singh, *id.* at 774, and Bhadbhade, *id.* at 2608.

580 See Bhadbhade, *id.* at 2600, citing an illustration to Sec. 19 of the repealed Specific Relief Act, 1877.

581 See, *e.g.*, Bhadbhade, *id.*, for references to further Indian case law.

582 See *id.* at 2602.

583 See *id.* at 2608 for references to Indian case law. Order II, Rule 2 of the Indian Code of Civil Procedure, 1908 provides the following rule:

> "Suit to include the whole claim – (1) Every suit shall include the whole of the claim which the plaintiff is entitled to make in respect of the cause of action; but a plaintiff may relinquish any portion of his claim in order to bring the suit within the jurisdiction of any Court.

According to Sec. 29 of the Specific Relief Act, a plaint for termination of the contract may also be brought in the alternative to a claim of specific relief (but not *vice versa*), *viz.* for the event that the court cannot or deems it inadequate to order performance.[584]

C. Comparative analysis

Due to their being interlinking with the three regimes' diametric conceptions of specific performance as a non-discretionary (Principles) and a discretionary remedy (Indian statutory contract law), their respective rules on the substitution of other remedies afford only limited grounds for comparison.

While protecting the aggrieved party by generally enabling it to shift freely to other remedies, the Principles also take into account the interests of the non-performing party acting in reliance on the former's claim of specific performance.[585] This is why, as long as a judgment has not been passed, the promisee may shift to claiming another remedy only if the promisor fails to perform (its non-monetary obligation) within a fixed additional period for performance or otherwise within a reasonable period of time after the initial claim of performance.[586]

By contrast, due to the fact that Indian law treats specific performance as a discretionary remedy, the Specific Relief Act leaves the decision over whether damages are to be *awarded* in lieu or substitution of (or in addition to) performance entirely up to the competent courts or arbitral tribunals. However, Indian courts have allowed the plaintiff to choose freely between its alternative *plaints* for specific performance and damages at any time during the proceedings,[587] *i.e.*,

---

(2) Relinquishment of part of claim – Where a plaintiff omits to sue in respect of, or intentionally relinquishes, any portion of his claim he shall not afterwards sue in respect of the portion so omitted or relinquished.

(3) Omission to sue for one of several reliefs – A person entitled to more than one relief in respect of the same cause of action may sue for all or any of such reliefs; but if he omits, except with the leave of the Court, to sue for all such reliefs, he shall not afterwards sue for any relief so omitted.

Explanation – For the purposes of this rule an obligation and a collateral security for its performance and successive claims arising under the same obligation shall be deemed respectively to constitute but one cause of action.

Illustration – A lets a house to B at a yearly rent of Rs. 1,200. The rent for the whole of the years 1905, 1906 and 1907 is due and unpaid. A sues B in 1908 only for the rent due for 1906. A shall not afterwards sue B for the rent due for 1905 or 1907."

584 See Singh, *supra* note 218 at 781.

585 See, *e.g.*, Antoniolli/Veneziano, *supra* note 442 at 362.

586 UPICC Art. 7.2.5(1); see also Comment C to PECL Art. 8:102.

587 See Bhadbhade, *supra* note 137 at 2602, for references to Indian case law.

irrespective of the passing of any fixed or reasonable period of time. Though Indian statutory law provides no express rule on whether such free shifting between two remedies is also permitted prior to the institution of judicial or arbitral proceedings, the aforementioned case law may certainly be perceived as an indicator that the promisee may *a fortiori* do so also before filing the suit.

According to the rule established by UPICC Art. 7.2.5(2), the Principles unconditionally permit a change from claiming specific performance to any other remedy if the contract later turns out to be unenforceable after a judgment ordering specific performance has been passed.[588] Indian statutory law remains silent in this regard, providing only that unless the aggrieved party had initially claimed *damages* in the alternative to specific relief or amended its plaint accordingly,[589] a subsequent claim of damages is barred once the court has passed a judgment awarding specific performance.[590] However, given that Indian law treats the contract as automatically void in cases of initial or subsequent impossibility,[591] it is obvious that if the judgment or award turns out to be unenforceable because performance has become impossible (and the contract void), the aggrieved party must necessarily be, subject to the applicable rules, entitled to damages for breach of contract instead.[592]

In the event of performance becoming impossible *during* the pendency of a suit for specific performance and damages in the alternative, the three regimes are, after all, quite likely to produce similar outcomes: subject to Sec. 21 of the Specific Relief Act, Indian law permits the courts to award damages in lieu and in substitution of specific relief if the contract cannot be enforced because performance has become impossible without the promisee's fault.[593] Under the Principles, the aggrieved party may (and usually will) shift to seeking damages as well, especially because impossibility excludes the remedy of specific performance.[594] An Illustration included in the repealed Specific Relief Act, 1877 exemplifies the proximity of the Principles and Indian law in this regard: "A, a purchaser, sues B, his vendor, for specific performance of a contract for the sale of a patent. Before the hearing of the suit the patent expires. The court may award A compensation for the non-performance of the contract, and may, if necessary, amend the plaint for that purpose."[595]

If governed by the Principles, the dispute would most likely lead to an identical outcome.

---

588 UPICC Art. 7.2.5(2); see also Comment C to PECL Art. 8:102.

589 Specific Relief Act Sec. 21(5).

590 Code of Civil Procedure, 1908 Order II, Rule 2(3) (*supra* note 583).

591 See *infra* Ch. VI(I)(B)(2).

592 See also Bhadbhade, *supra* note 137 at 1188.

593 Specific Relief Act Sec. 21(2) and Explanation to Specific Relief Act Sec. 21.

594 UPICC Art. 7.2.2(a); PECL Art. 9:102(2)(a).

595 For a reproduction of the entire set of Illustrations accompanying Sec. 19 of the repealed Specific Relief Act, 1877, see, *e.g.*, Singh, *supra* note 218 at 774.

Chapter VI: Termination of contracts

I. Grounds and means of termination

A. Principles

1. Generally

A remedy for both excused and unexcused non-performance and generally independent of any prior period of grace, termination of the contract under the Principles releases both parties from their obligations to tender and accept future performance, and usually entails restitution of what has previously been exchanged.

By allowing for termination of the contract only if the non-performance in question reaches a certain degree of severity, the Principles seek to balance the parties' conflicting interests affected by this incisive remedy:[596] having lost its right to or interest in performance or facing a situation where it is likely that the promisor will neither be able to perform nor to pay damages, the aggrieved party is best protected if it has a far-reaching right to terminate the contract. On the other hand, the non-performing party's interests may be worthy of protection as well, for instance if the non-performance is excused, if it has already incurred considerable expenses in preparing to perform, or if the level of specification of goods or services contracted for makes it impossible to offer them to another customer. In order to balance these two positions, the Principles generally allow for termination of the contract only if the non-performance is *fundamental* and termination would not pose too heavy a detriment to the defaulting party,[597] or upon the fruitless expiration of an additional period for performance granted by the promisee.[598] In other words: beyond the threshold of fundamentality, the Principles consider it justified to discard the concepts of *pacta sunt servanda* and *favor contractus*; if, on the other hand, the non-performance is not fundamental, it is assumed that other available remedies – most notably damages – adequately protect the interests of the aggrieved party and the drastic measure of termination can therefore be avoided. In light of these considerations, the fundamentality test

596 See *cf.* Comment 2 to UPICC Art. 7.3.1 and Comment A to PECL Art. 9:301.

597 See *infra* 2(a).

598 See *infra* 2(b).

for the remedy of termination of the contract again exemplifies the Principles' aim to preserve the contract to the furthest possible extent.[599]

A court order is not necessary for termination to take effect. Rather, the aggrieved party may terminate the contract on its own by giving notice to the non-performing party.[600] Serving as another safeguard for the promisor, the notice requirement prevents the promisee from speculating upon a favourable development of the market before opting to terminate the contract instead of claiming performance or damages, thereby minimizing the promisor's uncertainty as to when termination will be effective.

While the conceptions of the right to terminate the contract found in the two sets of Principles are basically similar and resemble (and in fact update or even advance) the corresponding rules provided by the CISG,[601] they also account for some notable structural differences. Reference to these divergences between the UPICC and the PECL will be made in the context where they appear throughout the following sections, which lay out the grounds on which the aggrieved party is entitled to terminate the contract.

2. Requisites of the right to terminate the contract

Except in a limited number of circumstances,[602] termination of a contract by the aggrieved party presupposes a fundamental non-performance and is to be executed by way of a termination notice given to the non-performing party.[603]

a. Fundamental non-performance

The right to terminate the contract is independent of whether the promisor is actually liable for the non-performance, *i.e.*, whether the default is excused or unexcused.[604] Rather, any type of default pertaining to any type of obligation may suffice as long as it constitutes *fundamental* non-performance. In general terms, fundamentality requires that the non-performance is material and not only of minor importance,[605] thereby destroying the promisee's expectations from the performance of the contract.[606] Aside from giving rise to the right to termina-

599 See, Rosett, *supra* note 6 at 447.

600 See *infra* 2(f).

601 See, *inter alia*, CISG Art. 25, 64, 72, 73 and 81 *et seq.*

602 See *infra* b to d.

603 See *infra* a and e, respectively.

604 See Comment 1 to UPICC Art. 7.3.1 and PECL Art. 8:108(2).

605 See Comment 2 to UPICC Art. 7.3.1.

606 See Magnus, *supra* note 5 at 272, who uses the German term "Wegfall des Vertragsinteresses".

tion, fundamentality also entitles the promisee to demand adequate assurance of performance,[607] and – under the European Principles – deprives the promisor of the right to cure a non-conforming tender.[608]

Clearly, the term needs to allow for a broad scope of interpretation in order for it to encompass the vast spectrum of situations where the aggrieved party may reasonably wish to terminate the contract. On the other hand, a high degree of flexibility necessarily entails a higher degree of unpredictability regarding the positions that courts may take on the question of whether a certain non-performance should permit the contract to be terminated. Balancing the protection of the aggrieved party and the need for "legal predictability" is especially crucial where performance is not delayed but the tender is otherwise non-conforming, because in this scenario the promisee cannot bypass the question of fundamentality by simply granting an additional period for performance and terminating the contract after the expiration of the same.[609]

Perhaps in response to the seemingly impracticable vagueness of the one-dimensional definition provided in CISG Art. 25,[610] the Principles seek to further substantiate the term by identifying a set of additional factors to determine what actually constitutes fundamentality. Still, though, UPICC Art. 7.3.1(2) ("*regard shall be had*, in particular, to whether" (emphasis added)) still refrains from establishing a clear-cut and compulsory definition; instead, it provides only a non-exhaustive list of circumstances that shall be relevant in assessing the substantiality of the non-performance. In reverse, this also means that a court may, at its own equitable discretion, treat a particular non-performance as non-fundamental even if one of these circumstances applies.[611] PECL Art. 8:103 takes a somewhat more

---

607 UPICC Art. 7.3.4; PECL Art. 8:105. See *infra* d.

608 See PECL Art. 8:104. Under the UNIDROIT Principles, fundamentality of the non-performance itself does not categorically *exclude* the right to cure (UPICC Art. 7.1.4(2); Comment 3 to Art. 7.1.4); however, the aggrieved party may terminate the contract or issue a notice of termination unless it has received an effective notice of cure from the promisor (UPICC Art. 7.1.4(3); Comment 7 to Art. 7.1.4). See also *supra* Ch. III(IV)(A).

609 UPICC Art. 7.1.5(3); PECL Art. 8:106(3).

610 CISG Art. 25 provides the following rule:

> "A breach of contract committed by one of the parties is fundamental if it results in such detriment to the other party as substantially to deprive him of what he is entitled to expect under the contract, unless the party in breach did not foresee and a reasonable person of the same kind in the same circumstances would not have foreseen such a result."

611 See *cf.* Tjakie Naudé, *Termination for Breach of Contract*, in Hector McQueen/Reinhard Zimmermann (eds.), *European Contract Law: Scots and South African Perspectives* (2006) at 286; and Düchs, *supra* note 161 at 217, for further references. See also Coen, *supra* note 204 at 231, who rightfully criticizes the UPICC's failure to back up their conception of termination (as a remedy which the aggrieved party is entitled to execute entirely on its own) by a compulsory definition of fundamentality, with the result that it is ultimately still up to the courts to decide whether the promisee was indeed entitled to terminate the contract.

terminal approach in providing that the factors set out therein are to be treated as binding parameters of fundamentality ("non-performance (...) *is* fundamental (...) if" (emphasis added)). However, as will be shown in the subsequent discussion of the factors set out in each of the Principles' black letter rules, neither approach offers a truly practicable solution to the ambivalence underlying the term, which is also that the very flexibility that is necessary for fundamentality to cover a multiplicity of situations in turn deprives the aggrieved party of a workable and reliable means to ascertain that the non-performance is indeed fundamental. Even under UPICC Art. 7.3.1 and PECL Art. 9:301, the question of whether the promise was indeed entitled to go ahead and terminate the contract is therefore likely to generate a comparably high volume of disputes and litigation.[612]

UPICC Art. 7.3.1(2) sets out a total of five factors to determine fundamentality which basically correspond to those provided in PECL Art. 8:103. The two provisions can therefore be presented jointly along the structure of the UNIDROIT Principles. Their core substantive divergences will be discussed in the context in which they occur.

(1) Non-performance substantially depriving the aggrieved party of what it was entitled to expect under the contract, the other party having foreseen or having reasonably been able to foresee this result (UPICC Art. 7.3.1(2)(a); PECL Art. 8:103(b)): looking at the gravity of the consequences of the non-performance, this first factor (the wording of which is almost identical in the two sets of Principles) comprises situations where performance is late or otherwise non-conforming to the extent that the promisee cannot use it for the intended purpose or is substantially deprived of its bargain.[613]

Just as under CISG Art. 25, the only certain consequence of this factor is that total and permanent impossibility of performance generally renders the non-performance fundamental.[614] But any attempt to apply this rule to a non-

612 For an assiduous discussion of three alternative regulatory conceptions by way of which revised versions of the CISG and the Principles could possibly tackle this dilemma in a more efficient manner (namely an expansion of the right to grant an additional period for performance; the introduction of prejudicial means of determining fundamentality; and the development of additional factors to determine fundamentality), see Düchs, *id.* at 371 *et seq.*

613 See, *e.g.*, Comment C to PECL Art. 8:103. It has been held that fundamentality in this sense can also be constituted by a failure to comply with a duty to apply its best efforts as per UPICC Art. 5.1.4(2) (see ICC Int'l Court of Arbitration, *Andersen Consulting Business Unit Member Firms v. Arthur Andersen Business Unit Member Firms and Andersen Worldwide Société Coopérative*, arbitral award no. 9797 (28 July 2000), available at http://www.unilex.info).

614 See, *e.g.*, Düchs, *supra* note 161 at 173. Comment B to PECL Art. 8:108 underscores that situations where the impediment already existed at the time of conclusion of the contract without the parties' knowledge are to be treated as matters of mistake as to facts or law, with the effect that the contract is avoidable subject to PECL Art. 4:103 – and therefore not as per Art. 9:301.

performance that falls short of total and permanent impossibility or refusal to perform uncovers its obvious weakness, that is, its unhelpful definition of fundamentality by way of a term that bears the exact same meaning: substantiality.[615] This being said, it is only a logical consequence that the Illustrations to both provisions provide hardly any foothold for an aggrieved party standing on the slippery grounds of the black letter rules of UPICC Art. 7.3.1(2)(a) and PECL Art. 8:103(b). Does a month's delay in the delivery of goods (in commercial transactions) generally constitute fundamentality if the buyer had requested their speedy delivery?[616] Exactly what severity of consequences (or perhaps: what size of a house) is required for a homeowner to be allowed to treat the defectiveness of a single heating pipe as substantially depriving it of the benefit which it was entitled to expect from the installation of a central heating system in its house?[617] The only general rule emanating from the Illustrations accompanying the two provisions is that fundamentality is not to be determined by objectively measuring the consequences of the non-performance, but by looking at its actual implications, *i.e.*, its substantiality, in each particular case.

The second element of UPICC Art. 7.3.1(2)(a) and PECL Art. 8:103(b) is at least a bit more tangible: even if the aggrieved party is substantially deprived of what it was entitled to expect, the non-performance is not fundamental if the promisor did not foresee and could not reasonably have foreseen this result at the time of conclusion of the contract, *viz.* if it did not expect and could not be expected to foresee that its default would be fundamental.[618] Evidently,

---

The UPICC's position on this issue is unclear: whereas Ill. 1 and 2 to Art. 7.1.7 indicate that the provision is not intended to encompass cases of initial impossibility or unlawfulness, either, Comment 1 to UPICC Art. 3.3 (according to which "initial impossibility of performance is equated with impossibility occurring after the conclusion of the contract," and which states that "the fact that the promisor (or the promisee) already knew of the impossibility of performance at the time of contracting" shall be taken into account in determining its consequences) suggests the opposite. See also Coen, *supra* note 204 at 388 *et seq.*

615 This circular reference is even more evident in some of the translations of the two sets of Principles. For instance, the German version of PECL Art. 8:103(b) uses identical words to define the terms "fundamental" and "substantially": "Eine Nichterfüllung ist für den Vertrag wesentlich, wenn (...) durch die Nichterfüllung der benachteiligten Partei im wesentlichen entgeht, was sie nach dem Vertrag erwarten durfte (...)."

616 See Ill. 2 to UPICC Art. 7.3.1.

617 See Ill. 4 to PECL Art. 8:103.

618 Even though Ill. 3 to UPICC Art. 7.3.1 provides reasonable grounds for a different interpretation of the wording of this passage, most observers seem to agree that this requirement does not relate to the question of whether or not the *non-performance* was foreseeable but to the consequences of the same, *i.e.*, the question of whether its *fundamentality* was foreseeable. See *cf.* Elbi Janse van Vuuren, *Termination of International Commercial Contracts for Breach of*

this also means that the promisee is also required to inform the promisor of any relevant circumstances due to which the prospective non-performance might give rise to consequences of otherwise unforeseeable severity.[619]

The overall diagnosis, however, is that while this first factor surely perpetuates the practically most relevant category of circumstances in which a party might opt for this remedy, the vagueness and unpredictability of the underlying terms render termination on this first category of grounds a fairly speculative choice under the Principles.

(2) Strict compliance with the obligation which has not been performed being of essence of the contract (UPICC Art. 7.3.1(2)(b); PECL Art. 8:103(a)): both the express stipulations of a contract as well as its implied terms, its nature, or circumstances surrounding it may render strict performance of a particular obligation of the essence of the contract.[620] In fact, as the parties are generally free to modify the Principles' provisions on non-performance,[621] they may even agree that *any* non-performance shall entitle the promise to terminate the contract. The Comments accompanying UPICC Art. 7.3.1(2)(b) and PECL Art 8:103(a) also indicate that other compulsory rules of law or even any applicable usages may also render performance of a particular obligation of the essence of the transaction[622]; typically, for instance, the time of delivery is considered to be of the essence of commercial sales contracts.[623]

It is especially with regard to this factor that the two provisions in question may actually generate different outcomes in practice: if a contract clause expressly states that timely delivery (or any other characteristics of the particular obligation) shall be of the essence of the contract, late performance – according to the compulsory definition of fundamentality provided in Art. 8:103(a)[624] – would necessarily need to be treated as fundamental non-performance under the PECL regardless of its actual consequences for the ag-

---

Contract: The Provisions of the UNIDROIT Principles of International Commercial Contracts, Arizona Journal of Int'l and Comparative Law 1998 at 583, 626 *et seq.*

619 See Ill. 3 to UPICC Art. 7.3.1 and Ill. 4 to PECL Art. 8:103.

620 See Comment 3(b) to UPICC Art. 7.3.1 and Comment B to PECL Art. 8:103.

621 See *supra* Ch. IV(I).

622 See Comment 3(b) to UPICC Art. 7.3.1 and Comment B to PECL Art. 8:103. UPICC Art. 1.9 and PECL Art. 1:105 also support the aforementioned Comments' statement that customs and usages may render time of the essence of the contract by establishing that the parties are bound not only by usages to which they have agreed but also by usages which would be considered as being generally applicable to persons in the same situation as the parties.

623 In this context, Ill. 2 to UPICC Art. 7.1.5 indicates that a party's failure to comply with a period fixed for the completion of performance of a commercial contract does not categorcially constitute fundamental non-performance.

624 According to PECL Art. 8:103(a), the non-performance is fundamental if "strict compliance with the obligation is of the essence of the contract."

grieved party.[625] By contrast, UPICC Art. 7.3.1(2)(b), under which this factor is only one of several indicators of fundamentality,[626] would in theory still permit the court to set aside such a clause when determining whether the non-performance was indeed fundamental.[627]

(3) Non-performance being intentional or reckless (UPICC Art. 7.3.1(2)(c)): under the UNIDROIT Principles, intentionality or recklessness also marks an indicator of fundamentality of the non-performance. Nonetheless, terminating the contract in response to an intentionally committed but insignificant non-performance may be contrary to good faith.[628]

The PECL, on the other hand, do not contain rules under which these two criteria alone suffice to constitute fundamental non-performance; however, the promisor's intentions come into play in the category of circumstances covered by UPICC Art. 7.3.1(2)(d) and presented in the next section.

(4) Non-performance giving the aggrieved party reason to believe that it cannot rely on the promisor's future performance (UPICC Art. 7.3.1(2)(d); PECL Art. 8:103(c)): the fourth factor to determine fundamentality is the question of whether or not the aggrieved party has reason to believe that there will be further non-performance(s) in the future. Under the UPICC, this factor is not necessarily dependent on whether bad faith or recklessness were involved on the promisor's end. Rather, the fact that the non-conformity of one instalment will recur in all future instalments is as much of a criterion as the untrustworthiness of a promisor that has acted fraudulently and thereby violated an accessory duty.[629]

---

625 See also Comment B to PECL Art. 8:103, according to which "[u]nder Article 8:103(a) the relevant factor is not the actual gravity of the breach but the agreement between the parties that strict adherence to the contract is essential and that any deviation from the obligation (...) (entitles) the other party to be discharged from its obligations under the contract." Nonetheless, Comment B to Art. 1:201 states that a merely trivial non-performance should not provide a grounds for termination even where strict adherence to the contract was of the essence.

626 UPICC Art. 7.3.1(2)(b) states that "[i]n determining whether a failure to perform (...) amounts to a fundamental non-performance, *regard shall be had* (...) to whether strict compliance with the obligation which has not been performed is of the essence under the contract" (emphasis added).

627 Even so, however, it appears unlikely that a court would actually disregard such a clause in a commercial contract stipulating that timely delivery is essential. See also Coen, *supra* note 204 at 233 *et seq.*

628 See Comment 3(c) to UPICC Art. 7.3.1. Considering the large variety of other situations where permitting termination of the contract would seem exaggerated in spite of the promisor's refusal to perform, some observers have argued that these two criteria should be treated as inferior factors and constitute fundamentality only in conjunction with other factors. See, *e.g.*, Coen, *id.* at 234, and Düchs, *supra* note 161 at 218.

629 See Comment 3(d) to UPICC Art. 7.3.1. The cumulative occurrence of two other factors listed in this article, namely those under UPICC Art. 7.3.1(2)(a) and (c), has also been considered to

Art. 8:103(c) of the European Principles goes a step further than the UPICC. Here, a non-performance that gives reason for the aggrieved party to believe that it cannot rely on future performance is fundamental only if it was committed *intentionally*. According to PECL Art. 1:303(3), intentionality in this sense includes recklessness, and the relevant Illustrations indicate that the term is intended to apply to a wide array of situations ranging from the promisor's mere knowledge of the respective non-performance to fraudulent conduct.[630] Given these circumstances, the contract may in principle be terminated even if the non-performance in question is itself insignificant or does not cause any harm to the aggrieved party.[631]

---

be enough to give the aggrieved party reason to believe that it cannot rely on the other's future performance (see *Centro de Arbitraje de México*, arbitral award of 30 November 2006, available at http://www.unilex.info).

630 Ill. 5 and 6 to PELC Art. 8:103. See also Antoniolli/Veneziano, *supra* note 442 at 366. Again, the downside of this wide scope conferred to the term "intentional" is that it results in a certain degree of unpredictability, especially if considering that it is hardly ever possible for the aggrieved party to make an accurate (and later provable) judgment of the promisor's state of mind. In fact, PECL Art. 8:103(c) anyway appears to extend the right to terminate the contract a bit too far: wouldn't the interests of the aggrieved party be sufficiently protected if the PECL would allow for termination only in cases of anticipatory non-performance, *i.e.*, if a previous non-performance makes it *clear* (as opposed to merely giving reason to believe) that there will be further *fundamental* non-performance in the future (Art. 9:304 (see *infra* c))? This seems even more so if one takes into account the fact that the aggrieved party is in any case entitled to withhold its own performance (Art. 9:201), require assurance of due performance (Art. 8:105 (see *infra* d)), and even terminate the contract to the extent that the existing non-performance is fundamental and concerns a separable part (Art. 9:302 (see *infra* e). This being said, it appears as though permitting a party to terminate the contract whenever it has reason to believe that a particular non-performance will be followed by further non-performance in the future invites abuse and unnecessarily compromises the core principle of *pacta sunt servanda*. Similar concerns come to mind with respect to the corresponding rule set out in Art. 7.3.1(2)(d) of the UNIDROIT Principles: though the latter do not provide for the possibility to terminate only a separable unperformed part of the contract (see *infra* c), it still appears exaggerated – and a prospective hotbed of disputes that are likely to be taken to the courts – to grant the aggrieved party a right to terminate the entire contract if only there has been a non-performance giving it a reason to believe that there will be any further non-performance in the future. Instead, it appears as though the combination of the right to termination where it is clear that there will be a future *fundamental* non-performance (UPICC Art. 7.3.3 (see *infra* c)) and the possibility to require assurance of due performance – and terminate the contract if assurance is not provided – (Art. 7.3.4 (see *infra* d)) would provide sufficient protection for the aggrieved party, especially as the substance of UPICC Art. 7.3.3 and 7.3.4 is at least a bit less vague than that of Art. 7.3.1(2)(d). See also Coen, *supra* note 204 at 235 and 263 *et seq.*

631 Despite this statement emanating from Ill. 5 and 6 to PECL Art. 8:103, Ill. 7 to the same shows that the actual gravity of the non-performance in question certainly also has an impact on the prognosis as to whether the aggrieved party can or cannot rely on future performance.

As this factor obviously does not play any role if there are no future obligations to be performed by the defaulting party, it is relevant mainly with respect to contracts for the performance of continuing obligations as well as contracts that are to be performed in multiple instalments.[632]

(5) Prevention of performance not causing any disproportionate loss to the promisor if the contract is terminated (UPICC Art. 7.3.1(2)(e)): finally, the UPICC introduce an indicator of non-fundamentality of a non-performance. If the respective promisor, having prepared or already tendered performance in reliance on the contract, would incur a disproportionate loss in case of termination of the same, the aggrieved party should not be allowed to invoke this remedy. According to Comment 3(e) and Illustration 5 to UPICC Art. 7.3.1(2)(e), regard is to be had in particular to whether the defective performance could still be of any value at all to the non-performing party (*e.g.*, whether it could resell the manufactured goods to other customers),[633] and to the time that it has already invested in preparing to perform.[634]

Regardless of any of the above factors, treating a non-performance as fundamental may be inappropriate if or to the extent that it was due to the promisee's own conduct.[635]

b. Termination after expiration of additional period for performance

Where performance is delayed but time is not of the essence of the contract, the non-performance in question is not to be treated as fundamental under UPICC Art. 7.3.1(2)(b) and PECL Art. 8:103(a), with the result that the aggrieved party would normally not be entitled to terminate the contract. Such an instance may occur if the contract merely provided that performance was to be tendered "within reasonable time" or "as soon as possible".

Yet based on the rather nebulous statement that late performance is "significantly different from other forms of defective performance",[636] UPICC Art.

632 See, *e.g.*, Comment D to PECL Art. 8:103 and Coen, *supra* note 204 at 263.

633 On the other hand, Ill. 5 to UPICC Art. 7.3.1 ("A tenders delivery (...), at which time B still needs the software") appears to indicate that termination shall nevertheless be permitted if performance is no longer of value to the *aggrieved party*.

634 The only other context in which the PECL's rules on non-performance and remedies take into account the *non-performing* party's interests is in their drafters' statement that a trivial non-performance should not allow for termination even where strict compliance with the obligation was of the essence of the contract. See Comment B to PECL Art. 1:201.

635 See Comment D to PECL Art. 9:301; this rule also emanates directly from UPICC Art. 7.1.2 and PECL Art. 8:101(3).

636 See Comment 1 to UPICC Art. 7.1.5. Admittedly, it remains unclear on what exact dogmatic grounds the Principles limit the right to grant additional time for performance to cases of "delay

7.3.1(3) and PECL Art. 9:301(2) – the Comments to which make express reference to UPICC Art. 7.1.5(3) and PECL Art. 8:106(3), respectively[637] – provide additional grounds of the right to termination: having set a reasonable additional period for performance, the promisee may terminate the contract upon expiry of this period even if the delay by itself did not constitute fundamental non-performance. Termination as per these provisions is subject to the following requirements:

(1) there is occurrence of an excused or unexcused[638] delay in performance that falls short of fundamental non-performance because time is not of essence of the contract;[639]
(2) the aggrieved party grants a reasonably long additional period for performance by way of a notice given to the non-performing party;[640]
(3) the promisor fails to tender performance within the reasonable additional period or – if the respite was not reasonably long – within an adequately extended period;[641] and

---

in performance". Moreover, it is hard to see why *late* performance is treated differently from "lateness of *conforming* performance", *e.g.*, cases where performance – though tendered on time and accepted by the promisee – was (non-fundamentally) *defective* and not cured by the time when performance was due. See also Coen, *supra* note 204 at 239 *et seq.* and 275 *et seq.*

637 See also *supra* Ch. III(V)(A).

638 While Comment B to PECL Art. 8:106 expressly states that Art. 8:106(3) also applies if the delay is excused due to a temporary impediment to performance, the same appears equally clear under the UPICC as well: first, UPICC Art. 7.1.5(3) is embedded in Art. 7.3.1, Comment 1 to which states that "(t)he rules set out in this Section are intended to apply to both cases where the non-performing party is liable for non-performance and to those where the non-performance is excused;" second, Art. 7.1.7(4) ("Nothing in this article prevents a party from exercising a right to terminate the contract") expressly underscores that excused non-performance give rise to the right to termination. See also Coen, *supra* note 204 at 243.

639 UPICC Art. 7.1.5(4) excludes the right to termination upon expiration of an additional period if the non-performance concerns only a minor part of the respective obligation. The PECL do not provide any indication to this extent; nonetheless, it can safely be assumed that termination of the entire contract in response to a trivial non-performance would normally violate the duty of good faith and fair dealing (Art. 1:201).

640 PECL Art. 8:106(3) requires the additional period to be of a *definite* duration. Hence, the notice must require performance "within two weeks" or "by July 1" and not merely "as soon as possible" (see *cf.* Comment D to PECL Art. 8:106). For the computation of such periods, see PECL Art. 1:304. According to PECL Art. 1:302, "[u]nder these Principles reasonableness is to be judged by what persons acting in good faith and in the same situation as the parties would consider to be reasonable. In particular, in assessing what is reasonable the nature and purpose of the contract, the circumstances of the case, and the usages and practices of the trades or professions involved should be taken into account."

641 Under the PECL, the question of which period is "reasonable" shall be determined in reliance on the factors laid out in Comment E to PECL Art. 8:106.

(4) the aggrieved party sends a notice of termination to the defaulting party after the expiration of the respite.[642]

In light of the Principles' emphasis on the principle of *favor contractus*,[643] the possibility of granting an additional period for performance is certainly also available where the delay already constituted fundamental non-performance.[644] However, if the promise makes use of this option in order to give the promisor a second chance to perform, the right to terminate the contract is barred until the expiration of the reasonable extra period.[645]

c. *Anticipatory non-performance*

Where it is already evident prior to the date when performance is due that there will be a non-performance by one party, the other party may be entitled to terminate the contract even before the actual due date. Pursuant to UPICC Art. 7.3.3 and PECL Art. 9:304,[646] termination in response to such "anticipatory non-performance" is allowed if and for as long as "it is clear that there will be a fundamental non-performance".[647] The reason for this equation of anticipatory non-

642 Alternatively, the aggrieved party may already state in the notice by which it sets the additional period that the contract shall terminate automatically upon the expiration of the respite (see UPICC Art. 7.1.5(3) and PECL Art. 8:106(3)). However, it should be a matter of good faith and fair dealing under both instruments that an additional confirmatory notice is nevertheless required if the promisor managed to tender performance within the additional period but this tender was non-conforming.

643 See, *e.g.*, Bonell, *supra* note 19 at 117.

644 Whereas this interpretation of UPICC Art. 7.1.5(1) and (2) is clearly purported by Comment 2 to UPICC Art. 7.1.5 ("The party who grant the extension of time cannot terminate (…) during the extension time."), the European Principles are admittedly somewhat unclear and even contradictory in this respect. Whereas on the one hand, Note 3 to PECL Art. 9:301 expressly states that "it should be noted that the Principles do not permit the non-performing party to be given extra time once the non-performance is fundamental," Comment C to PECL Art. 8:106 unambiguously indicates that this is indeed possible: "even where the delay or other non-performance is fundamental, and thus the aggrieved party has the right to terminate immediately, it may not wish to do so (…). The procedure set out in Article 8:106 permits it to give the debtor a final chance to perform." Against this background, the most convincing interpretation of PECL Art. 8:106 appears to be that – just as under UPICC Art. 7.1.5 – the right to set an additional period is also available where the delay itself already constituted fundamental non-performance.

645 UPICC Art. 7.1.5(2); PECL Art. 8:106(2). See *cf.* Comment A to PECL Art. 8:106.

646 See also CISG Art. 72(1). The concept of anticipatory non-performance originates from the common-law concept of *anticipatory breach* but has also been adopted in some recently revised continental European statutes. See generally Treitel, *supra* note 159 at 643 *et seq.*, and Zimmermann, *supra* note 161 at 485.

647 See UPICC Art. 7.3.3 and PECL Art. 9:304. Whereas it is made clear at least in a Comment to PECL Art. 9:304 (see Comment D to PECL Art. 9:304) that anticipatory non-performance also

performance and actual non-performance is that once it is sufficiently certain that the other party will fail or refuse to perform, it is usually useless or even harmful to the aggrieved party to wait until the date of performance before terminating the contract.

While neither Principles provide a clear-cut definition of what it takes for a party's prospective failure to perform to be regarded as being "clear" in this sense, the Comments to these two almost *verbatim* provisions offer a few indicators. First, neither a suspicion – even if it is well-founded – nor mere doubt as to a party's willingness and ability to perform shall suffice.[648] Rather, the expected failure or refusal must be manifest;[649] this may be the case because the promisor has declared its unwillingness to perform or because the circumstances clearly indicate that there will be a fundamental non-performance.[650]

If the anticipated fundamental default is not (yet) clear but the promisee has reason to believe that it will occur, it may resort to less incisive measures, namely to withhold performance or demand assurance of due performance, and to terminate the contract if the promisor fails to provide such assurance.[651]

d. Failure to provide assurance of due performance within reasonable time

Where the prospect that there will be fundamental non-performance is less "clear" than in cases of anticipatory non-performance, an promisee may still have an interest in obtaining certainty as to whether the other party is still able and willing to perform, primarily to prevent unnecessary losses that it might incur if it were compelled to wait until the agreed date of performance. For this purpose, the practically identical provisions of UPICC Art. 7.3.4 and PECL Art. 8:105(2) allow a party to demand adequate assurance of due performance if it reasonably[652] believes that there will be fundamental non-performance, *e.g.*, in cases of insolvency of the other party. If the latter subsequently fails to provide such

---

entitles the promisee to invoke any other compatible remedies, the UPICC do not make any mention of this by no means self-evident but clearly important rule.

648 See Comment to UPICC Art. 7.3.3 and Comment C to PECL Art. 9:304.

649 See Comment C to PECL Art. 9:304.

650 See Comment to UPICC Art. 7.3.3.

651 For a discussion of the different remedies available if it is clear or if the promisee reasonably believes that there will eventually be fundamental non-performance, see also Comment C to PECL Art. 9:201.

652 According to PECL Art. 1:302, "[u]nder these Principles reasonableness is to be judged by what persons acting in good faith and in the same situation as the parties would consider to be reasonable. In particular, in assessing what is reasonable the nature and purpose of the contract, the circumstances of the case, and the usages and practices of the trades or professions involved should be taken into account."

assurance within reasonable time, the former may terminate the contract.[653] The PECL underscore that they technically consider the failure to provide adequate assurance of due performance within reasonable time to be itself a fundamental non-performance.[654]

What constitutes "adequacy" of the assurance depends on the circumstances of the particular case, including the standing and integrity of the respective promisor and its conduct in connection with the contract.[655] The assurance may take a multiplicity of forms ranging from the promisor's mere declaration that it is still willing and able to perform or an explanation of how it intends to do so to the provision of security or guarantee by a third person.[656]

e. Contracts to be performed in parts

The European Principles admit "partial termination" of a contract that is to be performed in a series of separable parts, provided there is a fundamental non-performance[657] regarding one of these units and that the counter-performance owed for this part can also be apportioned (Art. 9:302).[658] The primary result of this rule is that the promisee is no longer obliged to accept performance of the unit in relation to which it has terminated the contract. PECL Art. 9:302 is therefore relevant especially with respect to contracts involving performance in multiple instalments that bear a separable price each and do not significantly affect the other instalments if they remain unperformed.[659] If there is no separable counter-performance or payment owed for the unperformed part – as is the case, for instance, in a contract for a continuing obligation – it is sufficient if it can be apportioned.[660] Art. 9:302 also reiterates that if the non-performance of a separable part constitutes fundamental non-performance of the *entire* contract, which

653 Once it has requested assurance of due performance, the promisee may also withhold performance of its own obligations under the respective contract until the promisor performs or provides the requested assurance, and for as long as it reasonably believes that there will indeed be fundamental non-performance.

654 See Comments A and C to PECL Art. 8:105.

655 See Comment D and Ill. 3 to PECL Art. 8:105.

656 See Comment 2 and Ill. to UPICC Art. 7.3.4 and Comment D to PECL Art. 8:105.

657 The PECL do not provide any particular guideline as to when such s non-performance of a separable unit is to be considered as being fundamental in relation to the respective part of the contract. As a result, at least PECL Art. 8:103(a) and (b) may need to be applied twice in a single case: first, to determine whether the non-performance is fundamental in relation to the contract as a whole, and second, to see whether it is also fundamental in relation to the respective part. See *cf.* Düchs, *supra* note 161 at 175 *et seq.*

658 See also CISG Art. 73.

659 See Comment A and Ill. 1 and 2 to PECL Art. 9:302.

660 See Comment B and Ill. 3 to PECL Art. 9:302.

may be the case particularly on the basis of Art. 8:103(c),[661] the promisee may certainly terminate the contract as a whole.

Apparently for no particular "policy reason",[662] the UNIDROIT Principles do not contain any provision corresponding to PECL Art. 9:302. Even so, they generate identical practical outcomes at least with regard to contracts that extend over a period of time and involve performance in instalments: by stipulating that termination releases both parties from their obligations to effect and receive *future* performance and that restitution may not be claimed for any divisible portions that have already been performed, the UPICC also provide that any instalments performed prior to the termination are not be restituted under this type of contracts.[663]

f. Termination notice

Termination by the aggrieved party on any of the grounds presented in the preceding sections[664] is to be effected by way of a notice of termination (UPICC Art. 7.3.2; PECL Art. 9:303). This requirement serves the purpose of letting the non-performing party know that the promisee will not accept performance, thereby giving the former a chance to prevent possible losses.[665] A termination notice is effective from the time when it reaches the other party.[666] It may be issued in writing or implicitly, that is by rejecting a late or non-conforming tender and (thereby) expressly or impliedly declaring that the contract shall be terminated.[667] In case

661 PECL Art. 8:103(c) provides that a non-performance is fundamental if the failure to perform (or, under Art. 9:302, to perform a separable unit of the contract) was intentional and gives the promisee reason to believe that it cannot rely on the promisor's future performance. See Ill. 2 to PECL Art. 9:302 and *supra* a.

662 See, *e.g.*, Bonell, *supra* note 19 at 348.

663 UPICC Art. 9.3.5(1) and 9.3.6(2). See also Ill. 5 and 6 to UPICC Art. 9.3.6 and *infra* II(A)(2)(a).

664 UPICC Art. 7.3.1(1); 7.3.1(2); 7.3.3; 7.3.4; and PECL Art. 9:301(1); 9:301(2); 8:105(2); 9:304; 9:302. For the only instances in which the contract may terminate without a termination notice, see *infra* 3 and 4.

665 See also CISG Art. 26. Emanating from the principle of good faith and fair dealing, the notice requirement is intended to protect the interests of the non-performing party in two ways: first, it seeks to avoid losses that might result from an uncertainty on the defaulting party's end as to whether the aggrieved party will accept late performance or a second (conforming) tender; second, it is intended to prevent the aggrieved party from speculating on a favourable development of the value of performance to the disadvantage of the party in default. See *cf.* Comment 1 to UPICC Art. 7.3.2 and Comment A to PECL Art. 9:303.

666 UPICC Art. 1.10(2); PECL Art. 1:303(2).

667 UPICC Art. 1.10(4); PECL Art. 1:303(6). See also Comment A to PECL Art. 9:303. Obviously, the express wording of Comment A to PECL Art. 9:303, according to which "[n]otice may be given by expressly declaring the contract terminated or by rejecting the tender of performance," needs to be understood in the context of other rules in the European Principles. This means that, whereas the act of rejecting the tender may simultaneously imply a declaration of termination,

the aggrieved party intends to terminate the contract after having granted an additional period for performance, it may already announce this consequence in the notice by way of which it sets the extra period.[668]

Where performance was actually tendered but the offer was late or otherwise non-conforming, the aggrieved party needs to issue the termination notice *within reasonable time* from when it knew or ought to have known of the tender or of the non-performance (UPICC Art. 7.3.2(2); PECL Art. 9:303(3)(a)). What is a reasonable period of time in this context depends on the circumstances of the particular case.[669] By any means, the aggrieved party shall be granted sufficient time to examine the tender to identify any defects and confirm its usability, and to decide how it wishes to respond to any shortcomings.[670]

If there has not yet been a tender of performance and the aggrieved party does not know whether the promisor still intends to perform, the constellation of interests and options is slightly different: if the aggrieved party is undecided or no longer interested in performance, it may simply wait and see whether the promisor will actually tender performance. If it opts for this alternative, it may claim damages for any losses incurred as a result of the delay and terminate the contract if the promisor indeed fails to perform altogether or if the eventual tender does not conform to the contract and thereby constitutes fundamental non-performance.[671] However, if the promisee is still interested in receiving performance even if it is delayed, it must claim specific performance within reasonable time after performance was due (UPICC Art. 7.2.2(e); PECL Art. 9:102(3)).[672]

---

it cannot by itself and without any further indication of the aggrieved party's intention to end the contract serve as a termination notice. Otherwise, an promisee could never claim repair, replacement or delivery of missing parts as per Art. 9:102(1) (see Comment C to PECL Art. 9:102) once it has rejected a non-conforming tender that constituted fundamental non-performance; similarly, mere rejection of a non-conforming tender that falls short of fundamental non-performance would always deprive the party in default of its right to cure (PECL Art. 8:104) and even render the aggrieved party liable to pay damages for unrightfully terminating the contract (see Comment A to PECL Art. 8:105). See also Coen, *supra* note 204 at 268 *et seq.*

668 UPICC Art. 7.1.5(3); PECL Art. 8:106(3). However, some observers have argued that, as a matter of good faith and fair dealing, the promisee should nonetheless be required to at least reconfirm the termination if the other party did indeed, yet non-conformingly, tender performance within the extra period. See also Coen, *id.* at 228.

669 See Comment 3 to UPICC Art. 7.3.2 and PECL Art. 1:301.

670 See Comment B to PECL Art. 9:303. If termination is declared in the course of a change of remedy, the time limit certainly needs to be extended accordingly (see Comment 4 to UPICC Art. 7.2.5). Similarly, where the aggrieved party has granted an additional period for performance, it is to be assumed that the reasonable period for issuing the termination notice starts to run only after the expiration of the same.

671 See Comment 2 to UPICC Art. 7.3.2 and Comment C(2) to PECL Art. 9:303.

672 See Comment 2 to UPICC Art. 7.3.2 and Comment C(1) to PECL Art. 9:303. See *supra* Ch. V(I)(A)(3)(e).

Finally, if performance is overdue but the aggrieved party nonetheless knows or has reason to believe that the promisor still intends to perform, it is required as a matter of good faith and fair dealing to notify the latter of its intention to terminate the contract and reject the tender within reasonable time. If it fails to give such notice, it loses the right to terminate the contract[673] and may be liable to pay damages[674] if the promisor actually manages to perform within reasonable time from the date when performance was due.

Except in this last instance, the consequences of a failure to give a termination notice within reasonable time are not entirely clear. Shall the right to terminate the contract be excluded perennially? The problem with this view is that it might cause a deadlock scenario: provided the aggrieved party fails to give notice of the termination in accordance with UPICC Art. 7.3.2 and PECL Art. 9:303 and at the same time fails to claim specific performance within reasonable time, both the right to claim performance and the right to reject a later tender would be lost coevally. What is more, damages would practically be incalculable because it might indefinitely remain unclear whether the other party will actually be able to perform.

One possible solution to this paradox could be to allow for the aggrieved party to somehow *regain* the right to terminate the contract, *e.g.*, by fixing an(other) additional period for performance as per UPICC Art. 7.1.5(3) and PECL Art. 8:106(3). Alternatively, it has been suggested that the right to termination should necessarily persist or "revive" despite a late termination notice if or once it is clear that there will indeed not be any performance at all.[675]

3. Contract terminated automatically

The European Principles pronounce the contract *automatically* terminated in cases where the non-performance is excused due to a total and permanent impediment (PECL Art. 9:303(4) and 8:108).[676] This exception – which does not appear in the UNIDROIT Principles[677] – certainly raises the question of why it should not apply

673 See Comment C(3) to PECL Art. 9:303.

674 See Comment 2 to UPICC Art. 7.3.2.

675 See *cf.* Coen, *supra* note 204 at 241.

676 Comment B to PECL Art. 9:103 also suggests that the contract could be considered automatically terminated where the aggrieved party has concluded a cover transaction as per Art. 9:101(2) (a) or (d) and the promisor is thus no longer entitled to tender its own performance or claim the counter-performance. (For the case where the former provides in the notice setsting an additional period for performance that the contract shall be terminated without further notice upon expiration of the extra period, see *supra* 2(b) and (f)).

677 As opposed to the PECL, the UPICC address another instance where the contract is considered automatically void, namely where a "permission affecting the validity of the contract" is refused (UPICC Art. 6.1.17(1)). The consequence of this rule – which is not a matter of non-

to cases of unexcused non-performance as well.[678] The primary reason for this differentiation appears to be that whereas in cases of *excused* non-performance it is unjustified to expose the innocent promisor to the situation where the promisee opts to keep the contract alive in order to still tender its own performance, there is no such need of protecting the former from being bound to accept the counter-performance at the latter's choice if the non-performance is *unexcused.*[679]

4. Judicial or arbitral termination

In cases of hardship,[680] both sets of Principles also permit a termination of the contract by the competent court or arbitral body. Provided the parties have conducted negotiations but failed to reach a mutual agreement on whether or how to adapt or perhaps to terminate the contract, they may resort to a court or arbitral tribunal to obtain a decision. Pursuant to UPICC Art. 6.2.3(4)(a) and PECL Art. 6:111(3)(a), the court or tribunal may terminate the contract if it finds that this is the only appropriate response to the change of circumstances. In any case, the court or arbitral body is not bound by the Principles' provisions on the effects of termination and restitution;[681] instead, it may freely determine the date and terms of the termination.

B. Indian statutory law

1. Generally

The Indian Contract Act, 1872 recognizes four general ways in which contracts may terminate: (1) performance of the obligations under the contract;[682] (2) termination by way of a mutual agreement between the parties to put an end to the contract;[683] (3) voidness due to impossibility of performance or unlawfulness of a

---

performance of contracts because obtaining the relevant permission is not necessarily a contractual obligation – is that "the contract is considered as never having come into being" (see Comment 2 to UPICC Art. 6.1.17).

678 See, *e.g.*, Hartkamp, *supra* note 116 at 353, and Coen, *supra* note 204 at 277 *et seq.*

679 In addition to the rule that the contract terminates automatically in cases of total and permanent impossibility, it should be noted that the PECL also establish that "[a] contract is of no effect to the extent that it is contrary to principles recognised as fundamental in the laws of the Member States of the European Union" (PECL Art. 15:101).

680 See UPICC Art. 6.2.2 and PECL Art. 6:111(2). See generally Perillo, *supra* note 395, and *supra* Ch. III(VII)(A)(1).

681 See *infra* II(A).

682 Indian Contract Act Sec. 31 *et seq.*

683 Indian Contract Act Sec. 62 to 67.

particular object or the consideration;[684] and (4) termination[685] at the option of the aggrieved party following a breach of contract.[686]

Breach of contract is constituted either by a (actual or anticipatory) failure or refusal to perform or by any action taken by one party which renders the other party's performance impossible or otherwise prevents it from performing its contractual obligations.[687] Whereas a contract is *automatically* void if performance is or becomes impossible or unlawful, termination at the option of the aggrieved party must be effectuated by way of a notice and is allowed only in a small number of circumstances.[688]

2. Contract automatically void due to impossibility, unlawfulness, or frustration

a. Grounds of automatic termination

Sec. 56 of the Indian Contract Act provides that a contract is automatically void if performance of it is or becomes impossible and unlawful. Whereas Sec. 56(1) of the Act deals with the situation where performance is impossible or unlawful at the time of conclusion of the contract ("initial impossibility"), Sec. 56(2) addresses cases of "subsequent impossibility" or unlawfulness due to a supervening event occurring after the conclusion of the contract. Sec. 23 and 24 of the Contract Act define what constitutes "unlawfulness" and also establish that illegality of an object or consideration[689] renders the entire contract void.[690]

---

684 Indian Contract Act Sec. 56 and 23 *et seq.*, respectively.

685 The Indian Contract Act and Specific Relief Act as well as the standard commentaries on Indian contract law use a variety of terms to circumscribe what the Principles unitarily refer to as "termination" of a contract that is terminable as a result of a party's non-performance. For the sake of uniformity and comparability, this survey consistently applies the term "termination" as a collective designation for what is known in India as "putting an end to the contract" (*e.g.*, Indian Contract Act Sec. 39, 53), "rescission" of a voidable contract (*e.g.*, Specific Relief Act Sec. 27 *et seq.*) or "voidance" (*e.g.*, Indian Contract Act Sec. 53 and 55).

686 See Indian Contract Act Sec. 39, 53 and 55. Termination at the option of the aggrieved party is considered as a specific relief converse to that of specific performance. See Bhadbhade, *supra* note 137 at 2644.

687 See generally supra Ch. III(I)(B).

688 See *infra* 3.

689 The terms "object" and "consideration" may in some cases refer to the same thing; usually, however, they have different meanings. For instance, where a debtor transfers certain property to a creditor for the purpose of giving the latter preference over other creditors, the consideration for the contract is the transfer of property, and the circumvention of the provisions of bankruptcy law is the unlawful object.

690 Generally, the following types of agreements are automatically void under Indian law: agreements involving a consideration and/or objects that are entirely or partly unlawful (Sec. 23 and 24); agreements without consideration (Sec. 25); agreements in restraint of marriage (Sec. 26);

The Indian Supreme Court has held that Sec. 56(2) of the Indian Contract Act transposes the doctrine of frustration into a general rule of statutory law,[691] and Illustrations (d) and (e) reflect its broad range of applicability. As a consequence, the term "impossibility" in this section is to be interpreted in a commercial rather than in its literal sense.[692] It thus covers supervening physical impossibility as well as a failure of the object of the contract, provided that the contract was previously valid and had not yet been performed entirely, and that the frustrating event was unforeseeable and occurred without either party's fault.[693] Against this background, Sec. 56(2) has been applied to the following main categories of circumstances:

- the destruction of subject-matter that the parties assumed would exist or continue to exist;
- the non-existence of circumstances the existence of which the parties had assumed and which formed assumed as the foundation of the contract;[694]
- the occurrence of circumstances that render performance impossible in the way it was contemplated, regardless of the fact that literal performance may still be possible;

---

agreements in restraint of trade (Sec. 27); agreements in restraint of legal proceedings (Sec. 28); uncertain agreements (Sec. 29); agreements by way of wager (Sec. 30); and agreements to do impossible acts (Sec. 56).

691 *Satyabrata Ghosh v. Mugneeram Bangur & Co.*, AIR 1954 S.C. 44 (1954). The transposition of the doctrine of frustration into an exhaustive rule of statutory law also has the effect that the different legal theories underlying the doctrine are inapplicable in India. See generally Bhadbhade, *supra* note 137 at 1117 *et seq.* For a more general overview of the doctrine of frustration, see *supra* Ch. III(VII(B)(1) and Treitel, *supra* note 159 at 649 *et seq.*

692 The following example (see Zweigert/Kötz, *supra* note 136 at 517) illustrates the dogmatic distinction between impossibility and frustration:

> "Suppose a manufacturer of fertilizer makes a long-term contract to produce a special fertilizer for tobacco plants and deliver it to a dealer for export to places overseas where tobacco is grown. If the fertilizer factory is then nationalized or if the manufacture of fertilizer is forbidden or if a government decree requires all fertilizers to be delivered to a state export organization, we have a case of *impossibility*. (...) *[F]rustration of purpose* would occur if the importation of fertilizer was forbidden in the consumer contract: it remains possible for the manufacturer to produce the fertilizer and for the dealer to accept and pay for it but it is now impossible to achieve the only purpose for which, as the manufacturer knew, the dealer entered the contract, namely to deliver the fertilizer to the consumer country."

693 See generally Treitel, *supra* note 159 at 652 *et seq.*

694 A contract which was agreed to be dependent on the occurrence of a certain contingency such as the granting of a public permission is void pursuant to Sec. 32 if the event becomes impossible ("Enforcement of contracts contingent on an event happening") rather than Sec. 56(2) of the Contract Act. Whereas Sec. 56(2) only deals with frustration due to circumstances caused by outside forces that are beyond the events contemplated by the parties, Sec. 32 applies to cases where the contract is dissolved as per its own terms.

- subsequent changes in law which render the contract or its performance unlawful; and
- death or incapacity of a party whose personal performance was required by the contract.[695]

By contrast, the section does not extend to cases of disappointed expectations or mere commercial hardship due, for instance, to a drastic decline in prices, devaluation of currency, or an unexpected obstacle to performance which only renders the same more difficult or costly.[696] Similarly, mere delay or a temporary impediment to performance shall not constitute frustration, either, unless the commercial purpose of the contract is destroyed.[697]

Sec. 56(1) of the Contract Act expressly deals only with physical impossibility that already existed at the time of conclusion of the contract.[698] Nonetheless, both Sec. 56(1) and (2) also apply to unlawfulness of performance. In cases of "subsequent unlawfulness", their applicability emanates directly from the wording of the second paragraph. With regard to "initial unlawfulness", Sec. 56(1) needs to be read in conjunction with Sec. 23 and 24 of the Contract Act, according to which a contract is void if it involves one or multiple objects or considerations that are (fully or in part) unlawful. Pursuant to Sec. 23 of the Act, an object or consideration under a contract is unlawful if it is fraudulent or forbidden by law (*e.g.*, the sale of liquor without a license); would defeat the law if permitted (*e.g.*, the conclusion of a transaction for the purpose of tax evasion); involves or implies injury to another person or property; or is to be regarded as being immoral or opposed to public policy (*e.g.*, trading with an entity in an enemy country or an exploitation of superior bargaining power).[699]

b. Consequences

In cases of frustration, the contract terminates automatically and irrespectively of the parties' intentions. Unless the contract provides for different consequences or

695 See Ill. (d) and (e) to Indian Contract Act Sec. 56 and Bhadbhade, *supra* note 137 at 1143. For a detailed discussion of the specific grounds of frustration recognized under Indian law, see, *e.g.*, Singh, *supra* note 218 at 341 *et seq.*

696 See generally Singh, *id.* at 339, and Bangia, *supra* note 182 at 254.

697 See cf. Bangia, *id.* at 251 and 253 *et seq.*, respectively. See also *infra* 3(c).

698 It is worth noting that where the parties act upon the mutual erroneous assumption that the non-existent subject-matter of the contract actually exists, the invalidity of the contract emanates from Sec. 20 ("Agreement void where both parties are under mistake as to matter of fact") rather than Sec. 56(1) of the Indian Contract Act. The effect of Sec. 20 is that the contract is void from the beginning.

699 See generally Singh, *supra* note 218 at 225 *et seq.*

risk-allocation, frustration excuses the performance of all obligations which are still to be performed at the time of its occurrence.[700] Contracts which have already been performed cannot be frustrated, and any transfers that have already been concluded remain unaffected by the termination. Provided the contract is divisible into lawful and unlawful units or performable and non-performable parts, the unaffected portions may remain valid and thus specifically enforceable unless the contract is frustrated as a whole.[701]

Finally, if the respective promisor knew or might reasonably have known of the impossibility or unlawfulness of the performance of one of its obligations at the time when it entered into the contract, it is also liable to make compensation of any losses sustained by the aggrieved party as a result (Indian Contract Act Sec. 56(3)).[702]

3. Termination of voidable contract

a. Repudiation and anticipatory breach

Where a party repudiates the contract by unrightfully refusing to perform ("renunciation") or disabling itself from performing a substantial portion of its obligations, the other party may terminate the contract pursuant to Sec. 39 of the Indian Contract Act. As in all common-law jurisdictions, repudiation of a contractual duty before the time for performance is known under Indian law as "anticipatory breach" or "anticipatory repudiation".[703] Sec. 39 applies to both anticipatory breach and to repudiation at the time for performance, with the right to terminate the contract being subject to the same test in both situations.[704]

Sec. 39 of the Contract Act sets out the following requirements for the right to terminate the contract: first, renunciation, *i.e.*, an unrightful refusal to per-

---

700 See, *e.g.*, Singh, *supra* note 218 at 357 *et seq.*

701 See Specific Relief Act Sec. 12(4) and Expl. to Specific Relief Act Sec. 12 (see *supra* Ch. V(I)(B)(2)(a)). For instance, where a sales transaction involves both legal and illegal goods, the contract remains valid with respect to the transfer of the legal goods if the price for these units can be apportioned. See *cf.* Bhadbhade, *supra* note 137 at 1140, for references to Indian case law.

702 See *infra* Ch. VII(I)(B)(1) and (2).

703 See generally Singh, *supra* note 218 at 386. Indian law also recognizes that anticipatory repudiation is possible with regard to contingent contracts even where the repudiating party refuses to perform or disables itself from performing before the occurrence of the respective contingency (see *cf.* Singh, *id.* at 387, and Bhadbhade, *supra* note 137 at 1006, making express reference to the English case of *Frost v. Knight* (L.R. 7 Ex. 111 (1872)). For an overview of anticipatory breach and its consequences under English law, see, *e.g.*, Hugh Beale, *Remedies for breach of contract* (1980) at 68 *et seq.*

704 See, *e.g.*, Bhadbhade, *id.* at 996.

form, presupposes that the repudiating party clearly and unequivocally declares or implies by its conduct its *intention* to be no longer bound by the contract.[705] Similarly, the second alternative of Sec. 39 requires the repudiating party to either deliberately disable itself from performing or to commit an act causing circumstances that render it unable to perform.[706]

Second, the refusal or self-induced disability to perform must either be absolute or affect a substantial part of the contract. Somewhat extending the scope of Sec. 39 beyond its express wording – which requires that the party in breach repudiates its "promise in its entirety" – Indian courts have recognized the English common-law rule that an unjustified refusal or self-induced disability to perform a part of the contract may also constitute repudiation if the breach goes to the root of the contract and deprives the aggrieved party of substantially its entire benefit under it.[707] To determine whether it does, regard is to be had, in each particular case, especially to the quantitative proportion of the concerned portion to the whole contract, and to the likeliness that the breach will be repeated. Moreover, the parties may agree that a certain contract term shall be essential in the sense that refusal or self-induced inability to comply with this term may also constitute repudiation.[708] As shown by Illustration (a) to Sec. 39, a party's refusal to perform even one in multiple instalments under a contract may give the other party a right to terminate the entire contract, if the instalment in question makes up an integral and essential part of it.[709]

Provided the aforementioned test under Sec. 39 of the Contract Act is met, the aggrieved party has two options: it may either accept the repudiation and terminate the contract, thereby releasing both itself and the promisor from their respective obligations (Indian Contract Act Sec. 64)[710] while retaining a right to claim damages for breach of contract;[711] alternatively, it may affirm the persistence of the contract and further insist on performance, for instance because it has reason to believe that the other party might eventually become able and willing to perform.

In cases of anticipatory breach, the aggrieved party may terminate the contract immediately, *i.e.*, even before the date when performance is due, and it may invoke this right for as long as the other party does not withdraw the repudiation.[712] If the

705 See *id.* at 994 and 997, and Singh, *supra* note 218 at 394. If the promisor does not express an intention not to perform, the promisee may terminate the contract only subject to Sec. 55 of the Indian Contract Act (see *infra* c).

706 See Bhadbhade, *supra* note 137 at 999.

707 See *cf.* Singh, *supra* note 218 at 394 and 397, and *id.* at 1000 *et seq.*, for references to Indian case law.

708 See Bhadbhade, *id.* at 1002 and 1003, and Singh, *id.* at 394.

709 See Bangia, *supra* note 182 at 243 *et seq.*

710 See *infra* II(B).

711 See Bhadbhade, *supra* note 137 at 1016.

712 See, *e.g.*, Bangia, *supra* note 182 at 244, for a reference to the English case of *Hochester v. De la Tour* (2 Ellis & Bl. 678 (1853)).

promisee instead opts to reject the repudiation and continue to treat the contract as valid, it may go ahead with its own performance while maintaining a chance for the repudiating party to eventually recall its repudiation and tender performance of its own; if, in turn, the latter is still unwilling or unable to perform at the time when performance is actually due, the aggrieved party may claim damages for breach of contract once this date has passed.[713] In the meantime, the promisee remains liable for all of its own obligations under the contract, and the repudiating party may take full benefit of any supervening event that might subsequently frustrate the contract or otherwise excuse its non-performance.[714]

The aggrieved party is required to communicate its decision to terminate or "acquiesce to the contract" to the repudiating party in accordance with Sec. 66 of the Indian Contract Act.[715] While such notification does not require any particular form and may be rendered expressly or impliedly, it must unequivocally communicate the fact of the termination or affirmation of the contract to the other party.[716] Mere silence and inaction in response to a repudiation are indicators of the promisee's acquiescence to the contract rather than its intent to terminate the same; accordingly, even silence or inaction must unequivocally indicate the decision to terminate the contract.[717] Finally, the wording of Sec. 39 ("unless he has signified (...) his acquiescence") evidently underscores that the aggrieved party's affirmation of the contract in response to the other party's anticipatory breach is irrevocable and the right to termination lost once the former's notification of its acquiescence has come to the latter's attention.[718]

b. Termination in response to being prevented from performing

Sec. 53 of the Indian Contract Act allows for termination of the contract by a party if the other has prevented it from performing a reciprocal obligation.[719] Moreover, the preventive act constitutes a breach of contract and thus gives the affected party a right to damages for any loss it incurs as a result of its inability to perform.

The term "prevention" relates to any "wrongful" action by which a promisee fails to comply with its own duty to cooperate or by which it impedes the occur-

713 See Singh, *supra* note 218 at 391.

714 See *id.*, making express reference to the English case of *Avery v. Bowden* (5 E. & B. 714 (1855)).

715 See Bhadbhade, *supra* note 137 at 1013, and *infra* d.

716 In any case, the contract is considered void from the time when it was terminated and not from the time of its repudiation. See generally Singh, *supra* note 218 at 388 and 390.

717 See, *e.g.*, *id.* at 394. Ill. (b) to Indian Contract Act Sec. 39 purports this assumption by stating that inaction of the aggrieved party is presumed to be an expression of its acquiescence to the contract.

718 See *cf.* Bhadbhade *supra* note 137 at 1009.

719 See also *supra* Ch. III(II)(B)(I).

rence of a condition precedent upon which the performance of the obligation was agreed to be contingent.[720] For instance, a promisee's failure to supply adequate machinery or material necessary for the other party to perform may be regarded as a wrongful act in this sense.[721]

c. Failure to perform at or within fixed time

Finally, Indian law provides for a right of termination where timely performance is so important that any delay materially affects the promisee's interest in receiving it. In this regard, Sec. 55(1) of the Indian Contract Act stipulates that if the parties had the intention that time should be of the essence of the contract, a party's failure to perform at or before a specified time entitles the other to reject the late tender and terminate the contract immediately.[722]

Whether time is of the essence of the contract primarily depends on the parties' express or implied intention, which is usually but not necessarily manifested in the contract. Against this background, a mere clause according to which performance should be tendered "as soon as possible" does not suffice to render timely performance of the essence; rather, the contract should provide that performance is due within "ten days or earlier" or on a specified date.[723] Ordinarily, time is presumed *not* to be of the essence of the contract, which means that the aggrieved party must usually prove that, according to the parties' mutual intention, it actually was. This presumption and the burden of proof are reversed in commercial transactions,[724] and in sales contracts, the time of shipment is usually considered to be of the essence.[725]

Subject to Sec. 63 and 66 of the Contract Act, Indian law also enables the aggrieved party to make time of the essence of the contract before or after the date when performance is due by subsequently issuing a notice by way of which requests the promisor to complete its performance within a fixed period of time of reasonable length.[726] According to the Indian Supreme Court, though, the prom-

720 See, *e.g.*, Bhadbhade, *supra* note 137 at 1073.

721 See, *e.g.*, Singh, *supra* note 218 at 321.

722 As in cases of repudiation, the delay itself does not entail termination of the contract, but the aggrieved party is given an option: it may either terminate the contract or it may accept performance despite the delay and at the same time claim damages for the delay provided it had announced its intention to do so at the time when it accepted the late tender (Indian Contract Act Sec. 55(3)).

723 See *cf.* Bhadbhade, *supra* note 137 at 1086 *et seq.*, stating that the parties' intention can be ascertained with reference to factors such as the express wording of the contract, the nature of the subject matter of the contract, the nature of the contract itself, and the surrounding circumstances.

724 See Singh, *supra* note 218 at 325 *et seq.*, and Bhadbhade, *id.* at 1103, for references, *inter alia*, to decisions of the Indian Supreme Court.

725 See Singh, *id.* at 327.

726 See *supra* Ch. III(V)(B).

isee cannot unilaterally extend the time for performance; rather, the notice to be given must be expressly or impliedly accepted by the promisor so as to constitute a mutual *agreement* upon the extension.[727] Unless the notice of the additional period for performance already provides that the contract shall terminate automatically if the promisor fails to perform within this time, termination is to be effected by way of a separate notice upon expiry of the respite.[728]

If time was neither intended to be nor later rendered of the essence of the contract, the aggrieved party is obliged to accept performance but retains a right to damages for any loss incurred due to the delay or failure to perform (Indian Contract Act Sec. 55(2)).

d. Means of effecting termination

If the contract is terminable as per the provisions examined above,[729] the aggrieved party may exercise this remedy by giving a notice of termination to the party in default. Sec. 66 of the Indian Contract Act provides that termination is to be effected in the same manner as the communication or revocation of a proposal; according to Sec. 3 of the Act, this may be done by way of any act or omission that has the effect of bringing the communicating party's intention to the attention of the other party. The termination notice does not require any particular form or wording and need not be delivered personally by the person that has issued it.[730]

In cases of repudiation by the promisor, the aggrieved party needs to clearly and unequivocally notify the other party of its acceptance of the repudiation and the consequential termination of the contract.[731] Mere silence and inaction in response to anticipatory breach are generally insufficient because these reactions normally indicate an affirmation of the persistence of the contract.[732] As Sec. 66 also applies to Sec. 55(1) of the Contract Act, termination of the contract after the expiration of an additional period granted for performance (by which time was made of the essence) requires a termination notice as well.[733] In any of those cases, the termination is effective[734] and irrevocable[735] from the time when the notice came to the other party's attention.

727 See *cf.* Bangia, *supra* note 182 at 263, for further references. See generally *supra* Ch. III(V)(B).

728 See *cf.* Bhadbhade, *supra* note 137 at 1092 *et seq.*

729 *I.e.*, under Indian Contract Act Sec. 39, 53 and 55(1), or upon fruitless expiration of an additional period for performance granted in accordance with Sec. 63 and 66 of the Contract Act.

730 See Bhadbhade, *supra* note 137 at 1013.

731 See *cf.* Singh, *supra* note 218 at 388.

732 See *id.* at 393 *et seq.* and Bhadbhade, *supra* note 137 at 1008.

733 See, Singh, *id.* at 334, for references to pertinent case law.

734 Indian Contract Act Sec. 4.

735 See Bhadbhade, *supra* note 137 at 1014 and 1333, and Specific Relief Act Sec. 27(2)(a).

A *suit* for termination of the contract[736] may be dismissed pursuant to Sec. 27(2) of the Specific Relief Act in four separate sets of circumstance, namely if (1) the contract, though it was terminable, was affirmed by the aggrieved party; (2) restitution is impossible because the positions of the parties have been altered to an extent where it is impossible to restore their original status, *e.g.*, the buyer has already resold the goods; (3) restitution would infringe with third party rights to the subject matter which were acquired for value during the period of time the contract was deemed valid; or (4) the promisee has sued for termination of a part that is actually not severable from the rest of the contract.[737]

C. Comparative analysis

1. Fundamental non-performance v. impossibility, frustration and repudiation

The Principles generally do not distinguish between excused and unexcused non-performance with regard to whether and how the contract may terminate. Instead, the only criterion is the materiality of the non-performance. The aggrieved party may terminate the contract if the default is to be considered as being "fundamental". As the Principles generally do not provide for automatic termination by force of law,[738] the consequences that these two instruments impose are contrary to the doctrine of frustration.[739]

736 Evidently, a "suit for rescission" is technically a suit for judicial declaration of the validity of the termination already effected by the plaintiff.

737 Unlike a suit for termination in the alternative for a suit for specific performance – *i.e.*, an alternative plaint for termination for the case that the contract cannot be specifically enforced – a plaint for specific performance in the alternative for a plaint for termination is not permissive under Indian statutory contract law (Specific Relief Act Sec. 29). See also Singh, *supra* note 218 at 781.

738 *Automatic* termination only occurs in one instance under each set of Principles. Under the PECL, a contract is terminated automatically where performance is entirely and permanently impossible or unlawful (see Ill. 3 to PECL Art. 8:108) due to a supervening event that is beyond the defaulting party's control and had not been contemplated by the parties (PECL Art. 9:303(4)); even though it is limited to cases of excused non-performance, this rule generally corresponds to Sec. 56 of the Indian Contract Act. The UPICC provide that the contract is void if "a permission affecting the validity of a contract" is refused (UPICC Art. 6.1.17(1)); this case would be governed by Sec. 32 of the Indian Contract Act. In fact, UPICC Art. 6.1.17(1) resembles the Indian case of *Punj Sons Pvt. Ltd. v. Union of India* (AIR 1986 Delhi 158 (1986)), where it was held that a contract is to be considered void if, due to a party's failure to obtain a release order for the necessary quota of an item that is required for performance (*e.g.*, non-availability of tin ingots with which the promisor was to coat milk containers it was to deliver to the promisee).

739 For an overview of the arguments in favour of and against each of the two approaches, see *infra* f.

Indian statutory contract law, on the other hand, incorporates the doctrine of frustration and thus distinguishes between cases of termination by force of law and those where the aggrieved party is entitled to put an end to the contract at its own option. Against this background, the Indian Contract Act presents a multi-layered system of termination: in cases of frustration due to impossibility or unlawfulness, the contract terminates automatically and regardless of the parties' intentions;[740] with respect to some other types of substantial non-performance, the Indian Contract Act, just like the Principles, confers a *right* to termination to the aggrieved party.[741]

Let aside these different *ways* in which a contract may become void in cases of non-performance, the *grounds* on the basis of which the three instruments determine what justifies termination are strikingly similar. In fact, many of the Principles' rules on termination were strongly influenced by English law[742] and therefore reflect a number of common-law concepts that also underlie the corresponding provisions of the Indian Contract Act.

In determining whether a particular non-performance entitles the promisee to terminate the contract, the criteria discussed in the following sections are to be taken into consideration under all three instruments.[743]

a. Severity of the non-performance

First, both the Principles and the Indian Contract Act recognize that a contract should be terminated or terminable where, in the words of the Principles, the non-performance substantially deprives the aggrieved party of what is was entitled

740 Indian Contract Act Sec. 56(1) and (2).

741 Indian Contract Act Sec. 39, 53 and 55. As another apparent result of its being rooted in the doctrine of absolute contractual liability, the Indian Contract Act also does not offer any means of termination whatsoever in cases where an outside event renders performance considerably more onerous (see, *e.g.*, Bangia, *supra* note 182 at 254); the Principles take a different route in recognizing that cases of hardship may allow for judicial or arbitral termination as a last resort if the parties fail to mutually adapt or terminate the contract in response to the change of circumstances (UPICC Art. 6.2.3(4)(a); PECL Art. 6:111(3)(a)).

742 See, e.g., Comment 1 to PECL Art. 8:108, Comment 1 to Art. 9:303, and Comment 1 to Art. 9:304.

743 The final factor listed in UPICC Art. 7.3.1(2) – namely that regard is to be had also to whether the termination would cause the non-performing party to suffer a disproportionate loss because it had already invested a high degree of effort or money in preparing to perform – does not appear in Indian statutory law. This is due to the fact that Indian law is based on the doctrine of absolute contractual liability, the essence of which is not to look at the position and interests of the party in breach and therefore to allow for exceptions (and hence for a termination of the contract) only in the well-established cases of frustration. As noted above (see *supra* A(2)(a)), the PECL also refrain from considering this aspect in determining whether the contract should be terminable.

to expect under the contract (UPICC Art. 7.3.1(2)(a); PECL Art. 8:103(b)).[744] The Indian Contract Act contemplates this factor in its provisions on frustration – that is, subsequent impossibility or unlawfulness of performance (Sec. 56(2)) – and on one party's refusal[745] or self-induced inability to perform its obligations in their entirety or to an extent where the promisee is substantially deprived of its benefit under the contract (Sec. 39).[746] As discussed, the three regimes only differ in their approaches on how the contract shall terminate, *i.e.*, whether it is automatically (Indian Contract Act Sec. 56(2)) invalid or terminable at the aggrieved party's option (UPICC Art. 7.3.1(2)(a); PECL Art. 8:103(b); Indian Contract Act Sec. 39).

However, a notable difference occurs with regard to initial impossibility of performance. whereas the Principles provide that the contract shall remain effective even if performance was impossible at the time when it was entered into (UPICC Art. 3.3; PECL Art. 4:102), Indian law prescribes the opposite (Indian Contract Act Sec. 56(1)).

b. Strict compliance with the contract

All three regimes also look at whether it was the parties' intention that strict compliance with the contract was of the essence of the particular transaction. In this respect, the Principles simply ask whether strict adherence to a particular obligation, most notably one to perform at a fixed time or within a fixed period, was of the essence of the contract.[747] Sec. 55(1) of the Indian Contract Act entitles the promisee to terminate a contract if the promisor fails to perform on a fixed date or within a fixed period and thus violates an essential term pertaining to the time of performance. Conversely, a party's refusal to adhere to or its self-induced non-compliance with any other essential term may constitute repudiation as per Sec. 39 of the Act and thereby render the contract terminable as well.[748]

c. Conduct of the non-performing party

The UNIDROIT Principles treat the questions of whether the non-performance was intentional or reckless (UPICC Art. 7.3.1(2)(c)) and whether the aggrieved

744 The Principles further require that the defaulting party did not foresee or could not have reasonably foreseen this result.

745 Indian Contract Act Sec. 39 addresses both anticipatory repudiation, *i.e.*, renunciation or self-induced inability to perform, and repudiation at the time of performance. See *cf.* Bhadbhade, *supra* note 137 at 996.

746 See *cf.* Singh, *supra* note 218 at 394 and 397, and *supra* B(3)(a).

747 UPICC Art. 7.3.1(2)(b); PECL Art. 8:103(a).

748 See, *e.g.*, Bhadbhade, *supra* note 137 at 1002 and 1003, and *supra* B(3)(a).

party may reasonably believe that it cannot rely on future performance (UPICC Art. 7.3.1(2)(d)) as two separate grounds on which it may terminate the contract. Under PECL Art. 8:103(c), these two factors together constitute one of the categories giving rise to the promisee's right to terminate the contract.

In India, those factors do not occur in a separate statutory provision, but they come into play under Sec. 39 of the Contract Act: if a party repudiates the contract at the time of performance by showing its intention to refuse to perform or by deliberately disabling itself from doing so, the aggrieved party has plenty of reason to believe that neither the immediately affected obligation nor any outstanding instalments or obligations will be performed. At least in this respect, intentional non-performance and a promisee's reasonable disbelief in the promisor's future willingness or ability to perform are recognized as possible grounds for termination under both the Principles and Indian statutory law.

d. Failure to perform within additional period for performance

Technically not being considered a factor to determine whether a non-performance is fundamental under the Principles, the case where a promisor fails to perform within an additional period for performance set by the promisee also justifies termination under all three instruments. Whereas the Indian Contract Act treats this constellation as a sub-category of non-performance on a set date or within a fixed period of time (Sec. 55(1)), UPICC Art. 7.3.1(3) and PECL Art. 9:301(2) both recognize it as an additional grounds of the right to termination. In any case, the implications are identical: if there is a delay in performance, the promisee may by way of a notice grant a reasonable additional period for performance and terminate the contract upon its expiration.[749] In fact, the three regimes even coherently enable the aggrieved party to declare already in the notice by which it grants the additional period that the contract shall be terminated after the same has expired.[750]

e. Anticipatory non-performance

As expressly confirmed by the drafters of the European Principles,[751] both sets of Principles transpose the common-law concept of anticipatory breach into a statutory rule. As a consequence, the substance of UPICC Art. 7.3.3 and PECL

749 UPICC Art. 7.1.5(3); PECL Art. 8:106(3). For the availability of this option under Indian Contract Act Sec. 55(1) and subject to Sec. 63 and 66, see *cf.* Bhadbhade, *id.* at 1101.

750 UPICC Art. 7.1.5(3) and PECL Art. 8:106(3). For the rule under Indian law, see, *e.g.*, *id.* at 1094.

751 See, *e.g.*, Note 1 to PECL Art. 9:304 and Zimmermann, *supra* note 161 at 485, both making express reference to the English case of *Hochester v. De la Tour* (2 Ellis & Bl. 678 (1853)).

Art. 9:304 is practically identical to Sec. 39 of the Indian Contract Act. While the Principles require that it is clear that there will be a fundamental non-performance, the Indian Act addresses the two instances that also pose the most relevant cases of anticipatory non-performance under the Principles: Sec. 39 allows for termination before the time when performance is actually due if the promisor refuses to perform a substantial part of the contract or disables itself from doing so. Consequentially, all three instruments also entitle the respective promisor to revoke its anticipatory repudiation until the promisee has issued a termination notice. As a result, termination prior to the due date of performance is permitted only for as long as the anticipatory non-performance is not revoked.

f. The concepts of fundamental non-performance and termination at the option of the aggrieved party as means of "improving" the doctrine of frustration?

Clearly, the Principles' rules on the requisites and ways of terminating a contract are aimed to strike a balance between the civil-law and common-law traditions. By the same token, their provisions on fundamental non-performance and termination – though they are by no means entirely self-contained or flawless – may be conceived as an innovative alternative to the requisites and consequences of the common-law concept of frustration of the contract. In this regard, two concepts found in the UPICC and PECL are particularly worth taking a closer look at.

First, the Principles depart from the (English) common law by expressly listing a number of factors that are to be considered in determining whether the aggrieved party is entitled to terminate the contract in the particular case.[752] The European Principles even go as far as conferring binding character to these black letter parameters. The aim of the Principles' conceptions is evident: a statutory enumeration (and thereby limitation) of the instances in which a non-performance is generally considered to be so material that the aggrieved party should be given a right to abandon the contract is intended to reduce uncertainty as to the grounds of this remedy.[753] To some extent, Sec. 56(2) of the Indian Contract Act does not emit such guidance and predictability. As the express rule under Sec. 56(2) wording speaks only of "impossibility" and "unlawfulness", the wide array of other instances of frustration to which this rule is also applicable[754] can only be ascertained by way of a thorough examination of English and Indian case law. From the perspective of international contract law harmonisation, the Principles' more clear-cut approach and shift to a statutory fixation of the traditionally purely judicial doctrine of frustration would obviously increase legal predictability among

752 See generally *supra* A(2)(a).
753 See also Naudé, *supra* note 611 at 285.
754 See *supra* B(2)(a) for references to the relevant decisions of the Indian Supreme Court.

parties as well as courts by minimizing the inevitable degree of vagueness that is required if such statutory rules are to cover the vast array of situations underlying the doctrine of frustration. On another note, the UPICC's approach of also taking into account the interests of the non-performing party[755] offers another idea that is unknown to the common-law concept of absolute contractual liability but has a potential of providing for a higher level of equity without overstretching the non-performing party's protection from the comparably harsh consequences of the remedy of termination.

Second, the idea of rendering a frustrated contract terminable at the option of the aggrieved party instead of pronouncing it automatically void certainly looks compelling at first sight. Why should it not be left up to the promisee to decide whether it wishes to terminate the contract or keep it alive in order to maintain the option of tendering its own performance or to retain non-separable parts of the respective contract?[756] The Principles seek to balance the parties' interests by (1) excluding the promisee's right to performance (in order to release the promisor from having to perform an obligation that is impossible of performance),[757] and by (2) in turn granting the promisee the option to terminate the contract and thereby providing it with a maximum range of remedies. This conception also serves the doctrines of *pacta sunt servanda* and *favor contractus*, which the drafters intended to be centres of gravitation of the Principles.[758]

The common-law rule, on the other hand, appears more practicable. The Principles' concept of leaving it up to the aggrieved party to decide whether the contract should terminate necessarily requires this party to ascertain and decide whether the requirements of this remedy are actually met in the particular circumstances. Especially in consumer transactions, this conception almost inevitably increase the likelihood of disputes over whether or not the promisee was indeed entitled to terminate the contract; as a result, the ultimate decision on whether the promisee could rightfully terminate the contract is shifted back to the courts.[759] Especially in international transactions, where diverging domestic standards and customs render it even more difficult for the parties to determine whether the requisites for termination are indeed fulfilled, the common-law approach – which was in part adopted in PECL Art. 9:303(4) – leaves the aggrieved party less options but

755 UPICC Art. 7.3.1(2)(e).

756 See Düchs, *supra* note 161 at 345 *et seq.*, who lauds the Principles' approach (*i.e.*, to leave it to up the aggrieved party to decide whether the contract should be terminated while releasing the non-performing party from the respective obligation) as a sufficient means of satisfying the civil-law principle of *impossibilium nulla est obligatio* and therefore considers it to be preferable over common-law tradition.

757 UPICC Art. 7.2.2(a); PECL Art. 9:102(2)(a).

758 See, *e.g.*, Bonell, *supra* note 19 at 117.

759 See also Coen, *supra* note 204 at 231, and *supra* A(2)(a).

appears to better serve the goal of providing for a high(er) degree of predictability. This is in line with the fact that, for the sake of clarity and persuasiveness, harmonised international legislation sometimes needs to limit the rights of the parties in favour of clear-cut rules and predictable consequences.

4. Failure to provide adequate assurance of performance

A right of the aggrieved party to request adequate assurance of performance or to terminate the contract if such assurance is not given (UPICC Art. 7.3.4; PECL Art. 8:105) are altogether unknown to both common law in general and Indian statutory contract law.[760] Instead, the only apparent means available under Indian law by which a party fearing that the other will not perform may obtain assurance would be to invoke the doctrine of "promissory estoppel". The term may be defined as "[t]he principle that a promise made without consideration may nonetheless be enforced to prevent injustice if the promisor should have reasonably expected the promisee to rely on the promise and if the promisee did actually rely on the promise to his or her detriment."[761]

Though acknowledging that it constitutes a departure from the otherwise fundamental requirement consideration as a requisite for a binding promise, the Indian Supreme Court has held that in India, promissory estoppel even furnishes a cause of action and may thus be specifically enforced.[762] As a result, a party may, for instance, provide effective assurance of performance by promising to pay a certain sum of money for the case that it fails to perform an obligation under an existing contract.

5. Termination in response to being prevented from performing

The Principles, in turn, do not generally entitle a party to terminate the contract if another party's act or omission has prevented it from performing. Instead, the consequences set forth by Sec. 53 of the Indian Contract Act (*i.e.*, that the contract shall be terminable at the option of the party being prevented from performing) may arise under the Principles only if the preventive act or omission constitutes a fundamental non-performance of the preventing party's duty to cooperate; for this purpose, the latter's conduct must either be intentional or reckless (UPICC Art. 7.3.1(2)(c)) or cast doubt on its future adherence to the contract (UPICC Art.

760 For the general position under the common law in this regard, see, *e.g.*, Note 1 to PECL Art. 8:105.

761 See Garner, *supra* note 141 at 247.

762 See *Motilal Padampat Sugar Mills Co. Ltd. v. State of Uttar Pradesh*, AIR 1979 S.C. 621 at 635 *et seq.* (1979), and generally Bhadbhade, *supra* note 137 at 300 *et seq.*

7.3.1(2)(d); PECL Art. 8:103(c)).[763] Quite obviously, this should be the case in most situations.[764]

6. *Termination notice*

Finally, the Principles and Indian statutory contract law unanimously require that the termination of a contract, if done at the option of the aggrieved party, is to be effected by way of a termination.[765] Neither instrument prescribes a particular form or wording in relation to the notice, which becomes effective when it reaches the non-performing party.

Yet, the Principles' additional requirement that the notice shall be given within reasonable *time* – and their statement that the aggrieved party loses the right to terminate the contract if it fails to comply with it – does not appear in Sec. 66 of the Indian Contract Act.[766] Rather, the only express time limit imposed under Indian statutory law is that a suit for termination of the contract must be brought within three years from the date when the facts giving rise to this remedy became known to the plaintiff.[767] However, at least in cases of anticipatory breach or repudiation at the time when performance was due (Indian Contract Act Sec. 39),[768] Indian law indirectly does force the aggrieved party to communicate its intention to the former: mere inaction or silence are generally presumed to indicate the former's acquiescence to the contract rather than its will to terminate the same.[769] Thus, waiting too long before deciding to terminate the contract and expressing this decision precludes the right to termination once the other party has gained the impression that the contract shall stand affirmed in spite of its repudiation.[770]

763 See also *supra* Ch. III(II)(A)(3)(a) and Comment B(iii) to PECL Art. 8:101.

764 In the rare case that a party's preventive conduct does not amount to fundamental non-performance, the contract may not be terminated but the other party's non-performance is still excused (UPICC Art. 7.1.2; PECL Art. 8:101(3)).

765 UPICC Art. 7.3.2; PECL Art. 9:303; Indian Contract Act Sec. 66. See also Note 1 to PECL Art. 9:303.

766 See also Bhadbhade, *supra* note 137 at 2647: "[A] party entitled to rescind is not bound to do so immediately, or within reasonable time, and he retains the right to make the election to rescind or not to rescind."

767 See Sec. 59 of the Schedule to the Limitation Act, 1963, which provides that the limitation period for a suit "[t]o cancel or set aside an instrument or decree or for the rescission of a contract" is three years starting "[w]hen the facts entitling the plaintiff to have the instrument or decree cancelled or set aside or the contract rescinded first becomes known to him".

768 See *supra* B(3)(a).

769 See *supra* B(3)(d).

770 See, *e.g.*, Ill. (b) to Indian Contract Act Sec. 39 and Specific Relief Act Sec. 24(2)(a).

II. Consequences of termination

A. Principles

1. General effects of termination

UPICC Art. 9.3.5 and PECL Art. 9:305 stipulate that the termination of a contract at the option of the aggrieved party does not take retroactive effect. Instead, the parties shall be released from their obligations to tender or receive any future performance under the terminated contract.[771] This rule emanates from the assumption that retroactive nullification would lead to inappropriate results in a number of respects. For instance, treating the contract as never having existed would bar the terminating party from claiming damages for the non-performance; what is more, retroactive nullification of the contract would necessarily comprise any clauses that are intended to determine the parties' rights and liabilities after termination, *e.g.*, dispute settlement provisions.[772]

The same considerations also form the basis of two other general consequences of termination, namely that any contract clauses which were intended to operate even after termination, *e.g.*, dispute resolution, confidentiality or non-compete clauses,[773] remain unaffected by the execution of this remedy,[774] and – as reiterated by Art. 7.3.5(2) of the UNIDROIT Principles – termination does not preclude a claim of damages for non-performance.[775]

UPICC Art. 7.1.4(2) provides that a termination notice does not preclude the non-performing party's right to cure its non-performance. This means that the

771 UPICC Art. 9.3.5(1); PECL Art. 9:305(1). Many observers have criticized the wording of the second part of PECL Art. 9:305(1) ("Termination (…) does not affect the rights and liabilities that have accrued up to the time of termination.") for its ambiguity and inaccuracy. Nonetheless, the drafters' intention behind this passage appears to be that except in the specific instances addressed by PECL Art. 9:306 to 9:308, the parties should neither be entitled to claim back nor be compelled to return or make compensation for anything that was performed or exchanged prior to the termination. See *cf.* Düchs, *supra* note 161 at 180.

772 See, *e.g.*, Comment B to PECL Art. 9:305.

773 See Ill. 2 to UPICC Art. 9.3.5 and Ill. 1 to PECL Art. 9:305. Obviously, this category also encompasses a wide array of other contract terms such as clauses on agreed payments for non-performance, penalty clauses or forum selection clauses. In fact, it has also been held that UPICC Art. 7.3.5(3) comprises contract terms that expressly entitle a party to claim restitution of promotional material as well as to clauses giving an agent a right to commission for orders that the principal had received before the date of termination (see *Camera Arbitrale Nazionale ed Internationale di Milano*, arbitral award no. A-1795/51 (1 December 1996), abstract available at http://www.unilex.info).

774 UPICC Art. 9.3.5(3); PECL Art. 9.3.5(2).

775 See also Comment to UP Art. 7.1.1 and Comment A to PECL Art. 8:102.

effects of a rightful termination are suspended until the time for cure has expired, provided that the promisor has issued a notice of cure without undue delay. Accordingly, the effective cure of a non-performance renders the termination notice inoperative.[776]

The Principles' rules on *restitution* (UPICC Art. 7.3.6; PECL Art. 9:306 to 9:309) differ fundamentally: whereas the UPICC prescribe mutual restitution as a general consequence of termination, the European Principles rule out restitution where both parties have already performed their obligations. Instead, the PECL arrange for restitution (or, if restitution is impossible, a monetary allowance) only as a means of re-establishing equity where one party has performed but not yet received or rightfully rejected the other party's performance.[777] Issues of unjust enrichment or third party rights,[778] on the other hand, are outside of the realm of either set of Principles and shall instead be realm governed by the applicable domestic (or international) laws.[779]

2. Restitution

a. Generally

Both the substantive merits and shortcomings of the Principles' provisions on restitution, as well as their value to the international legal harmonisation process, have been discussed extensively in a number of books and articles.[780] Being aimed to compare the Principles with Indian statutory law rather than to examine in detail whether and how they could be improved, this survey is limited to a presentation of the substance of the relevant black letter rules and explanatory comments.

The Principles' provisions on restitution arguably contain the most fundamentally dissimilar rules found in their respective chapters pertaining to with non-performance.

---

776 See Comment 8 to UPICC Art. 7.1.4. As argued earlier in this survey (see *supra* Ch. III(IV)(A)), Art. 8:104 of the European Principles should be construed so as to permit cure also after the promisor has received a termination notice from the aggrieved party.

777 See *infra* 2.

778 Third party rights in this context include the rights of the buyer's creditor or of a *bona fide* purchaser.

779 See, *e.g.*, Comment 5 to UPICC Art. 7.3.6 and Comment B to PECL Art. 9:308.

780 See, *e.g.*, Coen, *supra* note 204; Rainer Hornung, *Die Rückabwicklung gescheiterter Verträge nach französischem, deutschem und nach Einheitsrecht* (1998); and Reinhard Zimmermann, *Restitutio in Integrum: The Unwinding of Failed Contracts under the Principles of European Contract Law, the UNIDROIT Principles and the Avant-projet d'un Code Européen des Contrats*, Uniform Law Review 2005 at 719.

UPICC Art. 7.3.6 is built upon the assumption that each party should generally be entitled to claim restitution of "whatever it has supplied" prior to the termination.

Conversely, PECL Art. 9:305(1) provides that this remedy generally "does not affect the rights and liabilities that have accrued up to the time of termination", thus providing for restitution only "where one party has conferred a benefit to the other party but has not received the promised counter-performance in exchange." Benefits in this sense relate to money paid, property supplied, or performances that cannot be restored in kind, *e.g.*, services or perished goods.[781] Where the parties have already exchanged performances, the aggrieved party has three options under the PECL:[782] first, it is entitled to reject property it has received if the value of the same has been fundamentally reduced as a result of the non-performance (PECL Art. 9:306). In the alternative to the first option, it may proportionately reduce the price for the defective performance (PECL Art. 9:401) or claim damages for the reduction in the value of performance (PECL Art. 9:502).[783] Finally, where the contract allows for partial termination, the aggrieved party may, in any of the above cases, also terminate any separable part as per Art. 9:302 and recover the property supplied under that part to the extent that it did not receive the respective counter-performance.[784]

Though duties to make restitution are not contractual obligations, the UNIDROIT Principles expressly subject them to the rules on the right to withhold performance and on specific performance of non-monetary obligations.[785] The PECL, in turn, emphasize that a party claiming restitution of money is also entitled to claim interest in accordance with PECL Art. 9:508.[786]

Neither set of Principles provides for reimbursement of any expenses that the parties may have incurred on top of the cost of their respective performances, *e.g.*, costs incurred in preparing to perform; however, the aggrieved party may be entitled to recover such expenses under the rules on damages.

781 See Comment A to PECL Art. 9:307.

782 See also *infra* b.

783 The remedies of price reduction and damages for the reduction of the value of performance are incompatible under the European Principles. See, *e.g.*, Comment D to PECL Art. 9:401.

784 See Comment D to PECL Art. 9:308.

785 See Comment 4 to UPICC Art. 7.3.6, according to which the aggrieved party therefore "cannot claim the return of goods when this has become impossible or would put the non-performing party to unreasonable effort or expense (see Art. 7.2.2(a) and (b))." Still, though, "the non-performing party must [instead] make allowance for the value of the property" pursuant to UPICC Art. 7.3.6(1).

786 See Comment D to PECL Art. 9:307.

b. Restitution in kind

Under UPICC Art. 7.3.6, each party may claim restitution of anything – including money, services or custody of goods[787] – it has supplied under the terminated contract subject to four conditions:

(1) restitution in kind is in fact possible[788] (for instance, restitution may be impossible with regard to service or lease contracts or if the purchased goods had already perished before termination took effect);
(2) restitution in kind is appropriate;[789] for instance, restitution in kind may be inappropriate in this sense if a party had received partial performance and wants to retain that part.[790]
(3) the party claiming restitution concurrently makes restitution of what it has received or, if it cannot make restitution in kind, allowance in money;[791]
(4) performance of the obligation in question did not extend over a period of time or is indivisible although it did stretch over a period of time.[792]

The European Principles take a fundamentally different route. As "rights and liabilities that have accrued up to the time of termination" are generally not affected by the termination,[793] the PECL allow for recovery of performance only excep-

787 See Comment 1 to UPICC Art. 7.3.6.

788 See *cf. infra* c.

789 See *cf. id.*

790 See Comment 2 to UPICC Art. 7.3.6. Unfortunately, neither the UPICC's black letter rules nor the respective drafters' comments narrow down the scenarios in which restitution ought to be considered as being "appropriate", and they fail to illustrate cases where one party's wish to keep what it has received ought to be regarded as being worthy of a higher level of protection than the other's interest in getting it back.

791 According to the ICC International Court of Arbitration's much-cited decision in *Andersen Consulting Business Unit Member Firms v. Arthur Andersen Business Unit Member Firms and Andersen Worldwide Société Coopérative*, the parties are released from their duties to make restitution altogether if one of them is unable to do so concurrently because the membership benefits it has received in exchange for transfer payments made under a membership agreement (*e.g.*, coordination of activities of individual member firms) cannot be restored, *i.e.*, if restitution would result in unjust enrichment on one side (*ICC Int'l Court of Arbitration*, arbitral award no. 9797, *supra* note 613). See also Michael Joachim Bonell, *A 'Global' Arbitration Decided on the Basis of the UNIDROIT Principles: In re Andersen Consulting Business Unit Member Firms v. Arthur Andersen Business Unit Member Firms and Andersen Worldwide Société Coopérative*, Arbitration International 2001 at 249, 258.

792 See *cf. infra* d.

793 PECL Art. 9:305(1). The striking contradiction in the terminology of this article has been subject to heavy criticism: providing first that "(t)ermination of the contract releases both parties from their obligation to effect and receive future performance," the black letter rule goes on to state in the second part that termination "does not affect the rights and liabilities that have

tionally, namely in favour of a party that did not receive the counter-performance it was to receive in exchange for money it had (pre)paid (PECL Art. 9:307) or for property it had supplied (PECL Art. 9:308).[794] In other words – and in contrast to the rule under UPICC Art. 7.3.6 – "it does not follow from the fact that the contract has been terminated that the party which has performed can get restitution of what it has supplied."[795]

Restitution of *money* under PECL Art. 9:307 may be claimed where the other party failed to supply the counter-performance or if the party claiming restitution rightfully rejected the other's tender of the counter-performance. *Property* is to be returned only where the other party actually failed to deliver what it was to perform in exchange for the transfer of property[796] (PECL Art. 9:308).[797]

---

accrued up to the time of termination." Evidently, this contradiction in terms is due to editorial impreciseness; instead of "rights and liabilities that have accrued" (emphasis added), Art. 9:305(1) is clearly intended to establish that what has been *performed* or *exchanged* shall remain unaffected except if Art. 9:306 to 9:308 prescribe that it should exceptionally be restored. See *cf.* Coen, *supra* note 204 at 281 *et seq.*, and Düchs, *supra* note 161 at 180.

794 Evidently, a party terminating only a part of the contract as per PECL Art. 9:302 may recover only what it had supplied under the terminated part. Furthermore, restitution pertaining to the terminated part is limited to the extent to which the aggrieved party did not receive the counter-performance the other party was to supply under that part (see Comment C to PECL Art. 9:307 and Comment D to PECL Art. 9:308).

795 See Comment A to PECL Art. 9:307.

796 Unlike PECL Art. 9:307 (according to which "a party may recover money paid for a performance which it did not receive or which it properly rejected"), neither the black letter rule of PECL Art. 9:308 nor the Comments to that provision give any indication to the extent that non-receipt of performance (entitling a party to recover what it supplied) may also be due to its rightful rejection of the respective counter-performance, *e.g.*, the payment for the property in question. Though he, too, considers such a distinction between the restitution of money and that of property as "troubling," Reinhard Zimmermann (*supra* note 780 at 724 *et seq.*; see also Naudé, *supra* note 611 at 298) acknowledges the literal meaning of Art. 9:308 and thus reiterates that this provision does not apply where the payment or counter-performance tendered in exchange for the respective property were rightfully rejected by the party claiming restitution.

797 What remains unclear is whether the phrasings of PECL Art. 9:307 ("a party may recover money paid for a performance which it did not receive or which it properly rejected") and 9:308 ("a party which has supplied property (…) for which it has not received payment or other counter-performance may recover the property") are to be read as implying that these provisions are intended to apply only to cases of total failure of counter-performance or also where the performance was merely incomplete or otherwise non-conforming. The two provisions' literal meaning and the PECL's obvious proximity to English law (see Notes to PECL Art. 9:305 to 9:309) certainly point toward the first of the aforementioned interpretations, with the result that restitution were to be made only in cases of total failure of the other party's performance (see generally Treitel, *supra* note 159 at 773 *et seq.*). Conversely, if restitution would also take place in cases of partial failure or mere non-comformity of the counter-performance were correct, the next question would be whether Art. 9:307 and 9:308 are intended to entitle the respective promisor to reclaim the full amount of money paid or recover the entire property supplied, or

As under the UPICC, the right to restitution is in principle available to both parties; thus, if the aggrieved party has terminated the contract before having tendered performance of its own, the non-performing party is also entitled to claim back its performance.[798] Restoration of "property" under PECL Art. 9:309 includes the reassignment or calling off of a transfer of securities, debts or intellectual property rights. Moreover, the parties may also recover any certificates or any tangible items to which such intangible assets are attached, *e.g.*, works of art or paper on which a copyrighted work is written or printed.[799]

As restitution is prescribed only for exceptional cases, the PECL give the terminating party a general right to return property[800] that it has received prior to the termination, provided that the other party's non-performance has fundamentally reduced the value of what had previously been supplied to the terminating party (PECL Art. 9:306). On these grounds, the terminating party may thus reject all previous instalments that have become useless to it because the other party has failed to deliver an essential later instalment.[801] Alternatively – and particularly if it had already paid for what was delivered prior to the termination – the aggrieved party may keep what was supplied to it and claim damages (PECL Art. 9:502) or reduce the price (PECL Art. 9:401) for the decrease in the value of the performance.

c. Allowance in money instead of restitution in kind

If restitution in kind is "impossible" or deemed to be "inappropriate", the UPICC provide that the party which has rendered the respective performance may recover a reasonable amount for its value, provided that claiming such an allow-

---

only to recover an appropriate portion. (See generally Zimmermann, *id.* at 723 *et seq.*; Coen, *supra* note 204 at 301 *et seq.*; and Naudé, *id.* at 298. To illustrate the different effects brought about under each of these two interpretations of Art. 9:307 and 9:308, Zimmermann (*id.* at 724) provides the following example:

> "If the seller has delivered the vehicle sold under the contract, but the buyer has only paid half of the contractually agreed price, then, according to a literal understanding of Article 9:308 PECL, it cannot be said that the seller has 'not received payment or other counter-performance' for the performance of its part of the contract. On termination, therefore, the seller cannot request that the vehicle be returned. This is patently unsatisfactory."

798 See Comment C to PECL Art. 9:308.

799 See Comments E and F to PECL Art. 9:308.

800 In light of the fact that Comments E and F to PECL Art. 9:308 extend the right to recover "property" to intangible assets, the term "property" under Art. 9:306 should be construed so as to include tangible property as well as intellectual property, securities, stocks or debts. See also Coen, *supra* note 204 at 299.

801 See Comment to PECL Art. 9:306.

ance is "reasonable".[802] For instance, if a purchaser, prior to the termination, had irrevocably resold and already transferred the goods supplied to it by the seller, or if the goods had perished, it is to pay an appropriate allowance for their value.[803] Restitution in kind may also be impossible due to the nature of the contract, *e.g.*, with respect to services contracts, hiring contracts or carriage contracts. Inappropriateness may be constituted by the fact that "the aggrieved party has received part of the performance and wants to retain that part;"[804] what is more, with reference to the fact that the UPICC's rules on specific performance are applicable to a claim of restitution,[805] it has been argued that inappropriateness of restitution in kind may also be due to its being "unreasonably burdensome or expensive" in the sense of UPICC Art. 7.2.2(b).[806]

Subject to their above-mentioned general limitation of restitution to exceptional circumstances,[807] the PECL also acknowledge that restoration in kind may be replaced by the payment of a reasonable amount (corresponding to the value of performance to the party owing restitution) if returning the performance in question is "impossible" (PECL Art. 9:309).[808] This option is especially relevant where the termination leads to an imbalance of the parties' positions, for instance because a party performed its obligation but the consideration was to become payable only at a time after termination.

Impossibility of restitution under PECL Art. 9:309 may arise either because the benefit received was a result of work that cannot be returned, or because the property supplied has been used up or destroyed.[809] Furthermore, restitution in kind cannot be claimed if returning or undoing the performance would require

802 See Comment 1 to UPICC Art. 7.3.6. According to Comment 2 to UPICC Art. 7.3.6, the term "reasonableness" in this context is intended to "make it clear that allowance should only be made if, and to the extent that, the performance received has conferred a benefit on the party claiming restitution." Notwithstanding this comparably clear-cut explanation, commentators have conferred various different interpretations to the phrasing "whenever reasonable." On another note, the Comments do not address the question of which party's perspective should be relevant in determining the "value of what [was] received", *i.e.*, on what basis the amount of the allowance should be calculated. See *cf.* Coen, *supra* note 204 at 252 *et seq.*, and Zimmermann, *supra* note note 780 at 723, according to whom the value of performance to the party that is to make restitution and at the time of termination should determine the amount of the allowance.

803 See Comment 1 to UPICC Art. 7.3.6.

804 See Comment 2 to UPICC Art. 7.3.6 and *supra* a.

805 See Comment 4 to UPICC Art. 7.3.6.

806 See *supra* Ch. V(I)(A)(3)(b).

807 See *supra* a and b

808 See also Düchs, *supra* note 161 at 181 *et seq.*, who argues that this right to "recover a reasonable amount for the value of the performance to the other party" also extends to any benefits earned during the time when the promisee had possession of it, *e.g.*, profits or interest.

809 See Comment to PECL Art. 9:309.

unreasonable effort or expense, *e.g.*, if the costs for the removal of a work of art are disproportionate to the other party's interest in getting it back or in having it removed.[810]

As indicated by the Comments to PECL Art. 9:309, which is similar to the rule established by UPICC Art. 7.3.6(1),[811] a right to allowance in money in lieu of restitution in kind presupposes that the party that is to pay an allowance has retained a benefit from the non-returnable performance.[812] Accordingly, both sets of Principles underscore that the allowance is to be calculated on the basis of the true value that the retained benefits confer to the party that is to pay the allowance.[813] This means that a purchaser is not protected from losing a good bargain as it may be compelled to refund a higher amount than the actual price it was to pay for the performance.[814] Yet, if the net benefit to the party that is to make restitution is less than the cost that the party to which restitution is to be made had incurred for its performance, the former is to pay only the equivalent of its net benefit.[815]

d. Restitution only for the time after termination

Finally, the parties are not entitled to claim restitution if performance extended over a period of time and the contract is divisible (UPICC Art. 7.3.6(2)). The illustrations to this provision indicate that the termination of long-term contracts for recurring services for which the promisee is to frequently pay a particular

810 See Comment H and Ill. 4 to PECL Art. 9:308.

811 See Comment 2 to UPICC Art. 7.3.6.

812 See Comment A and Ill. 1 to PECL Art. 9:309. Yet, the PECL fail to pinpoint whether the time of receipt of the property or the time of termination (at which the property may have already perished or been destroyed) shall be relevant in calculating the benefit. See *cf.* Naudé, *supra* note 611 at 299.

813 See Comment 2 and Ill. 3 to UPICC Art. 7.3.6, and Comment B to PECL Art. 9:309.

814 See Comment 1 to UPICC Art. 7.3.6 and Comment G to PECL Art. 9:308. This aspect is well-illustrated by Ill. 3 to PECL Art. 9:308:

> "A has sold a Renoir painting to B for USD 200,000; the true value of the painting is over USD 250,000. When the picture is delivered to B, he does not pay for it. A is entitled to claim back the painting."

If B cannot return the painting because he has already resold and disposed of it, A is entitled to claim an allowance of USD 250,000 even though under the contract B was to pay only USD 200,000. However, Comment B to PECL Art. 9:309 makes clear that the allowance is limited to the net benefit by which the respective party is actually enriched – which would, in the present example, be USD 250,000, but may also be nil, for instance in cases where work that is left unfinished cannot be completed by another contractor.

815 See Comment B to PECL Art. 9:309. If, on the other hand, "the net benefit to the recipient is greater than the cost of providing it (...) the recipient should not be liable (...) for more than an appropriate part of the contract price" (see Comment B and Ill. 4 to PECL Art. 9:309).

remuneration gives the promisee of the services a right to restitution only in relation to any advance payments for which no counter-performance was received.

Conversely, restitution of what was previously exchanged is *not* excluded where the performance, though stretching over a period of time, is indivisible, for instance because the first five out of a total ten instalments are of no value to the promisee if the other instalments remain unperformed.[816]

In this respect, the UPICC actually adopt the approach underlying the European Principles' entire restitution regime, which is "geared chiefly to cases involving contracts for the performance of a recurring obligation".[817] According to the PECL, performances under divisible contracts for recurring obligations or divisible contracts that are to be performed over a period of time can be claimed back only to the extent that the other party failed to deliver the respective counter-performance.[818]

B. Indian statutory law

1. General effects of termination

As per Sec. 56 of the Indian Contract Act, physical impossibility, unlawfulness or frustration render a contract automatically void.[819] In cases of initial impossibility, unlawfulness or frustration, the contract is void *ab initio*, *i.e.*, from the time of its conclusion. If one of these grounds arises after the time when the contract was entered into, performance is excused for both parties from that time on, but liabilities already accrued remain unaffected.[820] *Restitution* of an automatically void contract is subject to Sec. 65 of the Contract Act.

With regard to situations where the contract is not void by force of law but terminable at the aggrieved party's option, Sec. 64 of the Indian Contract Act establishes that termination in response to a refusal or self-induced disability to perform (Indian Contract Act Sec. 39)[821] releases the repudiating party from

816 See Ill. 5 and 6 to UPICC Art. 7.3.6. Unfortunately, the UPICC fail to provide a clear-cut guideline to determine the instances in which a contract ought to be considered "divisible" under Art. 7.3.6(2). (In fact, this failure is exemplary of both Principles' general lack of definitions of abstract terms appearing in their provisions on restitution.)

817 See Zimmermann, *supra* note 780 at 723, and Ill. 2 to PECL Art. 9:305.

818 See Comment C to PECL Art. 9:307 and Ill. 4 to UPICC Art. 7.3.6.

819 See *supra* I(B)(2).

820 See, *e.g.*, Bhadbhade, *supra* note 137 at 1471.

821 Despite its seemingly unambiguous wording ("When a person *at whose option the contract is voidable* rescinds it" (emphasis added)), Sec. 64 apparently does not extend to contracts that have been terminated pursuant to Sec. 53 ("the contract becomes voidable at the option of the

having to perform its own obligations from the time when the innocent party has validly accepted the repudiation and thereby terminated the contract.[822] Having chosen to terminate the contract in accordance with Sec. 39, 53 or 55 of the Contract Act, the innocent party is released from having to perform its obligations as well, but may be liable to make restitution under Sec. 64 and 65; however, it can reject further performance by the promisor and may be entitled to damages pursuant to Sec. 75.[823]

The Indian Contract Act does not contain any rules on whether contract clauses concerned with dispute resolution shall remain valid after termination. Yet, there is a fair amount of case law on this issue: whereas it has been held that termination at the option of the aggrieved party in response to a breach of contract, *e.g.*, by way of acceptance of a repudiation (Sec. 39), does not affect an arbitration clause contained in the contract, such clauses have not been enforced where the contract was void *ab initio*, for instance due to impossibility or unlawfulness (Sec. 56).[824]

2. Restitution

a. Restitution of benefits received under a terminated contract by force of law

Based on the principle of *restitutio in integrum*, Sec. 65 of the Indian Contract Act aims to prevent unjust enrichment in cases where the contract is void *ab initio* as well as where it terminates at a later stage.[825] The rule established by this provision is that "any person who has received any advantage under [a contract discovered to be or having become void] is bound to restore it, or to make compensation for it, to the person from whom he received it."[826]

Voidness, or automatic termination, as referred to in Sec. 65 of the Contract Act may be due in particular to physical impossibility or unlawfulness of per-

---

party so prevented" (see *supra* I(B)(3)(b)) and Sec. 55 ("the contract (...) becomes voidable at the option of the promisee" (*supra* I(B)(3)(c)) of the Indian Contract Act. See *cf.* Bhadbhade, *id.* at 1274, for references to Indian case law.

822 See Singh, *supra* note 218 at 390.

823 See *infra* Ch. VII(I)(B)(1) and Bhadbhade, *supra* note 137 at 1471, for references to relevant case law.

824 See Bhadbhade, *supra* note 137 at 1019, for references to Indian case law.

825 For a comparison of Sec. 65 with the rules on restitution under English law, see *id.* at 1311 *et seq.*

826 The distinction between the terms "agreement" and "contract" in Sec. 65 ("When an agreement is discovered to be void, or when a contract becomes void") stems from Sec. 2(h) of the Indian Contract Act, according to which a contract presupposes an agreement that is enforceable by law; as a result, an agreement does not constitute a contract under Indian law if the performance of the agreed obligations is already impossible or unlawful at the time when it is made (see, *e.g.*, Bhadbhade, *id.* at 1281 *et seq.*).

formance or to frustration of the contract.[827] For instance, where performance becomes impossible due to illness of a singer who is to sing on a particular date, the contract becomes void as per Sec. 56(2) of the Contract Act and the singer is to repay any advance payment received for the appearance in question.[828] Regarding such subsequent voidness, what had been exchanged before the contract became void is to be restored; benefits received after the occurrence of the event that renders the contract void cannot be claimed back even if the parties were unaware of the event at the time of performance.[829] Instead, any performance after the time of termination is a matter of unjust enrichment and thus subject to Sec. 70 of the Contract Act.

The phrase "is discovered to be void" indicates that Sec. 65 presupposes that the initial impossibility or unlawfulness of performance were unknown to the parties at the time when they entered into the contract (*e.g.*, due to mutual mistake) and discovered only at a later stage.[830]

The term "advantage" used in Sec. 65 is considered to be identical to what is termed "benefit" in Sec. 64 of the Indian Contract Act.[831] Both terms do not "refer to any question of 'profit' or 'clear profit'" and are independent of "what the party receiving the money may have done with it."[832] As a result, restitution as per Sec. 65 does not extend to the recovery of expenses or compensation for any losses sustained by the parties[833] or to the net profits or interest earned by a party as a result of its use of the performance.[834] Instead, both parties may deduct any expenses they legitimately incurred in connection with the performance that

---

827 Indian Contract Act Sec. 56(1) and (2). The second major category of cases to which Sec. 65 applies are those where a "contingent contract" is void due to subsequent impossibility of an event upon the occurrence of which performance was to be dependent (see Indian Contract Act Sec. 39).

828 See Ill. (d) to Indian Contract Act Sec. 65.

829 See, *e.g.*, Singh, *supra* note 218 at 361, for references to Indian case law.

830 See Bangia, *supra* note 182 at 257, and Singh, *id.*

831 See *infra* b.

832 See Bhadbhade, *supra* note 137 at 1312, for references to Indian case law, and at 1318 for an apt illustration of the scope of restitution pursuant to Sec. 65, which has been derived from the Supreme Court's decision in *State of Rajasthan v. Associated Stone Industries (Kotah) Ltd.* (AIR 1985 S.C. 466 (1985)):

> "Where the grant of lease by the state for excavation of stone was subsequently found to be void, compensation was payable to the state for the stone already excavated in the amount of a reasonable royalty for the excavated stone, and compensation for exclusive rights granted to him. The net profits earned by the grantee after marketing the excavated stone could not be said to be an advantage received by him under the agreement; the net profit resulted from the processing of stone done by him and from his business activities."

833 See Bhadbhade, *id.* at 1315. However, any losses or expenses may be recoverable by way of damages for breach.

834 See Singh, *supra* note 218 at 365, and Bhadbhade, *id.* at 1317.

they are to *return*, *e.g.*, costs for the storage or preservation of the goods supplied under the contract.[835]

Sec. 65 equally compels both the aggrieved party and the party in breach to make restitution. If the benefits received cannot be restored in kind, the respective party owes an amount of money that is equivalent to the benefit received.[836] Losses incurred as a result of the breach of contract itself, on the other hand, may only be recovered by way of a claim for damages.[837]

b. Restitution of benefits received under a contract terminated at the aggrieved party's option

Where the contract is terminable at the option of the aggrieved party, *e.g.*, in response to the promisor's repudiation of the same (Indian Contract Act Sec. 39),[838] restitution is subject to Sec. 64 of the Indian Contract Act. Provided the aggrieved party indeed opts to terminate the contract, it is liable to restore any benefit it has received. As opposed to the above-mentioned Sec. 65 of the Contract Act, this provision therefore deals only with the terminating party's liability to make restitution. In fact, Indian law provides a rule that a judgment in favour of a party suing for termination presupposes that the plaintiff restores the benefits it has received under the contract.[839]

Restoration of any "benefit" refers to restitution of what was actually received under the contract. The term does not refer to profits that were or could have been drawn by a party that had received services or the goods contracted for.[840]

A claim of damages for breach of contract does not exclude a claim for restitution.[841] Hence, having terminated the contract, the aggrieved party may set off what it is to restore against any damages to which it is entitled for the breach.[842] Sec. 64 of the Contract act is also applicable if both parties have committed a breach of contract.[843]

---

835 See Bhadbhade, *id.* at 1314.

836 See *id.* at 1317.

837 See *id.*

838 With respect to termination following a breach of contract (as opposed to other instances where Indian law treats the contract as terminable at the option of one of the parties), Sec. 64 of the Indian Contract Act is apparently limited to cases of repudiation (Sec. 39). See *supra* 1.

839 Specific Relief Act Sec. 30. See also Bhadbhade, *supra* note 137 at 1275.

840 See *id.* at 1276 and *supra* a.

841 See Singh, *supra* note 218 at 399.

842 See Bhadbhade, *supra* note 137 at 1276 *et seq.*, for references to Indian case law.

843 See *id.* at 1277.

As noted above, Sec. 64 of the Contract Act only deals with the terminating party' obligation to restore the benefits it has received under the contract. Restitution of any benefits retained by the party in breach is therefore subject to the general rule set out in Sec. 65, which operates in both directions. Where, for instance, the aggrieved party has terminated the contract upon wrongful repudiation by the other party (Indian Contract Act Sec. 39), the former is to make restitution pursuant to Sec. 64 whereas the repudiating party is to restore what it received as per Sec. 65.[844] Accordingly, the Illustrations accompanying Sec. 65 refer to two particular categories of cases in which the contract is terminable at the aggrieved party's option, namely in response to repudiation (Sec. 39)[845] and in cases of late performance of contracts under which time was of the essence (Sec. 55(1)).[846]

c. *Quantum meruit*

In the context of repudiation, Indian law also allows for a claim for *quantum meruit*,[847] which is generally considered to be an alternative remedy to damages.[848]

The doctrine's applicability to situations of breach or automatic voidness of a contract emanates from the following considerations: traditionally, where the contract provided that a fixed remuneration was to be paid only upon *completion* of the work, English common law did permit the courts to interfere with the parties' bargain by ordering the promisee to pay a reasonable remuneration for work or services that were left unfinished. As a consequence, if the promisor only failed to complete its performance of the respective work or services, it could not even recover a portion of the agreed remuneration.[849] The categorical strictness of this rule prompted English courts to gradually recognize a number of circumstances in which disregarding it as a matter of equity appears justified, and Indian courts have in principle adopted these guidelines.

Two of these exceptions are particularly relevant in the context of restitution: first, where a party starts to perform and is then prevented from completing that performance due to the other party's breach of contract, it is entitled to a reasonable remuneration, or *quantum meruit*, for the value of the work that it had already

844 See id. at 1306 *et seq.*, stating that the Law Commission of India in fact suggested "suitable changes in [Sec. 65] to make it applicable to contracts avoided by a party entitled to do so."

845 See Ill. (b) to Indian Contract Act Sec. 65, which corresponds to Ill. (b) to Indian Contract Act Sec. 39.

846 See Ill. (c) to Indian Contract Act Sec. 65.

847 For other fields of applicability of the doctrine of *quantum meruit* under English common law, see, *e.g.*, Treitel, *supra* note 159 at 780.

848 See generally Bhadbhade, *supra* note 137 at 1326, and Bangia, *supra* note 182 at 311. Nonetheless, Singh (*supra* note 218 at 364) has classified *quantum meruit* claims as claims for damages.

849 See *cf.* Treitel, *supra* note 159 at 781.

completed.[850] Second, where the contract is discovered to be void or illegal in the sense of Sec. 56 of the Indian Contract Act, a party may recover the value of what it had supplied before the discovery.[851] These examples underscore that a claim of *quantum meruit* is a restitutionary (as opposed to a compensatory) remedy aimed at reasonable remuneration, thus being closely related to the right to restitution established by Sec. 65 of the Contract Act. Consequently, *quantum meruit* claims do not entitle the promisor to recover of any profits that the promisee has gained as a result of using the performance.[852]

In cases where the promisee has prevented the promisor's performance, a *quantum meruit* claim presupposes that the parties are actually discharged from their obligations because the contract is terminated by force of law or because the party prevented from performing has elected to terminate the contract for breach or contract.[853] If and for as long as the contract remains in effect, the promisor is only entitled to damages for the breach constituted by the promisee's preventive act.

The recoverable amount is to be determined on the basis of the price agreed by the parties, or, in absence of an express agreement, with reference to the current market rate.[854]

C. Comparative Analysis

1. General effects of termination

As for the general consequences of termination, the two sets of Principles and Indian statutory contract law share a considerable degree of conceptual simi-

---

850 See Bangia, *supra* note 182 at 284 and 311 *et seq.*, who also provides an example of these grounds of a *quantum meruit* claim:

"For instance, if A agrees to deliver B 500 bags of wheat and when A has already delivered 100 bags, B refuses to accept any further supply, A can recover from B the value of wheat which he has already supplied."

851 See *id.* at 312 and Bhadbhade, *supra* note 137 at 1329. The rule stems from the English case of *Craven-Ellis v. Cannons Ltd.* (2 K.B. 403 (1936)), which Treitel (*supra* note 159 at 782) has summarized as follows:

> "In *Craven-Ellis v. Cannons Ltd.*, the plaintiff worked for the defendant company as managing director. His service agreement with the company was void as neither he nor those who appointed him held the necessary qualification shares. Thus he could not recover his agreed pay. But the Court of Appeal held that he was entitled to a *quantum meruit*. Where the express contract is a nullity, the argument that the court must not interfere with the bargain between the parties loses much of its force."

852 See Singh, *supra* note 218 at 364.

853 See Bangia, *supra* note 182 at 311, and Bhadbhade, *supra* note 137 at 1329.

854 See *cf.* Bhadbhade, *id.* at 1331.

larity. Just as UPICC Art. 7.3.5 and PECL Art. 9:305, the Indian Contract Act recognizes that it would be inappropriate to treat a terminated contract as never having come into existence altogether. On this basis, the Contract Act provides that termination of the contract only discharges the parties from their obligations under the same.[855] In principle, all three instruments thus resemble the common-law tradition as well as those legal systems under which termination does not take retroactive but rather "prospective" effect.[856] Accordingly, Indian courts have held that termination, both by force of law and at the option of the aggrieved party (*e.g.*, under Sec. 39) does not nullify an arbitration clause contained in the contract;[857] this is different only where the contract is void *ab initio*, *e.g.*, as per Sec. 56 of the Indian Contract Act. It is therefore only in cases of frustration (or, under the Principles, *force majeure*) and initial impossibility that Indian law and the Principles, under which a contract remains valid even if performance was already impossible or unlawful at the time of its conclusion,[858] actually provide for fundamentally different consequences of termination.

Sec. 56 of the Indian Contract Act – according to which the contract is terminated *ab initio* in cases of frustration or initial impossibility or unlawfulness of performance – merely covers one particular part of the Principles, namely that of PECL Art. 9:303(4). In this regard, the UPICC take a different stance by providing that the contract remains valid even in cases where performance is entirely and permanently impossible.[859]

The three instruments also concur with regard to the relationship between termination and damages: UPICC Art. 9.3.5(2), PECL Art. 8:102 and Sec. 75 of the Indian Contract Act unanimously grant the aggrieved party a right to damages even if it has chosen to terminate the contract.

2. *Restitution*

Regarding restitution, the three instruments emanate from an identical point of departure, too: as the right to terminate a contract is entirely independent from whether the non-performance is due to the non-performing party's fault, both

---

855 See Indian Contract Act Sec. 64 and *supra* B(1).

856 See also Notes to PECL Art. 9:305 to 9:309 and Zimmermann, *supra* note 780 at 723.

857 Due to a lack of express references to case law in the major commentaries on the Indian Contract Act, it is impossible to derive a precise statement in relation to whether other contract terms that were intended to operate after the contract has been terminated, *e.g.*, penalty clauses or forum selection clauses, should "survive" the same. Even so, there is no apparent reason to assume that Indian courts (would) actually treat dispute settlement clauses differently from other clauses that the parties intended to operate after termination.

858 UPICC Art. 3.3(1); PECL Art. 4:102.

859 See generally *supra* I(A)(3).

parties are equally obliged to make restitution. Beyond this shared bottom line, however, the UPICC and Indian statutory contract law on the one hand and the European Principles on the other radiate into fundamentally different directions.

a. UNIDROIT Principles and Indian statutory contract law

Both UPICC Art. 7.3.6(1) and the Indian Contract Act, in Sec. 64 and 65, prescribe concurrent restitution of what the parties have received under the contract – including money or services – before its termination.[860] Whereas the UNIDROIT Principles expressly condition each party's claim to restitution in kind or allowance in money upon its own simultaneous restoration of what the other party had supplied under it, Sec. 65 of the Indian Contract Act simply provides that both parties are equally obliged to make restitution.

The terms "whatever (...) supplied" (UPICC Art. 7.3.6(1)), "advantage (...) received" (Indian Contract Act Sec. 65) and "benefit" (Indian Contract Act Sec. 64) essentially have the same meaning. Under all three provisions, any goods, money or property received are to be restituted, but the parties are not required to return any profit or interest derived from what they are to restore, or to compensate the other party for any expenses it incurred in connection with its performance or preparation of performance.[861]

In addition, the UPICC require that restitution in kind is both appropriate (*i.e.*, that the respective party does not wish to retain the goods or property) and possible (UPICC Art. 7.3.6(1)). If restitution is impossible or inappropriate, Art. 7.3.6(1) requires the respective party to pay an adequate allowance in money.[862]

Sec. 65 of the Indian Contract Act does not render restitution dependent on the parties' possible desire or interest in keeping what each one of them has received under the contract. However, Indian law certainly addresses cases where restitution in kind is impossible; here, a party that is to make restitution is compel must pay a monetary equivalent to what was supplied to it.[863] What is more, the principle of *quantum meruit*, in services or work contracts, ensures that a reasonable remuneration is paid for work or services that were performed in part but left unfinished due to a preventive act committed by the promisee or because the

860 In cases of automatic termination due to subsequent impossibility or unlawfulness of performance or frustration (Indian Contract Act Sec. 56(2)), restitution is to be made only of what was exchanged prior to the occurrence of the event that led to its voidness. Regardless of the parties' actual awareness of the voidness, anything supplied after the time when performance became impossible or the frustrating event occurred is to be returned only subject to Sec. 70 of the Contract Act. See *supra* B(2)(a).

861 See *supra* B(2)(a) and B(2)(c).

862 See *supra* A(2)(c).

863 See *supra* B(2)(a).

contract has terminated as a result of illegality or impossibility of performance.[864] Under the UPICC, the exact amount to be paid where restitution in kind is impossible (or inappropriate) is to be determined with reference to the value of the respective promisee's performance;[865] in India, regard is to be had to the monetary "equivalent" to the benefit received.[866]

The UNIDROIT Principles provide for an exception to the above-mentioned principles of restitution in cases where performance stretches over a period of time or is divisible into a multiplicity of separate portions or instalments (UPICC Art. 7.3.6(2)); here, restitution is only to be made with "prospective" effect, *e.g.*, by returning money advanced for an undelivered or non-conforming instalment.[867] A similar rule has been established under Indian law, where it has been held that a lessee, having paid a year's rent in advance, is entitled to a refund of an appropriate portion of the rent under Sec. 65 of the Contract Act if the contract is frustrated or terminated at the option of the lessee after less than the agreed term.[868] Moreover, Sec. 12(4) of the Specific Relief Act provides that where the contract is divisible into lawful and unlawful units or performable and non-performable parts, the performable parts of the contract may be treated as valid and what was supplied under the same is therefore not to be restituted unless the contract is frustrated as a whole.[869]

b. Principles of European Contract Law

According to PECL Art. 9:305(1), termination generally "does not affect the rights and liabilities that have accrued up to the time of termination." Thus, both parties are entitled to claim back what they supplied under the contract – namely property (PECL Art. 9:307) or money (Art. 9:308) – only if they did not receive or, in relation to monetary obligations, rightfully rejected the counter-performance. If restitution in kind is impossible, either party is entitled to a reasonable amount of money reflecting the value of what it has supplied (Art. 9:309). Similarly, if the aggrieved party wishes to return what it received, it may do so only if the value

864 See *supra* B(2)(c).

865 See Comment 2 and Ill. 3 to UPICC Art. 7.3.6.

866 See *supra* B(2)(a). *Quantum meruit* claims are to be assessed with reference to the price agreed by the parties for the respective work or services, or, if no price was agreed, to the current market rate.

867 See *supra* A(2)(d).

868 See *cf.* Bhadbhade, *supra* note 137 at 1309 and 1318, for references to Indian case law.

869 See Specific Relief Act Sec. 12(4) and Expl. to Specific Relief Act Sec. 12 (see *supra* Ch. V(I)(B)(2)(a)). For instance, where a sales transaction involves both legal and illegal transfers of goods, the contract remains valid with respect to legal transfers if the price for these units can be apportioned.

of that performance has been reduced substantially as a result of the other party's non-performance (Art. 9:306); alternatively, it may keep what it has received and claim damages for non-performance[870] or proportionately reduce the overall price it was to pay under contract.[871]

Finally, as opposed to the UPICC and Indian statutory law,[872] the European Principles expressly state that a party being obliged to restore money as per PECL Art. 9:307 is also bound to pay interest in accordance with Art. 9:508.

c. Evaluation

While the system of restitution established by Art. 7.3.6 of the UNIDROIT Principles has been lauded for its clarity and simplicity, it has also been criticized for allowing restitution "perhaps (…) too liberally"[873] and for failing to address a number of important issues such as restitution of benefits (*e.g.*, a possible profits or interest earned during the time when the promisee was in possession of the property or funds it is to restore)[874] or the distribution of risk (most importantly the risk of destruction of the subject matter) during the period between the termination and restitution.[875] Overall, however, observers have mostly welcomed the UPICC's approach of "mutual restitution" as a valuable contribution to the process of international contract law harmonisation, especially as Art. 7.3.6 closely corresponds to the already field-tested and well-established rules on restitution of the CISG.[876]

As examined in the preceding subsections, Indian statutory contract law is structurally akin to the regime presented by the UPICC. In fact, by providing that the parties are to mutually restore what they have received under a terminated contract, Sec. 64 and 65 of Indian Contract Act mark a significant departure from the very common-law tradition that apparently inspired the drafters of the PECL.[877]

---

870 See PECL Art. 9:502.

871 See PECL Art. 9:401.

872 For Indian law, see *cf.* Bhadbhade, *supra* note 137 at 1317.

873 See Hartkamp, *supra* note 116 at 354.

874 See, *e.g.*, Düchs, *supra* note 161 at 181 *et seq.*, and Zimmermann, *supra* note 34 at 30. Apparently, the unwinding of failed contracts in general is actually one of the main focus areas of the current revision and the drafting of a third version of the UNIDROIT Principles (see, *e.g.*, Kronke, *supra* note 82 at 8, and UNIDROIT Institute, *Implementation of Work Programme 2006-2008 – UNIDROIT Principles of International Commercial Contracts*, Uniform Law Review 2006 at 336). See also *supra* A(2)(c).

875 In fact, this issue is left unregulated by both the UPICC and the PECL. See, *e.g.*, Zimmermann, *supra* note 34 at 30 and note 780 at 725, and Naudé, *supra* note 611 at 304.

876 See, *e.g.*, Zimmermann, *supra* note 780 at 733, and Coen, *supra* note 204 at 415.

877 See, *e.g.*, Zimmermann, *id.*, and Naudé, *supra* note 611 at 298.

The European Principles' system of restitution has been criticized primarily for a number of doctrinal reasons. First, PECL Art. 9:306 to 9:309 are "geared chiefly to cases involving contracts for the performance of a recurring obligation",[878] thereby arranging for restitution of simple synallagmatic contracts only exceptionally. Especially with a view on international business transactions, this "unnecessarily complex"[879] conception is diametric to the actual practical relevance of each of these contract types and therefore appears inferior to the approach taken by UPICC Art. 7.3.6.[880] Second, the black letter rules of PECL Art. 9:307 and 9:308 signify that only a *total* default in relation to the counter-performance shall give the aggrieved party a right to claim restitution.[881] This conception is similar to English law, under which, subject to certain exceptions, money paid can only be recovered in cases of total failure of consideration, *i.e.*, where the debtor has received not even a portion of what it had bargained for.[882] However, a limitation of restitution to cases of total non-performance appears highly inconvenient and even contradictory to the primary purpose of Art. 9:307 and 9:308, that is, to restore equity. On a similar note, it is unclear why PECL Art. 9:306, if taken by its literal meaning, was devised to entitle a promisee to return property only if the value of the same has been substantially reduced in value as a result of the non-performance, but not if it was merely defective or non-conforming.[883] The UNIDROIT Principles and the Indian Contract Act both avoid these inconsistencies by providing for mutual restitution as the standard consequence of the termination of a contract.

Furthermore, commentators cite a number of editorial and substantive flaws and inconsistencies in the European Principles. For instance, the infelicitous phrasing of some of the relevant provisions – most strikingly that of Art. 9:305(1)[884] – and their sometimes unnecessary complexity[885] further add to the superiority of the system of restitution presented by the UPICC and Indian law over the PECL's current rules on the subject.

---

878 See Zimmermann, *id.* at 731.

879 See *id.* at 723.

880 See *id.* at 731; Coen, *supra* note 204 at 283; and Naudé, *supra* note 611 at 296 *et seq.*

881 See, *e.g.*, Zimmermann, *supra* note 780 at 724, and Naudé, *id.* at 298. See also *supra* A(2)(b) and note 797.

882 See generally Treitel, *supra* note 159 at 773 *et seq.*

883 See also Naudé, *supra* note 611 at 298.

884 See *supra* A(2)(b).

885 For instance, it is unclear why the PECL, though treating the two types of performances almost identically, contain two separate provisions for the restitution of money paid and for the restoration of property supplied under the terminated contract. See also Zimmermann, *supra* note 780 at 723.

Therefore, the overall conclusion drawn by this survey, too, is that the rules on restitution not only mark a substantial parting of ways between the UNIDROIT Principles and the PECL. More importantly, they fortify the conclusion that, especially with a view on each instrument's value to international business transactions (which almost always involve synallagmatic contracts), the UPICC's approach appears clearly superior to the concept underlying the European Principles.

Against this background, the proximity of Indian statutory law to the UPICC in relation to the subject of restitution marks another example of the Indian Contract Act's substantive quality. In fact, the two instruments' broad correlation can be perceived as another indicator of Indian law's being well-equipped to generate results may be regarded as equitable by both Indian and foreign – especially European – parties. In turn, the proximity of Indian statutory contract law and the UPICC also affirms the value of the latter instrument as a sophisticated set of principles of international contract law that effectively combines and strikes a workable compromise between the world's major legal traditions.

Chapter VII: Damages

I. Right to Damages

A. Principles

1. Generally

Subject to the provisions contained in Section 4 of the UNIDROIT Principles and Section 5 of the European Principles, UPICC Art. 7.4.1 and PECL Art. 9:501(1) (in conjunction with Art. 8:108) confer to the aggrieved party a general right to damages,[886] which is excluded only if the particular non-performance is excused. Under the Principles, the right to damages is thus based on the concept of no-fault liability, or "strict" liability,[887] for non-performance, according to which this remedy is available irrespective of whether the failure to perform was actually due the defaulting party's fault.[888]

Despite their different wordings, the black letter rules of UPICC Art. 7.4.1 and PECL Art. 9:501 establish identical tests pertaining to the right to damages by setting out the following requirements:

(1) non-performance of a contractual obligation;
(2) a (foreseeable)[889] harm sustained by the aggrieved party;
(3) a causal link between the non-performance and the harm; and
(4) the non-performance being unexcused.

Subject to the test set out above, the aggrieved party may choose to claim damages either exclusively or – subject to the respective (additional) requirements – in conjunction with other remedies. For instance, it may terminate the contract if the non-performance is fundamental and simultaneously claim damages as compensation[890] of the loss arising from the default; it may combine a claim

886 The term "damages" may be defined as "[m]oney claimed by, or ordered to be paid to, a person as compensation for the loss or injury." See Garner, *supra* note 141 at 170.

887 See Lando/Beale, *supra* note 47 at XXXVIII.

888 See, *e.g.*, Comment 1 to UPICC Art. 7.4.1 and Comment B to PECL Art. 9:501.

889 See UPICC Art. 7.4.4 and PECL Art. 9:503, and generally *infra* III(A).

890 The term "compensation" may be defined as "[p]ayment of damages, or any other act that a court orders to be done by a person who has caused injury to another and must therefore make the other whole." See Garner, *supra* note 141 at 118.

of specific performance with a claim of damages for the delay in performance and for any additional expenses incurred due to the delay; or it may claim damages in conjunction with other adequate remedies provided by law or in the contract, *e.g.*, cure or the publication of an admission of error.[891] Evidently however, if the aggrieved party has opted to reduce the price as per PECL Art. 9:401 (which provides a remedy that is unavailable under the UPICC), it may not claim damages for the reduction in the value of what it has received in comparison with the hypothetical value of a conforming performance of the contract; to this extent, price reduction and damages are incompatible remedies.[892]

2. Non-performance of a contractual obligation

As discussed,[893] statutory definitions of the term "non-performance" are provided in UPICC Art. 7.1.1 and in PECL Art. 8:101(1) and 1:301(4), respectively. The drafters' comments to these provisions emphasize that the remedy of damages is applicable irrespective of whether the non-performance concerns a "principal" or an "accessory" obligation.[894] Even where the aggrieved party is entitled to certain remedies for non-performance, its own conduct, *e.g.*, its partial interference with the other party's performance may have, also amounted to a non-performance and thus render it liable to pay damages as well.[895]

The only distinction between different types of obligations occurs in Comment B to PECL Art. 9:501. The distinction made here is whether the obligation in question is to produce a certain result or merely compels the promisor to apply reasonable care and skill or best endeavours. Whereas damages for non-performance of the first of these two types of obligations are available whenever the agreed result is not achieved, a right to damages for non-performance of the latter type presupposes a failure by the promisor to apply the agreed level of care or effort – a requirement which practically marks an exception from the principle of "no-fault liability".[896] This distinction appears to be unknown to Art. 7.4.1 of the UNIDROIT Principles, Comment 1 to which merely

891 See, *e.g.*, Comment 2 to UPICC Art. 7.4.1 and PECL Art. 1:301(4) and Comment D to PECL Art. 9:304, which also reiterates that the aggrieved party is entitled to damages also where it has terminated the contract in response to an anticipatory non-performance.

892 See Comment D to PECL Art. 9:401.

893 See, *e.g.*, *supra* Ch. III(I)(A).

894 See Comment 1 to UPICC Art. 7.1.4 and Comment B to PECL Art. 9:501.

895 See, *e.g.*, Comment D and Ill. 2 to PECL Art. 9:301.

896 See Comment B and Ill. 2 to PECL Art. 9:501, according to which, in absence of a clause specifying the level of care or skill to be applied, fault practically constitutes an additional requirement of the right to damages for non-performance of an obligation to use reasonable or best care

requires "the aggrieved party to prove (…) that it has not received what it was promised."[897]

Aside from this differentiation under the PECL between duties to produce a specific result and duties to use reasonable care and skill, neither set of Principles' concept of damages distinguishes between the particular types of non-performance, *viz.* delay or initial or subsequent impossibility. Situations where a party's particular conduct during the pre-contractual period may render it liable to pay damages, on the other hand, are addressed by a number of provisions outside the Principles' sections on damages.[898]

Unlike several civil-law systems, neither set of Principles requires the aggrieved party to give notice of the non-performance to the non-performing party before claiming damages.[899]

3. Harm sustained by the aggrieved party

According to UPICC Art. 7.4.2(1), the harm for which the aggrieved party may claim compensation "includes both any loss which it suffered and any gain of which it was deprived". The term "loss" is hence understood in a wide sense.[900] The black letter rules in Art. 9:501 of the European Principles only speaks of "loss caused by the other party's non-performance". However, the Comments accompanying the provision clearly imply that the term "loss" is intended to be as broad as the term "harm" used in the UNIDROIT Principles.[901] Both sets of Principles distinguish between material and non-material, *viz.* non-pecuniary, harm (UPICC Art. 7.4.2; PECL Art. 9:501).

The terms "loss" or "harm" not only relate to any reduction of the aggrieved party's assets but also to an increase in its liabilities, which may be due to its having to borrow money because the other party has failed to pay money owed under the contract, or to expenditures such as repair costs or higher interest caused by a late payment. Similarly, a loss of profit constitutes a loss in the sense of UPICC Art. 7.4.2(1); the term "loss of profit", which is also known as a type of "consequen-

---

and skill; with regard to duties to produce a result, mere (unexcused) failure to achieve the same entitles gives rise to liability for damages.

897 See also UPICC Art. 5.1.4(2) and Antoniolli/Veneziano, *supra* note 442 at 443 *et seq.* For a critical analysis of this distinction under the PECL, see, *e.g.*, Düchs, *supra* note 161 at 184 *et seq.*

898 See, *e.g.*, UPICC Art. 2.1.15 and PECL Art. 2:301(2) (negotiations in bad faith), or UPICC 2.1.16 and PECL Art. 2:302 (breach of confidentiality).

899 See *cf.* Note 3 to PECL Art. 9:501.

900 See Comment 2 to UPICC Art. 7.4.2.

901 See Comments E and F to PECL Art. 9:501.

tial loss" under (English) common law,[902] relates to losses due to personal injury or damage to property other than the goods contracted for. The aggrieved party's consequential loss hence extends to any profit of which it is deprived as a result of the non-performance. Where the exact amount of the profit was still uncertain, this also includes the loss of a chance or opportunity (UPICC Art. 7.4.3(2)).[903]

Moreover, liability for damages includes compensation for non-pecuniary harm. This includes physical suffering, emotional distress, loss of certain amenities of life, aesthetic prejudice, inconvenience (*e.g.*, with a view on travel contracts),[904] harm resulting from attacks on the aggrieved party's honour or reputation, or even the loss of a chance to become better-known.[905]

Finally, *future* harm such as profits prevented by the non-performance, or other prospective losses that are reasonably likely to occur after the time when the court makes its assessment of the amount of compensation, may also be recovered by way of damages.[906]

4. Causal link between non-performance and loss

The requirement of a causal link between the non-performance and the harm sustained by the aggrieved party is derived from the respective language of UPICC Art. 7.4.2(1) ("harm sustained *as a result of* the non-performance" (emphasis added)) and PECL Art. 9:501(1) ("loss *caused by* the other party's non-performance" (emphasis added)).

As emphasized in Comment D to PECL Art. 9:501, this means in turn that damages cannot be recovered for any losses that are *not* directly caused by the non-performance. For instance, where the chain of causation is interrupted by events like a fire destroying the goods contracted for or a trade embargo or export ban imposed by government, the connection between the failure to perform and the harm may be too indirect for the harm to be considered as having been caused

902 See, *e.g.*, Comment 2 to UPICC Art. 7.4.2 and Comment B and Ill. 2 to PECL Art. 9:502. The term "consequential damages" denotes "[l]osses that do not flow directly and immediately from an injurious act, but that result indirectly from the act." See Garner, *supra* note 141 at 170.

903 See *cf.* UPICC Art. 7.4.3(1) and Comment 2 to UPICC Art. 7.4.2, and Comment F to PECL Art. 9:501. See also *infra* II(A).

904 See, *e.g.*, Ill. 7 to PECL Art. 9:501.

905 See Comment 5 to UPICC Art. 7.4.2 and Comment E to PECL Art. 9:501. For the additional requirement of certainty of harm, which is of particular relevance in this context, see *infra* II(A). In this context, the *Camera Arbitrale Nazionale ed Internazionale di Milano* has held that compensation for emotional suffering and distress is excluded if the aggrieved party is a corporate entity. See *Camera Arbitrale Nazionale ed Internazionale di Milano*, arbitral award no. A-1795/51 (1 December 1996), available at http://www.unilex.info.

906 UPICC Art. 7.4.3(1); PECL Art. 9:501(2)(b). See generally *infra* II(A).

by (and being a foreseeable result of) the non-performance.[907] Conversely, if an intervening event or action would not have affected the contract if the non-performance had not occurred, it is *not* to be treated as breaking the causal link.[908]

5. Non-performance not excused

The promisor's liability for damages arises independently from the question of whether the non-performance is due to its fault ("no-fault liability"). Instead, the promisor can exculpate itself from liability for its non-performance if (and to the extent that)[909] the same is excused due to certain external factors.[910] A non-performance may be excused (1) as a result of the aggrieved party's conduct (*e.g.*, its interference with the other party's performance (UPICC Art. 7.1.2; PECL Art. 8:101(3)),[911] (2) as a consequence of *force majeure* (UPICC Art. 7.1.7; PECL Art. 8:108),[912] (3) due to an exemption clause (UPICC Art. 7.1.6; PECL Art. 8:109),[913] or (4) because the non-performing party is entitled to withhold its performance as per UPICC Art. 7.1.3 and PECL Art. 9:201.[914] The burden of proof for the defence that the non-performance is excused generally lies with the non-performing party.[915]

If the non-performance is indeed excused, the aggrieved party may claim neither damages nor specific performance; yet it may be entitled to withhold performance or terminate the contract and recover money paid or, under the PECL, accept the non-conforming tender and proportionately reduce the price payable for the performance.[916]

6. General measure of damages

In principle, a party owes full compensation for the harm caused by its non-performance (UPICC Art. 7.4.2(1)), or, in other words, "[t]he general measure of

---

907 See also Comment 3 to UPICC Art. 7.4.3.

908 See *cf.* Comment D and Ill. 4 to 6 to PECL Art. 9:501.

909 The German translation of PECL Art. 9:501(1) unambiguously provides that the defaulting party's liability for damages is excluded only to the extent that its non-performance is excused ("außer *soweit* die Nichterfüllung (...) entschuldigt ist" (emphasis added)). For the German translation of the PECL, see von Christian von Bar/Reinhard Zimmermann, *Grundregeln des Europäischen Vertragsrechts, Teile I und II* (2002).

910 UPICC Art. 7.4.1; PECL Art. 9:501(1) and Art. 8:101(2).

911 See generally *supra* Ch. III(II)(A).

912 See generally *supra* Ch. III(VII)(A).

913 See generally *supra* Ch. III(VI)(A).

914 See generally *supra* Ch. III(III)(A).

915 See *cf.* Comment 1 to UPICC Art. 7.4.1; Magnus, *supra* note 5 at 266 *et seq.* and 275; and Zoll, *supra* note 15 at 246.

916 See generally supra Ch. III(III)(A).

damages is such sum as will put the aggrieved party as nearly as possible into the position in which it would have been if the contract been duly performed" (PECL Art. 9:502, which thereby expressly reflects the principle of *restitutio in integrum* or full compensation).

This means that the non-performing party is bound to restore the aggrieved party's "expectation interest", which includes the value of both the defeated contractual expectation – *i.e.*, any losses incurred by the aggrieved party (*damnum emergens*) – and any consequential losses such as the profit of which it was and/or will be deprived (*lucrum cessans*) as a result of the default.[917] With a view on sales contracts, this means that the aggrieved party is entitled to recover damages for (1) a lost bargain, *i.e.*, the difference between the contract price and the market price, (2) any expenditures made in reliance on the contract, and (3) any (foreseeable) consequential loss.[918] Finally, liability for damages generally includes a duty to pay interest from the date when the loss occurred until the time of payment.[919]

Equally, however, "[d]amages must not enrich the aggrieved party."[920] This means that any *gains* which the aggrieved party accounts for as a result of the non-performance – for instance because it has resold the goods by way of a cover transaction[921] or because the non-performance has allowed it to avoid expenses such as storage costs – are to be set off against the amount of compensation for its losses.[922] Such "compensating gains" may arise automatically from the non-performance, *e.g.*, if, as a result of the same, the aggrieved party has been discharged from a future performance that would have involved expenditures, or if it has avoided a loss because the contract was a bad bargain.[923] Alternatively, compensating gains may be the result of events or actions occurring between the non-performance and the judgment or arbitral award, for instance where the aggrieved party manages to resell the goods by way of a cover transaction.[924]

The strict wording of UPICC Art. 7.4.2(1) and PECL Art. 9:502 does not authorize the courts to reduce the amount of compensation as appropriate in cer-

917 As underscored by the example given in Ill. 4 to UPICC Art. 7.4.2, the UNIDROIT Principles expressly differentiate between "loss (…) suffered" and "gain of which (the aggrieved party) was deprived" as two separate types of harm giving rise to a claim of damages. PECL Art. 9:502 draws a similar distinction between "loss (…) suffered" and "gain of which (the aggrieved party) has been deprived".

918 See, *e.g.*, Comment A to PECL Art. 9:502 and Comment B and Ill. 2 to PECL Art. 9:502.

919 UPICC Art. 7.4.10; PECL Art. 9:508. See *infra* VII(A).

920 See Comment 3 to UPICC Art. 7.4.2.

921 See *cf. infra* III(A).

922 See Comment 3 and Ill. 5 to UPICC Art. 7.4.2, and Comment C and Ill. 3 and 4 to PECL Art. 9:502.

923 See Comment 3 to UPICC Art. 7.4.2 and Comment C and Ill. 4 to PECL Art. 9:502.

924 See Comment 3 and Ill. 5 to UPICC Art. 7.4.2, and Comment C and Ill. 3 to PECL Art. 9:502.

tain circumstances (as allowed in some legal systems). According to the UPICC's drafters, this restriction is intended to avoid the high degree of uncertainty that any such judicial discretion and its multifarious use and interpretation by courts in different countries would bring about especially with respect to international transactions.[925] As a consequence, the amount of compensation may be limited only (1) as a result of the above-mentioned rule that compensating gains are to be set off against the amount of damages owed for the non-performance, or (2) because the aggrieved party is partly responsible for the harm or its extent.[926]

If the aggrieved party has undertaken a cover transaction or if there is a current price for the performance, the amount of damages is to be measured with reference to the cover transaction price or the current price, respectively.[927] In cases of non-pecuniary harm, the courts are free to determine the particular means of compensation. This means that, apart from awarding monetary compensation, they may also grant other types of redress such as publication of an admission of error in a newspaper.[928]

B. Indian statutory law

1. Generally

In accordance with common-law tradition, Indian law provides that any breach of contract gives rise to a cause of action for damages.[929] Unlike specific relief, the remedy is therefore not subject to the courts' discretion but arises as a matter of right upon any breach unless the parties have excluded it by way of a contractual provision.[930] Damages for breach of contract are awarded with the objective of placing the aggrieved party in the position that it would have been in had the

925 See, *e.g.*, Comment 1 to UPICC Art. 7.4.2.

926 UPICC Art. 7.4.7 and 7.4.8; PECL Art. 9:504 and 9:505. See *infra* V(A) and VI(A).

927 See generally *infra* IV(A)(1) and (2).

928 See, *e.g.*, Comment 5 to UPICC Art. 7.4.2.

929 See, *e.g.*, Treitel, *supra* note 159 at 686; Bhadbhade, *supra* note 137 at 994; and H.K. Saharay, *Dutt on Contract – The Indian Contract Act, 1872* (10th ed., 2006) at 612. In common-law jurisdictions, the term "damages" may be defined as "[m]oney claimed by, or ordered to be paid to, a person as compensation for the loss or injury." See Garner, *supra* note 141 at 170.

930 See, *e.g.*, Bhadbhade, *id.* at 1466 and 1468. (However, it should be mentioned that, despite the automatic and non-discretionary availability of this remedy as a matter of right, a claim for (non-liquidated) damages gives rise to a *debt* only from the time when the defaulting party's liability has been adjudicated and the amount of damages assessed by a court. See *cf. id.* at 1491 *et seq.*, and Singh, *supra* note 218 at 421.)

contract been performed, *i.e.*, to compensate the latter for any loss or damage[931] it has sustained as a result of the breach.

In synchrony with English common law,[932] Indian statutory law does not require the breach of contract to be the result of the defaulting party's fault. Similarly, due to the compensatory – as opposed to punitive – character of damages under the common law, the motive for and the manner of the breach are not to be taken into account because the objective of damages in contract law is not to penalize the promisor but solely to compensate the promisee for any losses sustained as a result of a promisor's failure to perform.[933]

While the Indian Contract Act deals with the aggrieved party's right to damages in a number of sections spread throughout the statute, Sec. 73(1), which is considered to be "declaratory of the common law on damages“,[934] sets out the general test for what the section heading refers to as "Compensation for loss or damage caused by breach of contract“. The requirements are as follows:

1. breach of a valid contract;
2. the promisee suffering a loss or damage;
3. the loss or damage having been caused by the breach;
4. the loss or damage not being "remote",[935] *i.e.*, having "naturally [arisen] in the usual course of things from such breach, or [having been known to] the parties (…), when they made the contract, [as being] likely to result from the breach."

The test established by Sec. 73(1) of the Contract Act is accompanied by a total of 18 Illustrations representing general rules that may be followed in interpreting the provision,[936] and by an Explanation pertaining to the estimation of the loss or damage.[937]

---

931 Under Indian law, the terms "damage" and "damages" are used to describe two separate items: whereas "damage" may be defined as the disadvantage suffered by a person as a result of another's act or default, "damages" generally refers to the recompense granted to the injured party by process of law for the actionable wrong which another person has committed. See *cf.* Bhadbhade, *id.* at 1484 *et seq.*, according to whom "[t]he term 'damages' is (…) used to mean 'nothing more than the compensation which the court determines in the circumstances of each case for the injury or loss which has been sustained by (a) party.'"

932 See, *e.g.*, Zimmermann, *supra* note 161 at 481, and Note 2 to PECL Art. 8:101.

933 See, *e.g.*, Treitel, *supra* note 159 at 691, and Singh, *supra* note 218 at 422.

934 See, *e.g.*, Bhadbhade, *supra* note 137 at 1469 and Singh, *supra* note 218 at 407, for references to observations made, *inter alia*, by the *Privy Council of India*.

935 See *infra* III(B).

936 See Bhadbhade, *supra* note 137 at 1465, and *infra* 2.

937 As opposed to Sec. 73(1), Indian Contract Act Sec. 73(2), according to the section heading, deals with "[c]ompensation for failure to discharge obligation resembling those created by contract"

Aside from the general rule that a breach of contract gives right to liability for damages (Indian Contract Act Sec. 73(1)), Sec. 75 of the Contract Act, which is supplementary to Sec. 39, 53, 54 and 55 of the Act,[938] establishes that "[a] person who has rightfully rescinded a contract is entitled to compensation" in five general sets of circumstances:[939]

- Upon termination of a contract under Sec. 39, the aggrieved party is entitled to compensation[940] for any loss it has sustained as a result of the breach of contract. Illustration (b) to Sec. 39 reiterates that this right to damages also comprises compensation for any harm caused an anticipatory breach. Accordingly, if the promisee chooses not to terminate the contract and instead wait to see if the other party might eventually perform despite its earlier repudiation, it may claim damages if the latter indeed fails to perform by the due date.[941]
- Sec. 53 – an official footnote to which makes express reference to Sec. 73 – deals with the liability of a party whose conduct prevents another party's performance.[942]
- Sec. 54 grants a right to damages to a party that is prevented from performing due to another party's failure to perform a reciprocal promise without the performance of which the former's promise cannot be performed.[943]
- Sec. 55(1), in conjunction with Sec. 55(3) of the Contract Act, provides that, where time was agreed to be of the essence of the contract, the aggrieved party may either reject the late tender and claim compensation for any loss sustained due to the breach, or it may accept late performance and claim damages provided it gives notice to the defaulting party of its intention to do so at the time of acceptance of the tender.[944]

(emphasis added). This type of obligation is generally governed by Sec. 68 to 72 of the Contract Act.

938 See *cf.* Saharay, *supra* note 929 at 685.

939 As this survey is concerned with the general Indian statutory law of contracts, more specific provisions such as Sec. 212 of the Indian Contract Act or Sec. 55 of the Sale of Goods Act, 1930 – which, though being based on the same general principles as Sec. 73 of the Contract Act, is regarded as more specific and therefore prevailing over the latter section in relation to the sale of movable property (see, *e.g.*, Bhadbhade, *supra* note 137 at 1567, for references to Indian case law) – are not subject to this comparison. For an overview of the law of damages for breach of particular types of contracts, see *cf.* Bhadbhade, *id.* at 1566 *et seq.* (on sale of goods contracts), 2219 *et seq.* (on agency), and 1588 *et seq.* (on employment contracts).

940 In common-law jurisdictions, the term "compensation" may be defined as "[p]ayment of damages, or any other act that a court orders to be done by a person who has caused injury to another and must therefore make the other whole." See Garner, *supra* note 141 at 118.

941 See *supra* Ch. VI(I)(B)(3)(a).

942 See *supra* Ch. III(II)(B)(1).

943 See *supra* Ch. III(III)(B)(2).

944 See *supra* Ch. IV(I)(B)(3)(c) and *infra* 5. See *cf.* Bangia, *supra* note 182 at 233.

– Sec. 55(2) reiterates that if time it not of the essence of the contract, a promisee – though it does not have a right to reject late performance – is entitled to compensation for any loss caused by the delay.[945]

With regard to damages in cases of unlawfulness or frustration (to which Sec. 75 of the Indian Contract Act is inapplicable because the contract is automatically void and therefore not terminable at the option of the aggrieved party), Sec. 56(3) provides that a party that knew or could reasonably have known that the performance of its promise would be impossible or unlawful due to a pre-existing impediment is liable to make compensation of any loss which the other party sustains as a result of the non-performance, provided the latter was unaware of the impediment.[946]

As all of the above-mentioned provisions of the Indian Contract Act merely establish that the aggrieved party has a right to damages and do not impose any additional requirements to those set forth in Sec. 73(1), the test underlying this remedy *is universal* and does not presuppose any differentiation between different types of breach of contract.[947] By contrast, the remedy of termination of the contract requires a distinction between delay (which, as per Sec. 55(1), entitles the promisee to terminate the contract only if time was of essence of the contract) and impossibility (which renders the contract automatically void (Indian Contract Act Sec. 56)) among others.

As for the compatibility of the remedy of damages with the aggrieved party's right to terminate the contract, the aforementioned Sec. 75 of the Contract Act stipulates that rightful rescission[948] of a contract generally entitles the rescinding party to compensation for any loss or damage it has sustained as a result of the underlying non-performance.

The general rule in relation to specific relief is that the aggrieved party is only entitled to damages for a breach of contract and cannot enforce performance unless the court considers damages to provide inadequate relief.[949] If a claim of specific relief is permitted under the Specific Relief Act, 1963, Sec. 21 of the same provides that "[i]n a suit for specific performance of a contract, the plaintiff may also claim compensation for its breach, either in addition to, or in substitution of, such performance." For instance, a claim of damages in addition

945 See *supra* Ch. III(IV)(B) and Ch. II(V)(B).

946 See *supra* Ch. VI(I)(B)(2)(b). See *cf.* Bhadbhade, *supra* note 137 at 1191 *et seq.*

947 The sole exception to this observation is the notice requirement in Sec. 55(3) of the Indian Contract Act. See *infra* 6.

948 The term "rescission" may be defined as "[a] party's unilateral unmaking of a contract for a legally sufficient reason, such as the other party's material breach." See Garner, *supra* note 141 at 606.

949 See *supra* Ch. V(I)(B)(1) and *cf.* Bhadbhade, *supra* note 137 at 1636 *et seq.*

to a suit for specific relief may be brought where the non-delivery of the goods contracted for has caused a loss of profit on the purchaser's end. A plaintiff claiming specific performance or damages in the alternative (as permitted by Sec. 21 of the Specific Relief Act) may elect between these two remedies at any time during the trial.[950] However, according to Sec. 24 of the Specific Relief Act, a suit for damages for breach of contract is barred after the dismissal of a suit for specific relief.[951]

2. Breach of a valid contract

The definition of the term "breach of contract" according to Indian law has already been described and discussed above.[952] In order to recover compensation from the party in breach, the aggrieved party must bring an action for damages and prove the breach.[953]

In addition to the types of breach mentioned in Sec. 39, 53, 54 and 55 of the Indian Contract Act, the Illustrations to Sec. 73 of the Act also stipulate a number of examples of other circumstances that give rise to the remedy of damages: for instance, a buyer's refusal to accept delivery or failure to perform its own obligations both constitute a breach of contract and entitle the seller to damages (Illustrations (c), (d) and (h) to Indian Contract Act Sec. 73). A seller, on the other hand, commits a breach if it fails to deliver performance (Illustrations (a), (j), (k), (o), (p) and (q) to Sec. 73) or comply with a warranty (Illustration (m) to Sec. 73).[954]

A contract which is automatically void due to frustration or unlawfulness does not fall within the realm of Sec. 73 and 75 of the Indian Contract Act; in such cases, damages may only be available under Sec. 56(3), *i.e.*, if one of the parties knew or could have reasonably known of a pre-existing impediment at the time of conclusion of the contract. Self-evidently, rightful withholding of performance in accordance with Sec. 51 and 54 of the Act does not constitute a breach of contract,[955] and a party's prevention of or its interference with another party's performance both exclude the latter's liability to pay damages, too.[956]

---

950 See *supra* Ch. V(I)(B)(3). See *cf.* Bhadbhade, *id.* at 2602 *et seq.*, for references to Indian and English case law.

951 See *supra* Ch. V(I)(B)(3).

952 See *supra* Ch. III(I)(B).

953 See, *e.g.*, Saharay, *supra* note 929 at 652.

954 See generally *id.* at 617.

955 See *supra* Ch. III(III)(B).

956 See *supra* Ch. III(II)(B).

3. Loss or damage sustained by the aggrieved party

As under English common law,[957] the objective of the remedy of damages is to put the aggrieved party in the position it would have been in if the contract had been performed.[958] For this purpose, regard is to be had either to its loss of bargain ("expectation interest") or alternatively to its "reliance interest".[959] By contrast, a profit made by the party in breach as a result of its non-performance is generally irrelevant in ascertaining the aggrieved party's recoverable loss.[960] The burden of proving the loss lies with the plaintiff.[961]

The term "loss or damage" used in Sec. 73 of the Indian Contract Act relates to three general categories of harm: (1) harm to property; (2) non-pecuniary harm; and (3) harm to the aggrieved party's economic position.[962] Whereas "harm to property" refers to damage to or the destruction of personal property, "harm to a party's economic position" comprises any pecuniary consequential loss, *viz.* loss due to personal injury or damage to property other than the goods contracted for.[963] Apart from losses of profit or opportunity,[964] this second category also includes pre-contractual expenses that the aggrieved party incurred in contemplation of the contract, *e.g.*, in preparing to perform, or after the breach (such as damages paid to compensate a third purchaser to which it had already resold the goods prior to the date when the seller was to deliver them).[965] A third category, damages for "non-pecuniary harm", or "personal harm", includes physical injury, loss of enjoyment or amenity, mental distress, inconvenience or disappointment, loss of publicity or opportunity to gain enhanced reputation, or vexation.[966]

957 See *cf.* D.R. Harris, *Chitty on Contracts, Vol. I* (27th ed., 1994) at 1198.

958 See, *e.g.*, Bhadbhade, *supra* note 137 at 1494.

959 See *infra* 6.

960 This principle corresponds to English common law. However, courts in common-law jurisdictions have in exceptional cases, awarded damages for the so-called "restitution interest" by ordering the defaulting party to disgorge its actual profit to the plaintiff ("account of profits") instead of compensating the loss caused by the breach. See *cf.* Bhadbhade, *supra* note 137 at 1494 and 1497 *et seq.*, and Treitel, *supra* note 159 at 687.

961 See, *e.g.*, Singh, *supra* note 218 at 400.

962 See, *e.g.*, Bhadbhade, *supra* note 137 at 1508.

963 See, *e.g.*, *id.* For the remoteness test, which is especially relevant with regard to claims of damages for any consequential loss, see *infra* III(B).

964 See *cf.* Saharay, *supra* note 929 at 624 *et seq.*, and Ill. (j) to Indian Contract Act Sec. 73.

965 See Ill. (k) to Indian Contract Act Sec. 73 and *cf.* Bhadbhade, *supra* note 137 at 1436 *et seq.*

966 However, Indian courts (just like English courts) have awarded damages for distress, vexation or loss of enjoyment only in exceptional cases (see, *e.g.*, Singh, *supra* note 218 at 430, and Bhadbhade, *supra* note 137 at 1466). See Singh, *id.* at 432 *et seq.*, for references to cases where English and Indian courts have awarded damages for non-pecuniary harm.

In addition to losses sustained at the time of the breach or up to the trial, harm in the sense of Sec. 73 also includes any future loss that the aggrieved party is to sustain after the passing of the judgment or award.[967]

4. Causal link between breach of contract and loss

Though the breach of contract in question need not be the sole cause of the harm sustained by the aggrieved party, the common law requires a causal connection between the breach and the loss.[968] In other words, the harm must be a "direct result" of the breach.[969] The chain of causation may be broken by intervening events or acts committed by the plaintiff or a third party, provided these constitute a new and independent cause of further harm.[970] In this event, the party in breach is liable only for the loss that had accrued before the occurrence of the intervening act or event.[971]

5. Specific requirements

Though Indian statutory law does not expressly provide that frustration of a contract does not give rise to liability for damages, a rule to this extent emanates from Sec. 56(3) of the Indian Contract Act. Under this provision, a party that knew or could reasonably have known that the performance of its promise would be impossible or unlawful due to a pre-existing impediment, is liable to make compensation of any loss sustained by the other party as a result of the non-performance, provided the latter was unaware of the impediment. In accordance with common-law tradition,[972] this rule thus signifies that frustration serves as an excuse to liability for damages as long as the respective promisor was unaware or could not have reasonably known of the impediment.[973]

If the parties had agreed that time should be of the essence of the contract, Sec. 55(3) of the Contract Act, in conjunction with Sec. 55(1), imposes an additional notice requirement: provided time was of the essence of the contract, the promisee is entitled to terminate the contract in response to the other party's failure to perform at the fixed time (Indian Contract Act Sec. 55(1)). However, if it accepts performance at any other than the agreed time, it can claim compensation of a

967 See, *e.g.*, Bhadbhade, *id.* at 1500.

968 See *cf.* Treitel, *supra* note 159 at 722, and Bhadbhade, *id.* at 1509 *et seq.*, for further references.

969 See, *e.g.*, Bhadbhade, *id.* at 1549, citing the Indian case of *Frederick Thomas Kingsley v. Secretary of State for India* (AIR 1923 Cal 49 (1923)).

970 See also *infra* III(B) for the remoteness of damages test.

971 See Treitel, *supra* note 159 at 723, making reference to the English case of *Weld-Blundell v. Stephens* ((1920) A.C.956).

972 See, *e.g.*, Note 2 to PECL Art. 8:101 and Note 1(b) to PECL Art. 8:108.

973 See, *e.g.*, Bangia, *supra* note 182 at 249.

loss caused by the delay only if it gave notice to the other party of its intention to do so at the time when it accepted the untimely tender.[974]

6. General measure of damages

Under Indian law, damages are of compensatory character and thus generally assessed in accordance with the actual loss sustained by the aggrieved party. Accordingly, Indian contract law – as opposed to tort law – strictly rules out the awarding of punitive damages.[975]

Instead, the remedy of damages primarily seeks restoration of the "expectation interest": the aggrieved party is to be put in the position it would have been in if the contract had been performed. If the injured party has sustained pecuniary harm, this involves compensation for its actual financial loss (caused, for instance, by the non-receipt of the performance) and for any gains that it had expected from making a particular use of the performance, *e.g.*, from reselling the goods contracted for.[976] Unless the contract provides for liquidated damages[977] or a contractual measure of damages,[978] the burden of proving or establishing reasonable certainty as to the existing and/or prospective financial loss as well as any lost profit or chances lies with the aggrieved party.[979]

In the alternative, or if the aggrieved party cannot prove the value of its expectation interest, it may recover its "reliance interest", the objective of which is to restore the position that this party would have been in if the contract had not been concluded. The reliance interest comprises any wasted pre-contractual expenditures the aggrieved party made in contemplation of the contract or its full performance, to prepare its own performance, or after the breach (*e.g.*, to pay compensation to a purchaser to whom it had already resold the goods prior to the time when they were to be delivered by the seller).[980]

---

974 See generally *id.* at 233.

975 See, *e.g.*, Bhadbhade, *supra* note 137 at 1467 and 1485.

976 See, *e.g.*, *id.* at 1466.

977 See *infra* X(B).

978 For instance, Sec. 62 of the Sale of Goods Act, 1930 permits the parties to agree upon a particular measure of the amount of damages for a breach of the contract. Act Sec. 62 of the Sale of Goods, 1930 provides the following rule:

> "Exclusion of implied terms and conditions – Where any right, duty or liability would arise under a contract of sale by implication of law, it may be negatived or varies by express agreement or by the course of dealing between the negatives or varied by express agreement or by the course of dealing between the parties, or by usage, if the usage is such as to bind parties to the contract."

979 See, *e.g.*, Singh, *supra* note 218 at 400, and Bhadbhade, *supra* note 137 at 1549.

980 See, *e.g.*, Bhadbhade, *id.* at 1486 and 1496. For an overview of the exceptional instances in which courts in common-law jurisdictions have awarded damages for the so-called "restitution interest" (*supra* note 960), see Bhadbhade, *id.* at 1497 *et seq.*, and Treitel, *supra* note 159 at 687.

The reason why the aggrieved party must normally choose between claiming damages for its expectation interest or for its reliance interest emanates from the principle that the amount of damages must not exceed the loss which it actually has or is likely to suffer.[981] As per this principle, any gain that it has made as a result of the breach is to be set off against its loss. The types of gains subject to this so-called "net loss approach" include tax savings, benefits gained from any partial performance that the defaulting party had rendered prior to the time of the breach, or savings that have arisen from the aggrieved party's release from its own obligations under the contract.[982]

Where no harm has occurred or where the aggrieved party did not sustain any substantial loss or damages or is unable to prove the same, Indian law allows for the awarding of "nominal damages".[983]

The exact amount of damages is to be assessed either on the basis of the cost of obtaining or completing performance ("cost of cure") or with reference to the difference in value between the non-conforming and the contractually agreed performance or a substitute ("difference in value").[984] If the performance in question has a market value – which is usually the case under commercial contracts –, damages are to be assessed on this basis.[985] In absence of a market value, the courts are to quantify the loss by looking at the cost of cure or by way of an estimation. Compensation for non-pecuniary harm, lost profits or prospective losses also requires an estimation or prognosis. Yet, whereas existing and prospective pecuniary losses may be measured separately, present and prospective non-pecuniary losses are to be quantified in a single amount.[986]

Generally, damages are due on and to be ascertained with reference to the time of occurrence of the breach.[987] While this is usually the time when performance is due, subsequent events can be taken into account to assess harm sustained after the breach, *e.g.*, where the breach gives rise to liability of a purchaser to its own customer.[988]

---

981 In turn, this means that the aggrieved party may combine its claims for expectation interest and reliance interest as long as it does not recover more than its actual loss. See Treitel, *id.* at 695.

982 See Singh, *supra* note 218 at 425, and Bhadbhade, *supra* note 137 at 1490 and 1560, for further references.

983 See *cf.* Singh, *id.* For the availability of nominal damages, *i.e.*, a nominal amount of compensation, under English common law, see, *e.g.*, Treitel, *supra* note 159 at 686. See also *infra* II(B).

984 See Bhadbhade, *supra* note 137 at 1550.

985 See generally *infra* IV(B).

986 See, *e.g.*, Bhadbhade, *supra* note 137 at 1500.

987 See Ill. (a) to Indian Contract Act Sec. 73 and Bangia, *supra* note 182 at 299.

988 See generally Bhadbhade, *supra* note 137 at 1560 *et seq.*, for references to relevant case law.

If, in cases of anticipatory breach, the aggrieved party accepts the repudiation and sues for damages before the date when the contract ought to be performed, the recoverable amount of damages is to be assessed with reference to (the presumptive market rate prevailing at) the due date and not to the time of the anticipatory breach. This is different only if the aggrieved party's duty to mitigate its loss requires it to make a substitute transaction after having accepted the repudiation.[989] If the aggrieved party, despite being entitled to terminate the contract as per Sec. 55(1) of the Indian Contract Act, chooses not to do so in order to possibly receive performance at the time when it is actually due, damages are available from and assessed with reference to the due date.[990]

C. Comparative analysis

1. Generally

With a view on the general requirements of the remedy of damages, a comparison of the Principles and Indian statutory contract law show only minor divergences. This is primarily because the Principles' conception of the remedy closely corresponds to that of English common law.[991]

A core dogmatic characteristic of both the Principles and the Indian Contract Act is that the aggrieved party has a non-discretionary right to damages regardless of whether the non-performance or breach of contract were due to the other party's fault ("no-fault liability"). In this sense, the Principles have been described as reflecting a tendency found among many of the world's contract law systems to "[depart] from the long civil-law tradition that regarded fault as a necessary element of a breach."[992] However, unlike Indian contract law – under which damages are the primary remedy and a claim of specific relief is entirely in the courts' discretion – the Principles treat specific performance and damages as equal and interchangeable forms of redress.

As for the compatibility of damages and other remedies such as specific relief and termination of the contract, the rules under Indian statutory law are similar to those presented in the Principles: whereas termination and damages are gener-

989 See, *e.g.*, Saharay, *supra* note 929 at 634 *et seq.* See also Treitel, *supra* note 159 at 711. For the aggrieved party's duty to mitigate its loss during the time between its acceptance of the anticipatory breach and the time when the contract ought to be performed, see *infra* VI(B).

990 See, *e.g.*, Bhadbhade, *supra* note137 at 1472. See also Treitel, *id.* at 711.

991 See generally Zimmermann, *supra* note161 at 481.

992 See Perillo, *supra* note 130 at 308. See also Zimmermann, *id.* at 481.

ally compatible remedies,[993] damages and specific performance are incompatible except if the claim for damages is only ancillary, *e.g.*, in cases where the aggrieved party claims compensation for losses caused by a late tender in addition to requesting performance of the contract.[994]

2. Non-performance/breach of contract

The first element of the test underlying the aggrieved party's right to damages under both the Principles and Indian statutory law is a party's failure to (fully) perform a contractual obligation. The characteristics of the term "non-performance" used in the Principles and of what is known as "breach of contract" under Indian law have been compared in detail above.[995] With the exception of the distinction between duties to achieve a certain result and duties to apply best efforts or reasonable skill as prescribed by the drafters of the European Principles (which does, however, not occur in any of the PECL's black letter rules),[996] neither UPICC Art. 7.4.1 and PECL Art. 9:501 nor Sec. 73(1) of the Indian Contract Act require a distinction between certain types of contractual duties such as primary or secondary obligations. What is more, the right to damages arises irrespectively of the exact type of non-performance; in other words, the question of whether the non-performance in question is constituted by delay or impossibility is relevant only with regard to other remedies such as termination or the right to withhold performance.[997]

The sole exception to this common pattern occurs in Sec. 55(3) of the Indian Contract Act, which (in conjunction with Sec. 55(1)) provides a somewhat extraordinary additional prerequisite of the right to damages for late performance: where time was agreed to be of the essence of the contract and the aggrieved party accepted a late tender of performance, it may claim damages for the delay

993 UPICC Art. 7.3.5(2); PECL Art. 8:102; Indian Contract Act Sec. 75 in conjunction with Sec. 39, 53, 54 and 55; and Indian Contract Act Sec. 56(3).

994 See, *e.g.*, Comment 2 to UPICC Art. 7.4.1 and Specific Relief Act Sec. 21.

995 See *supra* Ch. III(I)(C). The main difference between the two terms is that whereas under Indian law (as well as under English common law), "breach of contract" presupposes liability for damages, *i.e.*, there is no breach unless the aggrieved party is entitled to claim damages, "non-performance" under the Principles occurs whenever a party fails to perform (see, *e.g.*, Lando, *supra* note 120 at 360). For the sake of uniformity, this section, too, will apply the term "non-performance" as a reference to both of those terms.

996 See Comment B to PECL Art. 9:501 and *supra* (A)(2).

997 As noted above, the different types of breach of contract covered by Sec. 39, 53, 54 and 55 of the Indian Contract Act do not establish any additional requirements but only confirm the aggrieved party's right to damages pursuant to Sec. 73 and 75. The notice requirement under Sec. 55(3) of the Indian Contract Act marks the only exception to this structure.

only if it has given notice of its intention to do so at the time of acceptance. This exceptional requirement is unknown to the Principles.

3. Harm caused by non-performance

Second, all three regimes recognize that both pecuniary and non-pecuniary harm as well as any consequential losses caused by the non-performance are to be compensated by way of damages. Whereas pecuniary loss in this sense may consist of a decrease of a party's assets or an increase of its liabilities, consequential pecuniary loss comprises lost profits or, where the profits were not yet quantifiable, the loss of a chance or opportunity.[998] Subject to the respective remoteness and foreseeability tests,[999] all three instruments also allow for the awarding of damages for any future harm caused by the non-performance.[1000]

As for non-pecuniary harm, the Principles and Indian law account for a slight but notable difference: whereas the three regimes unanimously treat non-pecuniary harm such as pain, suffering or physical inconvenience as fully triggering a right to compensation, Indian courts award damages for vexation, distress or loss of enjoyment only in exceptional circumstances, namely where such mental suffering results from physical discomfort or inconvenience caused by the breach or where the contract is for the provision of enjoyment.[1001] While this restriction is based on the rules established by English courts, it is more strict than the proposed interpretation of the relevant provisions in the Principles.[1002]

Indian law and the Principles also unanimously require a causal link between the non-performance and the harm sustained by the aggrieved party, and all three regimes recognize that this link may be interrupted by an intervening event or third-party act.

4. Non-performance not excused

The Principles' general requirement that non-performance must not be excused is unknown to Sec. 73(1) of the Indian Contract Act. In principle, however, Indian

998 See Comment 2 to UPICC Art. 7.4.2 and Comment B to PECL Art. 9:502, and Bhadbhade, *supra* note 137 at 1547 *et seq.* English law allows for the recovery of damages, too (see Treitel, *supra* note 161 at 705).

999 See *infra* II and III.

1000 See UPICC Art. 7.3.1(1), PECL Art. 9:501(2)(b), and, *e.g.*, Bhadbhade, *supra* note 137 at 1500.

1001 See *cf.* Singh, *supra* note 218 at 430, and Bhadbhade, *supra* note 137 at 1540 *et seq.* For a description of this rule under English common law, see, *e.g.*, Treitel, *supra* note 161 at 731 *et seq.*, and Note 4(b) to PECL Art. 9:501.

1002 See Comment 5 to UPICC Art. 7.4.2 ("loss of certain amenities of life") and Comment E and Note 4 ("inconvenience following from (…) disappointment or vexation") to PECL Art. 9:501.

law recognizes all major instances in which non-performance is excused under the Principles: the *force majeure* defence;[1003] exemption clauses;[1004] rightful withholding of performance;[1005] and interference by the promisee with the performance in question.[1006]

First, frustration of the contract or impossibility and unlawfulness of performance – which broadly correspond to the situations underlying the *force majeure* defence under the Principles – render the contract automatically void and thus discharge the parties from their contractual obligations.[1007] In other words, performance is excused. The only exception to this general rule under Indian law is that if the promisor knew or could have reasonably known of a pre-existing impediment to its performance when entering into the contract, it is liable to pay damages if the promisee was unaware of these circumstances (Indian Contract Act Sec. 56(3)). (In fact, even the rule provided in Sec. 56(3) of the Indian Act is likely to be recognized under the Principles, too, because a party's violation of its duty of good faith and fair dealing (UPICC Art. 1.7; PECL Art. 1:201) also constitutes non-performance[1008] and thus gives rise to a right to damages in favour of the party that was unaware of the pre-existing impediment.)

Second, similar to the Principles, Indian law permits that the parties exclude the right to damages for breach[1009] by way of a contractual exemption clause.

Third, in India, too, the rightful withholding of performance of a reciprocal promise in accordance with Sec. 51 and 54 of the Indian Contract Act rules out a breach of contract for as long as the withholding party is entitled to exercise this right.[1010]

Finally, if a promisee wrongfully prevents another party's performance (Indian Contract Act. Sec. 53), fails to provide facilities that are necessary for the promisor's performance (Sec. 67) or unrightfully rejects a valid tender (Sec. 38), both Indian law and the Principles recognize that the non-performance is excused and the promisor exempt from liability to the extent that it is innocent.[1011]

1003 UPICC Art. 7.1.7; PECL Art. 8:108.
1004 UPICC Art. 7.1.6; PECL Art. 8:109.
1005 UPICC Art. 7.1.3; PECL Art. 9:201.
1006 UPICC Art. 7.1.2; PECL Art. 8:101(3).
1007 See *supra* Ch. III(VII)(B)(2) and Ch. VI(I)(B)(2)(b).
1008 See, *e.g.*, Comment 2 to UPICC Art. 7.3.2.
1009 See, *e.g.*, Bhadbhade, *supra* note 137 at 1468.
1010 See *supra* Ch. III(III)(B).
1011 See *supra* Ch. III(II)(B).

5. General measure of damages

The primary objective of UPICC Art. 7.4.2 and PECL Art. 9:502 as well as of Sec. 73(1) of the Indian Contract Act is to restore the aggrieved party's "expectation interest", *viz.* to put it in the position which it would have been in if the contract had been performed.[1012]

The remedy of damages is thus compensatory in nature, and neither of the three instruments permits the awarding of punitive damages for non-performance or breach of contract.[1013] Indian contract law, however, follows common-law tradition in allowing the courts to award nominal damages if the promisee did not sustain or is unable to prove any harm;[1014] the drafters of the Principles have consciously ruled out this alternative.[1015]

A slight divergence also occurs with regard to the measure of damages: whereas the Principles strictly stick to the expectation interest as the presumptive means of ascertaining of the amount of compensation,[1016] the Indian Contract Act – in synchrony with the rule under English law – allows for the computation of damages with reference to the aggrieved party's "reliance interest" alternatively to its expectation interest. However, this choice conferred to the aggrieved party under Indian law is generally limited where the recovery of the reliance interest would put it in a better position than a restoration of its expectation interest. The recovery of wasted expenditures is therefore impossible under all three instruments.[1017]

All three regimes provide that any ("compensating") gains that the aggrieved party has earned as a result of the other party's non-performance are to be set off against its loss.

Considering that Sec. 73 of the Indian Contract Act is considered to be "declaratory of the common law on damages",[1018] the observation that "the general principles governing the measurement of damages are quite similar in the com-

---

1012 For the currency in which damages shall be assessed, see *infra* IX.

1013 See, *e.g.*, Zimmermann, *supra* note 161 at 482.

1014 See, *e.g.*, Singh, *supra* note 218 at 425, for Indian law, and Treitel, *supra* note 159 at 686, for English law.

1015 See Comment 2 to UPICC Art. 7.4.3 and Comment A to PECL 9:501. See also *infra* II(A).

1016 The only instances in which a court might award damages solely for the reliance interest are where the occurrence of any harm is highly uncertain and the amount of damages thus speculative, or where the aggrieved party cannot prove its expectation interest. Such uncertainty may prompt the court to make use of its discretion to assess the amount of compensation (UPICC Art. 7.4.3(3)) and award damages only for the expenses that the aggrieved party had incurred in contemplation of the performance of the contract. See *cf. infra* II(A).

1017 See, *e.g.*, Bhadbhade, *supra* note 137 at 1496, and Note 5 to PECL Art. 9:502.

1018 See, *e.g.*, Bhadbhade, *id.* at 1469, and Singh, *supra* note 218 at 407, for references to observations made, *inter alia*, by the *Privy Council of India*.

mon-law and civil-law systems"[1019] to a certain extent also explains the wide-ranging substantive parallels between UPICC Art. 7.4.2, PECL Art. 9:502 and the law derived from Sec. 73(1) of the Indian Contract Act. In fact, this conclusion can even be extended to the three instruments' rules on the general requirements of this remedy, which – save with respect to a few minor issues such as the notice requirement established in Sec. 55(3) of the Indian Act or the possibility of awarding nominal damages or damages for loss of enjoyment – are broadly similar as well.

II. Certainty of harm

A. Principles

Under both sets of Principles, any recoverable loss is to be established with reasonable certainty, the requirement of "certainty of harm" being a necessary prerequisite for a claim of damages. Whereas the drafters of the UNIDROIT Principles have devoted a separate article – UPICC Art. 7.4.3 – to this requirement, the PECL contain a corresponding rule as part of their general provision on damages (Art. 9:501(2)(b)). However, in spite of this eye-catching structural difference, UPICC Art. 7.4.3 and PECL Art. 9:501(2)(b) are regarded as "corresponding provisions" that reflect "basically the same solutions" and therefore do not account for any substantive divergences.[1020]

Based on the assumption that the non-performing party in default should not be required to compensate a loss that may in fact not have occurred or may never occur, UPICC Art. 7.4.3(1) compels the aggrieved party to establish a reasonable degree of certainty as to both the occurrence of any harm as well as to its extent.[1021] Certainty as to the occurrence and the extent of harm is especially crucial with respect to damages for future losses that are to arise after the time of judicial or arbitral assessment of the damages, because the court needs to make a prognosis regarding both the likelihood of such harm as well as the appropriate amount of compensation. If the aggrieved party claims damages for the loss of a chance, UPICC Art. 7.4.3(2) provides that the amount shall be in proportion to the probability of the occurrence of the chance; in other words, the plain value of the particular opportunity (*e.g.*, the prize money which the purchaser of a race horse would have earned if the purchased horse had been delivered in time for and won

1019 See Perillo, *supra* note 130 at 308.

1020 See, *e.g.*, Bonell/Peleggi, *supra* note 116 at 316 and 317, and Bonell, *supra* note 19 at 342.

1021 See Comment 2 to UPICC Art. 7.4.3. See also Comment F to PECL Art. 9:501.

a particular race) is to be reduced by an appropriate amount that reflects the probability of the actual occurrence of the contemplated event (*e.g.*, the odds that the horse would have actually won the race).[1022]

Finally, UPICC Art. 7.4.3(3) establishes that "[w]here the amount of damages cannot be established with a sufficient degree of certainty, the assessment is at the discretion of the court." An important implication of this rule is that the courts may not award nominal damages; instead, an award for damages must be based on an equitable quantification of the harm sustained by the aggrieved party as a direct result of the non-performance.[1023] For instance, the discretion conferred by Art. 7.4.3(3) may prompt the courts to award damages for the so-called reliance interest if the promisee cannot prove its expectation interest.[1024]

B. Indian statutory law

Whereas Indian statutory law does make any express provision in this respect, Indian courts have adopted the position of English common law and required the aggrieved party to establish reasonable certainty as to the amount of damages.[1025] What is more, it has been stated that "[t]he mere fact that it is somewhat difficult to assess the damages, with certainty or precision, does not disentitle the plaintiff to compensation for the loss suffered."[1026] Subject to the certainty requirement, damages may therefore also be awarded for prospective harm or for the loss of a chance,[1027] and the courts may make an estimate of the amount of damages if certainty can be established only with regard to the occurrence but not the extent of the future harm.[1028]

1022 See Comment 1 to UPICC Art. 7.4.3. In stating that in calculating, for instance, the damages payable for the wrongful dismissal of an employee, "due allowance (is to be) made for her prospects of finding another job", Ill. 8 to PECL Art. 9:501 signifies that the European Principles also acknowledge the rule that damages for the loss of a chance are to be quantified in proportion to the probability of its occurrence.

1023 See Comment 2 to UPICC Art. 7.4.3.

1024 See, *e.g.*, Perillo, *supra* note 130 at 309.

1025 See, *e.g.*, Bhadbhade, *supra* note 137 at 1549, for a reference to Indian case law. For the corresponding rule under English common law, see, *e.g.*, Treitel, *supra* note 159 at 694, and Note 6 to PECL Art. 9:503.

1026 See Bhadbhade, *id.* at 1501.

1027 See, *e.g.*, *id.* at 1548, and Treitel, *supra* note 159 at 705, both of which make reference to the English case of *Chaplin v. Hicks* ((1911) 2 K.B. 786), in which a girl recovered damages for losing the chance to appear in the final selection of a beauty contest as a result of the organizer's negligence.

1028 See Bhadbhade, *id.* at 1549, citing the Indian case of *Frederick Thomas Kingsley v. Secretary of State for India* (AIR 1923 Cal 49 (1923)).

In cases where, despite a breach of contract committed by the promisor, the promisee is unable to prove that it has sustained any harm, Indian courts have recognized the possibility of awarding nominal damages for the purpose of establishing that there has been a breach of contract.[1029]

C. Comparative analysis

Except for their positions on the awarding of nominal damages, Indian contract law and Principles fully concur with regard to the rules set out in UPICC Art. 7.4.3.

First, all three regimes require the aggrieved party to establish reasonable certainty as to the occurrence and the extent of the harm for which it claims damages.

Second, it can be assumed that both the PECL and Indian law concur with the rule set out in UPICC Art. 7.4.3(2), according to which the amount of compensation for the loss of a chance is to be quantified in proportion to the probability that the chance would have actually materialized. In relation to the PECL, this assumption is based on the wording of Illustration 8 to PECL Art. 9:501[1030] and on the fact that Art. 9:501(2)(b) and UPICC Art. 7.4.3 are commonly classified as "corresponding provisions" that reflect "basically the same solutions".[1031] Regarding Indian contract law, where Sec. 73 of the Indian Contract Act in considered to be "declaratory of the common law on damages",[1032] the applicability of the rule is strongly purported by the position under English common law, under which "[t]he quantification of damages in such cases (…) depends on the value of the expected benefit and the chance that the plaintiff had of actually getting it."[1033]

Finally, both sets of Principles and Indian law acknowledge that, where the aggrieved party is unable to establish reasonable certainty as to its harm, the assessment of the amount of damages is left to the courts' discretion.[1034] In this context, however, there is one divergence between the Principles and Indian statutory contract law: whereas Indian courts may award nominal damages if the aggrieved

1029 See *cf.* Singh, *supra* note 218 at 425. For the availability of nominal damages, *i.e.*, a nominal amount of compensation, under English common law, see, *e.g.*, Treitel, *supra* note 159 at 686.

1030 See *supra* note 1022.

1031 See, *e.g.*, Bonell/Peleggi, *supra* note 116 at 316 and 317.

1032 See, *e.g.*, Bhadbhade, *supra* note 137 at 1469, and Singh, *supra* note 218 at 407, for references to observations made, *inter alia*, by the *Privy Council of India*.

1033 See Treitel, *supra* note 159 at 705.

1034 See UPICC Art. 7.4.3(3) and, *e.g.*, Bhadbhade, *supra* note 137 at 1558, respectively.

party is unable to prove the occurrence of any harm,[1035] this option is unavailable under the Principles.[1036]

III. Foreseeability of harm

A. Principles

UPICC Art. 7.4.4 and PECL Art. 9:503 unanimously provide that damages can be recovered only for harm that the non-performing party foresaw or could reasonably have foreseen as a likely result of its non-performance at the time of conclusion of the contract. A party's liability is thus limited to the harm that it ought to have anticipated as a likely consequence of its non-performance and for the occurrence of which it could have taken precautions such as insurance or an appropriate adjustment of the price.

According to the drafters of the UNIDROIT Principles, it is sufficient if the non-performing party (or its servants or agents[1037]) foresaw or ought to have foreseen the *nature* of the harm; foreseeability of the extent of the same is generally irrelevant.[1038] The test for determining foreseeability is whether, at the time of conclusion of the contract, a normally diligent person would or could reasonably have foreseen the particular harm in the ordinary course of things and under the particular circumstances of the contract. For instance, where A was unaware of the fact that its purchaser (B) would lose an exceptionally valuable contract with its own customer (C) as a result of A's late delivery of the goods, A is not liable for the profits that B would have made from the resale to C.[1039]

However, the two sets of Principles account for a substantial divergence in that the European Principles do not impose the foreseeability requirement if the non-performance was intentional or grossly negligent (PECL Art. 9:503). This limitation, under which deliberate, grossly negligent or, as per PECL Art. 1:301(3), reckless[1040] non-performance entitles the promisee to recover even unforeseen

1035 See, *e.g.*, Singh, *supra* note 218 at 425, and Bhadbhade, *id.* at 1553.

1036 See Comment 2 to UPICC Art. 7.4.3 and Comment A to PECL 9:501.

1037 See Comment to UPICC Art. 7.4.4.

1038 See *id.* This statement implies that the drafters of the UPICC intended to stress that the loss of an exceptionally valuable contract (for which liability is excluded in the example given in Ill. 1 to UPICC Art. 7.4.4) does not increase the aggrieved party's lost profits but constitutes harm of a separate nature.

1039 See *id.* and Ill. 1 to UPICC Art. 7.4.4, and Ill. 1 to PECL Art. 9:503.

1040 Unfortunately, the PECL lack a precise differentiation of the terms "grossly negligent" and "reckless".

losses, does not appear in the UPICC.[1041] Instead, the UPICC's drafters have merely called for a narrow interpretation of the principle of foreseeability and granted the courts flexibility and "a wide measure of discretion" in applying it.[1042]

B. Indian statutory law

In India, in accordance with English common law,[1043] the issue of limiting a party's liability for breach of contract to harm which it ought to have contemplated when it entered into the contract is treated as a question of "remoteness of damage". According to Sec. 73(1) of the Indian Contract Act, the recoverable harm is limited to "that which naturally arose in the usual course of things from [the] breach, or which the parties knew, when they made the contract, to be likely to result from the breach of it." Sec. 73(1) marks a statutory fixation of the principles established in the English case of *Hadley v. Baxendale*.[1044] The remoteness test is intended to ensure "fairness, reasonableness, avoidance of unduly harsh results, and the need for economic efficiency and avoidance of waste" by encouraging the promisee to disclose any unusual circumstances to enable the promisor to take appropriate precautions such as insurance against its liability for a possible breach.[1045]

In *Hadley v. Baxendale*[1046] it was held that "[t]he damages (...) should be such as may fairly and reasonably be considered *either* as arising naturally, *i.e.*, according to the usual course of things, from such breach of contract itself, *or* such as may reasonably be supposed to have been in the contemplation of both parties at the time they made the contract as the probable result of the breach."[1047] If the aggrieved party fails to establish either one of these two standards, or "branches",

1041 See Comment B and Ill. 3 to PECL Art. 9:503. Michael Joachim Bonell has characterized this divergence as being of "technical nature." See, *inter alia*, Bonell, *supra* note 19 at 345 and *supra* note 29 at 237.

1042 See Comment to UPICC Art. 7.4.4.

1043 See generally Treitel, *supra* note 159 at 713 *et seq.*

1044 See, *e.g.*, Bangia, *supra* note182 at 289, and *Hadley v. Baxendale*, (1854) 9 ExCh. 341, respectively.

1045 See Bhadbhade, *supra* note 137 at 1519.

1046 Treitel (*supra* note 159 at 713) has provided the following summary of the facts underlying the case:

> "A shaft in the plaintiffs' mill broke and had to be sent to the makers (...) to serve as a pattern for the production of a new one. The defendants agreed to carry the shaft (...) but in breach of contract delayed its delivery so that there was a stoppage of several days at the mill. The plaintiffs claimed damages (...) in respect of their loss of profits during this period."

1047 *Hadley v. Baxendale*, (1854) 9 ExCh. 341 at 354.

the harm is considered as being too remote for the party in breach to be liable to compensate it.[1048] In *Victoria Laundry (Windsor Ltd.) v. Newman Industries Ltd.*[1049] – the facts of which reappear in Illustration (i) to Sec. 73 of the Indian Contract Act – these two standards were interpreted as establishing that the harm must be "reasonably foreseeable as liable to result from the breach".[1050] (The House of Lords later emphasized in *The Heron II*[1051] that the interpretation applied in the aforementioned case of *Victoria Laundry* should not be understood as meaning that the remoteness test under contract law is identical to the "reasonable foreseeability" requirement applicable to torts. Instead, the court held that the parties' contemplation in contract law requires a comparably higher degree of probability.[1052]) Bearing to the nature of these types of harm, the remoteness test is especially relevant with regard to lost profits, pre-contractual expenditures and non-pecuniary harm.[1053]

The first branch of the rule provided in *Hadley v. Baxendale*, which is that liability for damages for breach of contract covers all harm that may reasonably be considered to arise naturally, *i.e.*, in the usual course of things, from the breach,[1054] therefore looks at the imputed knowledge of the parties. In India, it has

---

1048 Treitel's summary (*supra* note 159 at 713) of the decision in *Hadley v. Baxendale* provides an illustration of the two branches of the principle provided in this case:

> "Here the stoppage was not the 'natural' consequence of the delay: it could not have been foreseen by a carrier that delay in delivering the shaft would keep the mill idle. (...) Nor could the stoppage, though it was no doubt anticipated by the plaintiffs, have been contemplated by both parties at the time of contracting as the probable result of breach. (...) 'The only circumstances here communicated by the plaintiffs to the defendants at the time the contract was made were that the article to be carried was the broken shaft of a mill, and that the plaintiffs were the millers of that mill.' The defendants were not told that any delay by them would keep the mill idle."

1049 (1949) 2 K.B. 528. Treitel (*id.* at 714) has summarized the facts and the decision in this case as follows:

> "The defendants sold a boiler to the plaintiffs, knowing that the plaintiffs wanted it for immediate use in their laundry business. The boiler was delivered some five months after the agreed date and as a result the plaintiffs suffered loss of profits. (...) Here the defendants knew that the plaintiffs wanted the boiler for immediate use in their business: they were thus liable for loss of profits that would ordinarily result from such use. But they were not liable for loss of exceptionally lucrative contracts with the Ministry of Supply, which the plaintiffs would have been able to make if they had received the boiler in time: they knew nothing of these contracts and could not reasonably have foreseen such loss."

1050 *Victoria Laundry (Windsor Ltd.) v. Newman Industries Ltd.*, (1949) 2 K.B. 528 at 539.

1051 *Koufos v. C. Czarnikow Ltd.*, (1969) A.C. 350.

1052 See *cf.* Treitel, *supra* note 159 at 715, for a reference to the decision in *Koufos v. C. Czarnikow Ltd.*

1053 See *cf.* Bhadbhade, *supra* note 218 at 1534 *et seq.*

1054 See Bangia, *supra* note 182 at 291 *et seq.*, for references to relevant Indian and English case law.

been held that the question is whether a "reasonable man" in the promisor's position ought to have foreseen the harm as arising in the usual course of things when entering into the contract.[1055] This means that a party performing late generally ought to foresee a depreciation in market value of the goods to be delivered,[1056] but also that "the loss of profits from a contract of which the defendant had no notice is clearly too remote".[1057] For instance, where a "seller of land knew that the purchaser was a dealer in real estate, but not that he required the land for developing it himself, the seller would be liable on breach only for the profits which the purchaser would have made on resale, and not the loss of profits on development by the purchaser."[1058]

The second branch of the remoteness test established in *Hadley v. Baxendale* requires that the harm in question was within the parties' reasonable contemplation because the promisee had communicated the unusual circumstances leading to the loss or damage (which did not arise "in the usual course of things" from the breach and are therefore not subject to the first branch of the rule) to the promisor before or at the time of the conclusion of the contract.[1059] If the party in breach was already aware of the relevant circumstances, their communication is not necessary.[1060] With a view on sales contracts, the second branch hence implies that "lost profits which were to accrue upon resale cannot be recovered unless it is communicated to the other party that the goods are for resale upon a special contract."[1061] Similarly, "where the contract states that the purchaser wants the article (...) in order to help him carry out another contract, the contractor, if he commits a breach in the delivery of the article, is liable for the loss sustained by the purchaser if he becomes unable to carry out that other contract."[1062]

C. Comparative analysis

Unsurprisingly, the concepts of "foreseeability" and "remoteness" as applicable under the Principles and Indian contract law are practically identical. The limita-

1055 See, *e.g.*, Singh, *supra* note 218 at 411, and Bhadbhade, *supra* note 137 at 1520 and 1523.

1056 See, *e.g.*, Bangia, *supra* note 182 at 292, and Bhadbhade, *id.* at 1522.

1057 See Bhadbhade, *id.* at 1525. See also Ill. (j), (k) and (l) to Indian Contract Act Sec. 73.

1058 See Bhadbhade, *id.* at 1535.

1059 See, *e.g.*, Bangia, *supra* note 182 at 290, and also at 295 *et seq.* for references to relevant Indian and English case law.

1060 See, *e.g.*, Singh, *supra* note 218 at 403, making reference to the English case of *Simpson v. London & North Western Railway Co.* ((1876) 1 Q.B.D. 274), and Bhadbhade, *supra* note 137 at 1523.

1061 See Singh, *id.* at 416.

1062 See Ill. (k) to Indian Contract Act Sec. 73 and Saharay, *supra* note 929 at 624.

tion of liability to foreseeable or contemplated losses, which was established in England by the decision in *Hadley v. Baxendale*, is equally known to a number of civil law systems.[1063]

"Foreseeability" as per UPICC Art. 7.4.4 and PECL Art. 9:503 requires that the promisor foresaw or could reasonably have foreseen the harm as a likely result of its non-performance at the time when the contract was entered into. The standard underlying this test is what a normally diligent person ought to have anticipated in the ordinary course of things under the particular circumstances of the contract.

The concept of "remoteness of damage" as codified in Sec. 73(1) of the Indian Contract Act denotes a limitation of liability to "proximate" harm which naturally arose in the usual course of things from the breach or which the parties reasonably contemplated at the time of conclusion of the contract to result from the breach. Just as under the Principles, the standard here is what was or ought to have been contemplated by a reasonable person in the ordinary course of things under the particular circumstances. In fact, both the UPICC and the Indian Contract Act make express reference to the facts underlying the English case of *Victoria Laundry (Windsor Ltd.) v. Newman Industries Ltd.*[1064] for the purpose of illustrating the rule that, whereas a seller is generally liable for a loss of profit caused by its late delivery of a machine that was intended for immediate use, it could not reasonably have anticipated that the purchaser would also lose a specially valuable government contract if it was unaware of the same.[1065]

As a general rule, the Principles only require that the non-performing party could have foreseen the *nature* of the harm, meaning that it is liable regardless of whether it also anticipated the extent of the aggrieved party's loss.[1066] While English courts appear to have taken a less definite stance on this issue, it has been held with regard to lost profits that, in accordance with the decision in *Victoria Laundry*, contemplation of the exact *quantum* of the loss is irrelevant unless the *quantum* itself arose from unforeseeable circumstances.[1067]

The European Principles' rule that the foreseeability test does not apply to intentional or grossly negligent non-performance is unknown to both English

---

1063 See, *e.g.*, Note 1 to PECL Art. 9:503 and Zimmermann, *supra* note 161 at 482.

1064 (1949) 2 K.B. 528. See *supra* note 1049.

1065 See Ill. 1 to UPICC Art. 7.4.4 and Ill. (i) to Indian Contract Act Sec. 73.

1066 See Comment to UPICC Art. 7.4.4. As mentioned above, this statement made in the Comment to UPICC Art. 7.4.4 implies that the drafters of the UPICC intended to provide that the loss of an exceptionally valuable contract (for which liability is excluded in Ill. 1 to UPICC Art. 7.4.4) does not increase of the extent of the aggrieved party's lost profits but constitutes harm of a separate nature.

1067 See, *e.g.*, Treitel, *supra* note 159 at 720 *et seq.*, for further references.

common law and Sec. 73(1) of the Indian Contract Act.[1068] The reason for this seemingly random deviation of the PECL from both common-law tradition and the UPICC (as well as the CISG[1069]) might be that this rule, which appears to be inspired by French law,[1070] is a result of the Lando Commission's endeavour to strike a balance between the common-law concept of no-fault, or strict, contractual liability and the fault requirement imposed by most civil-law systems.

IV. Proof of harm in case of replacement transaction and by current price

A. Principles

In practically identical terms, the two sets of Principles provide two means of establishing and quantifying the loss in an abstract and therefore easier way. First, UPICC Art. 7.4.5 and PECL Art. 9:506 provide that, if the aggrieved party has terminated the contract and concluded a replacement transaction, it may recover the difference between the contract price and the price of the substitute transaction. Second, if the promisee has not carried out a replacement transaction but there was a "current price" of the goods or service, it may recover the difference between the contract price and the price current at the time of termination (UPICC Art. 7.4.6; PECL Art. 9:507).

1. Proof of harm in case of replacement transaction

Provided the contract was terminated and a substitute transaction carried out within a reasonable time and in a reasonable manner, the aggrieved party may recover – as a minimum – the difference between the contract price and the price for the replacement transaction without having to provide further proof of its loss (UPICC Art. 7.4.5 and PECL Art. 9:506). In addition to this presumptive loss, it may, subject to the general provisions on damages and the specific rules set out in UPICC Art. 7.4.3 and PECL Art. 9:501(2)(b), claim damages for any further harm such as expenses incurred for arranging the substitute transaction or a loss of profit caused by the delay in performance.[1071]

1068 See, *e.g.*, Note 5 to PECL Art. 9:503.
1069 See CISG Art. 74.
1070 See Zimmermann, *supra* note 161 at 483.
1071 See Comment 2 to UPICC Art. 7.4.5 and Comment A to PECL Art. 9:506.

A replacement transaction may be motivated by the aggrieved party's voluntary decision to obtain performance from another source. Alternatively, it may be compulsory as per a usage,[1072] as a result of the promisee's duty to mitigate the harm,[1073] or because the option of reasonably obtaining performance by way of a cover transaction excludes a claim of specific performance.[1074]

UPICC Art. 7.4.5 and PECL Art. 9:506 require that a replacement transaction has actually been carried out.[1075] According to the drafters' comments to the UNIDROIT Principles, this is not the case if the aggrieved party has itself performed the respective obligation, *e.g.*, if it has carried out repairs that were to be performed by the other party.

As for the additional harm for which damages may be claimed in accordance with the general rules set out in the Principles' relevant sections on damages, the requirement that the cover transaction shall be carried out in a "reasonable manner" sets a limit to the expenses that the aggrieved party may recover in this respect. In other words, expenses incurred in connection with the replacement contract cannot be recovered if they are unreasonably high or unnecessary,[1076] or if the transaction is so different in value or in kind that it cannot be considered a substitute for the unperformed contract.[1077]

In accordance with UPICC Art. 7.4.2(1) and PECL Art. 9:502, any compensating gains which the aggrieved party has made in connection with or as a result of the substitute transaction are to be deducted from the amount of damages, *viz.* from the difference between the contract price and the substitute contract price.[1078] What is more, the aggrieved party cannot recover the full difference between the contract price and the price of the cover transaction if it was partly responsible for the non-performance or if the same was otherwise excused.[1079]

1072 See Comment 1 to UPICC Art. 7.4.5 and also UPICC Art. 1.9 and PECL Art. 1:105.

1073 See Comment 1 to UPICC Art. 7.4.5 and *infra* VI(A).

1074 See UPICC Art. 7.2.2(c) and PECL Art. 9:101(2)(a) and Art. 9:102(2)(d). See also *supra* Ch. V(I)(A)(2)(b) and Ch. V(II)(A)(3)(c).

1075 See Comment 1 to UPICC Art. 7.4.5 and Comment A to PECL Art. 9:506.

1076 See Comment A and Ill. 1 to PECL Art. 9:506, according to which the costs incurred for changing the address on leaflets and posters because the venue for a particular event had become unavailable and needed to be replaced by another one are reasonable expenses.

1077 See Comment B and Ill. 2 to PECL Art. 9:506, according to which unavailability of a rental car only entitles the customer to rent the nearest available equivalent of the original rental car in size and value.

1078 See, *e.g.*, Comment C to PECL Art. 9:502.

1079 Though this rule is not stated in any of the drafters' comments to either set of Principles, it appears to be a self-evident result of the rules found in UPICC Art. 7.1.1 and 7.4.7 as well as PECL Art. 9:501(1), 8:101(3) and 9:504. See also Düchs, *supra* note 161 at 194.

2. Proof of harm by current price

If the aggrieved party decides not to obtain performance from an alternative source but there is a current price for the undelivered goods or the unperformed services, UPICC Art. 7.4.6 and PECL Art. 9:507 provide a presumption that its loss consists of the difference between the contract price and the price of a hypothetical cover transaction at the time when the contract was terminated. Unlike the European Principles, UPICC Art. 7.4.6(2) provides a statutory definition of the relevant standard: "current price is the price generally charged for goods delivered or services rendered in comparable circumstances at the place where the contract should have been performed or, if there is no current price at that place, the current price at such other place that appears reasonable to take as a reference." Usually, the current price in this sense corresponds to the market price.[1080]

As in cases where the aggrieved party has concluded a replacement transaction, the presumptive loss only constitutes the minimum *quantum* of the recoverable loss, and it may also claim damages for any additional harm caused by the non-performance or the termination of the contract. Nevertheless, damages for both the presumptive loss and any further harm are subject to the Principles' general provisions on this remedy, with the result that even the minimum amount of damages may be reduced if the non-performance was partly excused or if the aggrieved party was partly responsible for the same.

B. Indian statutory law

With regard to measuring the "expectation interest" in cases of breach of sale of goods contracts, Indian courts have adopted the relevant rule under English law, according to which the amount of damages is *prima facie* determined by the difference between the contract price and the market price of the goods at the time of the breach.[1081] The rule applies equally to non-delivery by the seller and to the purchaser's failure or refusal to accept the goods.[1082] (In disputes involving other

1080 See Comment 2 to UPICC Art. 7.4.6 and Ill. 2 to PECL Art. 9:507.

1081 See, *e.g.*, Ill. (a) and (o) to Indian Contract Act Sec. 73. See *cf.* Bangia, *supra* note 182 at 299, and Saharay, *supra* note 929 at 615, for further references.

1082 See Bangia, *id.*, for the following illustration of this rule:

> "For instance, A agrees to supply B a watch on 1st January for Rs. 1,000. If A fails to supply the watch and the market price of the watch on that date is Rs. 1,200, B will be entitled to recover from A Rs. 200 as damages. The reason is that the loss suffered by the buyer is Rs. 200 because due to rise in the market price of the watch, he will have to pay that much extra if he purchases the watch from the market. Similarly, if the buyer (B) refuses to take the watch on the due date, the seller will also be entitled to recover the difference between

types of contracts than sale of goods contracts, courts in both England and India sometimes award damages for the expectation interest on a "cost of cure" basis as opposed to the aforementioned market price or "difference in value" basis. For example, damages for breach of building contracts have been measured with reference to the amount of the cost for undoing the defective work or completing the building.[1083])

The general standard hence being the price of a hypothetical replacement transaction, it is not necessary that the goods were actually resold or repurchased.[1084]

If the aggrieved party indeed carries out a cover transaction, it is generally required to resell or repurchase the goods at the market rate in order to recover the full difference in price.[1085] However, commentators also cite single cases where Indian courts have awarded damages for the difference between the contract price and a "slightly higher price" a buyer has paid for "the nearest substitute of the goods of a slightly superior quality".[1086] Conversely, if a seller managed to resell the goods at a price that was higher than the market rate, its loss is to be measured with reference to the actual resale price as it would otherwise make a gain from the breach.[1087]

The term "market price" denotes the price at which the purchaser can obtain equivalent goods of equal quality at the time when and the place where they were to be delivered.[1088] If a market price is unavailable, the respective price prevailing at the nearest available market is to be taken into consideration.[1089] The burden of proof for showing the market price lies with the aggrieved party.[1090]

With a view on whether the purchaser can recover any further loss it has sustained as a result of the non-delivery of the goods, it has been observed that "[h] e is entitled to deal with the goods 'in any reasonable way' *e.g.* by adopting them to suit another customer, and his damages will then include the cost of adoption and also of the loss of profit on the first sale."[1091]

---

the contract price and the market price on 1st January. For instance, the market price of the watch on that date is R. 800. A's loss is Rs. 200 in respect of the transaction, because from another customer A can get only Rs. 800 whereas B had promised to pay Rs. 1,000 for the same. A can recover Rs. 200 from B."

1083 See, *e.g.*, Singh, *supra* note 218 at 412 *et seq.*, and generally Treitel, *supra* note 159 at 697 *et seq.*

1084 See, *e.g.*, Ill. (a) to Indian Contract Act Sec. 73 and Singh, *id.* at 415 *et seq.*

1085 See, *e.g.*, Ill. (k) to Indian Contract Act Sec. 73 and Singh, *id.* at 416, for further references.

1086 See, *e.g.*, Saharay, *supra* note 929 at 618, for further references.

1087 See, *e.g.*, Singh, *supra* note 218 at 419, with reference to the English case of *Wertheim v. Chicoutimi Pulp Co.* ((1911) A.C. 301).

1088 See Bhadbhade, *supra* note 137 at 1552, for further references. See also Ill. (a) and (o) to Indian Contract Act Sec. 73 and Bangia, *supra* note 182 at 299.

1089 See, *e.g.*, Saharay, *supra* note 929 at 615, and Bhadbhade, *supra* note 218 at 1556.

1090 See, *e.g.*, Bhadbhade, *id.* at 1551.

1091 See Saharay, *supra* note 929 at 618, for references to Indian case law.

C. Comparative analysis

Whereas the two sets of Principles expressly provide two presumptive means of measuring the harm sustained by the aggrieved party, namely the difference between the contract price and the cover price or the difference between the contract price and the current price, Indian contract law generally recognizes only the latter measure. What is more, the applicability of the market price rule in India is limited to sale of goods contracts. With regard to services contracts, the Principles hence provide for more uniform and more foreseeable results.

To the extent that it is applicable, however, the Indian market price rule in principle corresponds to what the UNIDROIT Principles denote as "measure of damages by current price". Where the goods contracted for have a market price, the aggrieved party may invoke the presumption that its recoverable loss is the difference between the contract price and the market rate.[1092] In the absence of a market price for the goods (or services) in the place of performance, regard is to be had to the rate at the nearest possible place.[1093]

However, the amount of compensation may nonetheless vary depending on which of the three regimes considered is being applied: whereas the relevant current price under the PECL and UPICC is the market rate prevailing at the time of termination of the contract,[1094] Indian contract law looks at the market price at the time when the goods were to be delivered.[1095]

As for the option of measuring the loss by way of the difference between the agreed price and the price of a (actually concluded) replacement transaction,[1096] neither Indian nor English courts appear to have specifically recognized a rule of law to this extent.[1097] Nevertheless, there have been single cases in England and India where, in consideration of the fact that the aggrieved party had carried out a cover transaction, damages were awarded in excess of the difference between the contract price and the market price.[1098]

In all, the Principles' provisions on the two presumptive means of ascertaining the aggrieved party's loss – both of which certainly reflect commercial practice – appear to offer solutions that are superior to those under than Indian law. First, there is no obvious reason why the market price rule should not also apply to services that have a market value. Moreover, the option of concluding a cover transac-

1092 See UPICC Art. 7.4.6, PECL Art. 9:507, and Ill. (a) to Indian Contract Act Sec. 73.
1093 See, *e.g.*, UPICC Art. 7.4.6(2) and Bhadbhade, *supra* note 218 at 1556.
1094 See, *e.g.*, UPICC Art. 7.4.6(2).
1095 See, *e.g.*, Ill. (a) and (o) to Indian Contract Act Sec. 73.
1096 UPICC Art. 7.4.5; PECL Art. 9:506.
1097 See, *e.g.*, Notes to PECL Art. 9:506.
1098 See *cf. supra* B.

tion and recovering the difference between the contract price and the actual cover price usually entails a higher level of (consumer) protection of the promisee; in fact, it even provides an incentive for the avoidance of economic waste by encouraging sellers or service providers to conclude substitute transactions even at (reasonable) prices below the market rate.

V. Harm due in part to aggrieved party

A. Principles

Both UPICC Art. 7.4.7 and – although in simpler terms – PECL Art. 9:504 provide that the amount of damages for a contractual non-performance shall be reduced to the extent that the aggrieved party's conduct or an event for which it bears the risk contributed to the occurrence or caused an increase of its harm. This rule stems from the general principle established in UPICC Art. 7.1.2 and PECL Art. 8:101(3), according to which a party may not resort to any remedies insofar as the non-performance was caused by its own conduct.[1099] Accordingly, UPICC Art. 7.4.7 and PECL Art. 9:504 address situations where aggrieved party's conduct (partly) caused the *initial* harm. UPICC Art. 7.4.8 and PECL Art. 9:505, on the other hand, deal with the promisee's *subsequent* failure to mitigate the harm initially caused by the non-performance.

The aggrieved party's partial responsibility for the harm may be due either to its contribution to the non-performance itself or to an "exacerbation of the loss-producing effects" of the same by its conduct. This may take the form of an act (*e.g.*, giving an incorrect address to a carrier), an omission (*e.g.*, failure to provide information), or an event for which it had assumed the risk (*e.g.*, contributory conduct of its servants or agents).[1100]

As for the apportionment of each party's responsibility for the harm, UPICC Art. 7.4.7 leaves a high degree of judicial discretion and simply prompts the courts to look at the "seriousness" of the relevant contributions as a primary guideline. If the promisee is fully responsible for the non-performance, its right to damages is excluded altogether.[1101]

1099 See *supra* Ch. III(II)(A).

1100 See Comment 2 to UPICC Art. 7.4.7 and Comments A, B and C to PECL Art. 9:504. Despite its somewhat simpler phrasing and the comparably less detailed guidance given in the accompanying comments, PECL Art. 9:504 is considered as being "corresponding" to and as reflecting "basically the same solutions" as UPICC Art. 7.4.7. See, *e.g.*, Bonell/Peleggi, *supra* note 116 at 316 and 317.

1101 See Comment 3 to UPICC Art. 7.4.7.

B. Indian statutory law

Indian courts have fully recognized the rule of English law under which the defence of "contributory negligence" is inapplicable to claims of damages for breach of contract unless the breach also constituted a tort.[1102]

In principle, the doctrine of contributory negligence is relevant only under tort law; it relates to situations where the claimant's own conduct has caused the loss or contributed its cause or increase. Accordingly, the English *Law Reform (Contributory Negligence) Act 1945* provides that where the harm sustained by the claimant was caused in part by its own "fault" and partly by the "fault" of another person, its claim shall not be defeated but the amount of damages is to be reduced in proportion to the degree of its own responsibility.[1103] Though it generally applies to torts only, courts in both England and India have held that the doctrine is not excluded merely because the parties had entered into a contractual relationship. Instead, it has been applied where a party breaches a contractual duty of reasonable care in a manner that would have been independently actionable under tort law.[1104]

For instance, a breach of the duty of care that professionals such as architects or lawyers owe to their clients – or similar contractual duties existing between carriers and passengers, employers and employees, bailors and bailees, or occupiers of premises and visitors – are generally regarded as giving rise to liability both under contract law and in tort.[1105] As a result, the promisor may invoke the contributory negligence defence and the promisee's claim for damages is to be reduced proportionately. Conversely, where a party commits a breach of a strict contractual duty without negligence and its conduct does not also constitute a tort, it is generally fully liable for the breach regardless of whether and to what extent the harm sustained by the promisee was in part due to its own careless behaviour.[1106]

C. Comparative analysis

Aside from their far-reaching similarities in the area of damages for breach of contract, the Principles and Indian contract law account for a significant di-

1102 See, *e.g.*, Singh, *supra* note 218 at 451; Bhadbhade, *supra* note 137 at 1466 and 1514; and generally Treitel, *supra* note 159 at 728 *et seq.*

1103 The Law Reform (Contributory Negligence) Act 1945 Sec. 1(1).

1104 See, *e.g.*, Bhadbhade, *supra* note 137 at 1514 *et seq.*, for references to English and Indian case law.

1105 See *cf.* Treitel, *supra* note 159 at 729.

1106 See *cf. id.* at 730.

vergence in their treatment of a promisee's partial responsibility for the harm brought about by a contractual non-performance: whereas UPICC Art. 7.4.7 and PECL Art. 9:504 fully acknowledge that a party's partial contribution to the non-performance or its loss-producing effects[1107] results in a reduction of the recoverable amount of damages, Indian courts have strictly followed English common law and generally ruled out the applicability of the contributory negligence defence in contract law. As a consequence, Indian law normally entitles the promisee to damages for the entire loss caused by the breach even if it was partly responsible for its occurrence or increase.[1108] However, where the careless conduct underlying the breach also constitutes a tort, the promisor may exceptionally invoke the doctrine of contributory negligence with the result that – just as under the general rule provided by the Principles – the promisee's careless contribution is taken into account for a proportionate reduction of the recoverable amount of damages.

VI. Mitigation of harm

A. Principles

Under the UNIDROIT and European Principles, the non-performing party's liability is excluded to the extent that the aggrieved party could have taken reasonable steps to mitigate the harm caused by the non-performance (UPICC Art. 7.4.8(1); PECL Art. 9:505(1)). As opposed to UPICC Art. 7.4.7 and PECL Art. 9:504, which deal with situations where the promisee is partly responsible for the occurrence of the non-performance or for its initial loss-producing effects,[1109] the present articles deal with the duty to take measures to curb or reduce the harm *after* the occurrence of a non-performance. UPICC Art. 7.4.8(2) and PECL Art. 9:505(2) provide the ancillary rule that the aggrieved party may recover any reasonable expenses it has incurred in attempting to comply with its duty to mitigate the harm.

Evidently, the promisee need not attempt to mitigate the harm immediately and at any cost. Instead, it is only obliged to take measures that are not unreasonably time-consuming or costly. Carrying out a replacement transaction in accordance with UPICC Art. 7.4.5 and PECL Art. 9:506 often marks a reasonable step to limit the loss. For instance, where a seller commits an anticipatory

1107 For the consequences of the aggrieved party's (partial) responsibility for a subsequent increase of its loss as a result of its failure to comply with its duty mitigate the same, see *infra* VI.

1108 See Zimmermann, *supra* note 161 at 483. See also Note 1(a) to PECL Art. 9:504 and 9:505.

1109 See *supra* V(A).

non-performance by refusing to deliver and the market price is likely to have risen by the time when the purchaser actually requires the goods, the latter is bound to buy them from another source as soon as reasonably possible.[1110] Similarly, where an unfinished building is exposed to bad weather and its condition would thus deteriorate if the owner failed to take interim protective measures, it is obliged to do so.[1111] Conversely, if a particular means of mitigating the harm would damage the promisee's commercial reputation, *e.g.*, because it would need to request its own customer to buy the defective goods without a price reduction, it is probably unreasonable.[1112]

Any expenses incurred for the purpose of reducing the harm are recoverable on top of the amount of compensation owed for the total loss, provided such expenses were themselves reasonable. Accordingly, if a reasonable attempt to minimize the loss in fact leads to an increase of the harm, the respective expenses are nevertheless recoverable so long as they were reasonable. This may be the case where a purchaser, upon the seller's refusal to deliver and in reasonable anticipation of a price hike, has carried out a cover transaction at a price that turns out to be way above the current price at the agreed time of delivery.[1113] However, if the promisee has taken measures in excess of what could reasonably have been expected to do to mitigate the harm, it cannot recover its related expenses.[1114]

B. Indian statutory law

Indian contract law, too, contains a statutory reference to the duty to mitigate damages. The Explanation accompanying Sec. 73 of the Indian Contract Act states that, "[i]n estimating the loss or damage arising from a breach of contract, the means which existed of remedying the inconvenience caused by the non-performance of the contract must be taken into account." In other words, the aggrieved party owes a duty of taking all reasonable steps to mitigate the loss caused by the breach and cannot claim damages for any loss that it could have mitigated by complying with this duty.[1115] (Evidently, however, a "violation" of the so-called "duty to mitigate" does not constitute a breach of contract or give rise to any liability on the promisee's end.)

1110 See Comment 1 and Ill. 1 to UPICC Art. 7.4.8, and Comments A and B to PECL Art. 9:505.
1111 See Comment 1 and Ill. 2 to UPICC Art. 7.4.8.
1112 See Comment B and Ill. 4 to PECL Art. 9:505.
1113 See Comment C and Ill. 7 to PECL Art. 9:505.
1114 See Comment E to PECL Art. 9:505.
1115 See, *e.g.*, Bangia, *supra* note 182 at 303, and Singh, *supra* note 218 at 443, for reference, *inter alia*, to the Privy Council of India's decision in *Jamal v. Moolla Dawood Sons & Co.* ((1915) 43 I.A. 6).

From a dogmatic perspective, the duty to mitigate may well be regarded as qualification of the above-mentioned principle that damages are to be quantified so as to put the aggrieved party in the position it would have been in if the breach had not occurred. If the promisee fails to take reasonable steps to minimize its loss, the party in breach may invoke this failure as a defence against its liability for the entire loss and with the effect of a proportionate reduction of the amount of compensation.[1116] In cases of anticipatory breach of contract, Indian courts generally distinguish between two situations: if the promisee does not accept the repudiation in order to keep the contract alive and wait if the promisor might change its position and tender performance at the due date, the former is not bound to mitigate its prospective loss in the meantime. Yet, if the promisee accepts the anticipatory repudiation, it is obliged to make reasonable efforts to minimize the loss even before the time when performance is due.[1117]

The standard for what steps of mitigating damages are considered "reasonable" under Indian law is generally what a "prudent person" would and could have done in the circumstances.[1118] On this basis, courts have usually considered a substitute transaction to be a reasonable measure to minimize the loss. Hence, it has been held with a view on sales contracts that a seller's failure to resell the goods at the market price upon the promisee's breach bars the former from to recovering its loss to the extent that it was later aggravated by a falling market.[1119] Similarly, if a seller of shares keeps them after the buyer has committed a breach of contract, it cannot recover the extra loss suffered due to a subsequent decline of the market.[1120] However, if the price paid in a substitute transaction is unreasonably high, the aggrieved party cannot recover the difference between the agreed price and the cover price.[1121] The obligation to make a substitute transaction usually also compels a wrongfully dismissed employee to take reasonable steps to obtain suitable employment even during the term for which the previous contract would have remained valid if the employee had not been dismissed.[1122]

1116 See, *e.g.*, Saharay, *supra* note 929 at 650, and Bhadbhade, *supra* note 137 at 1610.

1117 See generally Bhadbhade, *id.* at 1018 and 1472.

1118 See *cf.* Bhadbhade, *id.* at 1611 *et seq.*, and Singh, *supra* note 218 at 450. In spite of their citing similar cases, commentators appear to disagree as to the burden of proof regarding the duty to mitigate. Whereas Bangia (*supra* note 182 at 303) has stated that "[t]he burden of proof that reasonable steps have been taken to mitigate the loss (…) is on the plaintiff," Bhadbhade (*id.* at 1623) has concluded that "the burden of proof is on the defendant to show that the plaintiff has failed to take reasonable steps to mitigate his loss."

1119 See, *e.g.*, Saharay, *supra* note 929 at 615, for references to English and Indian case law.

1120 See, *e.g.*, Bangia, *supra* note 182 at 303.

1121 See, *e.g.*, Singh, *supra* note 218 at 447.

1122 See, *e.g.*, Bangia, *supra* note182 at 304. For an overview of additional illustrative cases, see, *e.g.*, Singh, *id.* at 444 *et seq.*, and Bhadbhade, *supra* note 137 at 1624 *et seq.*

For the purpose of mitigating its loss, the aggrieved party is generally not bound to take any steps that would have an adverse effect on its commercial reputation; also, it need not accept a tender that is different in quality from what was to receive under the contract.[1123]

Indian law also provides that any expenses incurred in attempting to mitigate damages are recoverable as additional loss. In fact, such expenses may be recovered even if they were fruitless or if the attempt to mitigate actually led to an increase of the loss.[1124] In turn, if the aggrieved party has taken steps that were *not* required under its duty to mitigate, any benefits brought about by these steps are anyway taken into account in assessing the amount of damages so long as these benefits are also a "direct result" of the breach.[1125]

C. Comparative analysis

In relation to the aggrieved party's duty of mitigation of the harm caused by a non-performance, there is full correspondence between the two sets of Principles and Indian statutory contract law. In fact, most of the Comments and Illustrations accompanying UPICC Art. 7.4.8 and PECL Art. 9:505 appear to be derived from English cases,[1126] and Indian commentators frequently cite very similar case law to illustrate the Explanation to Sec. 73 of the Indian Contract Act.[1127]

All three regimes provide that the aggrieved party must take reasonable steps to mitigate the loss caused by the (anticipatory or actual) non-performance, and that its right to recover the loss is excluded to the extent that it fails to comply with this duty. Moreover, the non-performing party is liable to reimburse the promisee for any reasonable expenses that the latter incurs in attempting to minimize the harm, even if the steps taken are fruitless or have actually lead to an increase of the loss.

1123 See *cf.* Bhadbhade, *id.* at 1618.

1124 See Bhadbhade, *id.* at 1614 and 1619.

1125 See *cf.* Treitel, *supra* note 159 at 726, for the position under English law.

1126 For an overview of the duty to mitigate under English law, see, *e.g.*, Beale, *supra* note 703 at 147 *et seq.*

1127 This is unsurprising considering the fact that Sec. 73 of the Indian Contract Act and the rule stated in the Explanation are regarded as reflecting English common law. See, *e.g.*, Saharay, *supra* note 929 at 649.

VII. Interest

A. Principles

1. Interest for failure to pay money

Both sets of Principles provide that a delay in the payment of money owed under a primary contractual monetary obligation gives rise to liability to pay interest upon that sum (UPICC Art. 7.4.9(1); PECL Art. 9:508(1)). Non-contractual, or secondary, debt such as damages or interest is not subject to these provisions.[1128]

Technically, UPICC Art. 7.4.9 and PECL Art. 9:508 establish a "special regime" governing a creditor's right to interest.[1129] This is because this right is not subject to the Principles' general provisions on damages such as those on the duty to mitigate, the means of quantifying damages, or the rule that the non-performing party is not liable to pay damages if its failure to perform was excused.[1130] Instead, it merely requires that payment is overdue as per each instrument's general rules on the time of performance.[1131]

Provided there is a delay in the payment of a debt, the creditor is automatically entitled to interest upon that sum from the time when the same was due until the actual time of the actual payment. According to UPICC Art. 7.4.9(3) and PECL Art. 9:508(2), if the delay caused further loss to the creditor, it may in addition recover damages for such loss subject to the Principles' general provisions on damages. For instance, where a lender, knowing that the borrower requires the money at a specific date in order to buy a business at a bargain price, fails to transfer the money on the agreed date, it is liable for the profit that the borrower would have made by reselling the business at the market price; however, its liability for such damages is excluded if the delay was excused, and it is, *inter alia*, subject to the

1128 While it is expressly stated in Comment B to PECL Art. 9:508 that the article does not apply to secondary monetary obligations, the UPICC provide a separate provision on interest on damages (UPICC Art. 7.4.10).

1129 See, *e.g.*, Comment 1 to UPICC Art. 7.4.9 and also Magnus, *supra* note 5 at 271. For a critical note on the Principles' rather commercial approach to interest on contractual debt and its relation to the PECL's proposed applicability also to consumer contracts, see Medicus, *supra* note 90.

1130 See Comment 1 to UPICC Art. 7.4.9 and Comment B to PECL Art. 9:508. The rule that a debtor owes interest regardless of whether the delay is excused stems from the drafters' consideration that "[i]f the delay is the consequence of *force majeure* (*e.g.*, the non-performing party is prevented from obtaining the sum due by reason of the introduction of new exchange control regulations), interest will still be due (...) as compensation for the enrichment of the debtor as a result of the non-payment as the debtor continues to receive interest on the sum which it is prevented from paying." (See Comment 1 to UPICC Art. 7.4.9.)

1131 UPICC Art. 6.1.1 and 6.1.2; PECL Art. 7:102.

requirement of foreseeability and the borrower's duty to mitigate the loss, *e.g.*, by borrowing the funds from another lender at reasonable terms.[1132]

As for the amount of interest owed, both sets of Principles provide a universal standard for the computation of the applicable interest rate. This means that, unless the parties have agreed upon a different interest rate or mode of calculation, the creditor is entitled to a lump sum and cannot recover a higher amount of interest even if it proves that it could have invested the money owed to it at a higher rate of interest.[1133] According to both UPICC Art. 7.4.9(2) and PECL Art. 9:508(1), the relevant standard is the average bank short-term lending rate to prime borrowers as applicable to the respective currency of payment at the agreed place of payment.[1134]

While this rule works in any of the Member States of the European Union and therefore throughout the countries in the PECL's primary sphere of application,[1135] the UPICC, due to their proposed applicability to international commercial contracts throughout the world, also take into account countries where it may be impossible to determine an average bank short-term lending rate to prime borrowers. For such cases, UPICC Art. 7.4.9(2) provides that the primary alternative shall be the average bank short-term lending rate to prime borrowers prevailing in the country of the currency of payment. If this primary alternative rate cannot be determined in the country of the currency, either, the interest rate fixed by the law of the country of the currency of payment or, where there are more than one legal interest rate, the one which appears to be most "appropriate for international transactions", shall apply. If there is no legal interest rate in the country of currency, the most appropriate bank rate in the country of the currency of payment shall be relevant.[1136]

In the absence of any contractual stipulation, the currency of payment is to be determined in accordance with UPICC Art. 6.1.9 or 6.1.10 and PECL Art. 7:108, and the place of payment is to be located with reference to UPICC Art. 6.1.6 and PECL Art. 7:101, respectively.

1132 See, *e.g.*, Ill. to UPICC Art. 7.4.9 and Ill. 2 to PECL Art. 9:508.

1133 See Comment 1 to UPICC Art. 7.4.9 and Comment B to PELC Art. 9:508.

1134 Though PECL Art. 9:508(1), unlike the UPICC, actually speaks of the "average *commercial* bank short-term lending rate to prime borrowers" (emphasis added), both articles clearly refer to the same rate. According to the Principles' drafters, this rate was considered to be suited best international trade (see Comment 2 to UPICC Art. 7.4.9) and also "the best yardstick for assessing the creditor's loss" (see Comment B to PECL Art. 9:508). The short-term rate was chosen to apply universally to all delays because the creditor is usually unable to anticipate the actual duration of the delay (see, *e.g.*, Comment B to PECL Art. 9:508).

1135 According to their Art. 1:101(1), the European Principles are primarily intended to serve as "general rules of contract law in the *European Union*" (emphasis added). See also *supra* Ch. I(E).

1136 See Comment 2 to UPICC Art. 7.4.9. See also Bonell, *supra* note 19 at 349.

2. Interest on damages

Unlike the European Principles, the UPICC contain a separate black letter rule dealing with interest on damages owed for the non-performance of non-monetary obligations (as per UPICC Art. 7.4.1 *et seq.*). Based on the commercial consideration that damages are quantified with reference to the time when the harm occurred and that the aggrieved party is therefore practically deprived of the interest it could have earned between that time and the date of actual payment of the damages, UPICC Art. 7.4.10 provides that interest on damages accrues from the time of the non-performance.

As neither the black letter rule nor the Comments accompanying UPICC Art. 7.4.10 give any indication as to the applicable rate of interest, it is assumed that the rate is to be determined in accordance with Art. 7.4.9(2).

The PECL, on the other hand, do not provide a separate statutory provision on interest on damages. PECL Art. 9:508 – just as UPICC Art. 7.4.9 – only applies to primary contractual debt and does therefore not give the aggrieved party a right to interest on secondary monetary obligations.[1137] As UPICC Art. 7.9.10 was apparently "included for no particular 'policy' reason in the UNIDROIT Principles but not in the European Principles",[1138] the reasons underlying this structural divergence are unclear.

However, it has been indicated elsewhere in the PECL that the absence of an express article on this issue does not mean that liability for interest on damages is altogether excluded.[1139] Instead, the aggrieved party may be entitled to recover such interest as consequential loss if it can establish that it would have earned interest on the amount of its loss (*e.g.*, on a prospective profit that was prevented by the non-performance) from the time when the loss occurred up to the date of payment of damages. (In this regard, the only difference remaining between UPICC Art. 7.4.10 and the position of the PECL is that under the latter, the recovery of interest on damages is subject to the general rules on damages, so that the aggrieved party must mitigate its loss and prove that it would have made a foreseeable profit if the non-performance had not occurred because it would have invested the lost profits at a certain interest rate.[1140]) Nonetheless, the express and much less conditional rule in UPICC Art. 7.4.10 appears superior as it more strongly discourages late payments of damages and therefore serves the principle of "full compensation"[1141] more effectively.

1137 See Comment B to PECL Art. 9:508.

1138 See Bonell/Peleggi, *supra* note 116 at 320 and 321.

1139 See Comment B to PECL Art. 9:502.

1140 PECL Art. 9:501 *et seq.*

1141 See UPICC Art. 7.4.2 and also PECL Art. 9:502.

B. Indian statutory law

1. Interest for non-payment of money

Though Indian law does not confer a general right to interest on overdue debt to the creditor, courts in India are authorized to award interest in three types of situations, *viz.* (1) if interest is payable by virtue of a custom or usage; (2) if there is an express or implied agreement under which interest is payable; or (3) subject to any provision of substantive law entitling a party to recover interest.[1142] Provisions of substantive law in the latter sense are Sec. 61 of the Sale of Goods Act, 1930,[1143] Sec. 78 to 81 of the Negotiable Instruments Act, 1881,[1144] and the

---

1142 See, *e.g.*, Bhadbhade, *supra* note 137 at 1600 *et seq.*

1143 Sec. 61 of the Sale of Goods Act, 1930 sets out the following rule:

"Interest by way of damages and special damages. (1) Nothing in this Act shall affect the right of the seller or the buyer to recover interest or special damages in any case whereby law interest or special damages may be recoverable, or to recover the money paid where the consideration for the payment of it has failed.

(2) In the absence of a contract to the contrary, the Court may award interest at such rate a it think fit one the amount of the price-

(a) to the seller in a suit by him for the amount of the price.- from the date of the tender of the goods or from the date on which the price was payable.

(b) to the buyer in a suit by him for the refund of the price in a case of a breach of the contract on the part of the seller- from the date on which the payment was made."

1144 Sec. 78 to 81 of the Negotiable Instruments Act, 1881 provide the following rules:

"78. To whom payment should be made. Subject to the provisions of section 82, clause (c), payment of the amount due on a promissory note, bill of exchange or cheque must, in order to discharge the maker or acceptor, be made to the holder of the instrument.

79. Interest when rate specified. When interest at a specified rate is expressly made payable on a promissory note or bill of exchange, interest shall be calculated at the rate specified, on the amount of the principal money due thereon, from the date of the instrument, until tender or realization of such amount, or until such date after the institution of a suit to recover such amount as the Court directs.

80. Interest when no rate specified. When no rate of interest is specified in the instrument, interest on the amount due thereon shall, notwithstanding any agreement relating to interest between any parties to the instrument, be calculated at the rate of eighteen per centum per annum, from the date at which the same ought to have been paid by the party charged, until tender or realization of the amount due thereon, or until such date after the institution of a suit to recover such amount as the Court directs.

81. Delivery of instrument on payment or indemnity in case of loss. (1) Any person liable to pay, and called upon by the holder thereof to pay, the amount due on a promissory note, but of exchange or cheque is before payment entitled to have it shown, is on payment entitled to have it delivered up to him, or, if the instrument is lost or cannot be produced, to be indemnified against any further claim thereon against him.

(2) Where the cheque is an electronic image of a truncated cheque, even after the payment the banker who received the payment shall be entitled to retain the truncated cheque.

sections of the Interest Act, 1978.[1145] Hence, unless there is an express or implied agreement under which interest is payable or excluded (Interest Act Sec. 3(3)(a)) or the awarding of interest on overdue debt is prescribed by a usage or by one of the aforementioned specific statutory provisions (Interest Act Sec. 4(1)), issues of interest are governed by the Interest Act, 1978.[1146]

a. Interest Act, 1978

The Interest Act confers a high degree of discretion to the courts and arbitral bodies as to whether a creditor of a contractual obligation to pay money may recover interest on that sum. According to its Sec. 3(1), a court or arbitral tribunal may, "[i]n any proceedings for the recovery of any debt or damage or in any proceedings in which a claim for interest in respect of any debt or damages already paid is made, (…) if it thinks fit, allow interest (…) at a rate not exceeding the current rate of interest." The term "debt" in this sense refers to "any liability for an ascertained sum of money and includes a debt payable in kind, but does not include a judgment debt" (Interest Act Sec. 2(a)).

As to the period for which interest may be awarded, Sec. 3(1) of the Interest Act provides that "[i]f the proceedings relate to a debt payable by virtue of a written instrument at a certain time, then [the court may award interest] from the date when the debt is payable to the date of institution of the proceedings." Alternatively, if the proceedings do not concern a debt payable by virtue of a written instrument at a certain time, the court may award interest "from the date mentioned in this regard in a written notice given (…) to the person liable that interest will be claimed to the date of institution of the proceedings." If the debt has been repaid prior to the commencement of the suit, interest shall not be awarded for the period after the repayment (Interest Act Sec. 3(1)). Moreover, whereas interest on interest may not be awarded (Interest Act Sec. 3(3)(c)), the statutory Comment accompanying the section provides that so-called "compound interest" may be awarded in certain circumstances, especially on debt arising from commercial contracts.[1147]

---

(3) A certificate issued on the foot of the printout of the electronic image of a truncated cheque by the banker who paid the instrument, shall be prima facie proof of such payment."

1145 Hereinafter also referred to as "Interest Act."

1146 As this survey is primarily concerned with the *general* Indian statutory law of contracts, the present section only examines the provisions of the Interest Act and leaves aside any of the rules found in specific statutes such as the Sale of Goods Act, 1930, the Negotiable Instruments Act, 1881 or the Code of Civil Procedure, 1908.

1147 See generally Bhadbhade, *supra* note 137 at 1606 and 1610, and Saharay, *supra* note 929 at 654 and 656. The term "compound interest" may be defined as "[i]nterest paid on both the principal and the previously accumulated interest." See Garner, *supra* note 141 at 362.

Notwithstanding the general rule established in Sec. 3(1), and provided interest is not payable or excluded under the contract or as per any specific statutory provision, Sec. 4(2) of the Interest Act lists a few exceptional cases in which the date from which interest may be awarded may vary. For instance, where money or other property was deposited as security for the performance of an obligation imposed by law or by contract, interest may be awarded from the date of deposit (Interest Act Sec. 4(2)(a)). Where the obligation to pay money or restore property stems from a fiduciary relationship, interest may be awarded from the date when the cause of action arose (Interest Act Sec. 4(2)(b)). Moreover, where money or other property is obtained or retained through fraud, interest may also be granted from the date when the cause of action arose (Interest Act Sec. 4(2)(c)).[1148]

Interest from the time when the suit was instituted to the date of judgment or even to the date of actual payment is not covered by Sec. 3(1) and thus not governed by the Interest Act. As confirmed by Sec. 5 of the statute, interest *pendente lite* or until the time of payment is instead subject to Sec. 34(1) of the Civil Procedure Code, 1908,[1149] which also grants the courts discretion as to whether such interest should be awarded at all.

Unless the parties have agreed upon a certain interest rate,[1150] the courts may determine a "rate not exceeding the current rate of interest" (Interest Act Sec. 3(1)). According to Sec. 2(b) of the Interest Act, the term "current rate of interest" refers to "the highest of the maximum rates at which interest may be paid on different classes of deposits (other than those maintained in savings accounts or those maintained by charitable or religious institutions) by different classes of

1148 See *cf.* Bhadbhade, *id.* at 1607 *et seq.*

1149 See, *e.g.*, Saharay, *supra* note 929 at 656 *et seq.*, and Bhadbhade, *id.* at 1610. Sec. 34(1) of the Civil Procedure Code, 1908 provides the following rule:

> "Where and in so far as a decree is for the payment of money, the Court may, in the decree, order interest at such rate as the Court deems reasonable to be paid on the principal sum adjudged, from the date of the suit to the date of the decree, in addition to any interest adjudged on such principal sum for any period prior to the institution of the suit, with further interest at such rate not exceeding six per cent, per annum as the Court deems reasonable on such principal sum from the date of the decree to the date of payment, or to such earlier date as the Court thinks fit:
> Provided that where the liability in relation to the sum so adjudged had arisen out of a commercial transaction, the rate of such further interest may exceed six per cent, per annum, but shall not exceed the contractual rate of interest or where there is no contractual rate, the rate at which moneys are lent or advanced by nationalised banks in relation to commercial transactions. (...)"

1150 See, *e.g.*, Bhadbhade, *supra* note 137 at 1608, for further references. According to the first Explanation to Sec. 74 of the Indian Contract Act, "[a] stipulation for increased interest from the date of default may be a stipulation by way of penalty"; in such cases, the consequence provided by Sec. 74 of the Contract Act is that the creditor is nevertheless entitled only to interest at a reasonable rate. See generally *infra* X(B).

Scheduled banks in accordance with the directions given or issued to banking companies generally by the Reserve Bank of India under the Banking Regulation Act, 1949 (10 of 1949)."[1151]

Where interest is awarded in a foreign currency, interest ought to be awarded at the rate prevailing in the commercial market of the respective country.[1152]

b. Recoverability of interest by virtue of damages?

As the issue of interest also occurs in Illustrations (n) and (r) to Sec. 73 of the Indian Contract Act, the question arises whether this provision might also entitle a creditor to recover interest, that is, as *damages*.

Prior to the enactment of the Interest Act, 1978, there was indeed considerable disagreement among Indian courts on the issue of whether, in cases where interest was irrecoverable under the Interest Act, 1839, it could be awarded by virtue of damages under Sec. 73 of the Contract Act. Today, however, that debate is no longer relevant as Sec. 3 of the Interest Act, 1978 (which succeeded the Interest Act, 1839) now establishes a general rule according to which interest on any type of overdue debt is recoverable subject to judicial discretion.[1153] Therefore, despite the fact that especially Illustration (n) to Sec. 73 of the Indian Contract Act appears to imply that the aggrieved party has a right to interest *on* damages for any breach of contract, the general rule today is that interest is to be awarded only if the parties have expressly or implicitly agreed that the money was to be paid on a specific date, or if the requirements of the Interest Act, 1978 are satisfied.[1154]

2. Interest on damages

In light of the above-mentioned rule that interest may not be awarded unless (1) it is payable by custom or usage, (2) there is an express or implied agreement to pay interest, or (3) the creditor is entitled to recover interest under a provision of substantive law,[1155] the recovery of interest *on* damages generally presupposes a statutory foundation.

1151 The Explanation to Sec. 2(b) of the Interest Act provides that "[i]n this clause, Scheduled bank means a bank, not being a Co-operative bank, transacting any business authorised by the Banking Regulation Act, 1949 (10 of 1949)."

1152 See, *e.g.*, Bhadbhade, *supra* note 137 at 1609, for further references.

1153 For an overview of the situation prior to the Privy Council's decision in *Bengal Nagpur Rly. Co. Ltd. v. Ruttanji Ramji* (AIR 1938 P.C. 67 (1938)) and the enactment of the Interest Act, 1978, see, *e.g.*, Bhadbhade, *id.* at 1601 *et seq.*, and Saharay, *supra* note 929 at 653 *et seq.*

1154 See, *e.g.*, Saharay, *id.* at 654 *et seq.*

1155 See, *e.g.*, Bhadbhade, *supra* note 137 at 1600 *et seq.*

In this context, the relevant statutory provision under which courts and arbitral tribunals may, at their discretion, award interest on the amount of damages is again Sec. 3(1) of the Interest Act, 1978.[1156] In short, Sec. 3(1) provides that unless the contract rules out interest on damages, the courts are authorized to award interest at a rate not exceeding the current rate of interest[1157] for the period from the date mentioned in a written notice that interest will be claimed to the date of institution of the proceedings.

In fact, if the judgment or award is, *inter alia*, for a sum exceeding INR 4,000 without interest and there are no specific reasons why the awarding of interest would be inappropriate, the court or arbitral body is bound to award interest on the amount of damages at a reasonable rate (Interest Act. Sec. 3(2)).[1158]

C. Comparative analysis

1. Interest for failure to pay money

Unlike UPICC Art. 7.4.9(1) and PECL Art. 9:508(1), Indian law does not recognize a general right to interest in cases of late payment of a contractual debt, and an action to recover the amount owed is the only non-discretionary remedy available for breach of an obligation to pay money.[1159] Sec. 3(1) of the Interest Act, 1978[1160] grants the courts wide discretion in deciding whether and at what rate interest should be awarded. Hence, while the rule under the Principles "should be familiar to every Continental lawyer",[1161] the position of Indian law is still closely related to English law, which also does not recognize a general obligation to pay interest on money owed under a contract.[1162]

At the outset, all three of the aforementioned provisions presuppose a delay in the payment of a contractual debt. Whereas neither UPICC Art. 7.4.9(1) nor PECL Art. 9:508(1) compel the creditor to give notice to the debtor of its intention to claim interest, Sec. 3(1) of the Indian Interest Act requires a notice if the contract does not fix a specific time for payment.

1156 For a detailed overview and discussion of Sec. 3(1) of the Interest Act, see *supra* 1.

1157 The term "current rate of interest" is defined in Sec. 2(b) of the Interest Act. See also *supra* 1.

1158 See generally Bhadbhade, *supra* note 137 at 1606 *et seq.*, for further references.

1159 See *supra* Ch. V(I)(B)(4).

1160 As discussed above, the Interest Act, 1978 applies where interest is not payable or excluded by virtue of the contract and under the condition that no usages or specific statutory provisions (namely Sec. 61 of the Sale of Goods Act, 1930 or Sec. 78 to 81 of the Negotiable Instruments Act, 1881) dealing with interest apply.

1161 See Zimmermann, *supra* note 34 at 30.

1162 See Zimmermann, *supra* note 161 at 283. See also Note 1 to PECL Art. 9:508.

As for the period for which interest is to be paid (or, under Indian law, may be awarded), the Principles prescribe that interest is due from the agreed time of payment, *viz.* the time when the non-performance occurred, up to the date of the actual payment. In cases where the parties had agreed on a specific date of payment, Sec. 3(1) of the Interest Act authorizes the courts to award interest from that date until the date of commencement of proceedings,[1163] and interest *pendente lite* may be awarded additionally subject to Sec. 34(1) of the Civil Procedure Code, 1908. However, Indian law does not allow for the recovery of interest for the period between the judgment or award until the date of the actual payment of the debt.

Unless the parties had agreed upon a certain rate of interest,[1164] UPICC Art. 7.4.9(2) and PECL Art. 9:508(1) provide that the rate at which interest can be recovered is irrespective of the creditor's presumptive use of the money. Instead, interest is to be awarded at the average bank short-term lending rate to prime borrowers for the relevant currency at the place of payment. (In contemplation of the fact that such a rate may not be available in all countries of the world, the UPICC, which are intended to be applicable to international commercial contracts throughout the world, also provide a number of alternative means of determining an appropriate interest rate.) In India, the determination of the appropriate interest rate is left to judicial discretion unless the parties have agreed upon a certain rate. However, Indian courts may not award interest in excess of the so-called current rate of interest (Interest Act Sec. 3(1)); this term refers to "the highest of the maximum rates at which interest may be paid on different classes of deposits [other than those maintained in savings account or those maintained by charitable or religious institutions] by different classes of Scheduled banks in accordance with the directions given or issued to banking companies generally by the Reserve Bank of India under the Banking Regulation Act, 1949 (10 of 1949)" (Interest Act Sec. 2(b)).[1165] If interest is to be awarded in a foreign currency, the relevant current rate of interest is the one prevailing in the country of that currency.[1166]

Finally, all three regimes allow for the recovery of any further damages caused by the delay in payment. A claim for damages for such losses is subject to the each regime's general provisions on damages.[1167]

1163 For a few exceptions to this rule with respect to the date from which interest may be awarded, see also Sec. 4(2) of the Interest Act.

1164 See Comment 1 to UPICC Art. 7.4.9 and Comment B to PECL Art. 9:508.

1165 According to the Explanation to Sec. 2(b) of the Interest Act, "Scheduled bank (in this clause) means a bank, not being a Co-operative bank, transacting any business authorised by the Banking Regulation Act, 1949 (10 of 1949)."

1166 See, *e.g.*, Bhadbhade, *supra* note 137 at 1609, for further references.

1167 UPICC Art. 7.4.1 *et seq.*; PECL Art. 9 :501 *et seq.*; and Indian Contract Act Sec. 73.

2. *Interest on damages*

Whereas under the PECL, interest on damages is recoverable as consequential loss in the form of lost profits and thus subject to the general rules on damages set forth in PECL Art. 9:501 *et seq.*, the UNIDROIT Principles take a different route by entitling the aggrieved party to recover interest on damages for non-performance of non-monetary obligations subject to the same requirements as interest on contractual debt.

As a result, interest on damages is subject to considerably different requirements under the two sets of Principles. What the two regimes do agree on, on the other hand, is that of interest on damages, interest on the amount damages accrues from the time of the non-performance until the time of actual payment of the amount of damages. Under UPICC Art. 7.4.10, the relevant interest rate is the one prescribed by UPICC Art. 7.4.9(2). The PECL, on the other hand, require the aggrieved party to prove that it would have made a foreseeable profit if the non-performance had not occurred; moreover, it needs to establish with certainty that it would have invested the profits at a certain interest rate.[1168]

Under Indian law, the awarding of interest on damages is subject to the Interest Act, 1978 as well. Sec. 3(1)(b) provides that the date from which interest may be awarded is the date mentioned in the written notice that interest will be claimed (which the aggrieved party needs to give to the party in breach). If, *inter alia*, the amount of damages without interest exceeds INR 4,000, the court or arbitral tribunal is bound to award interest on the amount of damages at a reasonable rate that must not exceed the current rate of interest as per Sec. 2(b) (Interest Act Sec. 3(2)); claims for interest on any smaller amounts of damages are subject to full judicial discretion (Interest Act Sec. 3(1)). In any of these cases, interest may be awarded until the date of commencement of the respective judicial or arbitral proceedings under Sec. 3(1) of the Interest Act, and from the time when the suit was instituted up to the date of the judgment or even of the actual payment (Sec. 34(1) of the Civil Procedure Code, 1908).

Unlike the Principles, the Indian Interest Act authorizes the courts to award compound interest in special circumstances, especially in disputes arising from commercial contracts.[1169]

3. *Evaluation*

Especially with a view on international transactions, the comparably wide judicial discretion provided under the Interest Act inevitably entails a higher level of

1168 See generally *supra* A(2).

1169 SeeComment to Interest Act Sec. 3.

uncertainty and unpredictability as to whether and at what rate interest is actually available. In fact, the respective rule under English law – which does not even recognize a general liability to pay interest on contractual debt – has been described as being "dissatisfactory"[1170] in this regard. And indeed, granting creditors a general right to damages on overdue debt at a predetermined rate by way of unconditional and clear-cut rules such as UPICC Art. 7.4.9 and PECL Art. 9:508 appears clearly superior.

The same reasoning applies to the issue of interest on damages. Here, UPICC Art. 7.4.10 clearly presents the most effective disincentive to delays in the payment of damages. As a result, it appears to provide the most efficient and predictable means of effectuating the fundamental objective underlying all three regimes' rules on damages, which is to put the aggrieved party in the position it would have been in if the contract had been performed.[1171]

VIII. Manner of monetary redress

Art. 7.4.11(1) of the UNIDROIT Principles establishes the general rule that damages are to be awarded and payable as a lump sum. The UPICC's drafters have deemed this rule to be working best in international trade.[1172] However, where the nature of the harm makes a payment in instalments more appropriate, the court or arbitral tribunal may also award damages in instalments. This alternative is especially useful in cases of "ongoing harm". For instance, where a wrongfully dismissed consultant was to be paid a certain percentage of the value of the company's production, it appears appropriate to pay monthly instalments for the remainder of the term of the contract or until the consultant finds new employment.[1173]

Where an instalment judgment is appropriate and an indexation permitted by the law of the forum, the judgment may be indexed in order to avoid the need to constantly review and adjust it to inflation (UPICC Art. 7.4.11(2)). For example, where a company's non-performance of a consultancy contract has led to the death of the consultant, the court may award a monthly allowance payable to the consultant's children, the instalments being adjustable in accordance with the relevant cost of living index.[1174]

1170 See Zimmermann, *supra* note 161 at 283 (translation from the German original). See also Note 1 to PECL Art. 9:508.

1171 UPICC Art. 7.4.2; PECL Art. 9:502; and Indian Contract Act Sec. 73. See also Perillo, *supra* note 130 at 311 *et seq.*

1172 See Comment 1 to UPICC Art. 7.4.11.

1173 See Comment 1 and Ill. 2 to UPICC Art. 7.4.11.

1174 See Comment 2 and Ill. 1 and 3 to UPICC Art. 7.4.11.

The PECL do not provide a rule corresponding to that of UPICC Art. 7.4.11. While this divergence is of merely "technical nature" and especially not attributable to these two instruments' different scopes of applicability,[1175] the UPICC's approach has been welcomed to the extent that "[w]e may take note of, and applaud, the drafters for their realism."[1176]

Similar to the PECL, neither Indian statutory contract law nor any other major common-law jurisdictions appear to have established any general rules on the issue.

IX. Currency in which to assess damages

A. Principles

While the issue of the currency in which damages are *payable* is governed by UPICC Art. 6.1.9/6.1.10 and PECL Art. 7:108, respectively,[1177] it may also be important in international transactions to determine the appropriate currency for *measuring* the amount of compensation. For this purpose, UPICC Art. 7.4.12 and PECL Art. 9:510 (which are, despite their different wordings, considered to be "corresponding provisions" reflecting "basically the same solutions"[1178]) establish that damages should be assessed in the currency that most appropriately reflects the loss sustained by the aggrieved party. The consideration underlying this rule is that fluctuating exchange rates may change the ratio between the currency of the contract and the currency of the loss during the period between the non-performance and the time when the amount of damages is assessed.

UPICC Art. 7.4.12 provides to the aggrieved party with a choice between the currency in which the contractual debt was to be paid and the currency or currencies in which the loss was sustained.[1179] The PECL do not expressly leave the choice to the aggrieved party as they merely state that the most appropriate currency shall be applied. However, as both articles seek to effectuate the principle of full compensation, *viz.* to avoid "over or under-compensation" of the aggrieved party,[1180] it is clear that the choice conferred under the UNIDROIT Principles should by no means lead to its enrichment.

1175 See, *e.g.*, Bonell/Peleggi, *supra* note 116 at 321, and Bonell, *supra* note 19 at 347.

1176 See Perillo, *supra* note 130 at 313.

1177 UPICC Art. 6.1.9 and 6.1.10 and PECL Art. 7:108 provide general rules on the currency of payment.

1178 See, *e.g.*, Bonell/Peleggi, *supra* note 116 at 316 and 317.

1179 See Comment to UPICC Art. 7.4.12.

1180 See *id.* and Comments A(1) and B to PECL Art. 9:510.

Cases where a choice between the contractual currency and the currency in which the loss arose may be relevant are those where the aggrieved party has incurred expenses or carried out a substitute transaction in a different currency than the contractual currency (*e.g.,* in its home currency), or where its loss consists of lost profits it would have made by reselling goods in a currency other than the one in which it had purchased them.[1181]

The drafters' comments to both articles also reiterate that interest and liquidated damages are to be assessed in the currency in which the respective obligation was expressed.[1182]

B. Indian statutory law

Indian commentators have cited a number of English decisions in relation to the issue of determining the currency that shall be relevant in measuring the amount of damages.[1183] In England and hence also in India, courts may award damages for breach of contract in a foreign currency even where the applicable *lex fori* is English law or Indian law, respectively.[1184] Similar to the UNIDROIT and European Principles, the question under English law is whether, to measure the loss, it is more appropriate to make reference to the contractual currency or to the currency in which the loss was sustained.[1185]

X. Agreed payment for non-performance

A. Principles

With a view on the Principles' purpose to present unitary solutions that bridge the dogmatic divide between the civil-law and common-law traditions, it has been observed that "[n]owhere in the law of contracts has the clash of common-law and civil-law notions seemed as irreconcilable as in the treatment of penalty clauses."[1186]

1181 See Comment to UPICC Art. 7.4.12 and Comment C and Ill. 1 and 2 to PECL Art. 9:510.

1182 See Comment to UPICC Art. 7.4.12 and Comment D to PECL Art. 9:510.

1183 See, *e.g.*, Bhadbhade, *supra* note 137 at 1630, for references to English case law.

1184 See *cf.* C.G.J. Morse, *Chitty on Contracts, Vol. I*, *supra* note 957 at 1579 *et seq.*

1185 See also Note 1 to PECL Art. 9:510. For an overview of the issue of currency of payment under Indian law including a comparison to UPICC Art. 6.1.9, see, *e.g.*, Bhadbhade, *supra* note 137 at 965 *et seq.*

1186 See Perillo, *supra* note 130 at 313.

Facing the two legal traditions' diametric positions on the issue, the Principles' drafters did not try to strike a balance but rather opted in favour of the most common civil-law approach, under which not only liquidated damages but also penalty clauses are generally enforceable unless they are exceptionally unfair.[1187] In fact, as penalty clauses are a frequently-used safeguard against non-performance in international contracts and the issue of their unenforceability in common-law jurisdictions is often simply avoided by way of alternative measures with the same effect such as standby letters of credit, the Principles' solution certainly also reflects the needs and practice of commercial reality.[1188]

UPICC Art. 7.4.13(1) and PECL Art. 9:509(1) provide that where a contract clause stipulates that the non-performing party is to pay the aggrieved party a specified sum for a non-performance, the latter is entitled to that sum irrespective of whether and to what extent it has actually sustained any harm. However, regardless of any possible agreement to the contrary, UPICC Art. 7.4.13(2) and PECL Art. 9:509(2) authorize the courts to reduce the specified sum to a reasonable amount if it is grossly excessive in relation to the actual harm or the other circumstances. If there has only been a partial non-performance, the courts may proportionately reduce the agreed payment unless the parties have agreed upon a different consequence.[1189]

According to the Principles' drafters, the term "agreement to pay a specified sum" is intentionally broad so as to cover both liquidated damages and penalty clauses.[1190] This term includes clauses stipulating only a minimum sum payable as damages while allowing the aggrieved party to recover a higher amount if it can prove that its harm actually exceeds the minimum payment.[1191] It also relates to agreements under which the aggrieved party is entitled to retain payments or deposits that it had already received as part of the price.[1192] Conversely, forfeiture clauses and similar clauses that allow a party to withdraw from the contract by not exercising an option to purchase while losing a deposit or to pay a certain sum instead of performing are not covered by UPICC Art. 7.4.13 and PECL Art. 9:509.[1193]

1187 See *cf.* Zimmermann, *supra* note 161 at 483.

1188 See, *e.g.*, Comment 2 to UPICC Art. 7.4.13 and Perillo, *supra* note 130 at 313.

1189 See Comment 2 to UPICC Art. 7.4.13.

1190 Liquidated damages are intended to facilitate the recovery of damages and reduce the uncertainty, time and expenses involved in proving the exact harm by entitling the aggrieved party to an amount of compensation that reflects a genuine pre-estimate of the probable harm. Penalty clauses, on the other hand, fix a disproportionately high amount of compensation for the primary purpose of discouraging non-performance.

1191 See Comment A to PECL Art. 9:509.

1192 See Comment 4 and Ill. 4 to UPICC Art. 7.4.13 and Ill. 2 to PECL Art. 9:509.

1193 See Comment 4 and Ill. 3 to UPICC Art. 7.4.13 and Comment D to PECL Art. 9:509.

For the purpose of balancing the parties' far-reaching autonomy in devising liquidated damages or penalty clauses, UPICC Art. 7.4.13(2) and PECL Art. 9:509(2) grant courts (and arbitral bodies) a certain degree of discretion to protect the weaker party from unfair clauses: even if the agreed payment for non-performance appeared reasonable at the time of conclusion of the contract, the court may reduce the sum payable if the same is "grossly excessive" in relation to the actual harm and/or the other circumstances.

A clear deficit of the Principles' rules is their lack of a precise definition or some kind of a yardstick regarding this term. Instead, they nebulously require a "gross disparity between the specified sum and the actual loss suffered by the aggrieved party" to the extent that "it is clear that the stipulated sum substantially exceeds the actual loss" or that the agreed payment "would clearly appear to be [grossly excessive] to any reasonable person".[1194]

Even if it finds the agreed figure grossly excessive, the court may not entirely set aside the parties' intention (to deter non-performance) by awarding an amount of compensation that exactly equals the harm sustained by the promisee. Instead, it is to award an intermediate figure.[1195] Conversely, if a liquidated damages or penalty clause has the effect of *limiting* the amount of damages payable to the aggrieved party, a court may award a higher figure only in accordance with UPICC Art. 7.1.6 and PECL Art. 8:109, *i.e.*, if enforcing the clause would be grossly unfair considering the purpose of the contract or contrary to good faith and fair dealing.[1196]

B. Indian statutory law

According to Sec. 74 of the Indian Contract Act, a breach of a contract in which "as sum is named (...) as the amount to be paid in case of such breach" or which "contains any other stipulation by way of penalty" entitles the aggrieved party to reasonable compensation not exceeding the stipulated amount regardless of "whether or not actual damage or loss is proved to have been caused thereby". By providing this unitary rule which does not distinguish between liquidated damages and penalties, Sec. 74 of the Contract Act thus marks a departure from the position in England, where liquidated damages are generally recoverable whereas penalty clauses are strictly unenforceable.[1197]

1194 See Comments B and C to PECL Art. 9:509 and Comment 3 to UPICC Art. 7.4.13, respectively.

1195 See Comment 3 to UPICC Art. 7.4.13 and Comment B to PECL Art. 9:509.

1196 See, *e.g.*, Comment 4 to UPICC Art. 7.1.6 and also *supra* Ch. III(VI)(A). For an analysis of the relationship between UPICC Art. 7.4.13 and 7.1.6., see *cf.* Fontaine, *supra* note 313 at 415 *et seq.*

1197 See generally D.R. Harris, *Chitty on Contracts, Vol. I*, *supra* note 957 at 1251 et seq.

Sec. 74 establishes that any such pre-determined amount of compensation constitutes the maximum amount of damages recoverable for a breach of contract. Within this limit, the courts have a wide discretion to assess the "reasonable compensation" that the aggrieved party should be entitled to. Though the express wording of the section allows the courts to award reasonable compensation "whether or not actual damage or loss is proved to have been caused" by the breach, it has frequently been held that the aggrieved party is not relieved from having to prove both the breach and a "legal injury", *viz.* that it has sustained any loss or damage at all.[1198] However, as liquidated damages or penalties make an exact quantification of the actual harm unnecessary, the plaintiff evidently need not prove its exact extent.[1199]

Despite the unitary approach of Sec. 74 of the Contract Act, the distinction between liquidated damages and penalties is not entirely irrelevant under Indian law. If the contract provides for an amount of liquidated damages that represents a mutual genuine pre-estimate of the probable extent of the harm, the courts generally enforce the clause as such and award the entire agreed sum.[1200] If, on the other hand, the clause is merely *in terrorem*, that is, intended to secure performance of the contract by fixing a sum which is manifestly supposed to exceed the likely loss, the court shall award only a reasonable amount.[1201] Whether a particular clause constitutes a penalty or merely liquidated damages is to be determined by way of construction and in consideration of various factors including the parties' intentions, the terms and circumstances of the contract and the purpose of the clause. Evidently, the description of the specified sum is only an indicator of its true character.[1202]

Where the contract provides for payment in instalments while stipulating that the whole amount owed shall become payable upon non-payment of any of the instalments, the court is to construe the relevant clause to ascertain whether it should be considered a penalty or not. If the nature of the debt had been such that normally the entire amount was due and the payment in instalments was

---

1198 Instead, it has been observed that "[t]he words in [Sec. 74] 'Whether or not actual damage or loss is proved to have been caused thereby have been employed to underscore the departure deliberately made by the Indian Legislature from the complicated principles of English Common Law and also to emphasize that reasonable compensation can be granted even in a case where extent of actual loss or damage is incapable of proof or not proved." See Bhadbhade, *supra* note 137 at 1665.

1199 See, *e.g.*, Saharay, *supra* note 929 at 661 and 662, and Singh, *supra* note 218 at 465 *et seq.*, for references, *inter alia*, to a decision of the Indian Supreme Court.

1200 See *cf.* Singh, *id.* at 460, and Bangia, *supra* note 182 at 309, for references to Indian case law.

1201 See *cf.* Saharay, *supra* note 929 at 663 *et seq.*, for references to Indian case law.

1202 See *id.* at 664 and *cf.* Bhadbhade, *supra* note 137 at 1650 *et seq.*, for references to illustrative case law.

only granted as a concession or facilitation of payment, a clause conditioning such a concession or facilitation upon prompt payment of each instalment is to be treated like a liquidated damages clause.[1203] Conversely, if the amount payable with each instalment shall merely become *due* on the date fixed for its payment, a clause providing that the entire balance shall fall due if the debtor fails to pay any one instalment is more like a penalty clause because it practically increases the amount due at the time of default by the sum of the outstanding instalments.[1204]

Sec. 74 not only applies to clauses under which the aggrieved party is entitled to a certain amount upon a breach, but also to clauses stipulating that an amount already received shall be forfeited. This means that the forfeiture of earnest money received under a contract for the sale of moveable or immoveable property does not constitute a penalty unless the amount to be forfeited is unreasonable in that it does not represent a genuine pre-estimate of the likely loss caused by a default.[1205] (In this regard, the Indian Supreme Court has held that a clause requiring the buyer to deposit 25 per cent of the total value of the purchased goods as earnest money and providing that this amount shall be forfeited by the seller if the buyer fails to pay the full price, is reasonable and thus enforceable.[1206]) Aside from earnest money – which is advanced as a part of the purchase price to guarantee performance of the contract – a security deposit – *viz.* money paid merely to secure due performance – may also be subject to a forfeiture clause if it represents a genuine pre-estimate of the probable loss.[1207]

Illustration (b) to Sec. 74 reiterates that penalties or liquidated damages may not only be employed to secure payment of money but also to ensure the performance of a collateral act. Moreover, as per a rule derived from the first statutory Explanation as well as Illustration (d) to the section, a stipulation under which the party in breach is to pay interest at an increased rate from the date of default may constitute a penalty if the interest rate is unreasonably high.[1208] In this context, it

1203 See Ill. (f) to Indian Contract Act Sec. 74.

1204 See Ill. (g) to Indian Contract Act Sec. 74 and *cf.* Bangia, *supra* note 182 at 309.

1205 See, *e.g.*, Bangia, *id.* at 309 *et seq.*, and Singh, *supra* note 218 at 462, for references to Indian case law.

1206 See Bangia, *id.* at 310, and Singh, *id.* at 467, for references to the Supreme Court's decision in *Shree Hanuman Cotton Mills v. Tata Aircraft Ltd.* (AIR 1970 S.C. 1986).

1207 See, *e.g.*, Bhadbhade, *supra* note 137 at 1693 *et seq.*, and Saharay, *supra* note 929 at 662, for references, *inter alia*, to the Supreme Court's decision in *Maula Bux v. Union of India* (AIR 1970 S.C. 1955).

1208 In spite of the rule derived from the first Explanation under Sec. 74 and from Ill. (d) to the same, it has been observed that "[p]enalties in the form of higher interest rate computations in the event of default are usually disregarded or recomputed by the court at reasonable rates." (See Chetan Nagendra, *A suitable law is not ready as yet*, The Financial Express (28 June 2005), available at http://www.financialexpress.com.)

has been observed that an agreement of compound interest is not by itself unreasonable or penal.[1209]

C. Comparative analysis

In relation to liquidated damages and penalty clauses, it is the very departure of the Indian legislature from the position under English law that moves Sec. 74 of the Indian Contract Act quite close to the relevant rules under the UNIDROIT and European Principles.

UPICC Art. 7.4.13(1), PECL Art. 9:509(1) and Sec. 74 of the Indian Act establish unitary rules on both liquidated damages and penalty clauses. Unlike English law, under which liquidated damages are generally recoverable whereas penalties are principally unenforceable, neither provision draws a categorical distinction between these two types of prefixed damages. What the Principles refer to as "specified sum payable for non-performance" is called "a sum named in the contract as the amount to be paid in case of such breach" or "any other stipulation by way of penalty" in Sec. 74 of the Indian Act. All three instruments hence treat both liquidated damages and penalties as generally enforceable. What is more, their unitary rules stem from a very similar reasoning: the drafters of the Principles have stated that the enforceability of clauses that provide for payment of a specified sum upon a non-performance reflects international contract practice;[1210] on similar grounds, Indian courts and commentators have confirmed that the Indian legislator "sought to cut across the web of rules and presumptions under the English common law, by enacting a uniform principle applicable to all stipulations naming amounts to be paid in case of breach."[1211]

Nonetheless, there is a slight divergence in relation to the effect that a valid liquidated damages or penalty clause has on the proof of harm requirement. Whereas under the Principles the aggrieved party is entitled to the specified sum

1209 See *cf.* Bhadbhade, *supra* note 137 at 1671 *et seq.* According to the second Explanation to Sec. 74, the section does not apply to any bail-bond, recognizance or similar instrument issued by for the performance of a public duty or an act in which the public is interested, provided the instrument is given under a law or government order. The person giving the instrument is therefore liable for the full amount stipulated therein.

1210 See, *e.g.*, Comment 2 to UPICC Art. 7.4.13.

1211 See Bhadbhade, *supra* note 137 at 1654, for a reference to the Supreme Court's decision in *Fateh Chand v. Balkishan Das* (AIR 1963 S.C. 1405). Zimmermann (*supra* note 161 at 483) has restated a similar consideration in relation to the Principles by observing that the (English) common law's distinction between penalties and liquidated damages brings about substantial difficulty in determining which of the two applies to a particular clause. The common law's strict distinction hence led to a loss of both legal certainty and case-by-case justice.

irrespective of whether it has proved any actual harm, Indian courts have applied a somewhat more differentiated interpretation of Sec. 74 of the Contract Act: while the plaintiff need not establish the exact extent or *quantum* of its harm, it does have to prove that it has sustained any loss or damage at all, *i.e.*, a "legal injury". If it fails to do so, it cannot recover any compensation at all.

The three instruments provide quite similar rules with respect to the limits of judicial interference with a liquidated damages clause. As a general rule, Indian courts are to award the full amount of liquidated damages if it represents a genuine pre-estimate of the harm that is likely to be caused by the non-performance. This is fully coherent with the position under UPICC Art. 7.4.13(1) and PECL Art. 9:509(1), which plainly state that the aggrieved party is entitled to the specified sum irrespective of its actual harm and as long as that sum is not "grossly excessive".[1212]

Regarding penalty clauses or unreasonably high liquidated damages, however, there is a notable divergence. Indian statutory law provides for wide judicial discretion by authorizing the courts to award "reasonable compensation" up to the agreed penalty. While this rule devises a seemingly effective means of preventing an exploitation of the weaker party, it certainly is a two-bladed sword as it considerably limits party autonomy and contravenes the commercial need for certainty and predictability. By permitting courts to reduce the specified sum only if it is "grossly excessive" (UPICC Art. 7.4.13(2); PECL Art. 9:509(2)), the Principles slightly raise the bar for judicial interference in favour of party autonomy. Yet, their lack of clear-cut definitions or yardsticks for the relevant thresholds of "gross excessiveness" and "reasonableness" of the awarded amount[1213] might turn out to provide too much of a back entrance for judges or arbitrators to apply their individual measures and thereby diminish legal certainty as much as the Indian position does.

As to the types of clauses covered by their relevant provisions, the Principles and Sec. 74 of the Indian Contract Act are quite similar as well. In India, the general rule today appears to be that both earnest money and security deposits may be subjected to forfeiture clauses.[1214] As a consequence, the court may only disregard the forfeiture clause and award a reasonable compensation as per Sec. 74 if the amount to be forfeited does not represent a genuine pre-estimate of the likely harm. The drafters of the Principles, too, have acknowledged that clauses accord-

1212 At least one tribunal has refused to apply the Principles' rule that the courts may appropriately reduce an unreasonbly high amount of liquidated damages in lieu of English law, to which such judicial interference is unknown. See *Tribunale Rovereto, Universal Pictures International No. 2 B.V. v. Curatela del fallimento academy pictures s.r.l.* (15 March 2007), available at http://www.unilex.info.

1213 See *cf. supra* A.

1214 See, *e.g.*, Bhadbhade, *supra* note 137 at 1695.

ing to which the aggrieved party may retain money advanced as part of the price (*viz.* payments corresponding to what is known under (English) common law as earnest money) are subject to UPICC Art. 7.4.13 and PECL Art. 9:509 and thus enforceable.[1215] Conversely, an amount of money which was not paid as an agreed payment for non-performance but only as a deposit for an option to purchase does not fall under these two articles and can therefore not be reduced by the court.[1216]

In all, both UPICC Art. 7.4.13 and PECL Art. 9:509 as well as Sec. 74 of the Indian Contract Act appear to effectively promote the two major purposes of liquidated damages and penalties, namely to avoid litigation and promote legal certainty by reducing the difficulties, time and cost involved in proving the actual harm caused by a non-performance, and to deter non-performance.[1217] In this sense, all three provisions have been conceived as preferable particularly over English common law as they avoid the difficult distinction between (generally enforceable) liquidated damages and (strictly unenforceable) penalties as well as the unpredictability that this distinction brings about.[1218]

1215 See Comment 4 and Ill. 4 to UPICC Art. 7.4.13.

1216 See Ill. 3 to UPICC Art. 7.4.13.

1217 See, *e.g.*, Comment 1 to UPICC Art. 7.4.13 and Comment A to PECL Art. 9:509. Joseph M. Perillo (*supra* note 130 at 314) has even stated that "[the UPICC adopt] a rule consistent with the modern civil law. So should we."

1218 For Indian Contract Act Sec. 74, see, *e.g.*, Bhadbhade, *supra* note 137 at 1654. For UPICC Art. 7.4.13 and PECL Art. 9:509, see, *e.g.*, Zimmermann, *supra* note 161 at 483, and Perillo, *supra* note 130 at 313.

Chapter VIII: Reduction of price

I. Principles

Unlike the UNIDROIT Principles, the PECL grant the aggrieved party a right to reduce the price if it has accepted a non-conforming tender of performance, thereby providing a fifth stand-alone remedy for non-performance. While this divergence between the two sets of Principles has been categorized as being of merely "technical nature", that is, not due to any "particular 'policy' reason",[1219] it clearly separates the UPICC not only from the PECL but also from the CISG[1220] and most civil-law jurisdictions, where this remedy is firmly established under the name of the term "*actio quanti minoris*".[1221]

Pursuant to PECL Art. 9:401(1), a party accepting a non-conforming tender may reduce the price by an amount that is proportionate to the difference between the value of the non-conforming performance at the time of the actual tender and the virtual value of performance as promised. Non-conformity in this context comprises any deficiency regarding quality, quantity, time of delivery or any other attribute of the respective obligation,[1222] and the price may be reduced regardless of whether the default is excused or unexcused.[1223] In fact, it is this very independence from the question of whether the promisor is at all liable for the default which renders this remedy a valuable alternative in cases where damages are unavailable because the non-performance is excused and the promisee is also not entitled or not willing to terminate the contract. What is more, a price reduction may even generate a higher amount of financial redress than damages if the contractually agreed price would have exceeded the actual financial value of performance.[1224]

If the promisee accepts the non-conforming tender and opts to reduce the price, it is entitled to withhold an appropriate portion of the same or, in the event that it has already paid a part of or the entire price, recover the sum exceeding the

1219 See, *e.g.*, Bonell/Peleggi, *supra* note 116 at 321, and Bonell, *supra* note 29 at 238.

1220 See CISG Art. 50.

1221 See *cf.* Note 1 to PECL Art. 9:401 and Magnus, *supra* note 5 at 273. In fact, at least one member of the Working Groups drafting the UPICC, Reinhard Zimmermann (*supra* note 34 at 30), has recommended the inclusion of a provision entitling the aggrieved party to reduce the price.

1222 See Comment A to PECL Art. 9:401.

1223 See Comment B to PECL Art. 9:401.

1224 See Ill. 2 to PECL Art. 9:401.

relevant amount (PECL Art. 9:401(2)). If, in turn, the aggrieved party rightfully rejects the tender, it may either terminate the contract and recover any payments it has already made (as per PECL Art. 9:301 *et seq.*), or claim damages subject to Art. 9:501 *et seq.*[1225]

PECL Art. 9:401(3) reiterates the evident limitation that the remedy of price reduction is incompatible with a claim of damages for the decrease in the value of performance. However, this loss does not limit the aggrieved party's right to recover any further losses caused by the non-conforming tender.[1226]

II. Indian statutory law

Price reduction as a means of balancing a loss incurred by the aggrieved party due to *incompleteness* of performance is known to Indian statutory contract law as well, albeit not as a remedy. Rather, where only a part of a contract can be performed, the courts may award specific relief with respect to the performable part and simultaneously order the promisor to refund the consideration that the aggrieved party had already paid for the non-performable part, or alternatively allow the latter to make an appropriate abatement from the price.

Subject to the court's discretion, Sec. 12(3)(i) of the Specific Relief Act, 1963 (the stipulations of which did not appear in the repealed Act of 1877) permits such coupling of an order of specific performance of a part of a contract with a price reduction under the following conditions:

(1) One party is unable to perform a considerable part of the contract (*i.e.*, a portion that is material regarding its quantity or quality), and it is therefore reasonable for the other party to reject performance of the non-performable part (Sec. 12(3)(a)).[1227]
(2) The non-performance of the non-performable portion can be compensated in money (Specific Relief Act Sec. 12(3)(a)). (Compensation in money for the non-performance of a part of a contract shall not be ordered if there is no way to ascertain a fair and reasonable amount that reflects the difference in value between what was promised and what can actually be performed, or, in other words, where it is impossible to make even a reasonable estimate.[1228])
(3) The plaintiff agrees to relinquish all claims to performance of the non-performable part as well as all claims to compensation for the incompleteness of

1225 See Ill. 1 to PECL Art. 9:401.
1226 See, *e.g.*, Ill. 4 to PECL Art. 9:401.
1227 See *cf.* Bhadbhade, *supra* note 137 at 2462.
1228 See *cf. id.*

performance itself and for any further loss or damages incurred as a result of the partial default (Specific Relief Act Sec. 12(3)(ii)).

Given the above requisites, the court may order that the performable part shall be performed and that the price (to be) paid shall be reduced by the consideration that was owed for that part. The fact that Sec. 12(2) of the Specific Relief Act may only be invoked by the promisee implicates that it has a choice: it may either (1) sue for performance of the performable part of the contract and in turn make a proportionate abatement, or (2) pay the full price and claim compensation for the loss caused by the incompleteness.[1229]

If the unperformed part cannot be compensated in money, the promisee may obtain an order of specific performance only upon payment of the price in full (Sec. 12(3)(i)).

III. Comparative analysis

Unlike the PECL and most civil-law systems, neither the UPICC nor (English) common law grant the aggrieved party a general right to reduce the price. The only remedies available for a non-conforming performance under the latter regimes are (1) damages for the difference between the value of performance as promised and the value of what has actually been delivered,[1230] or (2) termination of the contract and recovery of the entire price. Both of these options are available as alternatives under the PECL, too.

As Indian statutory law generally corresponds with common-law tradition in this area, it is clear that the dogmatic meaning of the term "reduced (…) consideration" in Sec. 12(3)(i) of the Specific Relief Act is quite different from the European Principles' conception of price reduction as a stand-alone remedy. This is particularly illustrated by the fact that Indian law – just like other common-law systems – provides for an abatement of the price only where performance is *incomplete*[1231] in a quantitative sense. Conversely, price reduction under the PECL Art. 9:401 is available for any non-conforming performance, including excused non-performance.[1232] Nevertheless, an arbitrary price reduction carried out by the aggrieved party (as under the PECL) on the one hand and a judgment ordering specific performance of a part of the contract coupled with a proportionate deduc-

1229 See, *e.g.*, Singh, *supra* note 218 at 738.

1230 The amount of damages payable as per this alternative may also be set off against the price. See *cf.* Note 2(a) to PECL Art. 9:401.

1231 See Note 2(a)(i) to PECL Art. 9:401.

1232 See Comment A to PECL Art. 9:401.

tion from the price (as under Specific Relief Act Sec. 12(3)(i)) on the other hand certainly bring about similar results in cases of incomplete performance.[1233]

In light of this observation and on the basis of the common understanding that the most practicable solutions to a particular issue should be transposed into harmonised laws, the conception of price reduction as a fully-fledged remedy appears to be the superior approach.[1234] This is not least because such a remedy provides an additional incentive for the aggrieved party to refrain from terminating the contract and thus promotes one of the centres of gravitation shared by many instruments of contract law harmonisation: the principle of preservation of the contract as far as possible, or *favor contractus*.

1233 See also Note 2 to PECL Art. 9:401.

1234 See also Magnus, *supra* note 5 at 274.

Conclusions

I. Generally

- The general finding of this survey is that the UNIDROIT and European Principles and Indian statutory contract law not only share a striking structural proximity in that their black letter rules are often accompanied by Explanations and Illustrations. In addition, their respective rules on non-performance and remedies in many respects either appear to be derived from the same legal concepts or (are likely to) lead to quite similar outcomes.
- The Principles are broadly similar in methodology, legal character, applicability, and contents.
- While both the UNIDROIT and the European Principles have served as sources of inspiration or model rules for new or revised legislation, especially the UPICC have been well-received by trade organizations and arbitral courts as a comprehensive set of rules that are eligible to govern contracts, and they have frequently been relied upon as sources of reference in interpreting contract laws. By this measure, the PECL have not been equally successful; yet, they play a pivotal role in the furtherance of European contract law harmonisation, namely by serving as a basis in the development of the Common Frame of Reference (CFR) and therefore also of a possible (optional) uniform instrument of EU contract law.
- Indian statutory law on contractual non-performance and remedies is mainly found in the Indian Contract Act, 1872, the Specific Relief Act, 1963 and the Interest Act, 1978.

II. Non-performance in general

- The Principles' notion of "non-performance" is based on a unitary concept: any failure to perform or any non-conforming performance of a contractual obligation, irrespective of its cause or consequences, constitutes non-performance. Hence, while the term non-performance serves as a general designation for what is described as "breach of contract", "default" etc. in other contract law systems, each remedy has particular requirements and it is only in this context that a distinction between excused or unexcused or fundamental or non-fundamental non-performance is of relevance.

- As opposed to the Principles, the Indian Contract Act does not provide an express definition of what this statute describes as "non-performance" or "breach of contract." While the term "non-performance" itself is used only sporadically, "breach of contract", in accordance with English common law, requires a failure to perform *and* a cause of action for the promisee to claim damages. This conception implies that breach of contract – just as under English common law – is to be asserted only if the non-performance is unexcused.
- All three instruments' notions of non-performance or breach of contract and the respective systems of remedies are based on the common-law doctrine of no-fault liability, according to which each party is strictly liable to perform its contractual obligations unless performance is *excused.*
- With regard to *prevention* of performance by the promisee, the scope of the Indian Contract Act corresponds to that of the Principles. All three instruments refer to an intentional and direct act of prevention as well as to any indirect conduct by the promisee that causes a failure of the other party to perform. However, Indian (and English) courts require any such conduct to be *wrongful.* However, the three regimes differ as to the consequences prescribed in cases where performance has been prevented by the promisee.
- As for the promisee's rejection of a valid tender of performance, all three instruments set forth requirements for a valid tender and agree that the promisee may not claim any remedies in this case.
- Both sets of Principles entitle the parties to withhold performance in three general situations: first, if the parties are to perform *simultaneously*, each of them may withhold performance until the other tenders performance or actually performs. Second, if the parties are to perform *consecutively*, the promisor may withhold performance until the party that is to perform first has performed its obligations. Finally, the promisor may, to a reasonable extent, partially withhold its performance if the promisee that is to perform first fails to perform fully. If a party is entitled to withhold performance, its own non-performance is *excused* until the other party actually performs or tenders performance. In relation to cases where the party that is to perform first seeks to withhold performance because it is *already clear* that the other will fail to perform its part, the UPICC and PECL account for a notable difference.
- The Indian Contract Act expressly entitles the parties to withhold performance in cases where the promisor (1) fails to perform a reciprocal promise that is to be performed simultaneously with the promisee's promise, or (2) fails to perform a reciprocal promise that is to be performed first. If the party that is to perform first fails to do so at the time of performance, it may not claim

performance of the reciprocal promise and must compensate the promisee for losses sustained by the failure.

- In accordance with their focus on encouraging performance and preserving the contract, both sets of Principles comprise a right to cure non-performance. However, the scope of their respective rules differs considerably. Subject to a fourfold test and provided that the contract does not require timely performance, the UPICC provide a comparably far-reaching right to cure. Based on a somewhat narrower concept than the UNIDROIT Principles, the PECL entitles the promisor to cure its non-performance only (1) if it has previously made a non-conforming tender that was rejected by the promisee and (2) if "the time for performance has not yet arrived or the delay would not be such as to constitute a fundamental non-performance", *viz.* time is not of the essence of the contract. The Indian Contract Act contains no express provision on the right to cure. However, it acknowledges that there are cases where the promisee must accept performance even if it is delayed. The Contract Act thus essentially corresponds to the UPICC in that, unless time is of the essence, performance may be rendered or non-performance cured even after the time when performance was due. As a consequence, both Indian law and the UPICC are plainly contrary to the strict rule set forth in the PECL.
- Based on the assumption that, if there is a delay in performance, the promisee is generally still interested in the performance of the contract, it may, without losing any of its remedies, give the other party a second chance to perform (and thereby indicate its continuing interest in performance). During the extra period, the aggrieved party may withhold performance of its own reciprocal obligations and recover damages for any loss caused by the delay; however, it is barred from invoking any other remedies such as terminating the contract or claiming specific performance. The Indian Contract Act permits the promisee to grant an extension of the time for performance. According to the Indian Supreme Court, the extension of time requires an *agreement* comprising mutual consent by the parties, which must be expressed orally, in writing or through their conduct. As for the effects of an extension, Indian law corresponds to the Principles.
- Under the UPICC, exemption clauses may not be invoked if they are "grossly unfair" in relation to the purpose of the contract, and the parties may not waive the restrictions imposed by this provision. In principle, the PECL provide a similar rule: "clauses excluding or restricting remedies" for non-performance may not be invoked if this were contrary to good faith and fair dealing. The PECL, unlike the UPICC, provide general rules on unfair contract terms that were not negotiated individually. Indian statutory contract law does not provide an express rule on the validity of exemption or limitation clauses. Instead,

the Indian Contract Act merely provides that contract clauses are void if they create unfair advantages because they are the result of a party's undue influence on the free will of the other party.

- Situations referred to, *inter alia*, as *force majeure* or impossibility due to unforeseen supervening events in civil-law systems or as frustration under English common law are addressed as "Force majeure" under the UPICC and "Excuse Due to an Impediment" under the PECL. Despite their use of different designations, the two sets of Principles' provisions on *force majeure* are very similar. Non-performance of any contractual obligation – including a total failure to perform or mere delay – is generally *excused* under the following conditions: (1) the non-performance is due to a supervening impediment which is beyond the promisor's sphere of control, and (2) the promisor could not reasonably have been expected to take the impediment into account at the time of conclusion of the contract or to avoid or overcome the impediment or its consequences. Impediments which are eligible to excuse the failure if they could not have reasonably been foreseen or avoided may be due to subsequent changes in law that render performance *illegal* as well as to physical factors that render it *impossible.* In the absence of any contrary contractual stipulation, *force majeure* operates as an excuse to non-performance. As a result, the promisor is not liable to pay any damages, liquidated damages or penalties, and *force majeure* also constitutes a defence against a claim of specific performance. (This may be different under the UPICC if a particular situation constitutes both *force majeure* and hardship.)

In synchrony with its common-law tradition, Indian law subjects cases where performance of a valid contract subsequently becomes impossible due to a supervening event beyond the parties' control to the doctrine of frustration. According to Sec. 56(2) of the Indian Contract Act, "[a] contract to do an act which, after the contract is made, becomes impossible (…), becomes void when the act becomes impossible (…)." The section thus marks an exception to the general common-law principle of "no-fault liability", *i.e.*, absolute liability of the parties for their obligations under a contract. "Impossibility" in this sense is not confined to its literal meaning. Instead, it addresses what is known under English law as frustration either due to physical impossibility of performance or to mere destruction of the commercial object of the contract. Mere commercial difficulty, *i.e.*, the fact that performance has only become unprofitable, more costly or otherwise more onerous, does not constitute frustration due to a change of circumstances. Impossibility and frustration in the above sense lead to *automatic* termination of the contract from the time of the occurrence of the supervening event (Indian Contract Act Sec. 56(2)). As a result, the failure to perform is excused and the promisor is not liable to pay damages; in other words, the promisor does not commit a breach of contract. Consequently, the aggrieved party's obligations are also discharged.

III. Specific performance

- The UNIDROIT and European Principles present widely identical systems of remedies. Both instruments provide four remedies for non-performance: the right to withhold performance; specific performance; termination; and damages. Unlike the UPICC, the PECL arrange for a fifth remedy, namely the aggrieved party's right to reduce the price in exchange for accepting a non-conforming tender of performance.
- Indian law distinguishes between damages as the presumptive remedy for breach of contract on the one hand and specific relief, preventive injunction and termination (which are available only in specific circumstances) on the other hand. Alternatively, the aggrieved party may also claim restitution of the value of what had been performed by the aggrieved party prior to the breach (*quantum meruit* claim).
- The Principles' provisions on the creditor's right to the performance of monetary obligations widely correspond to the situation under Indian law, under which the promise actually has a *right* to performance of contractual monetary obligations due to their being primary contractual duties. As a result and unlike generally (*viz.*, in relation to non-monetary obligations), specific performance of these obligations is neither an exceptional remedy nor left to the courts' discretion.
- Unlike their rules on the performance of monetary obligations, the Principles' rules on specific performance of non-monetary obligations are structurally diametric to those under Indian law. Whereas the UPICC and PECL grant the promisee a non-discretionary right to performance under two conditions, namely that the contract is valid and has not been terminated and that none of the general exceptions and limitations set out in the relevant black letter rules apply, Indian law generally qualifies specific relief as an exceptional remedy awarded at the sole discretion of the courts and only where damages would provide inadequate relief or in lack of a standard for determining the exact amount of payable damages. Consequently – and similar to English and Scottish law but in contrast to the Principles – neither the Specific Relief Act nor Indian case law provide any indication whatsoever as to whether the promisee shall have a right to claim cure of defective performance of non-monetary obligations. However, in spite of their fundamentally different conceptions of

this remedy, the Principles and the Indian Specific Relief Act share a number of very similar rules in relation to the instances in which the promisee's right to specific performance is excluded (Principles) or in which the courts shall not award specific relief (Indian law), respectively.

- Pursuant to the UNIDROIT Principles, a party may abandon its claim for performance and instead invoke any other remedy if a judgment ordering the other party to perform has not yet been rendered or if performance has not been received within an additional period for performance fixed by the aggrieved party or otherwise within a reasonable period of time. If the aggrieved party has already obtained a judgment ordering performance of the contract, Art. 7.2.5(2) allows for an *immediate* shift to another remedy. The black letter rules of the European Principles do not expressly address the option of shifting from specific performance to another remedy. However, substantive divergences between the two instruments have been characterized as emanating from "no particular 'policy' reason" and therefore being of merely "technical nature."

  Absent any express rule to the contrary, the Indian Specific Relief Act generally allows for free shifting between different remedies until a court has passed a judgment ordering performance of the contract. Provided that the plaintiff has sued for compensation in the alternative to specific performance or amended its plaint accordingly during the proceedings, the court may at its discretion award damages if it opines that specific relief should not be awarded but that there has indeed been a breach of contract for which the aggrieved party should be compensated.

IV. Termination of contracts

- A remedy for both excused and unexcused non-performance and generally independent of any prior period of grace, termination of the contract under the Principles releases both parties from their obligations to tender and accept future performance, and usually entails restitution of what has previously been exchanged.
- Except in a limited number of circumstances, termination of a contract by the aggrieved party presupposes a fundamental non-performance. The right to terminate the contract is independent of whether the promisor is actually liable for the non-performance, *i.e.*, whether the default is excused or unexcused. In general terms, fundamentality requires that the non-performance is material and not only of minor importance, thereby destroying the promisee's expectations from the performance of the contract. The Principles seek to further sub-

stantiate the term by identifying a set of additional factors to determine what actually constitutes fundamentality.

- Where it is already evident prior to the date when performance is due that there will be a non-performance by one party, the other party may be entitled to terminate the contract even before the actual due date. The Principles also allow a party to demand adequate assurance of due performance if it reasonably believes that there will be fundamental non-performance, *e.g.*, in cases of insolvency of the other party. If the latter subsequently fails to provide such assurance within reasonable time, the former may terminate the contract.
- Termination by the aggrieved party on any of the grounds presented in the preceding sections is to be effected by way of a notice of termination. However, the European Principles pronounce the contract *automatically* terminated in cases where the non-performance is excused due to a total and permanent impediment.
- The Indian Contract Act provides that a contract is automatically void if performance of the same is or becomes impossible and unlawful. This rule also applies to unlawfulness of performance. In cases of frustration, Indian law provides that the contract terminates automatically and irrespectively of the parties' intentions.
- Where a party repudiates the contract by unrightfully refusing to perform ("renunciation") or disabling itself from performing a substantial portion of its obligations, the other party may terminate the contract. Provided the test under Sec. 39 of the Contract Act is met, the aggrieved party has two options: it may either accept the repudiation and terminate the contract, thereby releasing both itself and the promisor from their respective obligations while retaining a right to claim damages for breach of contract; alternatively, it may affirm the persistence of the contract and further insist on performance. The aggrieved party is required to communicate its decision to terminate or "acquiesce to the contract" to the repudiating party.
- The Indian Contract Act also allows for termination of the contract by a party if the other has prevented it from performing a reciprocal obligation. Moreover, Indian law provides for a right of termination where timely performance is so important that any delay materially affects the promisee's interest in receiving it, *viz.* if the parties had the intention that time should be of the essence of the contract.
- As the Principles generally do not provide for automatic termination by force of law, the consequences that these two instruments impose are contrary to the doctrine of frustration. Indian statutory contract law, on the other hand, incorporates the doctrine of frustration and thus distinguishes between cases

of termination by force of law and those where the aggrieved party is entitled to put an end to the contract at its own option.

- The grounds on the basis of which the three instruments determine what justifies termination are strikingly similar. In fact, many of the Principles' rules on termination were strongly influenced by English law and therefore reflect a number of common-law concepts that also underlie the corresponding provisions of the Indian Contract Act. What is more, the criteria that are to be taken into account in determining whether a particular non-performance entitles the promisee to terminate the contract are fairly similar.
- The rights of the aggrieved party to request adequate assurance of performance or to terminate the contract if such assurance is not given are altogether unknown to both common law in general and Indian statutory contract law. Instead, the only apparent means available under Indian law by which a party fearing that the other will not perform may obtain assurance would be to invoke the doctrine of "promissory estoppel".
- The Principles stipulate that the termination of a contract at the option of the aggrieved party does not take retroactive effect. Instead, the parties shall be released from their obligations to tender or receive any future performance under the terminated contract. Contract clauses which were intended to operate even after termination, *e.g.*, dispute resolution, confidentiality or non-compete clauses, remain unaffected by the execution of this remedy, and termination does not preclude a claim of damages for non-performance. The Principles' rules on *restitution* differ fundamentally: whereas the UPICC prescribe mutual restitution as a general consequence of termination, the European Principles rule out restitution where both parties have already performed their obligations. Instead, the PECL arrange for restitution (or, if restitution is impossible, a monetary allowance) only as a means of re-establishing equity where one party has performed but not yet received or rightfully rejected the other party's performance. The UPICC, the PECL and the Indian Contract Act unanimously grant the aggrieved party a right to damages even if it has chosen to terminate the contract.
- As per the Indian Contract Act, physical impossibility, unlawfulness or frustration render a contract automatically void. In cases of initial impossibility, unlawfulness or frustration, the contract is void *ab initio*, *i.e.*, from the time of its conclusion. If one of these grounds arises after the time when the contract was entered into, performance is excused for both parties from that time on, but liabilities already accrued remain unaffected. With regard to situations where the contract is not void by force of law but terminable at the aggrieved party's option, the Indian Contract Act establishes that termination in response to a refusal or self-induced disability to perform releases the repudiating party

from having to perform its own obligations from the time when the innocent party has validly accepted the repudiation and thereby terminated the contract. The Indian Contract Act does not contain any rules on whether contract clauses concerned with dispute resolution shall remain valid after termination. Yet, there is a fair amount of case law on this issue.

- In the context of repudiation, Indian law allows for a claim for *quantum meruit*, which is generally considered to be an alternative remedy to damages. A claim of *quantum meruit* is a restitutionary (as opposed to a compensatory) remedy aimed at reasonable remuneration, thus being closely related to the right to restitution.
- The rules on restitution not only mark a substantial parting of ways between the UNIDROIT Principles and the PECL. More importantly, they fortify the conclusion that, especially with a view on each instrument's value to international business transactions (which almost always involve synallagmatic contracts), the UPICC's approach appears clearly superior to the concept underlying the European Principles. In India, the rule established with a view on restitution is that "any person who has received any advantage under [a contract discovered to be or having become void] is bound to restore it, or to make compensation for it, to the person from whom he received it."

V. Damages

- The Principles confer to the aggrieved party a general right to damages, which is excluded only if the particular non-performance is excused. Under the Principles, the right to damages is thus based on the concept of no-fault liability, or "strict" liability, for non-performance. Neither set of Principles' concept of damages distinguishes between the particular types of non-performance, *viz.* delay or initial or subsequent impossibility. The harm for which the aggrieved party may claim compensation "includes both any loss which it suffered and any gain of which it was deprived." The term "loss" is hence understood in a wide sense.
- The promisor's liability for damages arises independently from the question of whether the non-performance is due to its fault ("no-fault liability"). Instead, the promisor can exculpate itself from liability for its non-performance if (and to the extent that) the same is excused due to certain external factors.
- Under the Principles, a party owes full compensation for the harm caused by its non-performance. This means that it must put the aggrieved party as nearly as possible into the position in which it would have been if the contract been

duly performed and is bound to restore the aggrieved party's "expectation interest". However, damages must not enrich the aggrieved party, and the courts are not authorized to arbitrarily reduce the amount of compensation as appropriate in certain circumstances.

- In accordance with common-law tradition, Indian law provides that any breach of contract gives rise to a cause of action for damages. Similarly, Indian statutory law does not require the breach of contract to be the result of the defaulting party's fault. Generally, Sec. 73(1) of the Indian Contract Act is considered to be "declaratory of the common law on damages." The term "loss or damage" used in Sec. 73 of the Indian Contract Act relates to three general categories of harm: (1) harm to property; (2) non-pecuniary harm; and (3) harm to the aggrieved party's economic position. –Moreover, Sec. 75 of the Indian Contract Act establishes that "[a] person who has rightfully rescinded a contract is entitled to compensation" in the five general sets of circumstances addressed by Sec. 39, 53, 54 and 55 of the Act.
- Under Indian law, the remedy of damages primarily seeks restoration of the "expectation interest": the aggrieved party is to be put in the position it would have been in if the contract had been performed. In the alternative, or if the aggrieved party cannot prove the value of its expectation interest, it may recover its "reliance interest", the objective of which is to restore the position that this party would have been in if the contract had not been concluded. Where no harm has occurred or where the aggrieved party did not sustain any substantial loss or damages or is unable to prove the same, Indian law allows for the awarding of "nominal damages".
- With a view on the general requirements of the remedy of damages, a comparison of the Principles and Indian statutory contract law show only minor divergences. This is primarily because the Principles' conception of the remedy closely corresponds to that of English common law. The Principles' general requirement that non-performance must not be excused is unknown to Sec. 73(1) of the Indian Contract Act. In principle, however, Indian law recognizes all major instances in which non-performance is excused under the Principles.
- Both sets of Principles unanimously provide that damages can be recovered only for harm that the non-performing party foresaw or could reasonably have foreseen as a likely result of its non-performance at the time of conclusion of the contract. However, the two sets of Principles account for a substantial divergence in that the European Principles do not impose the foreseeability requirement if the non-performance was intentional or grossly negligent. In India, in accordance with English common law, the issue of limiting a party's liability for breach of contract to harm which it ought to have contemplated when it entered into the contract is treated as a question of "remoteness of damage".

According to the Indian Contract Act, the recoverable harm is limited to "that which naturally arose in the usual course of things from [the] breach, or which the parties knew, when they made the contract, to be likely to result from the breach of it". The concepts of "foreseeability" and "remoteness" as applicable under the Principles and Indian contract law are therefore practically identical.

- As the remedy of damages is compensatory in nature under all three instruments, neither one of them permits the awarding of punitive damages for non-performance or breach of contract.
- Unlike Indian contract law – under which damages are the primary remedy and a claim of specific relief is entirely in the courts' discretion – the Principles treat specific performance and damages as equal and interchangeable forms of redress.
- Both the UPICC and – although in simpler terms – the PECL provide that the amount of damages for a contractual non-performance shall be reduced to the extent that the aggrieved party's conduct or an event for which it bears the risk contributed to the occurrence or caused an increase of its harm. Indian courts have fully recognized the rule of English law under which the defence of "contributory negligence" is inapplicable to claims of damages for breach of contract unless the breach also constituted a tort. Instead, it has been applied where a party breaches a contractual duty of reasonable care in a manner that would have been independently actionable under tort law.
- Under the UNIDROIT and European Principles, the non-performing party's liability is excluded to the extent that the aggrieved party could have taken reasonable steps to mitigate the harm caused by the non-performance. The Principles provide the ancillary rule that the aggrieved party may recover any reasonable expenses it has incurred in attempting to comply with its duty to mitigate the harm. Indian contract law, too, contains a statutory reference to the duty to mitigate damages. Under the Indian Contract Act, the aggrieved party owes a duty of taking all reasonable steps to mitigate the loss caused by the breach and cannot claim damages for any loss that it could have mitigated by complying with this duty. Any expenses incurred in attempting to mitigate damages are recoverable as additional loss.
- Both sets of Principles provide that a delay in the payment of money owed under a primary contractual monetary obligation gives rise to liability to pay interest upon that sum. Non-contractual, or secondary, debt such as damages or interest is not subject to these provisions. The right to interest on contractual debt is not subject to the Principles' general provisions on damages such as those on the duty to mitigate, the means of quantifying damages, or the rule that the non-performing party is not liable to pay damages if its failure to perform was excused. As for the amount of interest owed, both sets of Principles

provide a universal standard for the computation of the applicable interest rate, namely the average bank short-term lending rate to prime borrowers as applicable to the respective currency of payment at the agreed place of payment.

- Indian law does not recognize a general right to interest in cases of late payment of a contractual debt. Instead, courts in India are authorized to award interest in three types of situations, *viz.* (1) if interest is payable by virtue of a custom or usage; (2) if there is an express or implied agreement under which interest is payable; or (3) subject to any provision of substantive law entitling a party to recover interest, most importantly the sections of the Interest Act, 1978. Under the Interest Act, a court or arbitral tribunal may, "[i]n any proceedings for the recovery of any debt or damage or in any proceedings in which a claim for interest in respect of any debt or damages already paid is made, (…) if it thinks fit, allow interest (…) at a rate not exceeding the current rate of interest." If, *inter alia*, the amount of damages without interest exceeds INR 4,000, the court or arbitral tribunal is bound to award interest on the amount of damages at a reasonable rate that must not exceed the current rate of interest; claims for interest for any smaller amounts of damages are subject to full judicial discretion.
- As per the Principles, damages should be assessed in the currency that most appropriately reflects the loss sustained by the aggrieved party. The question under English law is similar, namely whether, to measure the loss, it is more appropriate to make reference to the contractual currency or to the currency in which the loss was sustained.
- Finally, under the Principles, not only liquidated damages but also penalty clauses are generally enforceable unless they are exceptionally unfair. According to the Principles' drafters, the term "agreement to pay a specified sum" is intentionally broad so as to cover both liquidated damages and penalty clauses. Hence, where a contract clause stipulates that the non-performing party is to pay the aggrieved party a specified sum for a non-performance, the latter is entitled to that sum irrespective of whether and to what extent it has actually sustained any harm unless the agreed sum is "grossly excessive". According to the Indian Contract Act, a breach of a contract in which "as sum is named (…) as the amount to be paid in case of such breach" or which "contains any other stipulation by way of penalty" entitles the aggrieved party to reasonable compensation not exceeding the stipulated amount regardless of "whether or not actual damage or loss is proved to have been caused thereby." Thus, as a general rule, Indian courts are to award the full agreed sum if it represents a genuine pre-estimate of the harm that is likely to be caused by the non-performance. This rule marks a departure from the position in England, where liquidated damages are generally recoverable whereas penalty clauses are strictly unen-

forceable. In relation to liquidated damages and penalty clauses, it is therefore the very departure of the Indian legislature from the position under English law that moves Sec. 74 of the Indian Contract Act quite close to the relevant rules under the UNIDROIT and European Principles.

VI. Reduction of price

- Unlike the UNIDROIT Principles, the PECL grant the aggrieved party a right to reduce the price if it has accepted a non-conforming tender of performance, thereby providing a fifth stand-alone remedy for non-performance. Pursuant to the PECL, a party accepting a non-conforming tender may reduce the price by an amount that is proportionate to the difference between the value of the non-conforming performance at the time of the actual tender and the virtual value of performance as promised.
- Price reduction as a means of balancing a loss incurred by the aggrieved party due to *incompleteness* of performance is known to Indian statutory contract law as well, albeit not as a remedy.

Bibliography

Antoniolli, Luisa; Veneziano, Anna (eds.) — *Principles of European Contract Law and Italian Law*, The Hague 2005

Bangia, R. K. — *Indian Contract Act*, 11th ed., Faridabad 2004

Bangia, R. K. — *Law of Contract*, Part II, Faridabad 2005

Basedow, Jürgen (ed.) — *Europäische Vertragsrechtsvereinheitlichung und deutsches Recht*, Tübingen 2000

Beale, Hugh — *The Future of the Common Frame of Reference*, European Review of Contract Law 2007 at 257

Beale, Hugh — *Remedies for breach of contract*, London 1980

Berger, Klaus Peter — *The lex mercatoria Doctrine and the UNIDROIT Principles of International Commercial Contracts*, Law & Policy in International Business 1997 at 943

Berger, Klaus Peter; Dubberstein, Holger; Lehmann, Sascha; Petzold, Viktoria — *The CENTRAL Study on the Use of Transnational Law in International Contract Law and Arbitration: Background, Procedure and Selected Results*, International Arbitration Law Review 2000 at 145

Bhadbhade, Nilima (ed.) — *Mulla, Indian Contract and Specific Relief Acts*, 12th ed., vol. I & II, New Delhi 2001

Blase, Friedrich — *Die Grundregeln des Europäischen Vertragsrechts als Recht grenzüberschreitender Verträge*, Münster 2001

Boele-Woelki, Katharina — *Principles and Private International Law*, Uniform Law Review 1996 at 652

Bonell, Michael Joachim — *The UNIDROIT Principles in Practice: The Experience of the First Two Years*, Uniform Law Review 1997 at 34

Bonell, Michael Joachim — *The UNIDROIT Principles for International Commercial Contracts and the Principles of European Contract Law: Similar Rules for the Same Purposes?*, Uniform Law Review 1996 at 229

Bonell, Michael Joachim — *UNIDROIT Principles 2004 – The New Edition of the Principles of International Commercial Contracts adopted by the International Institute for the Unification of Private Law*, Uniform Law Review 2004 at 5

Bonell, Michael Joachim — *The UNIDROIT Principles and Transnational Law*, Uniform Law Review 2000 at 199

Bonell, Michael Joachim — *A 'Global' Arbitration Decided on the Basis of the UNIDROIT Principles: In re Andersen Consulting Business Unit Member Firms v. Arthur Andersen Business Unit Member Firms and Andersen Worldwide Société Coopérative*, Arbitration International 2001 at 249

Bonell, Michael Joachim — *The UNIDROIT Principles and CISG – Sources of Inspiration for English Courts?*, Uniform Law Review 2006 at 305

Bonell, Michael Joachim — *Towards a Legislative Codification of the UNIDROIT Principles?*, Uniform Law Review 2007 at 233

Bonell, Michael Joachim — *The UNIDROIT Principles in Practice, Caselaw and Bibliography on the Principles of Commercial Contracts*, New York 2002

Bonell, Michael Joachim — *An International Restatement of Contract Law*, 3rd ed., Ardsley (NY) 2005

Bonell, Michael Joachim — *The UNIDROIT Principles in Practice, Caselaw and Bibliography on the Principles of Commercial Contracts*, 2nd ed., New York 2006

Bonell, Michael Joachim; Peleggi, Roberta — *UNIDROIT Principles of International Commercial Contracts and Principles of European Contract Law: a Synoptical Table*, Uniform Law Review 2004 at 315

Bonell, Michael Joachim; Peleggi, Roberta	*UNIDROIT Principles of International Commercial Contracts and Draft Common Frame of Reference: a Synoptical Table*, Uniform Law Review 2009 at 437
Busch, Danny; Hondius, Ewoud	*Ein neues Vertragsrecht für Europa: Die Principles of European Contract Law aus niederländischer Sicht*, Zeitschrift für Europäisches Privatrecht 2001 at 223
Coen, Christoph	*Vertragsscheitern und Rückabwicklung*, Berlin 2003
Council of the European Union	*(Draft) Report to the Council on the setting up of a Common Frame of Reference for European contract law* (as endorsed by the Council as Council position on 18 April 2008 (document no. 8286/08))
DiMatteo, Larry A.	*Contract Talk: Reviewing the Historical and Practical Significance of the Principles of European Contract Law*, Harvard International Law Journal 2002 at 569
Drobnig, Ulrich	*The UNIDROIT Principles in the Conflict of Law*, Uniform Law Review 1998 at 385
Düchs, Constantin	*Die Behandlung von Leistungsstörungen im Europäischen Vertragsrecht*, Berlin 2006
European Commission	*A more Coherent European Contract Law – An Action Plan*, Communication from the Commission to the European Parliament and the Council, COM(2003) 68 final (12 February 2003)
European Commission	*Commission Decision 2010/233/EU of 26 April 2010 setting up the Expert Group on a Common Frame of Reference in the area of European contract law*, O.J. 2010, L-105 (26 April 2010)
European Commission	*European Contract Law and the Revision of the Acquis: The Way Forward*, Communication from the Commission to the European Parliament and the Council, COM(2004) 651 final (11 October 2004)
European Commission	*Communication from the Commission to the Council and the European Parliament on European Contract Law*, COM(2001) 398 final (11 July 2001)

European Commission	*Green Paper from the Commission on policy options for progress towards a European Contract Law for consumers and businesses*, COM(2010) 348 final (1 July 2010)
European Commission	*Green Paper on the Review of the Consumer Acquis*, COM(2006) 744 final (8 February 2007)
European Parliament	*European Parliament resolution of 12 December 2007 on European contract law* (12 December 2007), available at http://www.europarl.europa.eu
Fontaine, Marcel	*Les clauses exonératoires et les indemnities contractuelles dans les Principes d'UNIDROIT: Observations critiques*, Uniform Law Review 1998 at 405
Fontaine, Marcel	*Le projet d'Acte uniforme OHADA sur les contrats et les Principes d'UNIDROIT relatifs aux contrats du commerce international*, Uniform Law Review 2004 at 253
Garner, Bryan A. (ed. in chief)	*Black's Law Dictionary*, Second Pocket Edition, St. Paul 2001
Goode, Roy	*International Restatements of Contract and English Contract Law*, Uniform Law Review 1997 at 231
Goode, Roy	*Commercial Law*, 3rd ed., London 2004
Goode, Roy; Kronke, Herbert; McKendrick, Ewan	*Transnational Commercial Law – Text, Cases, and Materials*, Oxford 2007
Goode, Roy; Kronke, Herbert; McKendrick, Ewan; Wool, Jeffrey	*Transnational Commercial Law – International Instruments and Commentary*, Oxford 2004
Gopalan, Sandeep	*The Creation of International Commercial Law: Sovereignty Felled?*, 5 San Diego International Law Journal (2004) at 267

Gopalan, Sandeep	*Transnational Commercial Law: The Way Forward*, 18 American University International Law Review (2003) at 803
Guest, A. G. (gen. ed.)	*Chitty on Contracts*, 27th ed., vol. I (*General Principles*), London 1994
Hartkamp, Arthur S.	*The UNIDROIT Principles for International Commercial Contracts and the Principles of European Contract Law*, European Review of Private Law 1994 at 341
Hartkamp, Arthur S. *et al.* (eds.)	*Towards a European Civil Code*, 3rd ed., Nijmegen 2004
Hauck, Brian	*Implementation of Work Programme 2006-2008 – UNIDROIT Principles of International Commercial Contracts*, Uniform Law Review 2006 at 336
Heiderhoff, Bettina	*Grundstrukturen des nationalen und europäischen Verbrauchervertragsrechts*, München 2004
Herber, Rolf	*„Lex mercatoria“ und „Principles“ – gefährliche Irrlichter im internationalen Kaufrecht*, Internationales Handelsrecht 2003 at 1
Hornung, Rainer	*Die Rückabwicklung gescheiterter Verträge nach französischem, deutschem und nach Einheitsrecht*, Baden-Baden 1998
IndLaw.com (not attributed)	*Bhardwaj says prospects are bright for making India an arbitration hub*, IndLaw.com, 20 October 2007
International Institute for the Unification of Private Law (UNIDROIT)	*UNIDROIT Principles of International Commercial Contracts*, Rome 1994
International Institute for the Unification of Private Law (UNIDROIT)	*UNIDROIT Principles of International Commercial Contracts 2004*, Rome 2004

International Institute for the Unification of Private Law (UNIDROIT) — *Implementation of Work Programme 2006-2008 – UNIDROIT Principles of International Commercial Contracts*, Uniform Law Review 2007 at 798

Kane, P. V. — *History of Dharmashastras*, vol. III, Pune 1946

Kessedjian, Catherine — *Un exercice de rénovation des sources du droit des contrats du commerce international: Les Principes proposés par l'Unidroit*, Revue critique de droit international 1995 at 641

Koch, Robert — *Whether the UNIDROIT Principles of International Commercial Contracts may be used to interpret or supplement Article 25 CISG*, Internationales Handeslrecht 2005 at 65

Kötz, Hein; Flessner, Axel — *European Contract Law*, vol. I, Oxford 1997

Kramer, Ernst A. — *Die Gültigkeit der Verträge nach den UNIDROIT Principles of International Commercial Contracts*, Zeitschrift für Europäisches Privatrecht 1999 at 209

Kronke, Herbert — *A Bridge out of the Fortress: UNIDROIT's Work on Global Modernisation of Commercial Law and its Relevance for Europe*, Zeitschrift für Europäisches Privatrecht 2008 at 1

Kronke, Herbert — *UNIDROIT Principles: New Developments and Applications*, International Court of Arbitration Bulletin, 2005 Special Supplement

Lando, Ole — *Salient Features of the Principles of European Contract Law: A Comparison with the UCC*, Pace International Law Journal 2001 at 339

Lando, Ole — *Principles of European Contract Law and UNIDROIT Principles: Moving from Harmonisation to Unification?*, Uniform Law Review 2003 at 123

Lando, Ole — *CISG and Its Followers: A Proposal to Adopt Some International Principles of Contract Law*, 53 American Journal of Comparative Law 2005 at 379

Lando, Ole — *The European Principles in an Integrated World*, European Review of Contract Law 2005 at 3

Lando, Ole — *The Structure and Legal Values of the Common Frame of Reference (CFR)*, European Review of Contract Law 2007 at 245

Lando, Ole; Beale, Hugh (eds.) — *Principles of European Contract Law, Parts I and II, Prepared by the Commission on European Contract Law*, Combined and Revised Edition, The Hague 2000

Law Commission of India — *199th Report on Unfair (Procedural & Substantive) Terms in Contract* (2006), available at http://lawcommissionof india.nic.in/reports/rep199.pdf

Law Commission of India — *13th Report (Contract Act, 1872)* (1958), available at http://lawcommissionofindia.nic.in/1-50/index1-50.htm

Leible, Stefan; Lehmann, Matthias — *Die Verordnung über das auf vertragliche Schuldverhältnisse anzuwendende Recht („Rom I“)*, Recht der international Wirtschaft 2008 at 528

Letterman, G. Gregory — *UNIDROIT's Rules in Practice: Standard International Contracts and Applicable Rules*, The Hague 2001

López Rodríguez, Ana M. — *Lex Mercatoria and Harmonisation of Contract Law in the EU*, Copenhagen 2003

Mahmood, Tahir — *The Muslim Law of India*, 3rd ed., New Delhi 2002

Magnus, Ulrich — *Wesentliche Fragen des UN-Kaufrechts*, Zeitschrift für Europäisches Privatrecht 1999 at 642

Magnus, Ulrich — *Das Recht der vertraglichen Leistungsstörungen und der Common Frame of Reference*, Zeitschrift für Europäisches Privatrecht 2007 at 260

Martiny, Dieter — *Europäisches Internationales Vertragsrecht in Erwartung der Rom-I-Verordnung*, Zeitschrift für Europäisches Privatrecht 2008 at 79

McQueen, Hector; Zimmermann, Reinhard (eds.) — *European Contract Law: Scots and South African Perspectives*, Edinburgh 2006

Mistelis, Loukas A. — *Regulatory Aspects: Globalization, Harmonisation, Legal Transplants, and Law Reform – Some Fundamental Observations*, International Lawyer 2000 at 1055

Nagendra, Chetan — *A suitable law is not ready as yet*, Financial Express, 28 June 2005, available at http://www.financialexpress.com

Perillo, Joseph M. — *Force Majeure and Hardship under the UNIDROIT Principles of International Commercial Contracts*, Tulane Journal of International and Comparative Law 1997 at 5

Perillo, Joseph M. — *UNIDROIT Principles of International Commercial Contracts: The Black Letter Text and a Review*, Fordham Law Review 1994 at 281

Perillo, Joseph M. — *Hardship and its Impact on Contractual Obligations, A Comparative Analysis*, Centro di studi e ricerche di diritto comparato e straniero: Saggi, Conferenze e Seminari, n. 20, Rome 1996

Rosett, Arthur — *UNIDROIT Principles and Harmonisation of International Commercial Law: Focus on Chapter 7*, Uniform Law Review 1997 at 441

Rösler, Hannes — *Hardship in German Codified Private Law – In Comparative Perspective to English, French and International Contract Law*, European Review of Private Law 2007 at 483

Saharay, H. K. — *Dutt on Contract – The Indian Contract Act, 1872*, 10th ed., Kolkata/New Delhi 2006

Sarin, Manmohan Lal — *Contract Unconscionability in India*, 14 Loyola of Los Angeles International and Comparative Law Journal (1992) at 569

Schulze, Reiner (ed.) — *Common Frame of Reference and Existing EC Contract Law*, Munich 2008

Singh, Avtar — *Law of Contract and Specific Relief*, 9th ed., Lucknow 2005 (reprinted, 2006)

Sivesand, Hanna — *The Buyer's Remedies For Non-Conforming Goods. Should there be Free Choice or are Restrictions Necessary?*, Munich 2005

Study Group on a European Civil Code; Research Group on EC Private Law (Acquis Group) — *Principles, Definitions and Model Rules of European Private Law – Draft Common Frame of Reference (DCFR) – Interim Outline Edition*, Munich 2008

Study Group on a European Civil Code; Research Group on EC Private Law (Acquis Group) — *Principles, Definitions and Model Rules of European Private Law – Draft Common Frame of Reference (DCFR) –Outline Edition*, Munich 2009

The Economist (not attributed) — *A bumpier but freer road*, The Economist, 2 October 2010 at 67

The Times of India (not attributed) — *Nobody can direct House on uniform civil code: SC*, The Times of India, 18 October 2008 at 15

Treitel, Guenter H. — *The law of contract*, 5th ed., London 1979

Treitel, Guenter H. — *Remedies for Breach of Contract – A Comparative Account*, Oxford 1988

van Vuuren, Elbi Janse — *Termination of International Commercial Contracts for Breach of Contract: The Provisions of the UNIDROIT Principles of International Commercial Contracts*, Arizona Journal of International and Comparative Law 1998 at 583

Vaquer, Antoni — *Tender of Performance, Mora Creditoris and the (Common?) Principles of European Contract Law*, The Tulane European and Civil Law Forum 2002 at 83

Vogenauer, Stefan; Kleinheisterkamp, Jan (eds.) — *Commentary on the UNIDROIT Principles of International Commercial Contracts*, Oxford 2008

von Bar, Christian; Zimmermann, Reinhard — *Grundregeln des Europäischen Vertragsrechts, Teile I und II* , München 2002

Work, Tracy S. — *India Satisfies Its Jones for Arbitration: New Arbitration Law in India*, 10 The Transnational Lawyer (1997) at 217

Zimmermann, Reinhard — *Konturen eines Europäischen Vertragsrechts*, Juristenzeitung 1995 at 477

Zimmermann, Reinhard — *Die „Principles of European Contract Law", Teil III*, Zeitschrift für Europäisches Privatrecht 2003 at 707

Zimmermann, Reinhard — *Die Unidroit-Grundregeln der internationalen Handelsverträge 2004 in vergleichender Perspektive*, Zeitschrift für Europäisches Vertragsrecht 2005 at 264

Zimmermann, Reinhard — *The UNIDROIT Principles of International Commercial Contracts 2004 in Comparative Perspective*, The Tulane European and Civil Law Forum 2006 at 1

Zimmermann, Reinhard — *Restituto in Integrum: The Unwinding of Failed Contracts under the Principles of European Contract Law, the UNIDROIT Principles and the Avant-projet d'un Code Européen des Contrats*, Uniform Law Review 2005 at 719

Zimmermann, Reinhard — *European Contract Law: General Report*, Europäisches Zeitschrift für Wirtschaftsrecht 2007 at 455

Zoll, Fryderyk — *UN-Kaufrecht und Common Frame of Reference im Bereich der Leistungsstörungen: Ein Beitrag aus der Perspektive der Acquis Group*, Zeitschrift für Europäisches Privatrecht 2007 at 229

Zweigert, Konrad; Kötz, Hein — *Introduction to Comparative Law*, 3rd ed., Oxford 1998

INTERNATIONALRECHTLICHE STUDIEN
Beiträge zum Internationalen Privatrecht,
zum Einheitsrecht und zur Rechtsvergleichung

Herausgegeben von Ulrich Magnus und Peter Mankowski

Band 1 Birgit Reimers-Zocher: Beweislastfragen im Haager und Wiener Kaufrecht. 1995.

Band 2 Lenja Vespermann: Schadensersatz bei Beeinträchtigung rechts- oder sittenwidriger Interessen im deutschen und französischen Recht. 1996.

Band 3 Peter Cypra: Die Rechtsbehelfe im Verfahren der Vollstreckbarerklärung nach dem EuGVÜ unter besonderer Berücksichtigung der Ausgestaltung in Deutschland und Frankreich. 1996.

Band 4 Brigitta Lurger: Regulierung und Deregulierung im europäischen Privatrecht. 1997.

Band 5 Uta Gutknecht: Das Nacherfüllungsrecht des Verkäufers bei Kauf- und Werklieferungsverträgen. Rechtsvergleichende Untersuchung zum CISG, zum US-amerikanischen Uniform Commercial Code, zum deutschen Recht und zu dem Vorschlag der Kommission zur Überarbeitung des deutschen Schuldrechts. 1996.

Band 6 Stefan Abel: Die Qualifikation der Schenkung. Zur Methode der Qualifikation im Internationalen Schuldvertragsrecht. 1997.

Band 7 Daniel Kötz: Verkäuferpflichten und Rechtsbehelfe des Käufers im neuen norwegischen Kaufrecht vom 13. Mai 1988 Nr. 27 im Vergleich zum UN-Kaufrecht vom 11. April 1980 (CISG). 1997.

Band 8 Olaf Beier: Grundsätze eines europäischen transportmittelübergreifenden Schadensrechts für den Gütertransport. Eine rechtsvergleichende Untersuchung unter besonderer Berücksichtigung der CMR, der ER/CIM 1990, des WA/HP und der HVR. 1999.

Band 9 Ulrich Krüger: Modifizierte Erfolgshaftung im UN-Kaufrecht. Die Haftungsbefreiung bei Lieferung vertragswidriger Ware gemäß Art. 79 CISG. 1999.

Band 10 Wolf-Henning Hammer: Das Zurückhaltungsrecht gemäß Art. 71 CISG im Vergleich zu den Kaufgesetzen der nordischen Staaten unter Einbeziehung transportrechtlicher Aspekte. Eine rechtsvergleichende Studie. 1999.

Band 11 Ulrich Quay: Der Consulting-Vertrag im Internationalen Privatrecht. 2000.

Band 12 Axel Halfmeier: Die Veröffentlichung privater Tatsachen als unerlaubte Handlung. Eine rechtsvergleichende Untersuchung. 2000.

Band 13 Stephanie Scholz: Lohngleichheit durch Verfahren. Eine Studie zur Förderung der Lohngleichheit durch verfahrensrechtliche Ansätze. 2000.

Band 14 Tarık Cebecioglu: Stellung des Ausländers im Zivilprozeß. Eine rechtsvergleichende Untersuchung des türkischen und deutschen Rechts. 2000.

Band 15 Gunnar Straube: Sozialrechtliche Eingriffsnormen im Internationalen Privatrecht. 2001.

Band 16 Daniela de Lukowicz: Divergenzen in der Rechtsprechung zum CISG. Auf dem Weg zu einer einheitlichen Auslegung und Anwendung? 2001.

Band 17 Mohamed Hassan Fadlalla Ali: Das islamische Ehe- und Kindschaftsrecht im Sudan. Mit Hinweisen zu den Lehren der Islamischen Rechtsschule, der anwendbaren Familienrechtsvorschriften für Nichtmuslime im Sudan und im deutschen Familienrecht. 2001.

Band 18 Ole Lando/Ulrich Magnus/Monika Novak-Stief (Hrsg./eds.): Angleichung des materiellen und des internationalen Privatrechts in der EU. Harmonisation of Substantive and International Private Law. 2003.

Band 19 Florian Schulz: Der Ersatzlieferungs- und Nachbesserungsanspruch des Käufers im internen deutschen Recht, im UCC und im CISG. Eine rechtsvergleichende Untersuchung unter Berücksichtigung der Schuldrechtskommission, der EG-Richtlinie 1999/44/EG und des Diskussionsentwurfs eines Schuldrechtsmodernisierungsgesetzes. 2002.

Band 20 Ingo Janert: Die Aufrechnung im internationalen Vertragsrecht. 2002.

Band 21 Armin Jentsch: Die Erhaltungspflichten des Verkäufers und des Käufers im UN-Kaufrecht im Vergleich zum US-amerikanischen Uniform Commercial Code und zum deutschen Recht. 2002.

Band 22 Martin Taschner: Arbeitsvertragsstatut und zwingende Bestimmungen nach dem Europäischen Schuldvertragsübereinkommen. Einheitliche Auslegung. 2003.

Band 23 Klaus Bitterich: Die Neuregelung des Internationalen Verbrauchervertragsrechts in Art. 29a EGBGB. 2003.

Band 24 Sascha J. Morgenroth: Umsetzung der Verbrauchsgüterkaufrichtlinie in Spanien und Deutschland. Umsetzung der Richtlinie 1999/44/EG des Europäischen Parlaments und des Rates vom 25. Mai 1999 zu bestimmten Aspekten des Verbrauchsgüterkaufs und der Garantien für Verbrauchsgüter in Spanien und Deutschland. 2003.

Band 25 Markus Renfert: Über die Europäisierung der ordre public Klausel. 2003.

Band 26 Henning Mordhorst: Die Behandlung vertraglicher Mobiliarsicherheiten im US-amerikanischen und deutschen Insolvenzrecht. 2003.

Band 27 Hans Markus Wulf: UN-Kaufrecht und eCommerce. Problembereiche bei der Anwendung des Wiener Übereinkommens auf Internet-Verträge. 2003.

Band 28 Julia Kaiser: Freiheit oder Schutz? Die Scheidungsfolgenvereinbarung im deutschen und im englischen Recht. 2003.

Band 29 Astrid Hillebrenner: Die private Zustimmung zu Rechtsgeschäften Dritter im englischen, dänischen und deutschen Recht. 2004.

Band 30 Irene von der Heyde: Das deutsche und italienische internationale Kindschaftsrecht im Rechtsvergleich. Favor filii oder favor filiationis? 2004.

Band 31 Sven-Michael Werner: Recht im Systemwandel. *Ein Land, zwei Systeme* und das Kontinuitätsproblem in Hongkong. 2004.

Band 32 Holger Ellenberger: Wirtschaftsrelevante Kollisionsnormen im japanischen internationalen Privatrecht. 2004.

Band 33 Sebastian Kaufmann: Parol Evidence Rule und Merger Clauses im internationalen Einheitsrecht. 2004.

Band 34 Britta Christina Weber: Eigentumsübertragung und gutgläubiger Erwerb beim Kauf von beweglichen Sachen im vietnamesischen Zivilgesetzbuch von 1995. Eine rechtsvergleichende Analyse unter Berücksichtigung des Eigentumsbegriffs im vietnamesischen Recht. 2004.

Band 35 Alexander von Saucken: Die Reform des österreichischen Schiedsverfahrensrechts auf der Basis des UNCITRAL-Modellgesetzes über die internationale Handelsschiedsgerichtsbarkeit. Ein Diskussionsbeitrag. 2004.

Band 36 Jasnica Garašićć: Anerkennung ausländischer Insolvenzverfahren. Teil 1 und Teil 2. Ein Vergleich des kroatischen, des deutschen und des schweizerischen Rechts sowie der Europäischen Verordnung über Insolvenzverfahren, des Istanbuler Übereinkommens und des UNCITRAL-Modellgesetzes. 2005.

Band 37 Eugenia Kurzynsky-Singer: Anknüpfung und Reichweite des Vollmachtsstatuts. 2005.

Band 38 Timo Utermark: Rechtsgeschichte und Rechtsvergleichung bei Ernst Rabel. 2005.

Band 39 Mohamed Lakmes: Die IPR-Anknüpfung der Schuldverträge. Ein Vergleich zwischen dem deutschen und dem syrischen Recht. 2005.

Band 40 Christian Haas: Vertragsstrukturen privatfinanzierter Infrastrukturprojekte. Nationale und internationale Perspektiven. 2005.

Band 41 Tanja Herzog-Engels: Gesellschaftsrechtliche Formvorschriften und Internationales Privatrecht. 2005.

Band 42 Hassan Siahpoosh: Das Familien- und Erbrecht im Iran. 2006.

Band 43 Carola Reifenrath: Das Vertragsrecht Hongkongs und dessen zukünftige Entwicklung. Unter besonderer Berücksichtigung des englischen Common Law. 2006.

Band 44 Arkadiusz Wudarski: Der Pfandbrief und sein Treuhänder. Eine rechtsvergleichende Untersuchung zum polnischen und deutschen Recht. 2006.

Band 45 Ulla Liukkunen: Cross-Border Services and Choice of Law. A Comparative Study of the European Approach. 2006.

Band 46 Claire Anna Reifner: Die Umsetzung der Verbrauchsgüterkaufrichtlinie in Italien und Deutschland. 2007.

Band 47 Shahriar Rabbanifar: Vergleich des Rechts der öffentlichen Unternehmen in Deutschland, Iran und Polen. 2007.

Band 48 Judith Farokhmanesh: Der Schutz des Urhebers im internationalen Vertragsrecht. Funktion, Reichweite und Effektivität zwingender Bestimmungen im deutschen, französischen und englischen Recht. 2007.

Band 49 Christoph Hellriegel: Schuldnerschutz in Polen. Rechtsvergleichende Untersuchung eines universalen Regelungsproblems. 2007.

Band 50 Ingemar Carl: Einstweiliger Rechtsschutz bei *Torpedoklagen*. 2007.

Band 51 Gabriele Wunsch: Möglichkeiten und Grenzen eines europäischen Hypothekarkredits. Problemanalyse und Lösungswege für die Schaffung eines Binnenmarktes für Grundpfandrechte unter Berücksichtigung des deutschen, englischen, schwedischen und spanischen Rechts. 2009.

Band 52 Sven Kuchmann: Die Haftung des Geschäftsführers einer deutschen GmbH und des Gerente einer argentinischen SRL im Rechtsvergleich. 2008.

Band 53 María Elena Alvarez de Pfeifle: Der Ordre Public-Vorbehalt als Versagungsgrund der Anerkennung und Vollstreckbarerklärung internationaler Schiedssprüche. Unter Berücksichtigung des deutschen, schweizerischen, französischen und englischen Rechts sowie des UNCITRAL-Modellgesetzes. 2009.

Band 54 Amir-Said Ghassabeh: Die Zustellung einer *punitive-damages*-Sammelklage an beklagte deutsche Unternehmen. Zugleich ein Beitrag zum „unnötigen" transatlantischen Justizkonflikt. 2009.

Band 55 Gunnar Lennart Schmüser: Das Zusammenspiel zwischen Haupt- und Sekundärinsolvenzverfahren nach der EuInsVO. 2009.

Band 56 Johanna Siemonsen: Die deutschen Ausführungsvorschriften zur Europäischen Insolvenzverordnung. 2009.

Band 57 Dan Malika Gunasekera: Civil Liability for Bunker Oil Pollution Damage. 2010.

Band 58 Sarah Mukaddes Oguz: Das türkische und das europäische Verbraucherrecht. Eine vergleichende Analyse mit Blick auf die Beitrittsbestrebungen der Türkei zur Europäischen Union. 2010.

Band 59 Niklas Wielandt: Die einseitig verpflichtende Schuldzusage. Eine rechtsvergleichende Untersuchung des abstrakten, kausalen und nicht rechtsgeschäftlichen Schuldanerkenntnisses und Schuldversprechens nach deutschem und englischem Recht. 2010.

Band 60 Lars Meyer: Non-Performance and Remedies under International Contract Law Principles and Indian Contract Law. A comparative survey of the UNIDROIT Principles of International Commercial Contracts, the Principles of European Contract Law, and Indian statutory contract law. 2010.